A CULTURAL HISTORY OF LAW

VOLUME 6

A Cultural History of Law
General Editor: Gary Watt

Volume 1
A Cultural History of Law in Antiquity
Edited by Julen Etxabe

Volume 2
A Cultural History of Law in the Middle Ages
Edited by Emanuele Conte and Laurent Mayali

Volume 3
A Cultural History of Law in the Early Modern Age
Edited by Peter Goodrich

Volume 4
A Cultural History of Law in the Age of Enlightenment
Edited by Rebecca Probert and John Snape

Volume 5
A Cultural History of Law in the Age of Reform
Edited by Ian Ward

Volume 6
A Cultural History of Law in the Modern Age
Edited by Richard K. Sherwin and Danielle Celermajer

A CULTURAL HISTORY OF LAW

IN THE MODERN AGE

*Edited by Richard K. Sherwin and
Danielle Celermajer*

BLOOMSBURY ACADEMIC
LONDON • NEW YORK • OXFORD • NEW DELHI • SYDNEY

BLOOMSBURY ACADEMIC
Bloomsbury Publishing Plc
50 Bedford Square, London, WC1B 3DP, UK
1385 Broadway, New York, NY 10018, USA
29 Earlsfort Terrace, Dublin 2, Ireland

BLOOMSBURY, BLOOMSBURY ACADEMIC and the Diana logo are
trademarks of Bloomsbury Publishing Plc

First published in Great Britain 2019
Paperback edition published in 2023

Copyright © Bloomsbury Publishing Plc, 2019

Richard K. Sherwin and Danielle Celermajer have asserted their right under the Copyright,
Designs and Patents Act, 1988, to be identified as Editors of this work.

Cover image: Klimt's Jurisprudence © Leopold Museum, Vienna

All rights reserved. No part of this publication may be reproduced or transmitted in
any form or by any means, electronic or mechanical, including photocopying,
recording, or any information storage or retrieval system, without prior
permission in writing from the publishers.

Bloomsbury Publishing Plc does not have any control over, or responsibility for,
any third-party websites referred to or in this book. All internet addresses given in
this book were correct at the time of going to press. The editor and publisher regret
any inconvenience caused if addresses have changed or sites have ceased
to exist, but can accept no responsibility for any such changes.

A catalogue record for this book is available from the British Library.

A catalog record for this book is available from the Library of Congress.

ISBN:	PB set:	978-1-3503-6891-0
	HB:	978-1-4742-1277-9
	PB:	978-1-3503-6870-5
	ePDF:	978-1-3500-7933-5
	eBook:	978-1-3500-7934-2

Series: The Cultural Histories Series

Typeset by Integra Software Services Pvt. Ltd.
Printed and bound in Great Britain

To find out more about our editors and books visit www.bloomsbury.com
and sign up for our newsletters.

CONTENTS

LIST OF FIGURES	VI
NOTES ON CONTRIBUTORS	IX
SERIES PREFACE	XII

Introduction   1
Richard Sherwin and Danielle Celermajer

1   Justice: Klimt's *Jurisprudence*—Sovereign Violence and the Rule of Law   27
    Desmond Manderson

2   Constitution: Performance Evidence in Aboriginal Land Claims   47
    Craig Elliott

3   Codes: Judging the Rwandan Soundscape   69
    James E.K. Parker

4   Agreements: Truth, Politics, and the Value of Performing Impersonations   87
    Diana Taylor

5   Arguments: Should Videos of Trees Have Standing?
    An Inquiry into the Legal Rites of Unnatural Objects at the ICTY   99
    Susan Schuppli

6   Property and Possession: On the Illegality of Situational Art   129
    Alison Young

7   Wrongs: A Conversation with Filmmaker Joshua Oppenheimer   145
    Richard Sherwin, Joshua Oppenheimer, and Danielle Celermajer

8   Legal Profession: Beaten Black and Blue—Lessons from Watching
    the Rodney King Case   169
    Christian Delage

NOTES	186
BIBLIOGRAPHY	202
INDEX	227

LIST OF FIGURES

JUSTICE

1.1 Gustav Klimt, *Jurisprudence* (University painting for the University of Vienna, 1903; destroyed by fire, 1945).   29

1.2 Isaac Oliver, *The Rainbow Portrait* (Hatfield House, Hertfordshire, 1600).   36

CONSTITUTION

2.1 Main tent and shade during the *Alyawarr* hearing at ALEPEYEWENH (Black Tank Outstation, Hatches Creek, site No. 32), September 2000.   59

2.2 Preparation for Women's Performance Evidence during the *Alyawarr* hearing, at site ATETYERRETYER (site No. 21), September 20, 2000.   60

2.3 Senior claimant Frankie Holmes Akemarr gives performance evidence during the *Alyawarr* hearing, at site ILENTYARLEWERREPP-ARRERNELHEW (site No. 37), September 27, 2001.   61

2.4 Main tent during the *De Rose* hearing at ILINTJITJARA, June-July 2001.   62

2.5 On-country evidence at site KANTJA (site No. 29, southern De Rose Hill pastoral lease) during the *De Rose* hearing, July 6, 2001.   63

2.6 Bush foods collected and displayed during evidence at site KANTJA (site No. 29) *De Rose* hearing, July 6, 2001.   64

CODES

3.1 Still from "20 Years Challenging Impunity".   71

3.2 Still from "20 Years Challenging Impunity".   76

3.3 Still from "20 Years Challenging Impunity".   78

3.4 Still from "20 Years Challenging Impunity".   86

AGREEMENTS

4.1 Lorie Novak Sin Maíz.   90

4.2 Monsanto and Motherland.   90

4.3 Beating Monsanto.   91

4.4 Jacques Servin's BBC DOW Announcement.   92

LIST OF FIGURES vii

ARGUMENTS

5.1 IT-95-13a: Dokmanovic [JPG] Video still of Exhibit D2 at
15:42. Date: 17/06/1998. 100

5.2–5.3 IT-95-13a: Dokmanovic [MPG] Video segment of alleged
locations depicted on exhibit D2 at 15:36 and 15:42. Date: 18/06/1998. 104

5.4 Courtroom of the International Criminal Tribunal, during a
swearing-in ceremony of judges. 106

5.5–5.6 Evidence vault of the Office of the Prosecutor OTP. 108

5.7–5.8 IT-98–32/1: Lukic et al. [MPG] Expert Witness Fire Inspector
Benjamin Dimas opening an examined sealed evidence bag.
March 24, 2009. 109

5.9–5.10 Audio-visual technology used in the Trial Chamber. 112

5.11–5.21 IT-99–36: Brdjanin [JPG] Multiple versions of the same
picture of the Omarska model, considered the most notorious concentration
camp of the Bosnian war. 113

5.22–5.23 IT-95-14/2: Kordic and Cerkez [PPT] Set of 54 photographs
of destroyed buildings in Han Ploca. 114

5.24 US Army staffers organize stacks of German documents collected by war
crimes investigators as evidence for the International Military Tribunal.
Nuremberg, Germany. November 20, 1945—October 1, 1946. 116

5.25 IT-95-13a: Dokmanovic [JPG] Photograph taken by witness
on February 12, 1998 depicting house at the alleged location recorded
on Exhibit D2 at 15:42. 119

5.26–5.29 IT-95-13a: Dokmanovic [MPG] Expert witness Paul
Tabbush describing the manner in which trees grow and comparing a
photograph of from February 12, 1998 and a video still of the same
tree from November 20, 1991. 122

5.30 Internal report 128

PROPERTY AND POSSESSION

6.1 Memorial tag for Dick Nose. 130

6.2 Piece by Slicer. 131

6.3 Tag by Fray. 132

6.4 Piece by Urban Cake Lady. 133

6.5 Piece by Be Free. 134

WRONGS

7.1 Dramatization scene from *The Act of Killing*. 147

7.2 Dramatization scene from *The Act of Killing*. 147

7.3 Fantasy scene from *The Act of Killing*. 148

7.4 Scene of Anwar Congo retching, from *The Act of Killing*. 149

7.5 Image of Adi from *The Look of Silence*. 150

7.6 Fantasy scene from *The Act of Killing*. 156

7.7 Daughter of perpetrator (in foreground) asks Adi for forgiveness in a scene from *The Look of Silence*. 158

LEGAL PROFESSION

8.1 Rodney King, photo taken three days after his March 3, 1991 videotaped beating, one of three introduced into evidence by the prosecution in the trial of four LAPD officers in Simi Valley, Calif. 175

8.2 An attorney points to still copies of a video of the Rodney King beating as the video is displayed on television monitor in a Simi Valley courtroom. 178

NOTES ON CONTRIBUTORS

Danielle Celermajer is a Professor in the Department of Sociology and Social Policy at the University of Sydney. Her research explores the multi-dimensional nature of injustice and the practice of human rights. She recently completed a European Union-funded multi-country project on the prevention of torture, focusing on everyday violence in the security sector. Her publications include *Sins of the Nation and the Ritual of Apology* (Cambridge, 2009), *Power, Judgment and Political Evil: Hannah Arendt's Promise* (Routledge, 2010) and *The Prevention of Torture: An Ecological Approach* (Cambridge, 2018). She is now researching practices that enhance forms of life conducive to respectful relationships between humans and the more-than-human world.

Christian Delage teaches at the University of Paris VIII, the Institute of Political Studies in Paris, and the Benjamin N. Cardozo School of Law. He has made over twenty films (documentary, fiction, and archival) including *From Hollywood to Nuremberg: John Ford, Samuel Fuller, George Stevens* (2013) and *Nuremberg: The Nazis Face Their Crimes* (2007). His written scholarship includes *The Truth through the Image: Nuremberg Milosevic Trial* (2014) and *Film in the Courtroom: From the Nuremberg Trials to the Trials of the Khmer Rouge* (2013). In 2010, he curated a special exhibit for the Shoah Memorial in Paris "*Filming the Camps: John Ford, Samuel Fuller, George Stevens, from Hollywood to Nuremberg.*"

Craig Elliott is a social anthropologist with qualifications from Macquarie University and Australian National University (ANU). He has taught anthropology at ANU, University of Canberra and New York University (Sydney campus). He has worked with Aboriginal people for thirty years as a consultant and senior anthropologist at Central Land Council (2006–2017). He has conducted anthropological research and authored reports in relation to applied public health, cultural heritage, intestate claims, and Indigenous land claims in Northern Territory, Queensland, South Australia, and Western Australia. He appeared as an expert witness before the Federal Court of Australia in the *Alyawarr* and *De Rose* cases.

Professor Desmond Manderson is jointly appointed in the ANU Colleges of Law and the Arts & Social Sciences at the Australian National University, where he directs the Centre for Law, Arts and the Humanities, designing innovative interdisciplinary courses with English, philosophy, art theory, history, among other fields, and pursuing collaborative projects with the National Library, the National Gallery, the Australian Broadcasting Corporation, and the Street Theatre. His books include *From Mr Sin to Mr Big* (1993); *Songs without Music: Aesthetic Dimensions of Law and Justice* (2000); *Proximity, Levinas, and the Soul of Law* (2006); and *Kangaroo Courts and the Rule of Law* (2012). Recent scholarship examines the intersection of law and the visual arts, notably *Law and the Visual: Representations, Technologies and Critique* (2018) and *Danse Macabre: Temporalities of Law in the Visual Arts* (forthcoming).

Joshua Oppenheimer is a writer and filmmaker. His debut feature, the documentary-fiction hybrid *The Act of Killing* (2012), won seventy-two awards including the Grand Jury Prize at the Venice Film Festival and was named Film of the Year in 2013 by *The Guardian*. *The Look of Silence* (2014) received seventy-two awards, including an Independent Spirit Award and a Gotham Award. He was nominated for an Academy Award for each film. Together these films have helped transform Indonesia's understanding of the 1965–1966 genocide—inspiring a movement for truth, reconciliation, and justice, as well as prompting the US Government to declassify 30,000 previously secret files detailing America's complicity in the massacres. In 2014, Oppenheimer was awarded a MacArthur Fellowship. He is a partner at Final Cut for Real ApS in Copenhagen and Professor of Film at the University of Westminster in London.

James E. K. Parker is a senior lecturer at Melbourne Law School, where he is also director of the research program "Law, Sound and the International" at the Institute for International Law and the Humanities. His research addresses the many relations between law, sound, and listening. He is the author of *Acoustic Jurisprudence: Listening to the Trial of Simon Bikindi* (Oxford University Press, 2015), which explores the trial of Simon Bikindi, who was accused by the International Criminal Tribunal for Rwanda of inciting genocide with his songs. In 2017, he was a Visiting Research Fellow with the Program on Science, Technology and Society at Harvard. His most recent work concerns the weaponization of sound and the legal history of eavesdropping.

Susan Schuppli is an artist and researcher whose work examines material evidence ranging from war and conflict to environmental disasters. She has published widely within the context of media and politics and is author of *Material Witness* (2018). Schuppli is Director of the Centre for Research Architecture, Goldsmiths University of London, and previously worked on the Forensic Architecture project.

Richard Sherwin is the Wallace Stevens Professor of Law and Director of the Visual Persuasion Project at New York Law School. His scholarship explores the relationship between law and culture, focusing in particular on legal narrative, visual communication, the legitimation process, and the genealogy of law's sovereignty. His books include: *Visualizing Law in the Age of the Digital Baroque: Arabesques and Entanglements* (2011) and *When Law Goes Pop: The Vanishing Line between Law and Popular Culture* (2000). In 2018, he was elected Visiting Fellow at Fitzwilliam College and Senior Research Fellow at the Centre for Research in the Arts, Social Sciences and Humanities at Cambridge University.

Diana Taylor is University Professor and Professor of Performance Studies and Spanish at New York University. She is the author of multiple books in English and Spanish, including *¡Presente! The Politics of Presence* (forthcoming), *Performance* (2016), *The Archive and the Repertoire: Performing Cultural Memory in the Americas* (2003), *Disappearing Acts: Spectacles of Gender and Nationalism in Argentina's "Dirty War"* (1997), and *Theatre of Crisis: Drama and Politics in Latin America* (1991). Taylor is the recipient of prestigious awards including a Guggenheim Fellowship in 2005. She was President of the Modern Language Association in 2017, and is Founder and Director of the Hemispheric Institute of Performance and Politics at NYU.

Alison Young is the Francine V. McNiff Professor of Criminology in the School of Social and Political Sciences at the University of Melbourne, and a Professor in the Law School at City University, London. She is the author of *Street Art World* (2016), *Street Art, Public City* (2014), *The Scene of Violence* (2010), *Street/Studio* (2010), and *Judging the Image* (2005), and numerous articles on the intersection of law, crime, culture, and public or private space. In 2015, *Street Art, Public City* was awarded the Penny Pether Prize for best book by the Australasian Association of Law, Literature and the Humanities.

SERIES PREFACE

The six volumes in *A Cultural History of Law* present a panorama of law's cultural significance over the span of several centuries, especially as it relates to the place of law in the arts and humanities. Each volume focuses on a distinct time period from antiquity to modernity and in each volume a chapter is devoted to one of eight legally significant themes: "Justice," "Constitution," "Codes," "Agreements," "Arguments," "Property and Possession," "Wrongs," and "The Legal Profession." The collection does not seek to provide encyclopedic coverage, but rather to present cultural case studies that highlight how particular cultural artifacts express and explore the key legal—and inevitably the key political and social—concerns of their time. The authors have picked flowers from their field of expertise—a play, a painting, a mosaic, a book, a film—which bring into close focus the cultural and legal flourishing of the time. The volume editors are internationally distinguished scholars with a passion and deep appreciation for the law and culture of their chosen period. Together with the experts that they have assembled to contribute chapters on the eight themes, they are reliable guides not merely to the facts about each period but to the feel of each period. Every volume has an ethos and a style that immerses the reader in the distinctive quality of its era. The series is indebted to the archivist's concern to discover and catalog historical materials, but what sets it apart is its concern to show how the materials of history are materially meaningful. In this way, our retrospective of more than 2,000 years continues to have relevance for lawyers and for all culturally concerned citizens today.

Sometimes we find that artifacts have lost the cultural meanings that first produced them. Likewise, we sometimes we find that artifacts are culturally meaningful today in ways that they were not at the time of their creation. Take the example of Magna Carta— The Great Charter of King John of England sealed at Runnymede on the Thames in 1215. Today, in the United States in particular, Magna Carta has been hoisted to totemic heights in the cultural imagination. It might therefore seem strange to us that William Shakespeare's play *King John* makes no reference at all to this great artifact. The reason for its omission is that for Shakespeare and his early modern contemporaries, the most dramatic historical event in the reign of King John was his surrender of the Crown to the papal legate and his receiving it again as a papal vassal. The modern significance of Magna Carta is largely a post-Enlightenment invention and its principal promoters were the great myth-makers who framed the American Constitution and created the idea of the United States. It is some proof of this that the Magna Carta memorial which stands at Runnymede today was erected by the American Bar Association. The small-scale temple, like the much larger Jefferson Memorial in Washington DC, has become a place of secular pilgrimage; a sanctuary to the values of political freedom and human rights under law.

In 2015, to mark the 800th anniversary of the sealing of Magna Carta, sculptor Hew Locke's "The Jurors" was installed at Runnymede. It comprises twelve bronze chairs, each of which (according to the official narrative) "incorporates symbols and imagery representing concepts of law and key moments in the struggle for freedom, rule of law and equal rights." In this respect, it performs a similar function to the eight bas-relief panels by sculptor John Donnelly Jr that adorn the great bronze doors of the United States Supreme Court in Washington DC. Shakespeare would have appreciated the performative purpose of these "solemn temples" but he would surely be surprised to see today how much has been made of Magna Carta. The rise of Magna Carta as an artifact of cultural history would certainly have amazed the landed aristocrats who first compelled King John to set his seal to the charter in the culturally Christian, monarchal, and feudal context of the High Middle Ages. The narrative accompanying "The Jurors" alerts us to the license that the sculptor has taken with the history of law. We are told that it is "not a memorial, but rather an artwork that aims to examine the changing and ongoing significance and influences of Magna Carta." It is, in short, a cultural reworking of an artifact that owes its great status to creative cultural appropriation. The actual provisions of Magna Carta that survive in law are impressively few, but the three survivors are perhaps all the more significant for their small number. Much is still made of the survival of the right to trial by jury. Rather less is made, nowadays, of the provisions that preserve the "liberties of the English Church" and the "privileges of the City of London." One of the most important contributions we can make to the appreciation of history is to show where cultures are selective in what they present as fact. The artifacts of history are always presented in the cabinets of culture.

The word "fact" comes, in fact, from the Latin *facere* ("to make") and it can be helpful to think of historical facts as things that are produced by the action of culture and as things which, in turn, produce cultures. Even where a society is collectively in error in its understanding of historical fact, a commonly held mistake inevitably becomes part of the cultural history of that society. The story becomes the history. One of the mistakes we often make, as the shifting status of Magna Carta indicates, is to suppose that the modern commentator can claim a monopoly in the present moment to determine "true" history from "false." Today's official history is only ever the history of the present. The past had its own histories. Cultural history allows an appreciation of the cultural stories that give meaning to societies in time and across time. From a cultural perspective, myths can be more meaningful, and in that cultural sense more "true," than many a cold matter of fact.

Another great and oft-repeated mistake that this book series seeks to remedy is the supposition that law can be meaningfully separated from the culture in which it exists. In *Law as Culture*, Lawrence Rosen observes that law:

> never stands apart from life—some refined essence of professional inquiry or arcane speech. Rather, it forms the conscious attention we give to our relationships. Like art and literature, through law we attempt to order our ties to one another ... However it is displayed, however it is applied, we can no more comprehend the roles of legal institutions without seeing them as part of their culture than we can fully understand each culture without attending to its form of law.[1]

There is an historical aspect to this understanding of law as culture. Pierre Legrand writes, for example, that:

> French law is, first and foremost, a cultural phenomenon, not unlike singing or weaving. The reason why the French have the *chanteurs* they have lies somewhere in their history, their Frenchness, in their identity. Similarly, the reason why the French have the legislative texts or the judicial decisions they have, say, on a matter of sales law, lies somewhere in their history, their Frenchness, in their identity.[2]

There are obvious limits to the mechanistic metaphor by which we talk of cultural history as something manufactured or fabricated. Human hands fashion historical artifacts, but legal artifacts grow out of a culture in a way that makes it hard to know where the artifact starts and the culture ends. It might be better to take the "culture" metaphor seriously and to suggest that laws grow out of a society organically and that the artificial intervention of human hands are like those of the gardener—taming, tending, and ordering wild growth. Thus the cultural history of law becomes something like a horticultural history. This is not such a strange thought when one considers that the English word for the "court" of law is derived from the Latin *hortus* (garden). Malcolm Andrews has suggested that "one could write an illuminating, if oblique, history of a nation's cultural development by examining its changing conception of the garden's scope, design and function."[3] The gardening metaphor may be especially useful in helping us to understand the cultural history of law, given the complex relation between natural justice and artificial laws in human society. Dress is another artificial creation of human craft which, as a cultural outworking of the complex relation between nature and human ordering, serves well as a way to understand the artificial and creative nature of law's contribution to culture. Laws are produced in society in much the same way that gardens, dress, and other products of complex cultural systems are produced in society. When we have completed our journey through the six volumes of this series we may conclude that the chief legislator across the ages has been no Parliament nor any body of the people politically represented, but that the great lawmaker has always been the deep, rich, and creative power of human culture.

Gary Watt, Professor of Law, University of Warwick, UK

Introduction

RICHARD SHERWIN AND DANIELLE CELERMAJER

This collection of essays seeks to illuminate through representative stories of conflict broader patterns in law and culture during the modern age since 1920. While each story is singular in its particularity, taken together these essays point toward a distinctive meta-story describing significant trends over the past century in the exercise, distribution, and contestation of state power under the rule of law.

Each chapter explores a particular human struggle—from challenges to corporate power through digital impersonation, to disputes over Aboriginal land claims, to aspirations toward social reconciliation in the aftermath of genocidal violence. Collectively, these accounts tell us something about the way meanings are made. More specifically, they prompt us to ask how, and with what effects, a particular expressive modality (ceremonial dance, live street theater, mixed-genre film, to name a few) helps to construct (or suppress) legal and political meanings in society.

By self-reflexively braiding medium and message, we hope to garner new insights about the way power circulates in society, including the terms by which it is named and deemed legitimate under law—or found worthy of resistance. We believe that the braid also helps to tell an important meta-story about hyper-awareness in late-modern culture regarding the construction and deconstruction of meaning. This awareness helps to account for late modernity's obsession with the interplay between authenticity and simulation.

Shifting the modality of communication brings to the fore diverse standards of truth-making and judgment in politics and law. Sometimes a particular expressive modality may be tethered to power, while at other times severed from it. During the twentieth century, many people witnessed this phenomenon in the rise of propaganda and public relations (the so-called "engineering of consent") which culminated in the widespread application of principles and techniques of marketing to politics and law more generally.

The illustrative stories that we present here fall under eight rubrics: justice, constitution, codes (norms), agreements, arguments (including rhetoric), property and possession, wrongs (including crimes), and the legal profession. Each rubric is illustrated in synecdochal fashion by a particular human conflict and a corresponding expressive medium. Making explicit the entanglement of historical content and disparate ways of knowing and communicating brings to the surface deeper issues across the entire period. In this way, we canvas a diverse range of representative cultural themes, coaxing into view (or sound or perhaps some other embodied form of knowledge) new ways of understanding the historical interplay of authenticity, power, and judgment under color of law.

We invite readers to join us in this high-stakes, high-wire act of balancing theory and practice. Together we will survey sites of conflict and suffering in order to assess the role law and its agents (or surrogates) play in the service of conflict resolution and the aspiration to justice. Our hope is that by traveling the path of recent history we will learn more about how best to calibrate the aesthetic and the ethical in law's ever shifting acculturated exercise of power and judgment.

Reflecting the spirit of perspectival openness that inspired and frames our approach in this volume, in what follows we offer a general historical overview in the form of a dialogue on law in the modern age.

* * *

The thing known is in the knower according to the mode of the knower (Huxley 1970: 146).

Danielle Celermajer ["D"]: The history of the modern age since 1920: is it possible to speak about such a thing? And that's even before we add the inflection of culture, another essentially contested concept (Gallie 1955).

Richard Sherwin ["R"] It's possible, if we can imagine how other people lived. If Vico was right when he said humans can understand what humans make (Vico 1976 [1744]). Humans make history, right?

[D] At the time, or retrospectively? I'm thinking about the difference between what we imagine we are doing as we are doing it, and the story we tell later, when we subsequently look back—not to mention how others interpret our actions over time.

[R] So many different interpretive lenses are in play.

[D] How does one keep track of them all given the great number of actors and interpreters involved?

[R] The historian's task is to discern dominant patterns across multiple networks of actions.

[D] How do we find the best narrative to fit the patterns encountered along the way? Is that not also an act of judgment?

[R] Which returns us to your question: is history a matter of capturing the meaning of a stream of lived "nows" or of retrospectively narrating them from some point in the future?

[D] Am I living my own history or the history of my time?

[R] Either way, wouldn't you agree that the narrative comes after the fact? It's like the paradoxical circle that Dupuy imagines: we project the future from the past, and we experience the past as being fulfilled in the future. And so we move forward toward a future that we narratively imagine. Cause follows effect (Dupuy 2013: 210).

[D] When we think about the inter-temporal connection between events in this way, a mechanistic or positivist understanding of causality seems hopelessly inadequate. It fails to capture the lived realities of human history and underestimates the indeterminacy of our actions and the multiplicity of factors that are at play from moment to moment.

[R] Yes. Benjamin's and Arendt's notions of historic elements that crystallize into an apparent whole only in the moment when we arrest them might provide a more productive metaphor (Arendt 1971: xv; Arendt 1994; Benjamin 2003[1940]: 395).

[D] So from this now time, gazing back at the twentieth century, what past do we create?

[R] Refracted through the present moment, the twentieth century seems to be the story of an ever accelerating falling away of any single foundational (or meta-) narrative in favor of a thousand cultural blossoms.

[D] The loss of a singular foundation, especially one that bears the credentials of metaphysics, is certainly one of the distinguishing qualities of the twentieth century. Arendt's notion that in the absence of such foundations, we must learn to "think without banisters" (Arendt 1979: 336) seems to aptly describe the predicament. Although of course, it was not only thinking that she had in mind, but also the action of creating through our words and deeds the structures through which we would govern ourselves and the principles that ought to regulate those structures, our relationships with each other, and the paths we carve towards the future.

[R] What a challenge, and how vertiginous: a source of both exhilaration and fear.

[D] And all the more so given the blow suffered by allegedly universal principles of rationality and progress associated with the Enlightenment. In Europe the Enlightenment story hit a dead end—shattered by the cumulative violence of the twentieth century.

[R] We're talking about the demise of a cultural legacy that stretches back more than two millennia: a shared belief in the universal, unalterable structure of reality. Of course, even in Europe, the rationalist Enlightenment always had its critics. One need only think of Vico's sense of historical cycles and the foundational power of providence and the poetic imagination (Vico 1976 [1744]), or Romantic thinkers and poets like Herder, Wordsworth, Coleridge, not to mention Schelling and Schlegel, and many others besides.

[D] Except that previously those voices spoke from the cultural margins. The shattering that occurred with the Shoah in Europe had cataclysmic repercussions for the twentieth century. The trajectory of Enlightenment ideas and their role in the constitutive identity of who people thought they were, and what they believed they were up to, had more or less been an article of faith, and the path of that trajectory was now unmistakably deflected.

The theoretical critique of rationality initiated by the early Frankfurt school thinkers became one of the keynotes of twentieth-century theory (Adorno and Horkheimer 1989), evident not only in post-modernism and post-structuralism (Derrida 1976; Kristeva 1980; Lyotard 1984), but also in the insistence that affect, the strata of materiality and the body, be included as bases for understanding, judging, and deciding (Bennett 2002; Gatens 1996; Irigaray 1985; Merleau-Ponty 2014).

So it was not only a loss of the ground of authority for morality, for law, for politics, and for religion but also a loss that had an affective dimension, a loss of faith that "Europeans" (and those they would make in their image) were in fact becoming ever more enlightened. Certainly, these streams of thought did not spring forth fully formed in the twentieth century, but they became a highly prevalent mood or hue tinging the century in an unprecedented way. And one encounters it in almost all fields of cultural production. In the early part of the century, for example, one thinks of Cubism, surrealism, and Dadaism—not to mention the atonal idioms of Schoenberg, Berg, and Varese.

[R] These developments reflect the emergence of radical pluralism and incommensurability.

[D] It was a time when people faced an unprecedented imperative to find new ways of constituting cultural and political orders and laws across vast differences.

In the field of legal and political practice, this trend toward heterogeneity, or the capacity of law to harmoniously encompass incommensurable narratives of truth and value, has perhaps been most evident in the movements of feminism, black liberation, Indigenous rights, multiculturalism, post-colonialism, GLBTI (gay, lesbian, bisexual, transsexual and intersex) rights—and more recently the claims for the rights of beings in the non-human world (including animals and the natural environment).

Though importantly different, in each of these movements people who looked to law and saw their absence, or their presence as "other," laid claim to being legitimate, rights-bearing subjects of law (Butler 2006; Eckersley 1992; Regan 2004; Said 1979; Tully 1995; Young 1990).

In some cases, this took the form of demands that law expand to cover new rights, or to cover existing rights in a manner that was more inclusive. In others, the demand was a more radical one, to recognize the structural exclusions at the heart of our inherited legal forms together with fundamental assumptions about the nature of personhood, the constitution of the subject, and the distinction between the human and the non-human world that conditions how we even understand law.

[R] Have you also noted at its outer limits, articulated for example in sub-altern studies (Spivak 1988) and in a somewhat different, but harmonious key in some branches of psychoanalysis (Castoriadis 1997: 283), a note of caution accompanying the aspiration to create space for the authentic voice of the excluded? As if the very act of "speaking for" were somehow compromised, or even interdicted by a politics of exclusion that insists upon structuring the production of speaking subjects.

[D] Yes. One might map these critical moves within a turbulent and perhaps endless dialectic of claims for recognition. At each stage, the identity that has succeeded in gaining such recognition itself becomes subject to claims that it, too, has elided difference.

In the name of feminism, for example, the demand was made that law not encode implicit gender biases. Then black and postcolonial feminists called out their feminist sisters for omitting issues of race and geo-politics and eliding critical differences (including differences of power) within the category of gender (Lorde 2012; Mohanty, Russo and Torres 1991), while women with disabilities pointed to their all but complete erasure within mainstream feminism (Ghai 2002), and so on. In each case, the accusation of exclusion and the call for recognition is made in the name of justice, but a justice never yet fully achieved. In Derrida's terms, it's the justice to come (Derrida 1992: 27).

The type of plurality I'm speaking about here is a plurality of perspectives or ways of being human. One of the achievements of your work has been to draw our attention to the pluralism of the aesthetic, or the pluralism of media of transmission and how different expressive forms alter what it is we can or do experience …

[R] Or judge …

[D] Okay, I don't mean to sever the normative dimension from the aesthetic. But my point is that it's not just a matter of pluralism in the absence of any over-arching meta-narrative or of any authoritative claim to a foundation for truth or right or good, but also with respect to the very expressive forms in which such claims are expressed in the first place. This is why one might say we are dealing with more than one form of pluralism.

[R] And once we see that this is the case, we also recognize the centrality of the kinds of questions that radical pluralism and incommensurability raise. Questions like: What realities under what circumstances with what effects (political, legal, affective, cognitive, and ethical) are produced, how, by the discrete logics of a given expressive medium? That in a nutshell describes the challenge of what might be called the politics of significance.

Viewed through the lens of the politics of significance, the history of twentieth-century culture beckons us to reckon with a plurality of worlds, together with the expressive communities (Rorty 1979) or discrete dialects (Sherwin 1988) whose meaning-making practices and modes of interpretation (Bruner 1986, 1991) produce and sustain different forms of life (Geertz 1973).

What binds together and authoritatively organizes a community made up of diverse and ultimately incommensurable beliefs and interpretive practices is one of the quintessential responsibilities of law, albeit with the mixed collaboration (both open and veiled) of politics and theology. Taken together, these are our shared cultural resources for normative order. But who decides, on what basis, under what circumstances? Which expressive community, for what reason, gets to say what about whom, with what authoritative effect?

[D] This means that we must cultivate multiple literacies in the constitutive dialects of reality making (Geertz 1983; Schechner 1985; Turner 1969, 1988)—not just in words, but also in sounds, feelings, colors, choreographed (or ritualized) bodily movements, as well as visual images, whether moving or still, lens-based or digitally simulated (Howes 2014).

[R] That is how the politics of significance is engaged: by entering the complex play of multiple forms of meaning or reality construction, self-consciously weighing the basis for the exercise of state power. After all, isn't this the way it always works? Those individuals, communities, and institutions in society that are invested with the most prestige get to have their preferred manner and matter of interpretation backed up by the force of the state (Cover 1983). As Harold Berman said: "Law—in all societies—derives its authority from something outside itself" (Berman 1983: 16).

[D] But given what we said earlier, that one of the markers of the twentieth century is precisely that radical doubt and disagreement gets cast on any source of authority outside law, what we then have is, to invoke Habermas, a legitimation crisis (Habermas 1975).

[R] As Berman observed, law in the modern era is becoming "more and more fragmented, more subjective, geared more to expediency and less to morality, concerned more with immediate consequences and less with consistency or continuity" (Berman 1983: 39).

[D] The most dangerous possibility in the face of this fragmentation and crisis of legitimate authority is one we know all too well: that the situation disintegrates into what Schmitt called the state of emergency in which the one who is sovereign simply decides.

[R] With that eventuality it's as if the whole Western legal tradition based on precedent and custom (which might well include the historical basis for "natural rights") were being eroded. As if the twentieth century were washing away the soil from which the deepest principles of the common law tradition had grown (Berman 1983: 39).

I think this poses a key element in the legacy of twentieth-century law and culture. How do we grasp the source of meaning and authority that legitimates law's power? What happens when you can't project into the future? Does the past collapse? Or is there a constellation of justice that would be an alternative to the state of emergency?

[D] Once we agree that an accelerating awareness of the constructedness and plurality of meaning (together with concomitant notions and practices of deconstruction [Derrida 1972, 1974]) is one of the key attributes of the history of late modern culture during the twentieth century running up to the present, it is but a small step to understanding law in this way as well.

[R] Yes, though an important shift ought to be noted during the early part of the twentieth century toward process theory (Bergson 1911, 1946; James 1925, 1956; Sherwin 2011: 123–125; Whitehead 1978) and the felt sense that one could discern forces immanent in history, or in the nature of things. Think of Bergson's notions of "*élan vital*" and "creative evolution," or what the American jurist Benjamin Cardozo referred to as "centres of energy" (Cardozo 1928: 4) and the "growth of the law" (Cardozo 1924). For a judge like Cardozo, the main challenge lay in responding to "pressures" generated by "the social mind" and putting oneself "within the heart and mind of others" (Cardozo 1928: 52, 55).

You spoke earlier about various aesthetic expressions of meaning's fragmentation, but these artistic forms, take Cubism, for example, also reflect an awareness of how different perceptual perspectives can be captured in new modes of expression, leading to novel forms of reality. Though I suppose you could also say that impressionism and neo-impressionism along with Fauvism were certainly getting at the same thing.

Twentieth-century poetic constructs by Mallarmé (among others, including William Carlos Williams and Wallace Stevens) and musical composition, like early twentieth-century twelve-tone scoring, similarly reflect the way different realities are constructed through discrete aesthetic choices. In this sense, perhaps John Cage's mid-century musical compositions based on chance operations represent a kind of crescendo of constructivist formalism in the service of letting some immanent event or "happening" simply occur (Cage 1961).

A similar fixation on immanent unfolding, or reality as endless process, also informs early twentieth-century legal realism (Cardozo 1921; Geny 1954 [1899]). For example, with the rise of process theory language began to lose its fixity, the capacity to maintain formal categories.

[D] In which case, law becomes more readily subservient to economics, its normativity reduced to a very localized utilitarian calculus. Not unlike the loss of ultimate purpose that characterized Deism and that Charles Taylor sees as the precursor for secularism (Taylor 2007).

[R] Yes. At the same time, we also witness many Legal Realists focusing on how irrational forces (desire, emotion, unconscious socially constructed prejudice, and so on) intrude upon law. As a result, formal notions of justice tend to give way to notions of public policy and contextualized fairness (Frank 2009 [1932]; Gadamer 1975 [1960]; Hutchson 1929).

Critical legal studies ("CLS") advanced this deconstruction of allegedly (but not really) rational forms in order to flesh out unconscious, or at least unexpressed political preferences in legal discourse (Unger 1986).

The Realists thought social science data would provide policy targets, but CLS substituted politics—conceding (with Weber) that the sciences can't answer normative questions. The ensuing rise of such diverse movements as feminist jurisprudence, law and literature, law and economics, legal cultural studies, among other scholarly developments, only fed the shared sense of radical plurality and incommensurability.

[D] The concern here would have to be that in the absence of stable formal categories there's nothing to protect us from endlessly changing policy preferences, shifting calculations of interest. As Jerome Bruner put it, we "compose and decompose worlds, impelled by different aims in doing so … and since all is in motion, the order and reordering we impose is a way too of imposing alternate stabilities" (Bruner 1986: 102–103).

[R] Bruner's understanding of the narrative construction of possible worlds makes me think of Dante and Vico and Wallace Stevens: it's the poet-legislator who invents the meaning of lived reality (Sherwin 2011: 183–187). This is a far cry from the Enlightenment's scientific or mathematical ideal of universal and objective truths, culled from the so-called "view from nowhere." The poetic *mythos* produces contingent worlds of meaning that are culturally distributed and that are made habitable by our shared cultural commitments.

[D] Bruner's hope was that the reordering of reality would be "principled rather than entirely fanciful," but there is of course no guarantee that it is principle that would be decisive. And even if it were, which principle would be in play? Within this fluidity and contestation—this "all in motion"—justice is left vulnerable, particularly where legal institutions themselves are captured by powerful private interests.

Even worse would be the possibility that the categories that seemed to ground core values, like equality or freedom, or like social justice and natural right, would be recast depending on whatever seems the most pragmatic thing to do at the time. That is certainly an accusation that has been leveled against human rights advocacy, and legitimately so given that at the end of the century, US President George W. Bush cited human rights as one of the justifications for invading Iraq.

[R] Allowing core inherited values to be reduced to the status of a plaything of fashionable policies and preferences is precisely what legal conservatives like US Supreme Court Justice Antonin Scalia feared most. And it was Strauss, wasn't it, who said this kind of instrumentalism is what leads to nihilism (Strauss 1965: 15–18).

[D] Hardly company I would have expected to find myself in. Although this also describes the legacy of Weber: reason breaking down into competing preferences, even with respect to basic principles—which devolves into an irresoluble contest setting my principles against yours. Or one that can only be resolved through force.

[R] Perhaps this is part of the ongoing epistemological oscillation between explanation and understanding (von Wright 1971). As the Weberian preference for a scientific explanatory method confronted one impasse after another, alternative theories and interpretive practices would arise to pick up the slack. This effort to adapt greatly complicated the positivist project and exerted pressure on the relatively thin behavioral models based around pain and pleasure that have influenced much of liberal political, jurisprudential, and economic theory in the modern era.

A utilitarian calculus that maximizes pleasure and minimizes pain not only failed to predict how political subjects actually behave, but it also failed to do justice to the plenitude of human passions, interests, and values which bind communities together and motivate action as well as belief and judgment.

[D] If political and legal realities on the ground seemed to elude the grasp of formal rules, including formal rules for rule making and interpretation (Hart 1961), it follows that we need a far richer archive of categories to capture the different dimensions of human motivation, belief, judgment and action; categories that will sometimes resist the criteria that the positivist mind can accept or imagine.

[R] Perhaps the tension between legal formalism and natural law theory operated as a proxy battle between competing notions of secular reason. To put it crudely, is reason a dispassionate calculation machine or a desire-inflected assemblage of time-resistant principles, norms, and categories—and let us include here categories of knowledge as well as feelings and other recurrent patterns of lived experience.

Viewing the political subject along behavioral and instrumentalist lines envisions secular reason as little more than a seething cauldron of competing affective intensities that take shape by virtue of radically divergent interest preferences seeking to maximize pleasure. But on that account how does one keep the liberal project from decaying into relativism, a contest in which the most powerful will wins? This is, of course, the familiar critique put forth by Carl Schmitt among other twentieth-century critics of secular liberalism, including communitarians like Michael Sandel and classicists like Leo Strauss (Sandel 1998; Schmitt 2005 [1922]; Strauss 1965).

[D] Well, it also may depend on whether you believe—as some critical and postmodern theorists would argue—that reason is an artifact of power, or whether, as Habermas wants us to consider, it is salvageable (Habermas 1984). In a post-foundational context, however, reason is achieved by dialogizing it, setting up a dynamic whereby differently situated subjects enter into a reason-giving activity and the reasoned consensus that they arrive at is the outcome of a process of mutual justification.

We are nevertheless left with the question of how wide that conversational circle can be or, put differently, what the fundamental rules or basic consensus needs to be, in order to sustain a dialogue that could potentially reach an unforced consensus. That debate is perhaps most alive today with respect to the possibility of including in our conversational circle people with strongly held politically illiberal or metaphysical (usually theological) commitments. In this regard, deep pluralism requires a form of inclusion that does not demand that participants bracket what Rawls called their comprehensive worldviews (Rawls 1985). Such bracketing was part of the original liberal secular response to the calamitous inter-religious violence that culminated in the Thirty Years War in Central Europe (1618—1648).

We might view these various reactions to the loss of foundations—the conservative desire to reinstate traditional values and the liberal desire to keep thick commitments out of politics—as different responses to the advent of radical pluralism. But each in their own way is left having to cordon off their space from the threat of the "other". This is so germane to issues of rhetorical construction.

[R] I agree. As a rhetorical or aesthetic matter, I see our task in this book as situating within the context of twentieth century culture the process of increasingly self-reflexive legal meaning making in the face of a multiplicity of discrete rhetorical tools for world making. This perspective helps to explain our decision to structure this book around diverse, yet singular modes of expressive communication.

These different rhetorical "fields" or "webs of significance" (to cite a catchy Geertzian phrase) construct different worlds for us to be in (Geertz 1973: 5). And so we need ask, what does it mean when a plurality of worlds is constructed on the basis of a plurality of world making tools? What's in our toolkit? How do we construct and take up residence with others in the contingent worlds that we inhabit, including the worlds of politics and law? What are the practical and moral consequences for law when this constructive process occurs?

[D] Constructivism, particularly once we understand it as a rhetorical act, a performance with formal as well as substantive dimensions, raises both ethical and aesthetic questions. Since the one interpenetrates the other it seems best for us not to treat the ethical and the aesthetic as autonomous or mutually exclusive domains.

[R] Yes, I heartily agree. Such an integrative approach allows us to ask more nuanced questions, like how certain normative preferences or options are affected—either encouraged or foreclosed—by our rhetorical choices? What is the relationship between mediated/constructed worlds of law—the *"nomoi,"* to use Robert Cover's term (Cover 1983)—and certain normative end points? This theme strikes me as endlessly rich in its ontological, epistemological, and phenomenological implications. These are themes famously dealt with by Plato in the *Republic* and *The Laws*, concerning the optimal function of discrete forms of discourse—like poetics/aesthetics versus politics/philosophy—when it comes to organizing society toward discrete preferences about "the good life" or "justice."

My own approach aims for at least the complementarity between, if not the integration of the ethical and the aesthetic. This harks back to the classical rhetorical ideal, articulated by pre-Socratic thinkers like Isocrates as well as later rhetors like Cicero, Dante, Vico and, in the twentieth century, Chaim Perelman, Richard Weaver, Donald Verene, Ernesto Grassi, and James Boyd White. The crux of it comes down to a fairly simple claim: Without philosophy rhetoric is blind, and without rhetoric philosophy is mute. There are various versions of this assertion. For example, when we speak of "blindness" is it in respect to knowledge, to the nature of the good? But integrating or at least correlating the aesthetic and the ethical is the gist.[1]

[D] And my approach, as you know, has been to enter into the *practice* of exploring the possibility that we humans, in all of our diversity and in the midst of all this contingency and motion might come up with some shared principles and practices that could support our flourishing, or give meaning across time to an idea like dignity. Human rights not as a closed set of substantive laws, but as a space to work out together how we can and must live together.

[R] The rhetorical basis for working out such a harmonious consensus is also what concerns me most. And I think dialogue, in whatever expressive medium it occurs, presupposes a shared understanding of equal dignity and the acceptance of mutual worth.

But what about those who see human rights advocates as clothing themselves in the universal, while underneath the familiar antinomies of Western liberalism continue to run their course?

[D] In other words, seeing human rights advocacy as a type of reaction formation in response to the threat of radical pluralism rather than working through and integrating pluralism into their understanding of rights.

I think the answer depends on whether you are a positivist about human rights or if you see it as a principle in the Arendtian sense—a possibility awaiting (always incomplete) fulfillment (Arendt 1977: 152). The objection that human rights *as instantiated in existing legal instruments* fail the test of robust universalism is absolutely correct. As promulgated, the rights instruments that stemmed from the Universal Declaration of Human Rights ("UDHR") encoded assumptions about gender and about culture that effectively undermined the claim that human rights equally promoted and protected the dignity of all human beings.

At the same time, if we view the twentieth-century development of human rights in historical terms, we can recognize in them an aspiration to promulgate a set of universal constitutional principles that would impede the self-legitimating ambition of power operating under the pretext of law or legitimate political authority. In this respect, the Nuremberg trials mark a legal watershed for the century, introducing a higher universal law that trumped the laws of the state where they authorized unconscionable acts. This aspiration is only worked out through the historical process of differently situated humans pointing out where the laws or norms that claim the status of the universal still exclude them and their perspective.

Which is exactly what has happened. Consistent with the radical pluralism that characterizes the century, the claim to universalism has been subject to searing critiques. Sometimes those critiques have been leveled in the name of a more authentic conception of human rights and a more inclusive conception of the human. Consider in this respect feminist scholars like Hilary Charlesworth who point to the gendered way in which rights and violations have been defined—the requirement, for example, that for an act to count as torture it must have been inflicted by state agents, or the correlative downgrading of violence predominantly experienced by women in the private sphere (Charlesworth, Chinkin, and Wright 1991). What the critics are calling for is an expansion of the rights framework to eliminate these implicit assumptions and biases. On this view, human rights, like radical democracy, is an ongoing project that includes the possibility that societies can be ordered in ways that allow for the representation of the interests and hopes of all human beings while also constraining illegitimate power and abuse.

Nevertheless, the question remains as to whether any universalist project will inevitably import assumptions that privilege certain perspectives or identities and marginalize others. When it encounters specific worlds, do human rights inevitably "foreignize" (to borrow a concept from Tihanyi's translation theory) imposing their own structures and logics (Tihanyi 2004)? A host of critiques, including those offered by critical or neo-Marxist scholars, along with myriad voices in the Global South, understand the human rights project as inevitably particularistic, principally because of the assumptions about the nature of persons and the structures of society and economy that any liberational discourse imports when it adopts the language of rights (Brown 2004).

[R] So even in the heart of a utopian longing for unfettered differentiation under the shared, protective canopy of universal human rights, one still has to wonder what would the realization of such a call to justice be like? It's not just the problem of what legitimates the kind of rights regime you describe, given our shattered faith in any unified metaphysical or other extra-legal ground for authority, but also what constitutes community in the face of such radical heterogeneity?

[D] I'd want to express some reservations about the word community here, perhaps because of its connotations of closure and pretense of harmony—not that I am advocating a permanent agonism (Mouffe 2000). Rather than unification coming from identity (as would seem to be implied by community), we might look to some shared commitment or open principle as that which creates an ongoing sense of a shared project. In that case, the question would be, what ought to be the orienting principles in a culture of radical pluralism? Or we might narrow that to "what constitutes justice" in the context of radical pluralism?

[R] I think those questions are well put, though I do not share your sense that it is necessary to read "closure" into the concept of community. When we talk about a "shared project," or shared fundamental principles of co-existence, I would say that one's public or political identity thereby extends to the political community at large. The same shared fundamentals help to constitute and sustain both political subjectivity and the social imaginary of the community. As De Tocqueville observed: "Each man in his sphere takes an active part in the government of society" (De Tocqueville 2006 [1835]).

In any event, the underlying tension remains. If justice is the name we give to what authorizes the power of law, including those core organizational principles or values beyond conventional rules of positive law, and if all we can say is justice is "to come," then what's left to us now as the basis for a shared political life amidst radical difference?

If the answer is "time will tell"—which is to say, if we can only recognize the unfolding of partial justice as we encounter it in the endless flux of contiguous nows—that means all we can do is live immanently, framing the meaning of things as they emerge, including the resolution of specific legal conflicts.

[D] But then we are still left with the question, what authorizes one preference or one value over another?

[R] One response is to turn to power itself, the quality of sheer intensity. We hear this in Baudelaire's Romantic credo: "Let the will become intoxicated by drugs or pain, dreams or sorrow, no matter by what, but let it break its chains" (Berlin 1991: 234). Or as Nietzsche presciently put it: "Life is will to power ... Moral evaluation is an exegesis, a way of interpreting. The exegesis itself is a symptom of certain physiological conditions, likewise of a particular spiritual level of prevalent judgments. Who interprets?—Our affects" (Nietzsche 1968: 148).

This is where late modern "process" or immanence-oriented thinkers like Deleuze and Massumi seem to come in. Massumi's brand of affect theory, and perhaps the school of thought known as bio-politics more generally, may be viewed, at least in part, as a reaction to the Derridean constructivist, radically pluralist world view in which it's constructs all the way down, where there is no respite from making moves in an endless game of interpretation (Bennett 2002; Connolly 2002; Deleuze 2001; Massumi 2002, 2015). In a Deleuzean world of "pure immanence," intensity of affect may be the ultimate self-authorizing value. As Massumi puts it, "Intensity is a value in itself" (Massumi 2015: 99).

The problem, of course, is by what intensities shall we be bound, or forced apart? To what acts of meaning do we say yes or no? And in so saying whom do we become? What kind of society do we create? These are questions that vitalists like Nietzsche and Massumi, or for that matter the neurobiology of autonomous affect, cannot adequately resolve. The defense of freedom in a resilient democratic society requires informed choice as well as informed deliberation in the decision-making process. Democracy cannot flourish as a non-cognitive phenomenon in which the supposed emancipatory power of affective intensity reigns supreme.

[D] And what about the flourishing of meaning in history: how can the shifting sands of momentary encounters—whether in the form of fleeting affects or intuitions—provide the ground for any continuity of practice or commitment?

[R] Surely any political community or legal order requires at least provisionally binding promises that link past to future.

[D] Well, whether immanentist intensities or claims of universal rights prevail, it remains the case that we're left with multiple worlds, constituted by multiple communities committed to their own unique expressive modalities in which competing sources of authority busily clamor for power and dominance.

[R] Yes, this is the point of departure for what James Boyd White has called the "constitutive rhetoric" of law and politics (White 1985: 205). The realities we know, or at least occupy (knowingly or not), are constituted by the stories we read and hear and tell, the images we watch, and the social and cultural performances that we engage and reproduce.

[D] By extension, the realities we are in, or that are in us, are also the byproducts of intrinsic operating systems—the various "logics" that constitute the particular medium in play.

[R] On this dispensation, images are irreducible to text, as is sound to image, word to sound, dance to word, and so on. Each medium is sustained by a uniqueness of production and expressive truth, a novelty of aesthetic fashioning, epistemology, ontology, perhaps even metaphysics.

We listen and look, but literacy is a relative thing. We do not always know what is there before us to be seen and heard, or what kind of absence silently beckons: whether in symptomatic slips of the tongue or structures of feeling hidden in an image—by Vermeer, say, or Rothko, or David Lynch. What does it signify? Different eyes, different hearts and minds, are attuned to different realities and the codes that constitute them. Common sense may lay claim to elementary levels of cultural literacy. But some codes require study. The uneducated eye or ear will miss much that is of significance. That is why it is important to ask, how is a particular image or text or sound or performance coded for meaning? In what aesthetic and ethical registers does it operate? Once we realize that the information that all of our senses provide is socially and culturally constructed, the need for this kind of decoding—in the present as well as throughout history—becomes self-evident.

[D] Your reference to the educated sense implies that we need to call into question what we assume about what it means to know, as well as the modalities of learning we have embraced. It also suggests a degree of humility in the face of those media of transmission to which we ought to admit we are color blind, tone deaf, smell hindered, and so on. Or even where we do have some sensual education, we would do well to be mindful of the depth and breadth of our capacities to "read" or interpret sensory data.

[R] For each medium (and each mediated reality) that we encounter there are extrinsic codes of organization (the order common sense is privy to) as well as hidden ones, what ethnographers respectively refer to as an "exoteric" order and an "esoteric" one. Consider, say, the exoteric nature of a Byzantine icon, or early modern legal emblem, or popular contemporary legal images—whether from a courtroom, TV show, film, or internet series. Each of these visual mediations can be described by its apparent ("self-evident") references to familiar cultural patterns: the iconic crucifixion, the popular explanation for the emblem's esoteric Latin motto, the familiar story genres, character types, and plot lines that we recognize when we watch moving images on electronic screens, large and small, inside the courtroom and in the court of public opinion.

[D] The exoteric is familiar enough to take us in, and hold us there. But there is also a larger culture of implicit references and meaning-making processes at work in every expressive medium. For example, the quality of affect being invoked has reference points inside and outside the context of the particular story that is being told. This includes, as Foucault taught, the way affect circulates within a larger network of power or authority in society.

[R] Yes, and investigating this broader context concerning the implicit or disguised flow of power initiates a more esoteric journey into the meaning-making process. For example, the emblem's image of a blind judge implicitly points to a disembodied vision of greater import and value than sensorial sight allows. That spiritual dimension, in turn, sanctions a hidden source of authority, a deeper knowledge, registering in the key of metaphysics, where an unwritten law guides (perhaps even commands) the written one (Goodrich 2014).

Likewise, the iconic crucifixion belies a deeper mystery, one that also resists sight altogether. The incarnation that seizes sight teaches the eye it cannot possibly see the infinitely merciful man-God who has been given, though iconophiles and iconoclasts beg to differ on these matters (Mondzain 2005)

So, too, in our secular or perhaps post-secular (Habermas 2008) encounters with screened legal displays a multitude of esoteric subtleties beckons. As when film director Joshua Oppenheimer invites us to relive the fantasies and terrors of Anwar Congo, a genocide perpetrator, whose heaving body in pain lures us into the enigmatic domain of the political unconscious, law in the flesh (Sherwin 2014)—the violently destructive or creative plenitude out of which one legal regime comes to an end and another one arises—if we have the eyes to see it, the heart to feel it, or the intellectual capacity to self-reflectively decode what is unfolding before us.

[D] Or, to take an epistemologically and ontologically less complex, though hardly self-evident level of aesthetic and ethical construction, we might consider the deliberate fragmentation and re-contextualization of screen images in a legal case like the one involving the Los Angeles police officers who surrounded and brutally beat Rodney King following a high-speed chase. These images, too, contest visual common sense, and depending on how we frame them, they can be (and were, to great effect) transformed in court from a story of brutal racialized violence into something quite different, a tale that featured the measured "escalation" and "de-escalation" of force by trained professionals.

[R] Or, shifting from the courtroom to the court of public opinion, we might ask how did it come about that in the popular TV show "Homeland" when a Hezbollah commander walked through a Syrian refugee camp in Lebanon he passed by a wall with graffiti scrawled in Arabic: "'Homeland' is racist." What secret flow of power and resistance is evident here? Or, for that matter, is present in the racial dynamics involved in shifting the source of aggression from perpetrator to victim in the Rodney King case?

[D] Whose space are we occupying? What secret flow of power do we encounter? What are we able to read, and what do we misread or fail to read altogether, assuming, as James Parker describes in Chapter 5, that it is mere noise, a kind of background static without meaning?

[R] Whether it is a subversive act of resistance in "Homeland," or one of acquiescence and control, as in Katherine Bigelow's film "Zero Dark Thirty"—in which harsh interrogation practices, such as water boarding, seem to demonstrate their efficacy by providing information leading to the capture and killing of Osama Bin Laden—viewers might well discern the covert circulation of power (particularly with regard to Bigelow's use of CIA-fed story elements).

[D] Or they might be swept into the flow of power without recognizing it as power at all and thereby find themselves unwittingly subject to its effects. That is very much the danger in the Bigelow film, no?

[R] Yes, I think you're right. Where should we draw the line that divides documentary film making from propaganda, or the line that separates factual truth from political ideology, or objective reality from irrational fantasy? And when might significant, albeit masked legal and political truths surreptitiously dwell in surreal fantasies, awaiting epiphanic insight through empathic interpretation, as Oppenheimer challenges us to experience in his film "The Act of Killing"?

What we readily see or hear or feel often belies a deeper truth, accessed by a deeper knowledge. Masked or otherwise hidden realities must be separated (perhaps excavated) from superficial, more readily apparent ones.

The exoteric disguises the esoteric. At the same time, an easily recognized exterior often imports a complex network of unrecognized assumptions and beliefs. Like that hidden puppeteer—theology—of which Walter Benjamin famously wrote in "The Concept of History":

> The story is told of an automaton constructed in such a way that it could play a winning game of chess, answering each move of an opponent with a countermove. A puppet in Turkish attire and with a hookah in its mouth sat before a chessboard placed on a large table. A system of mirrors created the illusion that this table was transparent from all sides. Actually, a little hunchback who was an expert chess player sat inside and guided the puppet's hand by means of strings. One can imagine a philosophical counterpart to this device. The puppet called "historical materialism" is to win all the time. It can easily be a match for anyone if it enlists the services of theology, which today, as we know, is wizened and has to keep out of sight (Benjamin 2003 [1940]: 389).

[D] You say that the hidden realities "must be" separated, but how? Who is able to do this? How do we even know when we are swept into the flow of power carried by the esoteric? To do so requires that we be hyper-literate, something that might not be attainable without guidance.

[R] Without a doubt, amid the plurality of narratively or visually or acoustically or performatively contrived realities, self-reflective interpretation and critical deconstruction present a great challenge. How could we be we literate enough, in whatever medium that is in play, to manage the critical burden of deciphering the esoteric power struggle—for authority, for mastery of meaning, for collective belief and the ongoing contest over its proffered hierarchies of knowledge that roil beneath the surface of exoteric spectacle in all its forms? That is what would be required for prudent judgment in the face of multi-modal forms of communication.

[D] True enough, but prudent judgment seems like such a tame phrase when so much is at stake. Consider the example of the veil that some Muslim women wear. In this case, there are multiple economies at work as well as interpretations of what those economies are, but the baring of those interpretations goes far beyond the question of attire or even how women's bodies are caught in circulations of power. Those referents are themselves caught up in larger political economies. Think of the way in which "liberating Muslim women" fed into the justifications for military action in Iraq and Afghanistan. At the same time, some Muslim women will insist that the association between the veil and oppression fails not only to encode their experience but is based on culturally distinctive understandings of freedom (Mahmood 2011).

[R] A more expansive approach to aesthetics and judging would encourage greater receptivity to diverse, underlying epistemologies, ontologies, and metaphysics. So, for example, when we ask (following William Mitchell's arch query) "what do pictures want" (Mitchell 2004) this not only implicates a dynamic range of subject/object entanglements (cognitively, affectively, culturally, unconsciously, and so on). It also prompts a host of related questions, such as: What does sound want? Or photographs? Or films? Or graffiti? Or dance? Or painting? Or digital simulation? Or any cultural performance for that matter.

Refracted through the critical lens of the politics of significance, I wonder whether the history of twentieth-century culture culminates in what might be described as synaesthetic jurisprudence. Synesthetic jurisprudence inquires into the various ways in which the embodied political subject acquires the capacity to think, feel, and judge as an inextricably entangled process. Judging in this sense is to a significant degree an offshoot of the orchestration of the subject's passions in accordance with the dictates (or "logic") of a given social imaginary.

Hence arises our intensified interest in diverse modalities of mediation or relation (between subject and object, context and idea, controversy and judgment) as part and parcel of the constitution of the political subject.

[D] But if each communicative medium operates according to its own logic, how could they be synthesized? And if each reaches to a rich and distinctive esoteric dimension, does not synthesis risk becoming a form of reduction?

[R] Must an integrated multi-modal performance necessarily reduce the singularity of its component parts? Must the singularity of a discrete rhetorical manner of minding the world and others around us necessarily refute universal values? Anti-Enlightenment thinkers like Vico and Herder rejected that premise (Berlin 1976).

Different cultures, even different historical periods within a given culture, may have their own sense of value. But it is important to note that incommensurability isn't the same thing as relativism. Plural systems of meaning, whether substantively or expressively, may be equally objective and equally knowable (Berlin 1976: 84), just as each may express or temporally partake of recurrent trans-temporal patterns or categories of meaning.

[D] But even if people living in the twentieth century were emancipated from the tyranny of universal, unalterable historical structures, that doesn't release them (or us) from the burden of constructive choice. Just the reverse: the lack of any single, invariable, overriding principle makes all the more urgent the need to choose and justify among multiple possibilities the creation of social structures that promote the greatest justice and foster social solidarity based upon one set of principles as opposed to another.

In accordance with what overriding value preference? The greatest individual freedom, or the greatest equality? The least oppression among its members, or the greatest economic or cultural productivity that can be attained? Or perhaps a larger vision that includes responsibility for those who cannot represent themselves within our political processes, including non-human animals and future generations—not to mention the planet itself. Any choice entails loss as well as gain, as does any decision-making principle we adopt. I suppose that might be the tragic dimension of freedom …

[R] Or the burden of freedom. In each instance of choosing, the case for the right or best outcome based on the right or best principle or expressive modality must be made.

At the same time, I wonder if we might agree that there may be some values we can't help but accept, or can't help experience their repudiation with anything but shock. So perhaps in this sense, even without the metaphysics of it, we may yet speak of a shared sense of attunement, perhaps as an offshoot of our nature as humans. Such a thought may garner support from the recurrent prestige of humanism—at least, humanism conceived as a way of thinking and judging that relies upon reasoned persuasion as its point of departure rather than some closed set of atemporal, a priori principles (Grassi 1988; Strauss 1965: 32–33, 105).

[D] If you're referring to some innate sense of "human nature," well that's a term that makes me uncomfortable, again because it seems to imply that the ontic, that which is stable and foundational, is in a realm called nature, and then through some other faculty, we (particular types of humans?) transcend this. It also implies that this source we are looking for is located within individual humans, as distinct from being a type of emergent property of relationships we have with each other and our embeddedness in a non-human world that also constitutes us (Coles 2016).

Your point though is, I think, more concerned with seeking a source of orientation—not a singular principle, but perhaps a few principles in the sense that Arendt used the term, where there exist myriad possibilities of instantiation of the principle and yet nevertheless, the principle is not just an empty signifier.

[R] Yes, I like that way of framing it. When we think about law and culture rhetorically, as a system of communication, we are saying that they operate by way of discrete codes and discursive practices that are characteristic of discrete discursive communities contextually and argumentatively endowed with the prestige necessary to warrant belief, and enforcement (Sherwin 1988; White 1985). To be sure, choices of value must be made and, at least in democratic societies, the process leading to their acceptance ought to be as open and self-reflective as possible. That's how law's legitimacy arises: with the political subject's capacity and willingness to accept political and legal obligation.

[D] But of course when you use the word "open" doesn't that raise the question of who counts as a political subject? Who gets to be included in the political community that legislates for itself, especially in a world where the community affected is likely to exceed the political community from which the power of law emanates?

In any event, as Foucault contended, the capacity and willingness of the subject you are referring to do not exist as dimensions of an autonomous subjectivity who then accepts or rejects, but are themselves effects of disciplinary regimes (Foucault 1978).

[R] OK, to integrate the Foucauldian insight, if the way political and legal subjects consent to authority (which is to say, if the way we attain consensus on a preferred source and flow of power in society) depends (at least in part) upon how subjects are constituted, and different expressive modes of communication constitute subjectivity in different ways, then the study of diverse modalities of expressive communication must be deemed essential to the study of law.

To paraphrase Kenneth Burke, not only is every form of knowing a form of repression (of alternative ways of knowing and thinking and communicating), but also an act of repression directed against disparate expressive communities. In a liberal democracy, any act of discursive or communicative closure must be exercised with great care. (Kahan 2009)

[D] So how does a given expressive medium of communication at a given time, under given cultural (social, political, economic, and theological) circumstances constitute the political subject? Which is to say, what is the basis for law's legitimation, and how is it sustained (or resisted or subject to decay and dissipation) over time?

[R] This is what the politics of significance sets out to address, and it points to one of the the overarching themes of this volume. For example, starting in chapter one, Desmond Manderson asks what it means to capture newly emerging notions of justice in the medium of painting. Through a close look at Gustav Klimt's lost masterpiece, *Jurisprudence*, Manderson examines the relationship between sovereign power, the abject subject, and the immanent third ("the citizen-spectator"). The painting itself, which depicts a suffering naked man surrounded by eyes, was commissioned to be hung in the Great Hall of the University of Vienna. That objective was never realized, and the painting itself was destroyed by a fire during World War II.

Manderson argues that in this work, produced at the very beginning of the twentieth century, Klimt eerily captures the relationship between 'sovereignty and bare life' a dynamic that, according to Giorgio Agamben, was re-forged and refined across the twentieth-century. In this sense, Klimt's complex, volatile image might well be the first, and perhaps still among the most comprehensive representations in modernity of the abject figure. Manderson's chapter explores how the late modern subject suffers the extra-legal power of sovereignty, on the one hand, while aspiring to the creative agency of a collective social imaginary, on the other.

[D] And in chapter two, Craig Elliot explores the conflict that arises when Indigenous peoples, perhaps the exemplary instance of the abject that the modern nation state has produced, draw on their own laws and use their own expressive modalities to mount claims against the constitution of the sovereign state. Song, dance, and story are for Aboriginal people the expressive modes through which they transmit their understandings of sovereignty, relationship, and law. This is the basis upon which they are able to establish ownership of land. But when they have sought to communicate the existence of such traditional forms of ownership, a variety of profound conflicts have ensued.

For one thing, the performative modalities that transmit these substantive claims challenge the assumptions that modern nation states and their legal systems make about how truth is transmitted. With their preference for documentation or oral testimony, the courts of the settler-colonial state are ill equipped to comprehend the messages that First peoples bring to them. A song that traces the Dreaming track that underpins relationships between a particular people and a tract of land is, by default, illegible in this context, and thus delegitimized by the courts. Absent access to a privileged set of expressive modalities, or at least courts becoming attuned to these modalities, the Aboriginal understanding of sovereignty and right that underpins their legal claims remains at risk of never gaining traction with the understanding of sovereignty that structures and informs the state's constitution.

Tracing a number of cases in which Aboriginal people have presented evidence of land ownership using performative media, Elliot analyses the conflict that ensues when profoundly divergent systems of law, meaning, and expression clash in court. The Australian legal system's efforts to 'accommodate' performance evidence by expanding their rules of evidence may have gone some way toward bridging the gap, but ultimately they prove inadequate in the face of profound disparities in knowledge and power. Insofar as Aboriginal song, dance, and performance are inseparable from their distinctive understandings of the sources of Indigenous law, sociality, and the relationship between people and the land, seemingly insuperable obstacles block their ability to be heard and seen in their own voice through their own customary practices. In this way, the chapter makes vivid the kinds of expressive, ontological, and constitutional conflicts that have played out during the twentieth century.

In chapter three, James Parker examines the case taken in the International Criminal Tribunal for Rwanda (ICTR) against Simon Bikindi, one of Rwanda's best known musicians and popular figures, whose songs – considered by many to be 'the soundtrack for genocide' – were transmitted through radios across the country. The case provides a window onto the ICTR's *sonic imagination*, which is to say, how the court conceived of the Rwandan soundscape and the role it played in the genocide. Parker demonstrates how the court's capacity (or incapacity) to discern the nature of the acoustic universe in which the case unfolded had a significant impact on its judgments of responsibility and exoneration. The chapter focuses specifically on how the tribunal conceived of radio, a technology and media apparatus that it insisted was central to the commission of genocide, but that it reduced to the status of a tool for the amplification of intentional human action. In the process, the tribunal overlooked the complex constitution of the acoustic medium itself. This failure points to an incapacity to decode how the acoustic medium shapes and reframes the sonic meaning of what was being transmitted.

This case prompts the question of how the significance of sound has been systematically neglected by legal scholars and jurists. Although law is deeply implicated in the fabrication of our sonic environments, matters of acoustics are routinely treated as self-evident. As a result, apparently self-evident, but unexamined assumptions are unwittingly smuggled into judicial judgments. For example, in the course of this chapter we learn that the International Court's inability to self-reflexively discern the difference between noise and sound had a significant impact on their rulings regarding institutional versus individual criminal responsibility. Parker leaves no doubt that sound's unique expressive modality requires legal practitioners and scholars alike to cultivate a new sensitivity regarding the juridical practice of listening – what Parker refers to as 'acoustic jurisprudence'.

The emergence of visual evidence in legal trials, including films, videos and photographs, represents one of the century's most significant legal shifts, charging legal practitioners to cultivate literacy in the visual arts alongside traditional text-based and verbal rhetorical strategies. In chapter four, Susan Schuppli explores the increasingly important role that non-human forms of testimony such as video footage are playing, thus positioning them as active agents in the production of jurisprudence.

The specific legal conflict that Schuppli considers is the trial of Slavko Dokmanović which took place before the International Criminal Tribunal for the former Yugoslavia (ICTY). Dokmanović was charged with participating in a mass execution in Croatia. He offered an alibi, supported by a video, allegedly taken en route, showing that he was in a part of the country remote from the massacre on the day that it took place. Although two human survivors gave testimony to having seen Dokmanovic at the site and on the day of the massacre, it was the combination of their human witness with what Schuppli calls the 'material witness' of a reconstructed video, deciphered for the court by an expert on trees, that constituted a narrative of sufficient credibility to disprove Dokmanovic's alibi. Along with the video of trees, Schuppli examines a range of materials that archive their complex interactions with the world, and which, through forensic decoding can be reassembled to provide courts with a type of access to a past that they did not witness, but which they must somehow come to know.

[R] Material witnessing through visual media is a fascinating development in modern legal culture. But live performance, and specifically street theatre, was also used with enormous creativity and to great effect throughout the twentieth century. Performance makes visible some of the deep-seated assumptions underpinning and normalizing contestable social, political and economic arrangements. As Diana Taylor argues in chapter five, legal regimes are themselves forms of performance that sanction certain preferred resource distributions and relationships to power, while repressing others. Sometimes, it takes the staging of a counter-performance to expose law's constructive function and the contingency of its choices. Such counter-performances make explicit the agreements to which political subjects implicitly assent, opening the way to a more reflexive process of critical evaluation so that the justice of those agreements may be duly challenged.

Taylor's chapter examines a series of performances involving the impersonation of the multinational agriculture corporation Monsanto. The performances were staged during the period when a decision was pending in regard to Monsanto's application to the Mexican government seeking permission to plant genetically modified corn (GMC). The performances included staging a fake website and a fake press release impersonating Monsanto announcing, and expressing its gratitude to the Mexican government for granting the corporation's request. The impersonation also announced a series of (fake) measures that Monsanto would take in response to anticipated critics.

In this way, activists were able to flag how Monsanto might readily counter protests concerning the impact of the government's decision on communities and the environment. While the performers were quick to publicly reveal the 'lie' (as the chapter puts it) of their impersonation, this did not keep them from successfully exposing the kinds of performative moves corporations make to quell dissent and, of course, garnering significant public attention to the issues at stake. In the course of exploring the legal limits of impersonation, freedom of speech (particularly academic freedom), and related ethical issues, the chapter casts light on the vicissitudes of social activism in the face of disproportionate corporate power.

Another expressive medium also has played a role in constituting law and late modern political subjects. Along the way, it has raised important questions about the state's power to delineate what is public space and what remains under the control of private property. In the latter half of the twentieth century, an illicit activity became both a significant art movement and a prevalent political and cultural practice. Street art and graffiti have in recent years come to signify urban creativity, while remaining firmly criminalized.

Although street art is increasingly present within mainstream cultural institutions as much as in city spaces, it remains an illicit activity that can lead to criminal sanctions against its practitioners. Street art and graffiti are thus currently positioned at a threshold of legitimacy: their histories derive from the illicit or semi-licit activities of protest movements, youth cultures, and punk, but their recent incorporation into the mainstream art world complicates the distinction between their status as art practices and their categorization as crimes.

In chapter six, Alison Young engages with the ways in which law responds to the urban images generated by street artists and graffiti writers, considering the interconnections of criminal law and property law as a means of *framing* words and images placed in city spaces without permission. Young raises challenging questions concerning citizen-artists whose use of illicit public art works calls attention to territorializing and de-territorializing strategies in modern society. Who owns the public spaces of cities? Might a new 'commons' help to constitute what it means to occupy the contemporary cityscape? Correlatively, how do graffiti artists disrupt legally instantiated ideas about property and individual rights, inscribing their presence often with a boldness that defies their putative exclusion?

In chapter seven, we explore in dialogue with director Joshua Oppenheimer what different genres of filmmaking can tell us about societal wrongs and, in particular, how political subjects collude in or resist systemic political violence. The chapter is based on our interview with Oppenheimer in New York City in 2015. It explores themes concerning the different ways in which documentary film has been deployed in the mediation and representation of massive human rights violations in the twentieth century.

The specific films in question (Oppenheimer's 'The Act of Killing' [2012] and 'The Look of Silence' [2014]) focus on genocidal violence committed by governmental agents and local citizen militias in Indonesia during 1965-66. The brief introduction by the editors considers questions of documentary truth as well as the promise of greater transparency in the representation of state wrongs. It also wrestles with the dangers associated with victor regimes intent on repressing or distorting across generations the rending effects of genocidal violence. The interview itself canvasses a number of key issues such as how film can be used to challenge dominant representations of the past while also opening up a space for the narratives of victims sacrificed to the tyranny of state imposed silence.

Along the way, the chapter elucidates how documentary films employ different aesthetic codes to constitute and convey different social, political, and psychological realities. This includes the respective roles and ethical choices of persecutors and their victims, and of the moviemaker himself whose visual rhetoric knits together the various parties' disparate narratives using diverse film genres and commingled registers of truth and fiction. The chapter explores various forms of guilt and denial that ultimately work to destabilize the perpetrator's identity. It also addresses the role of ethical clarity, dignity, and moral courage on the part of Adi, a victim who defies decades of state imposed silence. In speaking back to the perpetrators - his neighbors - who have for three decades remained in power, Adi models the difficult but necessary process of seeking moral accountability. It is this process that prefigures the possibility of political truth, social reconciliation, and liberatory forgiveness. Woven throughout the discussion we encounter the thematic entanglement of empathy, responsibility, love, and their relationship to justice.

In chapter eight, Christian Delage extends the exploration of visual media by examining how techniques of visual and verbal narration can be used in court to constitute (and re-constitute, or annul) the meaning of racialized violence. Delage's exploration of these issues reverberates within the tortured history of racial discrimination in the United States. Representations of this history over the last century range from popular literary and cinematic figures like Atticus Finch in *To Kill A Mockingbird*, who heroically stands up in court against the injustice of racial prejudice, to TV images of the trial of African-American football hero and pop culture figure O.J. Simpson. In the latter instance, Simpson oscillates, paradoxically, between celebrity, perpetrator (of a double homicide), and victim (of endemic police racism). Against this cultural backdrop, Delage probes the criminal trial of the four white Los Angeles police officers who were fortuitously filmed by an amateur videographer as they surrounded and furiously beat African-American motorist Rodney King following a high-speed chase on a California freeway. But what do these images show? Did the twelve jurors in court (not to mention the millions of citizens across the US who watched the televised proceedings as jurors in the court of public opinion) witness a racially motivated, morally abhorrent exercise of excessive state violence, or the professional 'elevation' and 'de-elevation' of force based on established norms of police training?

In drawing out the unprecedented challenges presented by the spectacle of 'trial-by-image' in the age of digital mass media, Delage raises difficult practical and ethical questions regarding the search for truth in contemporary, image-saturated courtrooms. How should trial lawyers go about the business of examining and cross-examining visual images along with the narratives strategically devised to amplify their putative truths? In its reflexive framing of the law's various accounts of alleged racial violence against Rodney King, this final chapter underscores how visual literacy (or its absence) affects the development and outcome of legal conflicts in contemporary society. In so doing, it also highlights a broader claim of this volume, namely: that literacy or its absence in *any* discrete expressive mode of communication is bound to have significant effects on the adjudicatory process. And so, in the end, we re-encounter a theme sounded at the beginning – judgments cannot be adequately understood apart from the tools we use to make them.

[D] I think this summary shows how each of our authors sets out to explore one or more of the plurality of worlds generated by a plurality of expressive modalities. The claim of this book is that attending to these constructs expands the archive of legal knowledge as well as the repertoire of legal interpretive and administrative or institutional practices, nurturing what we are calling synaesthetic jurisprudence.

[R] Improving our literacy in different expressive modalities helps us to recognize what is being claimed and how. This increased awareness also allows us to provide a better response to the Foucauldian question concerning how power circulates in society. When we are able to identify which form of knowledge, in which mode of expression, is being privileged over others under a given set of circumstances, we are also able to say which discursive community is being elevated over others. For the very act of privileging a particular way of knowing correlatively privileges the discrete community with which that knowledge is associated (Kahan 2009). At the same time, empowering particular modes of knowing also elevates implicit assumptions and hidden values. To the extent they remain veiled, covert forms of empowerment impair the deliberative process in which ideas and preferences compete for social and political ascendancy in the larger contest for knowledge and power in the community at large.

And so aesthetic clarity prepares the field of judgment. In democratic societies, where transparency in the deliberation process is deemed a virtue, literacy is a valuable cultural asset.

[D] Yes, but this volume also addresses a further ambition, namely: to go beyond simply fostering greater literacy in the various expressive media that make up the social imaginary, including the domains of law and politics, to open up the question of justice itself

[R] I agree. Sharpening our aesthetic capacities should work hand in hand with deepening our ethical capacities – the possibility of our making judgments that are capaciously just under conditions of radical plurality.

CONCLUSION

[R] So how should we conclude these introductory thoughts?

[D] Well, for one thing, if the loss of foundations and the rise of radical pluralism and incommensurability during the twentieth century constitute, as we have been suggesting, the unavoidable context in which legal and political choices are to be made, then the emergence of synaesthetic jurisprudence makes sense. Synaesthetic jurisprudence will not mandate specific choices in the ongoing search for right or just outcomes in particular legal or political conflicts, but insofar as it recognizes the need to "read across difference" it affords us the type of open orientation that may best equip us to undertake that search.

[R] Yes. The challenge is how to proceed in the absence of stable meta-narratives. Under such conditions the specter of legitimation crisis hovers close by. How do we negotiate a path between the opposing threats of illiberalism (whether in the form of Schmitt's decisionism or Nietzsche's will to power) on the one hand, and an incoherent, unsustainable relativism on the other?

[D] And beyond working out what such a path might look like, it seems equally important to ask, what are the subjective capacities needed for us to remain on that path? What is it that sustains us in the give and take of dialogic process, or any collaboration in the performance of meaning, whatever its expressive mediation?

[R] What challenging questions! At first blush, one might respond by exploring the various ways in which particular passions, desires, and emotions propel— and perhaps bind us to—the different meanings that the discrete logics of multiple modes of communication express. But I suspect there is also a deeper dimension here, the matter of accounting for the invisible social bond that holds us together.

Might we speak of some originary, unitary force that binds us like refracted rays of light whose distinctive hues are preserved while held in spectral unity? Is this the binding power that mysteriously echoes in the ancient and recurrent term "*Eros*"?

[D] Perhaps the core normative idea is that the very act of communicating presupposes a capacity and willingness to be present with, and receptive to difference.

[R] This may well be the most fundamental ethical premise one could imagine.

Writing, conversation, legal argumentation, the act of persuasion, and of expressive communication as a whole all presuppose a desire to share a certain urgency within a given historical context, together with the concomitant belief that others want to know, and can at least to some extent enter into an otherness for the sake of some shared meaning.

[D] The very act of "entering into" is the ethical key—even if full understanding is lacking, or impossible. And regardless of agreement or disagreement, which are ancillary.

[R] As Richard Schechner puts it, we recover ourselves by going out of ourselves in our meeting with others (Schechner 1985: 112). Such a capacious dialogic attunement to harmony and difference allows us to sustain a robust pluralism. Which means it serves society as a stable platform for freedom.

[D] Yes, I think that's right. But I'd also say the type of freedom authentic attunement makes available is larger still. As Levinas has said, "To approach the Other in conversation is to be welcome to his expression, in which at each instant he overflows the idea a thought would carry from it. It is to receive from the Other what is beyond the capacity of the I" (Levinas 1969: 51).

[R] These are beautiful and profound words. I think it is this kind of attunement to otherness that we encounter in time-transcending forms of art, such as the endlessly rich humanism of Shakespeare (Dawson 2014).

Perhaps attunement of this sort is capacious enough for us to imagine how Josh Oppenheimer could befriend someone like Anwar Congo, a perpetrator of genocide—acts of killing that Oppenheimer repudiates with every moral fiber in his being.

[D] Attunement capable of reaching that far across otherness allows us to enter realms that are likely to feel alien and sometimes repellant, like Congo's perverse imagination—replete with wild fantasies and self-exonerating rationalizations—while still being able to recognize him as human, a member of a shared cultural community whose stories, images, and affects link us together.

Perhaps it is this spirit of attunement that also allows us to understand a man like Adi, the protagonist in "The Look of Silence," who confronts the violent perpetrators, whether government officials or members of the powerful para-military shadow government, who live all around him in contemporary Indonesia, perhaps including those who ordered the violent death of Adi's own brother.

Indeed, perhaps Adi, who literally adjusts the lenses of the perpetrators so that they may better see, models this capacity to be present with them, even as he holds true to an ethical compass that gauges the horror of their acts.

[R] Might this suggest an ethical substrate within which the disparate elements of radical pluralism flow? A larger source that contains disparity ... How about *agapé*?

[D] Levinas invites us not to be afraid to use that word, to "say this quite plainly, what is truly human is love … even with everything that burdens love, or … responsibility is actually love" (Levinas 2001: 143).

[R] The capacity to love, which is but another way to describe the capacity to understand, to listen and watch across vast differences within the plenitude of human nature.

If we were to agree with Plato and Freud that *eros* is a natural force in the human world, that would place an interesting spin on how we might humanize, for political purposes, affect—the intensity fields that swirl around and within us. Perhaps this converges with the approach to affect that Martha Nussbaum has recently taken up (Nussbaum 2013), not to mention Hardt and Negri in *Commonwealth* (Hardt and Negri 2009).

[D] Generosity towards the other. Radical pluralism and incommensurability—sustained not necessarily by agreement, which may be impossible, but by a willing engagement with difference, based on a deeper sense of shared humanity. And I would hope, a movement across difference beyond the human, based perhaps on a deeper sharing of the conditions of life and our interdependencies, including ones that we have not yet identified.

[R] That may well be an important part of the ethical meaning of Oppenheimer's film work, the ethical symbolism that his stories allegorically perform. Such generosity of heart and mind would certainly allow the give and take of persuasion to flourish, the kind of collective negotiation of mutually sustainable worlds of meaning that is necessary for a robust and just coexistence.

[D] This suggests a more vibrant, receptive-expressive space where solicitude for each other calls forth rich multimodal articulations of our different experiences of the world.

[R] Reflecting the way the members of a community actively engage in the quest for unity amidst diversity, how each may seek to persuade the other about what is best or just, or worth pursuing as the most meaningful or valuable kind of life we can think of, the kind of life that makes the reality of being human strike us anew as the miraculous gift that it is.

CHAPTER ONE

Justice

Klimt's Jurisprudence—*Sovereign Violence and the Rule of Law*

DESMOND MANDERSON

INTRODUCTION

There is something uncanny and prophetic about painter Karl Klimt's lost masterpiece. *Jurisprudence*, a suffering naked man surrounded by eyes, eerily captures the relationship between "sovereignty and bare life" that Agamben argues was re-forged and refined across the twentieth century—a particular construction of legality that grants to executive power an uncanny freedom of action, and in the process both dominates and shapes the bodily experience of human beings subject to it. Klimt's image might perhaps be regarded as the very first, and perhaps still among the most comprehensive representations of this abject modern figure.

But how can a painting which no longer exists, by an artist long since dead, be "about" a book by Agamben written in 1998? One answer lies in the social and legal landscape already emerging in 1903. The seeds of Agamben's analysis of the relationship between sovereignty and law are to be found in the work of earlier writers such as Carl Schmitt (2005) and Walter Benjamin (2007), much closer to Klimt's time and place. More than this historical connection, the meaning of a work of art is a function not just of the artist's intention but of the richness of quotation and cultural resonance that grows up about it (Bal 1999: 1–23). Art does not lose currency in changed social contexts, but *accumulates* it, like a snowball tumbling down a hill. For those of us trained in jurisprudence, this will not seem so strange. It is the central predicate of legal judgment (Dworkin 1985). A decision is not settled when it is first expressed: the full extent of its implications unfold and ramify over many years. Thus this chapter, in its exploration of an emerging theme of justice, attempts to draw out the full implications of Klimt's compelling image by reference to the cultural and legal forces in circulation at the time, *and* by reference to how they have unfolded in the hundred years since.

Klimt, however, does not merely exemplify the force field of jurisprudential violence laid plain by Agamben; he complicates and interrogates it. In this chapter I first introduce the basic themes and background of the picture, highlighting the inadequacies of a merely iconographic reading. After that, I offer alternative interpretations of the image and particularly of the naked man at its heart. I first interpret the picture through one of the most important cultural events that took place in Vienna while Klimt was working on

Jurisprudence—the first German production of the *Oresteia*. This reading highlights Klimt's critique of legal formalism, and closely connects it to the concept of *homo sacer*. I then develop a very different understanding of bare life via Freud's *Interpretation of Dreams*—published, once again, at the very same time that Klimt was thinking about *Jurisprudence*.

The two readings I propose hover in an uneasy relationship. They draw our attention to a tension within Agamben's relationship between sovereign power and law—one, sovereignty's conversion of human beings into legal *objects*; the other, the psychic life of the legal *subject*. The possibility of a third reading, critical or inter-subjective, sheds new light on some of the puzzles and anomalies in Klimt's complex painting. If *homo sacer* illustrates the vulnerability of human life to the "force of law"—the figure of the sovereign being both a creature of the law and exterior to it—it also testifies to its resistance to that force and to our responsibility with respect to it. These three readings—the objective, the subjective, and the critical—develop three understandings of the relationship between the sacred man and the law. This relationship is of increasing importance in a world in which the power of the sovereign state to protect itself seems increasingly to justify all manner of actions in the name of the law, and yet to undermine it.

BEYOND KARL KRAUS

Gustav Klimt was Lord of the Ring—the *Ringstrasse* that is, home and monument to bourgeois Austrian legality (see Schorske 1980). In 1894, sustained by a well-burnished respectability, he was commissioned to produce three paintings for the ceiling of the Great Hall of the University of Vienna. They were to represent the Faculties of Philosophy, Medicine, and Jurisprudence (Klimt 1903–1907, 1899–1907, 1898–1907; see also Novotny and Dobai 1968; Whitford 1990). It was to be an ode to the spirit of enlightenment. But by the time he came to fulfill the commission, Klimt had changed, artistically and intellectually. In 1900 and 1901, his first two paintings, *Philosophy* and *Medicine,* were excoriated (Schorske 1980: 231–243). *Philosophy* showed "unclear ideas through unclear forms," (in Whitford 1990: 50) darkness and fog abounding; *Medicine* showed not the science of healing but bodies in pain and ecstasy, death, sex and life writhing across the canvas (Marlowe-Storkovich 2003). Reason and science are in each case subjugated to primal forces. Questions were asked in Parliament; petitions were raised against the works; the ministry was pressured to withdraw the commission; the university's new chair of aesthetics famously declared "We are not opposed to nakedness or to the freedom of art, but we are opposed to ugly art" (Schorske 1980: 235–239). In 1901, when Klimt began work on *Jurisprudence* (Figure 1.1) he knew what to expect (Schorske 1980: 246–247). Although there are clear thematic connections between it and the earlier pictures, it was already apparent that the canvases would never be hung as originally planned. In style, palette, and texture, the treatment of the final picture marks more of a rupture with the other two than their continuation. The canvas was not designed with a ceiling, or with its companions, in mind. When it was first exhibited, as part of the Secession exhibition of 1903, Karl Kraus, Vienna's most prominent critic, dismissed it as bringing the grandeur of law into disrepute. The viewer might respond to the work, he suggested, with "ridicule or pity" as the mood took them (Kraus 1903).

Klimt had committed the unpardonable sin of turning his back on conventional wisdom. The painting was not called *Recht* or *Rechtswissenschaft* or *Gerechtigkeit*. No mystery there; *Jurisprudenz* was what he had been commissioned to depict—the proper name of the oldest Faculty in the second-oldest university in the German-speaking world

FIGURE 1.1 Gustav Klimt, *Jurisprudence* (University painting for the University of Vienna, 1903; destroyed by fire, 1945). Source: Leopold Museum, Vienna.

(Minkkinen 1999: 183). But a "Faculty of Jurisprudence" stakes a claim to treat law as a coherent object of study. In the civil law tradition, *die Jurisprudenz, la jurisprudence*, connects philosophy to practical wisdom through an underlying logic. Klimt sought to illuminate a relationship between theory and practice—precisely a "jurisprudence"—radically different from this self-image. He paints a portal into the faculty. We are allowed to furtively peer through the keyhole into the inner recesses of the law, but the scene we glimpse there is visceral and disturbing. No wonder they hated it. Bitter recriminations followed. The Faculty Paintings were never displayed at the university, let alone installed in the Great Hall. Klimt returned the commission and refused to hand over the paintings. They were sold to the Lederer family at the end of the First World War, only to be "Aryanized" by the Nazis after the *Anschluss*. In 1943, they were removed for safe-keeping to a castle in lower Austria. There, they sat out the war, only to be destroyed in a fire, along with about seventy works by Klimt and others (Nebehay 1994: 76–77; Whitford 1990: 62).

Jurisprudence no longer exists. We have nothing except a few brief descriptions of it and a black-and-white reproduction. The one thing we *cannot* do any more is simply look at the work, since before it we are all now color blind. Its monochrome drabness immediately suggests black-letter law and gray-haired lawyers. But this only serves to persuade us that reading a work of art—any work of art—requires the exercise of the imagination. The original experience of looking at Klimt's canvas was not dull but shocking. The vast canvas, over 4 meters high, was dominated by the use of only three strong colors—black, gold, and red (Whitford 1990: 61). The swirling Furies have red hair; the currents that flow around them and give the picture a sense of giddy movement are black; gold illuminates the three goddesses that stand in the background. The creature in the middle is red.

It is worth beginning with Karl Kraus, not only because he was so prominent in Viennese critical and cultural circles at the time, but because his analysis of *Jurisprudence* is the fullest contemporary discussion of it we have. Writing in *Die Fackel*, Kraus treated Klimt's tonal "symphony" as a kind of visual slander—the scurrilous appropriation of a combination of colors "strictly frowned upon by the Austrian authorities" (Kraus 1903). By adopting the three colors of the imperial coat of arms, Klimt equates law with the power of the state, and implies that its trappings of patriotism and nobility only disguise its underlying violence. Throughout Europe, the judiciary almost always wore crimson robes and hats; in that way too red and black signify judicial authority, violence, and power.

In the distance, among the clouds, Klimt shows three conventional allegorical figures: *Nuda Veritas,* the naked truth (see Klimt 1899; Schorske 1978); *Justicia* in the middle; *Lex* cradling the word of the law, literally. They appear totemic, static, indurate. Beneath this celestial frieze, a scene of submarine horror unfolds. The three Furies are animated by swirling black lines that suggest the currents of a fast-flowing river or ocean (see e.g., Klimt 1898). Yet in the midst of this turbulence, two figures are locked together in an eternal embrace: an abject everyman with head bowed, and a monster. The association between Hobbes' Leviathan (1968; Minkkinen 1999: 184) and the state springs to mind, but Leviathan was a dragon or sea-serpent, or more generally a whale.[1] No, Klimt has drawn a Kraken, the giant octopus of northern legend (e.g., Bergen 1753; Tennyson 1830). The German word for octopus is *Krake,* but the older word *polyp* conjured more sinister resonances. The term was commonly used as a metaphor for the state and its agents—tentacular, dark-lurking, "blood-sucking," furtively deploying its many limbs in all directions.[2] In Klimt's Vienna, to put it bluntly, *polyp* was slang for a policeman: the long arm of the law. As Kraus puts it, the artist is "getting away with a painted insult" (Kraus 1903; Nebehay 1994: 74). An image is also a text, and here a verbal pun—*polyp/polizei*—has been literalized visually, or visualized literally.

Kraus complains that while "at the beginning of the twentieth century ... no symbol can reveal relations that are richer than that of jurisprudence," Klimt has merely equated law with punishment, smuggling in veiled insults to the imperial family, the judiciary, and the police along the way. Iconography—reading the image "for what it is not," as

Norman Bryson put it turns the image into a textual element (1983; see Bal 1991, chapter 1 and 177–189). Even Kraus' interpretation of Klimt's colors relies not so much on a keen eye as a sharp tongue (see Timms 1986). The colors themselves are not replicated by Klimt—the "gold" on the imperial flag was not, we can be sure, Klimt's gold—but only their *names*. Kraus uses the same words to describe different sensory phenomena and then connects their connotations. Through this chain of extended signification, imperial honor becomes tainted with blood lust. But Kraus fails to see how his textual approach actually invites a broader linguistic point. Klimt's wordplay is paralleled in the structure of the picture, in which Latinate virtues—*lex*, abstract and remote—are contrasted with everyday speech. Hifalutin legal language, Klimt implies, is a facade. Down in the slangy streets, some poor sap is having the life sucked out of them by the fuzz, much to the delight of a bunch of harpies. Slang, translated into images, is the secret code that slips past the censors and the cops.

But this semantic analysis cannot come to terms with the dynamic complexity of Klimt's image—its style, composition, erotics, affect, and "mysterious atmospheric depth" (Schorske 1980: 273). For Carl Schorske, *Jurisprudence* marks a turning-point in Klimt's career. He reads it as the last gasp of a wounded narcissism: a self-portrait of the artist as martyr (Schorske 1982: 44–45; see Kann 1981: 179).[3] Certainly a radical shift took place in the years following Klimt's original 1898 composition study for the painting. In that version, an all-powerful Justice wields a mighty sword to slay her tentacular enemies (Klimt 1897–1898; Novotny and Dobai 1968: cat. 86). By 1902, a revised composition sketch reflects Klimt's radical rethinking. Justice has retreated and now the hideous sea monster holds center stage (Strobl 1980: No.l 942).[4] Abject and naked, the central figure, who has no place in the mythopoetics of the earlier sketch, elicits our attention and our sympathy. For centuries, the figure of justice had been idealized, and the state legitimated as its embodiment. Klimt produces something quite different: law from the point of view of its victims.

According to Schorske, *Jurisprudence* was Klimt's parting shot. Thereafter, he retreated from the real world to "an ornamental two-dimensionality, itself an index of utopian complacency." "Wherever European artists made the difficult attempt to grapple with an existing order," writes Schorske, "as they so often did in the nineteenth century, social realism emerged as a dominant literary mode" (1980: 273–279). He is not alone in making this argument. Kraus condemned Klimt as a mere aesthete. The architect Adolf Loos accused Klimt and the Secession of applying "a layer of whitewash ... in collusion with a reactionary order of state" (Hofmann 1972: 9; see also Timms: 3–17; Loos 1982, 1998). But utopia is not a denial of politics; it is an expression of it. Thomas More did not write the original *Utopia* (1965) as a "retreat" from the world. He wrote it *as* a critique. Both utopian and dystopian texts have performed that function ever since. Indeed if the reputation of utopianism has been tarnished over the past century, it is on account of its political zeal rather than any complacency (Kateb 1972; Mannheim 2013).

Furthermore, and Schorske to the contrary, there is *nothing* real about realism (Bal 1990). Modernism was determined to reject the pseudo-realism of mimesis (Gay 2010; Manderson 2012: 23–26; Burrow 2000). Abstraction for example, recognized the reality of paint and the actual "two-dimensionality" of the canvas far more honestly than the *trompe l'oeil* of perspective and figurative art (Bal 1990, 1999). Modernism took as its point of departure the gap between the world and our representations of it. That has been the starting point of every social critique since (Burrow 2000: 235–238). Certainly, Klimt's *Faculty Paintings* reject art's arrogant claims to objectivity and realism—just as they reject the arrogant claims of philosophy, medicine, and jurisprudence. That is not an apolitical position; far from it.

So Klimt's *Jurisprudence* shows how ornament and style can be incorporated *as* critique. The aesthetic dimension of law—its gilded forms and abstract reasons—is juxtaposed against the lonely figure with heavy irony. This makes *Jurisprudence* very different from its sister-works. Both *Philosophy* and *Medicine* evoke ethereal spaces with soft lines and flowing contours. Obscurity and uncertainty are their subject and their form. Klimt showed what these disciplines, for all their claims to scientific precision, could not cure, could not understand, and could not perhaps even see. *Jurisprudence* takes the opposite tack. Its subject and its form focus on clarity and definition. The lines are etched with greater force, and the figures more sharply demarcated. The geometric designs in the background, the swooping curves of the women's hair, and the circles that stud the sea creature create two-dimensional shapes rather than three-dimensional volumes. In all these ways, Klimt conveys the rigidity and force of law. If Klimt attacked the disciplines of philosophy and medicine by portraying what their arrogant claims to sovereignty could never reach, *Jurisprudence* took the reach of law's sovereignty very seriously indeed. There are obvious connections between Klimt's portal to the law and the gatekeeper who stands "before the law" in Franz Kafka's parable (1953: 173–175; Minkkinen 1994). But the "inside" of the law, which is forever hidden from Kafka's "countryman," is pitilessly exposed by Klimt. The Kafkaesque might have looked something like the other Faculty Paintings—tableaus of misty mystery. But *Jurisprudence* treads a different path. It does not minimize law's pretensions to total knowledge, but shows instead its effects on human bodies. Klimt does not suggest that the law fails too often, but that it succeeds too well.

AGAINST *ORESTEIA*

Jurisprudence developed this critique in dialogue with one of the richest dramatic works ever written about law—Aeschylus' *Oresteia*, a trilogy first performed in Athens in 458 B.C.E.[5] The influence of Greek tragedy on nineteenth-century Germanic culture—on Richard Wagner for example (Ewans 1982), and later on Sigmund Freud—cannot be overstated. Constructed from 1893 to 1902, a monumental statue of Pallas Athene (the key figure in *Oresteia*) stands guard outside the Austrian Parliament. Yet the first complete German language performance of the trilogy did not take place until the end of 1900. Berlin and Vienna both put on performances based on the same new translation within weeks of one another (Aeschylus 1900; Hardwick 2011; Macintosh 2004: 366–368; Schlenther 1900). The modern approach of the Austrian production at the *Burgtheater* was particularly influential (Mikhalis; Hardwick 2011; *Neue Freie Presse* 1900: 1–2).[6] There are enough internal references within Klimt's image to be confident that he saw it. The play is said to tell the story of Athens' transition from a primitive vendetta culture, represented by the Erinyes—the Furies—to the founding of the Areopagus, the development of independent courts, and something like the rule of law. In the first play, *Agamemnon*, the Chorus insists on unquestioning obedience to two laws. Zeus' infallible law that wisdom comes only through suffering (A 177–78) is one; the *lex talionis* is the other. "Blood grudge for blood grudge, blood let for blood let," they intone. "He who has wrought, shall pay; *that is law*" (A 1564). The Furies are the bailiffs of this law. In return for fair winds when his fleet set sail for Troy, King Agamemnon sacrificed his own daughter Iphigenia. For this shocking and callous act, his wife Clytemnestra plots a terrible vengeance. On his victorious return from the war, she tangles him in a net and stabs him to death. In *The*

Libation Bearers, their son Orestes exacts retribution on his mother. Now the Furies, mere metaphors and allusions in the earlier plays, take visible form. Clytemnestra demands that they revenge *her* death, as Orestes avenged Agamemnon's, and Clytemnestra, Iphigenia's.

> "In return for hostile words, let hostile words be paid!" —
> in exacting what is due, Justice shouts that aloud,
> and "In return for bloody blow, let bloody blow repay!"
> "For the doer, suffering" is a saying three times old. (L 310–3)

The Furies pursue Orestes. "They come like gorgons, they wear robes of black, and they are wreathed in a tangle of snakes. I can no longer stay ... These are no fancies of affliction! They are clear, real, and here; the bloodhounds of my mother's hate" (L 1048–54).

In *Eumenides*, the final play, Orestes seeks Apollo's protection, and Pallas Athene is called upon to arbitrate between the claims of Apollo and the Furies. She breaks the cycle of vengeance, acquitting Orestes and insisting that justice does not condemn us to eternal repetition. She designs the Areopagus to include the participation of Athenian citizens, and shifts its focus from tribe to city, and from honor to welfare. The Erinyes are renamed Eumenides, "kindly" or "awesome" ones. They cede part of their vengeful role and become the guardians of creation—of fertility, productivity, and the land—before being led "deep in the earth's primeval hidden places," there to "keep holy silence" for all time. Guided by Athene's wisdom, and with feeling put to sleep, the rule of law begins.

But in Klimt's *Jurisprudence* something has gone wrong. The Furies have just woken up and circle around a figure that might be Orestes. In the distance, the virtues that might, in their splendour and association, be called Apollonian, appear powerless to intervene. Schorske concludes that Klimt re-runs the drama; only this time, the Furies win. Law is still governed by vengeance, reason stands far off, and Athene is "simply absent" (Schorske 1980: 251). This is only half-right. Although the figures of legitimacy are distant and static, this should not be taken to imply impotence. On the contrary, law's legitimacy *relies* on its removal from the day-to-day violence that enforces it. Law's ornamental trappings are a mantle that protects the legal system, keeping its hands clean but complicit in its excesses. In Klimt's rendition, Truth holds no mirror[7]; Justice has a sword but no scales (see De Ville 2011: 346). The gilded forces of legal order—the word of the law, the beauty of truth, the majesty of justice—have not been sent packing by the passions. They stand and watch; they give it the thumbs up.

This is not just autobiography. *Jurisprudence* is, well, jurisprudence. Vienna, as Kraus would famously remark in 1914, was "an experimental laboratory for the end of the world" (Timms 1986: 10). Klimt's painting reflects critical features of his legal culture as well as our own—the ascendancy of legal positivism, on the one hand, and the critique of legal reason on the other (Burrow 2000; Dyzenhaus 2006, 1998; Manderson 2012: 25–51). These two forces were already on a collision course that would shake the twentieth century. In Austria, the *Allgemeines bürgerliches Gesetzbuch* (ABGB) had been promulgated in 1811, but Pandectism across the continent led to an approach to law that was increasingly systematic, metaphysical, and abstract. The German civil code, the *Bürgerliches Gesetzbuch* or *BGB*—widely perceived as the most ambitious and influential product, indeed the apotheosis, of "legal science"—came into effect on January 1, 1900 (Berkowitz 2006). In due course, Hans Kelsen would give this science its most uncompromising theoretical justification. In 1901 he was only a law student; in the Faculty of Jurisprudence at the University of Vienna (Dyzenhaus 1998; Kelsen 1967). Carl Schmitt's mature work (e.g., 2005, 2008) also dates from the inter-war years, although his early monograph on decisionism appeared before the start of the Great War (1969; see Kennedy 2004). He argued there that within every moment of legal judgment lay a fundamental indeterminacy which could not be controlled by rules. It would not strain matters too much to read Klimt's *Jurisprudence* in this light. The Furies of arbitrary power engulf the solitary figure, while rule-bound legality stands idly by. Klimt chastises pompous legality for the forces it could not control; and popular legality for the violence it unleashed. The question of the balance of these forces was already an important one at the turn of the century, though its most important theoretical exposition was yet to come (see Schorske 1961, 1973). Klimt prefigures Schmitt's ridicule of the impotence of Kelsen's "legal science." But he also prefigures Kelsen's warning (1934) as to the dire consequences of Schmitt's "political theology" (2005). Can one take both sides to task? Certainly one can if, like Klimt's abject man, one suffers from the aloofness of one and the violence of the other, adding the insult of one to the injury of the other.

Giorgio Agamben (1998, 2005) elaborates the contemporary understanding of sovereignty, as the *id* of law, we might say, the moment where the legal rules break down and the power of the executive to enforce its will proves unstoppable. He traces its origins from Roman law to the concentration camps of the twentieth century, glossing Schmitt's observation that "sovereign is he who decides on the exception" (2005: 7). The sovereign declares as a conclusory fact that this or that person or group or race or class are outside all legal protection. His is the power to declare an exception or an emergency to which the rules no longer apply. Now Schmitt's initial insight was that *all* legal circumstances contain some unique kernel, some element of difference and exceptionality, which might let this anomic genie out of the bottle. There is therefore an intrinsic, albeit paradoxical, relationship between legal rules and rule-less sovereignty. *Homo sacer* is the figure formed by this power—he could be any one of us, reduced to a pure animal existence without political status, legal identity, or recourse. As Agamben explains, "bare life" is "included" in the legal order only "by exclusion" (1998: 65). To take another instance, one might say that, like the outlaw or *werewolf* of the Middle Ages, he is subject neither to legal norms nor religious rites; neither is the state subject to them with respect to him. He is outcast from law by law. This intertwined logic of absolute sovereignty cast its longest, darkest shadow over Europe under the Third Reich, where the forces of legal order were complicit in the extermination of many millions of human beings, stripped of all belonging and exposed to the sadistic pleasure of the furies. The extermination of the Jews was "neither capital punishment nor a sacrifice, but simply the actualization of a mere 'capacity to be killed' inherent in the [factual] condition of the Jew as such" (Agamben 1998: 114–115). Their death was not, strictly speaking, a punishment, but only the outcome of a factual determination to which law was utterly indifferent.

But this is just the terrain on which Klimt and Agamben meet. The Third Reich did not come from nowhere. The British had already constructed "concentration camps," so-called, during the Boer War, which began in 1899 and claimed 9,000 lives. In some ways the war was quickly won; but Boer *commandos* continued to mount a successful guerrilla operation in the countryside. In 1900, to cut off their supply lines, the British Army interned well over 100,000 civilians, mainly women and children. Within a year, nearly 30,000 had died from disease and starvation. After Emily Hobhouse exposed these atrocious conditions, the British Government was forced to appoint a Commission which investigated the concentration camps in the second half of 1901 (1901; see also Agamben 1998: 166–180; Judd and Surridge 2013; Pakenham 1997; Seibold 2011). The Boer War was the most important topic of Austro-Hungarian foreign policy that year. During 1900 and 1901, anti-British sentiment in Germany and Austria ran high. There was uproar in the press, and in the Austrian Parliament (Bridge 1972: 247–248). The Emperor stood by his British cousins. Perhaps he had an eye on the German Empire's own "exception" in southern Africa. Only a couple of years later, the Herero people of German South-West Africa were driven into the Namib desert by General von Trotha, and prevented from leaving: hounded "like a wounded beast," reported the German general staff, "until finally he became a victim of his own environment" (Bley 1996: 162). Up to 100,000 died of starvation and thirst, the rest reduced to slavery. It was the first attempted genocide of the twentieth century (Whitaker 1985).

The violence that sovereign power would unleash could not have been imagined by Klimt or his viewers. But it had its roots in the legal context that was already taking shape. Klimt seems to have captured with uncanny prescience the *danse macabre* between its component parts—"the tinsel of legal form" whose hands are tied, the tentacular state whose arms are long, the rabid furies of sovereign power, and in the middle, *homo sacer*, a "bare life" abandoned to its fate like a wounded beast (Figure 4). If, as Agamben argues, sovereignty exists precisely *by virtue of* its capacity to constitute and exploit bare life, then *homo sacer* is produced by the exercise of that sovereign power. There is a strange symmetry between them; on one side a power that exposes all men to the exteriority of the law, and on the other a vulnerability so absolute that any man might freely exert sovereignty over them: a prison guard, a bureaucrat, or even another internee. The sovereign is a beast, it is said, just as the outlaw is nothing but an animal (Agamben 1998; Manderson 2003); both are included by jurisprudence only by being excluded from it (Agamben 1998: 28; Derrida 2009). *Both* exist outside the governance of law.

This is exactly the relationship at the heart of Klimt's *Jurisprudence*—a sovereign power beyond juridical control, and a bare life beneath it, circling one another. What shape does this sovereignty take? It is a torus, a circular body which encloses empty space, generating but never entering the anomic field. That is the shape of Klimt's Kraken—neither *polyp* nor *homo* actually touch one another, though no doubt a magnetic force holds them in place. Klimt portrays "the force of simultaneous attraction and repulsion that ties together the two poles of the sovereign exception: bare life and power, *homo sacer* and the sovereign" (Agamben 1998: 110). The bareness of life, "which is invoked today as an absolutely fundamental right in opposition to sovereign power, in fact originally expresses precisely both life's subjection to a power over death and life's irreparable exposure in the relation of abandonment" (Agamben 1998: 83). The sovereign needs bare life and bare life cannot evade it; legality hovers in suspended animation in the clouds.

Agamben is not alone in thinking that we are witnessing the normalization of the figure of *homo sacer* along with the endemic practices of sovereign violence that reduce human beings to it. We see it in the administration of humanitarian intervention, and in places like Guantanamo Bay and Abu Ghraib (see Greenberg and Dratel 2005; Goldstein 2007; Humphreys 2006). We see it in stealth bombings, drones, and targeted assassinations authorized by—what?—an executive authority that does not presume to make a legal decision but only to declare certain facts. We see it in internment of refugees and displaced persons (e.g., Manderson 2013a, b). In Australia, a person who wishes to claim protection to which they are legally entitled is automatically stripped of those self-same rights, prevented from accessing them, or accessing knowledge of them, or even accessing information about the denial of them. By law this doesn't happen in Australia; since

May 2013 the whole continental mainland has been legally removed from Australian territory for the purposes of immigration (*Migration Amendment Act 2013*). The whole of Australia, Agamben would say, is only included in the law to the extent that it has been excluded from it. Sovereign power is then free to unleash its inner fury. This structure of excision and exception, "black holes," secret violence and active surveillance, seems increasingly invasive of our physical existence.

Look at the pre-eminent role of eyes and vision in Klimt's painting. The Furies stare wildly; the Virtues look into the distance. There are further small figures behind the Furies, all watching on inquisitively. The circles and spots that form the cloak of the law, and splatter truth and justice—they too resemble pupils in a glaucous jelly. Above all, look at the Kraken. Its single eye—clearly marked in Klimt's revised composition sketch—stares fixedly ahead. But its arms and body are covered in thousands more eyes, emphasizing the idea of the state as an organ of unblinking surveillance. The image is not new. Legal emblems depicting the sovereign wearing a "coat of eyes" frequently signified an omniscient power (Goodrich 2014). The "Rainbow Portrait" of Elizabeth I (Oliver 1600–1602; Figure 1.2) is the best-known example. She wears a cloak covered in uncannily realistic eyes and ears, the better to spy on her enemies. One looks from kraken to queen and from queen to kraken; but already it is impossible to say which is which.

FIGURE 1.2 Isaac Oliver, *The Rainbow Portrait* (Hatfield House, Hertfordshire, 1600). Source: Bridgeman images.

WITH FREUD

All the same, this reading fails to account for critical characteristics of Klimt's style and composition. The rounded volumes of the central figure give it a powerful embodied reality; but the sacred man is circled by a cartoon monster, stylized, flat gorgons, and highly ornamented goddesses. They float in two-dimensional space. Those in the foreground are dynamic but spectral; those in the background suggest a monument or a statue. What they share is this sense of hovering disembodiment, symbolic rather than real, unanchored in physical space. The image transpires in an ether, alien to the logic of perspective, like a painting of angels from the Middle Ages. Even the clouds (see Damisch 2002) at upper right, and the unpainted space across the middle, suggest an absolute contrast between transcendent forms outside the world, and the immanent body of the naked man, firmly rooted in it. They seem to inhabit categorically incommensurable realms. When could they ever meet?

Freud knew the answer: in a dream. That's where reality becomes a representation and representations become real. *The Interpretation of Dreams,* was published in November 1899. The resonances between Klimt's visual, and Freud's verbal, pre-occupations are well known. Both associate dreaming with *eros* and *Thanatos* (Frodl and Klimt 1992: 88). And both find in Greek myths the archaic and instinctual undertows of our lives (Schorske 1980: 220–221). But in what follows I want for the first time to read Klimt's work directly in relation to Freud's classic work. Klimt's painting records a dream, and the dreamer with it and in it, eyes closed, drawing our attention inside his unconscious. It is one thing to explain *Jurisprudence* as an avatar of Klimt's unconscious, as does Schorske (Schorske 1980; see also 1973). It is quite another to explain the unconscious as an avatar of jurisprudence.

In *The Interpretation of Dreams,* Freud lays down the law: "The dream is the fulfilment of a wish" (1953: 103). But we experience "a feeling of repulsion towards this wish. And in consequence of this repulsion the wish is unable to gain expression except in a disfigured state" (1953: 120). In order to evade the internal thought police, dreams communicate our desires in disguised form. They have a "latent content" (or meaning) that must be distorted in order to sneak past the mind's "censor," often resorting to puns, proverbs, or colloquialisms to get its point across. The connection Freud draws between the governance of the subconscious and legal regulation was not a coincidence. Law was explicitly the model for his entire analytical structure.

> The political writer who has unpleasant truths to tell to those in power finds himself in a like position. If he tells everything without reserve, the Government will suppress them ... [H]e therefore moderates and disguises the expression of his opinions ... The detailed correspondence between the phenomena of censorship and the phenomena of dream-distortion justifies us in presupposing similar conditions for both. (1953: 51)

Freud goes on in thoroughly legalistic terms:

> We should then assume that in every human being there exist, as the primary cause of dream-formation, two psychic forces (tendencies or systems), one of which forms the wish expressed by the dream, while the other exercises a censorship over this dream-wish, thereby enforcing on it a distortion ... Nothing can reach consciousness from the first system which has not first passed the second instance ... (1953: 121)

Freud's jurisprudence leads to an amendment of his original law. "The dream is the (disguised) fulfillment of a (suppressed, repressed) wish" (1953: 136). Freud provides many examples, from the most straightforward (dreams motivated by thirst, or the urge to urinate) to complex dreams employing elaborate techniques to encode their meanings—rebuses or picture puzzles, the "condensation" of multiple experiences into a single figure, and the "displacement" of central themes (1953: 261–304; 399–402). He might have been talking about *Jurisprudence*. In order to evade government censorship, Klimt disguised his latent content by means of extensive wordplay, codes, and metaphor.

So *Jurisprudence* is a dream, and a dream is the fulfillment of a wish. But what wish? Freud struggles to explain how anxious or shameful dreams can fulfill a wish when they seem to do the exact opposite. His response to these "apparently invincible objections" is not entirely convincing. Most of the time, Freud says, the wish being fulfilled in "painful and terrifying dreams" is to prove him wrong. The dream fulfills the wish by not fulfilling a wish (1953: 48). But fortunately Freud does not leave it at that: "[D]isagreeable dreams contain, as a matter of fact, something which is disagreeable to the second instance [the internal censorship mechanism], but which at the same time fulfils a wish of the first instance" (1953: 51). Blondie notwithstanding, dreams are not free. The unconscious has an internal revenue service—guilt, shame, and anxiety are the taxes it levies on our desires.

Jurisprudence in fact illustrates a very common dream that Freud considers at length. He calls it "the embarrassment dream of nakedness," typically staged while figures of authority, or strangers, look on—

> when one wishes to escape or to hide, and when one feels the strange inhibition of being unable to stir from the spot, and of being utterly powerless to alter the painful situation ... According to our unconscious purpose, the exhibition is to proceed; according to the demands of the censorship, it is to come to an end. (1953: 79–81)

Such dreams, for all the discomfort they cause, reveal an underlying desire, which might be termed the desire to achieve legal subjectivity: to be seen by the law, to be exhibited before it, not in a partial or abstract way, but "as we really are," in complexity, innocence, pain, and pleasure. The man in Klimt's painting is old, worn, and weary. He is not one of those idealized figures that the legal system constructs or supposes—not the virtuous citizen, or *bonus pater familias*, or the reasonable man. He is a man of everyday feelings, needs, and desires. This is literally what he stands for, against the wholly symbolic and abstract forms that encircle him. Freud observes that a dream cannot directly express a negation. Instead, elements of form and absurdity critique the manifest content of the dream and direct us toward its secret message (1953: 304–307, 341). The form of *Jurisprudence* conveys clarity, force, and separation. But the Kraken strikes a satirical note which made Kraus uneasy. The noble figures, immobile and far away, demonstrate their ignorance. The figure of humanity yearns for a responsiveness they cannot give him, an understanding they do not possess, an intimacy of which they are incapable. Klimt's dream expresses a desire for *recognition*.

Up close, the "first instance" of desire is found in the dynamic and dangerous movement of the libidinous figures that swirl around him. In the distance, the "second instance" of repression looks on, static and authoritative, commanding us to *stop* in the name of the law. Caught in the middle, abjectly exposed to the gaze of others, both desire and shame course through the naked man. The censors of the dream-work pervert this desire for recognition, but nevertheless hold our feet to the fire, *preventing* our escape. In Klimt as in Freud, the man is unable to move.

What is the meaning of the sensation of inhibited movement which so often occurs in dreams, and is so closely allied to anxiety? One wants to move, and is unable to stir from the spot; or wants to accomplish something, and encounters obstacle after obstacle. (1953: 110–111)

The abject man clasps his *own* hands behind his back. Nothing ties his wrists together, and indeed the Kraken's limbs do not at any point touch him either (a modification of Klimt's own preliminary sketch). Mieke Bal (1991: 167) sees the position of the hands in works of art as forms of visual "speaking." But in *Jurisprudence* the hands are holding back not reaching out. The goddesses express forbearance or disinterest: justice wards us off; law clutches its own word tight. The hands of the Furies do not grab, or consume, or entice. They seek their own flesh, each hand caressing only its mate. "Inhibited movement," expressing a frustrated will to communicate, marks not only the abject man but all the hands in the painting. There is a complete breakdown of relations, an alienation of its component parts.

The same lack of relation characterizes the treatment of eyes which dominates the picture. In Francisco de Goya, *El tres de mayo de 1808* (1814) shows a complex interplay of eyes. The soldiers who are about to execute the young man look at their target but their faces are hidden from us. The witnesses cover their eyes from the violence to come; the eyes of the dead are closed. So the former cannot be seen, and the latter cannot look. Only the central figure returns the gaze of the firing squad. *Jurisprudence* presents a very different relationship. It shows us every eye *except* the victim's. A man stands: head bowed, gaze averted. As opposed to Goya, it is the man that turns inward, and everyone else that sees, a classic instance of Freud's shamed visibility. Panu Minkkinen is wrong to conclude, however, that "all eyes are on him: the goddesses,' the Furies', ours" (1999: 187). Of all those eyes *not a single one* looks at the central figure.

Klimt gives us ideals that do *not* speak, hands that do *not* touch, and eyes that do *not* see. The dream expresses and fulfills a wish for recognition and communication. But the eyes do not have it; they look the other way. Klimt's dream represents the experience of a thwarted desire for recognition, a feeling of impotence accompanied by only the traces of a lost desire: in the dream-like and innermost posture of the man and the libidinous forces of the swirling female figures that surround him, searching for a liberation that cannot be consummated.

Throughout the twentieth century, the jurisprudence of recognition has taken many forms: philosophies of human rights, legal pluralism, legal realism, critical legal studies, feminism, race theory, and post-colonialism, to name a few.[8] In very different ways, they all start from the experiences and needs of human existence and human societies rather than imposing idealized forms and normative strictures onto human life. But once again, Klimt's treatment forcefully suggests Agamben's critique of this rhetoric. Bare life has two faces: the face of bio-political subjection, and the face of legal recognition. They are not opposed but mutually implicated. "The spaces, the liberties, and the rights won by individuals in their conflicts with central powers always simultaneously prepared a tacit but increasing inscription of individuals" lives within the state order, thus offering a new and more dreadful foundation for the very sovereign power from which they wanted to liberate themselves (Agamben 1998: 121). In this, he broadly follows Foucault's critique about law's creeping discipline of bodily existence. Although their approaches are quite different and related to distinct projects, both writers conceive of the relationship between power and bodies as marking a profound shift towards more intimate and invasive practices of administration and governance, as opposed to the periodic and spectacular displays of sovereign power. Pierre-Joseph Proudhon observed this change in 1851:

> To be *governed* is to be watched, inspected, spied upon, directed, law-driven, numbered, regulated, enrolled, indoctrinated, preached at, controlled, checked, estimated, valued, censured, commanded ... and to crown all, mocked, ridiculed, derided, outraged, dishonored. That is government; that is its justice; that is its morality. (1923: 293–294)

The promulgation of various rights to life, body, and so on were partial political responses *to* these developments. Agamben (1998: 125) mentions the writ of *habeas corpus* (1679) (see also Haverkamp and Vismann 1997). A legal command is issued to bring before the court not a person or citizen or a name, but a body. It is released from custody but subjugated before a greater authority. The "*corpus* is a two-faced being, the bearer both of subjection to sovereign power and of individual liberties" (Agamben 1998: 125). Klimt's figure might well be called *Habeas Corpus*, too—for behold the body of the legal subject, exposed to the judgment and use of the law and the sovereign. No doubt the extent to which this argument can be pressed is open to dispute, specifically in relation to the liberatory potential of the writ (e.g., Fitzpatrick 2001; Norris 2005). But Agamben's broader point is that the desire for exposure, for recognition—to be seen by the law—is the perverse complement of our subjection. In Klimt too, desire and subjection change places before our eyes. In fact, the central role of the naked figure in both aspects, stages this ambiguity with unprecedented clarity.

Yet *Jurisprudence* resists this argument. Klimt reminds us that the bareness of life is not simply a legal construct. We *are* bare life. Sickness, mortality, poverty, and aging remind us of the desires and needs which we share with human and animal life. My mother is very old. She is incontinent; she remembers little; she finds it hard to produce the simplest sentence. She is constantly perplexed, anxious, and lost. She is utterly dependent on others. Her life is bare. But Mardi—her name is still hers—still has needs and desires. If anything they have become more urgent in her fading days. She still enjoys the sun on her back and the song of the birds. She still needs to be touched with love and companionship. She needs to be comfortable: she needs to be comforted. Her existence has been reduced to these elemental needs; but their pulse can be felt in all of us. Our defenseless nudity makes demands on others, and reveals a truth about ourselves.[9]

For Agamben, *homo sacer* was constituted by sovereign power as an object that could be killed with impunity, neither the legal consequences of a murder nor the ethical consequences of a sacrifice pertaining to it. For Levinas—writing several years earlier but in a register which has not ceased to haunt more recent debates on the relationship between ethics and law—the nudity and defenselessness of life is precisely that which cries out for a sacrifice. The difference is that this sacrifice is not made *by* the sacred man, but *for* him. According to Agamben, *homo sacer* is constituted as an unacknowledged sacrifice in the interests of sovereignty: the concentration camp is its regulatory exemplification. According to Levinas, he is constituted as a sacrifice at the expense of our sovereignty: the concentration camp is its regulatory contradiction (Levinas 1988; see also Diamantides 2007; Manderson 2009). The hidden face of Klimt's central figure, turned away from recognition, only intensifies the interruptive silence of suffering, which breaks up the world of knowledge and narrative closure (see Diamantides 2003, 2000; Minkkinen 2008: 82). The naked man, precisely by resisting our efforts to impose a settled meaning on him, produces an ethical demand that is singular without being individuated. As Schopenhauer—whose influence on Klimt is well-established—said, the fully realized human subject is capable of "regard[ing] the endless sufferings of all that lives as his own, and thus take upon himself the pain of the whole world" (in Marlowe-Storkovich: 245).

The paradox is that this human body is both the expression of our plea for recognition *and* the vehicle of our subjection. Klimt's painting shows us two ways of looking at the very same flesh and blood, one by eliciting our compassion and the other by dramatizing our power. *Jurisprudence* is suspended between these two discourses. On the one hand, sovereignty's demand on human life—*habeas corpus,* give me the body; and on the other hand, humanity's demand on sovereign power—*ave verum corpus,* behold my body's truth. These two sides are not related as right to wrong, or false consciousness to true, or cause to effect. They express the inescapable irony of the "two poles, irreconcilable but indissociable" (Derrida 2002: 51–54; Manderson 2012: 147–148) of our relationship to law.

FOR ATHENE

Two opposed readings of Klimt's painting, then, one focusing on the power of sovereignty within law and the other on the claims of bare life against it. This presents a problem—sovereignty helps constitute the desire for recognition but also perverts and exploits it. The answer may lie with a brief return to Aeschylus' trilogy, which I have discussed at greater length elsewhere.[10] The trilogy begins with two legal norms—"learning through suffering," and "the doer must suffer." These are initially treated as two formulations of the same strict rule. But they are not the same (Conacher 1987: 83–85; Zak 1995: 38–39). The Furies' law, the *lex talionis*, implies a stasis and a cycle of repetition from which the House of Atreus could not escape. But Zeus' law, as it is called, wisdom or learning through suffering, implies the possibility of growth and change. The House of Atreus was condemned to the eternal repetition of blood for blood by virtue of its *failure* to learn from its own suffering. In fact the Furies are—and this is the critical point—the most legalistic of all the characters in the play. Like legalists, positivists, and fundamentalists everywhere, they claim they cannot *choose*, but merely follow the law, time after time after time. Finally, however, by dint of Athene's persuasive force, even they come to acknowledge that things do not have to stay the same for ever.

The curse of blind repetition is of course the curse of law. Athene invites us to see in the passage of time and the subtleties of circumstance, the *difference* rather than the sameness of our acts. Human time, the very element that myth ignores, becomes law's defining feature. "*En krono,*" writes William Zak about this conclusion (1995: 87), "we may come to wisdom not merely after the fact of our failures but 'in time' to avoid repeating all the same catastrophes over again." Athene achieves this resolution by yoking the moment of judgment to persuasion, difference, and time. Contrary to most orthodox interpretations of the play, she does not stand for reason against the passions, but for a discourse of judgment against the merely repetitious word of the law.

With that in mind, let us return one last time to the puzzles of Klimt's *Jurisprudence*. Who is the man? What is everyone staring at? And where in the world is Athene? The answers are connected. Here is a scene from a play—a play that Klimt saw on a winter's night, in Vienna, 1900. Klimt positions the viewer on-stage, painting the audience in the background, peering out of the darkness, only their heads visible. In the middle stands Orestes surrounded by the Legal Furies, just woken up but baying for his blood. In the distance, perhaps, stand the avatars of Apollo: shellacked in gold, high-handed and arrogant. Klimt has depicted a very *specific* moment in the story: the moment of decision, when the very future of the law was at stake, and *before* Athene inaugurates a new legal discourse that will shatter the yoke of the past.

Indeed, Athene's decision creates an extraordinary parallel with the argument of Agamben in *Homo Sacer*—but with a significant difference. Athene can be precisely described in Schmitt's famous words (2005: 7; see Agamben 1998, 2005: 1–31): "Sovereign is [s]he who decides on the exception." Indeed Agamben follows the logic of the plays even more closely. The *lex talionis,* he concludes, is just the repetition of a sanction. The *juridical* "constitutes itself through the repetition of the same act without any sanction, that is, as an exceptional case ... In this sense, the exception is the originary form of law" (Agamben 1998, 2005: 26). If this claim seems far-fetched, the *Oresteia* illustrates it perfectly. Athene's ability to judge singular facts, and to break with the past by identifying the exception, truly inaugurates the juridical order. The exception is the origin of the law. Schmitt and Agamben only push this to its logical conclusion, showing us the paradox nestling at the heart of the legal order. Schmitt writes that *"All* law is situational law. The exception reveals most clearly the essence of legal authority ... To produce law it need not be based on law" (2005: 13; see also 1912). Thus he opens the door for the exercise of sovereign power purely on the basis of a factual circumstance of which the sovereign alone is competent to judge (Agamben 2005: chapter 1). The appearance of *homo sacer,* the exceptional figure of abjection who is excluded from the rules, is but the *reductio* of this irreducible sovereign power. Orestes, answering Athene's writ of *habeas corpus,* is "a two-faced being, the bearer both of subjection to sovereign power and of individual liberties" (Agamben 1998: 125). His freedom comes at a terrible price.

Yet Aeschylus resists this conclusion. What ultimately separates Athene's advocacy of the rule of law from untrammelled sovereignty or exceptionalism, are the external structures of abnegation and accountability to which she willingly submits herself. Athene demonstrates a vision of judgment as a participatory and transformative process. This she does in two ways. First, she insists on the involvement of the *whole* community in the act of judgment, establishing the Areopagus in which Athenians themselves would have a meaningful say in decision-making.

> The matter is too big for any mortal man
> who thinks he can judge it. Even I have not the right.
> ... Then, since
> the burden of the case is here, and rests on me,
> I shall select judges of manslaughter, and swear
> them in, establish a court into all time to come. (E 470–84)

Second, she shows the essential role of *peitho*—rhetoric or persuasion—in a discourse of legal legitimacy. Aeschylus understands, better than a great many people before or since, that a legal system does not depend on whether the winners accept the verdict, but whether the losers do (Lind and Tyler 1988). Both Apollo and the Furies connect *dike* with *nike*—δικε and υικε justice and victory; Athene rejects the association (e.g., E 795–6; see Goldhill 2004: 239–245). Indeed, it is a striking feature of the drama that so much of the last play takes place *after* the decision, highlighting the critical moment for any legal system not as one of judgment but of justification (Lebeck 1971: 20–21). Athene does not treat *peitho* as a legal pathology, as do the Furies (and as indeed does Schmitt, in no uncertain terms). She shows how its "sweet beguilement" (E 885) can be enlisted in the service of wisdom and judgment.

> I admire the eyes
> of Persuasion, who guided the speech of my mouth
> towards these, when they were reluctant and wild. (E 970–74)

By exposing our discussions to ongoing dispute and negotiation, sovereignty is made continually answerable to everybody.

The *Oresteia* begins by presenting the indeterminacy of language as law's curse, and the certain application of the law its cure; it concludes by radically reframing the question. Now it is the certain application of law which is the curse—and the indeterminacy of language its cure (Goldhill 2004). The indeterminacy of Klimt's image between the two readings I developed above is in fact its critical feature. Orestes is shown at the very moment of indeterminacy, his visage concealed from us and his body suspended between possible futures of recognition and exploitation, between the arrogance and humility of sovereign power. Klimt generates this suspense by introducing not one but two distinct centers of focalization (e.g., Bal 1991: 159). The internal focalizer draws us into Orestes' psyche and invites us to engage empathetically with his experience and dreams. But the many eyes of the picture constitute an external locus of focalization, which addresses the viewer directly. By inviting us to inhabit these two positions *at once,* Klimt places us in exactly the position of the judgment of Athene. He makes possible both the recognition and the opportunity to which the canvas draws our attention.

No wonder, then, Klimt's painting is dominated by eyes that look expectantly *out* of the frame. They are looking at us. Athene is not "simply absent" at all. In fact, if we really are on-stage, the part we are playing is hers. As she says in the *Oresteia,* she is immanent from that moment on in the sense of responsible judgment she argued for and the social institutions she set up. All the other figures—even the Kraken—interpellate us directly. They are waiting for us to deliver our verdict.[11]

Jurisprudence thus condenses three readings of the relationship between sovereignty and law into a single scene. Law is described in the real world of the first reading in terms of exploitation and violence. This objective or external perspective treats the abject man as a legal object, to be governed and disciplined by sovereign power. In the imaginary world of the second reading, law is described in terms of an unrealized potential. This subjective or internal perspective imagines the man as a legal subject, whose identity is constitutive of legality and legitimacy itself. In the symbolic world of the third reading, law is transformed into an ongoing and collective responsibility (Freud 1961: 243–341, 311). This critical or inter-subjective reading goes beyond either an absolutist understanding of the power of the sovereign, or a reductionist or positivist understanding of the rule of law. It differs from them both, from Kelsen on the one hand and Schmitt on the other, by deferring the responsibility for the development of legal practices to the community as a whole. It is they—we—who are charged by Athene and by Klimt with its stewardship.

These readings are held together by the gravitational force of the naked and abject figure at their cross-roads. He shifts between the expression of a desire that is at one moment crippled, the next dormant, and then aroused. His "bare life" is simultaneously legal violence, human vulnerability, and social responsibility. Like an optical illusion, Klimt's painting thus switches between three different but nonetheless necessary perspectives: law as it is (which has something to do with society); law as we imagine it (which has something to do with philosophy); and law as it might be (which has something to do with politics). The proper name for the study of their relationship is *jurisprudence*.

The end of *Jurisprudence* demonstrates just how unwelcome its study can be. Two days after the German surrender in May 1945, Soviet troops took over *Schloss Immendorf*. Fire broke out soon after and German soldiers, including the castle's owner, returned to put it out. A few days later, another fire broke out in the basement, where over seventy works by Klimt, Schiele, and others were held. All were burnt to ashes. It is no longer possible to determine how the fire started or whose fault it was. But it doesn't matter. One fire may be regarded as a misfortune—two looks like a Freudian slip. Klimt's Faculty Paintings were stored away from the rest of the Österreichische Galerie. Disavowed by the Austrians, abandoned by the Nazis, left to the Soviets, the loss of *Jurisprudence* seems a predictable coda to its sad history of neglect. Klimt's *Jurisprudence* implicates law in violence and oppression, no doubt. But perhaps just as awkwardly, it implicates the jurisprudent in the future of law. It brings the Faculty of Jurisprudence into a more direct relationship with the state on the one hand, and the legal subject on the other. No doubt a lot of people would rather forget the whole thing. The tentacular state, the lofty idealists, the venal Furies—everyone must have breathed a sigh of relief when *Jurisprudence* went up in smoke.

The story of the legalistic Furies is one of the sublimation of law. Repression is the opposite of sublimation—one drives down our desires, whereas the other elevates them to a higher sphere. It is the essence of civilization, as Freud was to argue, to endeavor to transform our darkest urges into a positive force, capable of expressing and fulfilling a finer and wider purpose (Freud 1961: 284–285). But the auto-da-fe of *Jurisprudence* was no such sublimation. Ironically perhaps, the powers that be proved the point of Klimt's masterpiece, promptly repressing his critique of repression, censoring his critique of censorship. We are left with only ashes and a colorless remainder, gone but not forgotten.

The radical nature of Klimt's work lies in two respects. First, *Jurisprudence* does not simply pit justice against the law, but depicts it purposefully on the side of injustice. The intimate relationship between eyes, hands, and sovereignty on the one hand, and the golden figures of privilege on the other, create a dynamic of legal power that is terrifying. In both cases, law is understood as a structure of *eros* not reason: the vengeful *eros* of Legal Practice, personified in the Furies, takes pleasure in the abjection of *homo sacer*, while the voyeuristic *eros* of Formal Law, in the figures of Truth, Justice, and Law, takes pleasure in withholding their power and observing the infliction of suffering. The former are the functionaries aroused by action; the latter are the officials and bureaucrats equally aroused by inaction.

Second, however, is Klimt's insistence that the study of jurisprudence provides a moment of intervention, both critical and active, in the pursuit of justice that the figures of law and sovereign power eschew. The naked body and hidden face of Orestes cry out for recognition. The absence of Athene does not merely signify the abandonment of *homo sacer;* rather she interpellates us to come to his aid, through the kind of critical understanding and agency that jurisprudence provides. As citizens, subjects, spectators, and as scholars, it is not the Gods alone, but we collectively who can exercise the disciplined *peitho,* uniting empathy and reason, to undo law's repetitive injustice. Klimt postulates the legal system as a *danse macabre* among power, subjection, and form. But so, too, does he postulate justice as originating in art: in an imaginative representation of power, subjectivity, and formal structures that neither abandons the naked man to his fate, nor yet surrenders our role in it. In the twenty-first century, when sovereignty and power seem intent on both intensifying their pleasures and concealing their role, this message (and art's role in bringing it to our aesthetic and ethical attention) seems ever more relevant and ever more urgent. The naked man is Everyman now. And it is only *this* recognition that can change the relationship between law and justice—not our recognition of him, but our recognition of *ourselves*.

CHAPTER TWO

Constitution

*Performance Evidence in Aboriginal
Land Claims*

CRAIG ELLIOTT

Constitutions, understood as legal documents or unwritten conventions, set out the highest principles of a state's laws, and establish the institutional structure of government. Approaching them more conceptually, they articulate the identity, ethos, and normative orientation of the state—the foundation from which particular political and legal actions may be elaborated. In the modern age, human rights and pluralism are among the most urgent constitutional issues that states have confronted. With respect to the former, advocates have demanded the entrenchment of human rights principles within constitutions at various junctures, particularly when nations are in transition following periods of systematic state abuse (in South Africa, for example). With respect to pluralism, increased recognition of the distinct rights of sub-state groups has led to increased advocacy for their constitutional recognition. This challenge is evident in multiethnic states as well as in postcolonial contexts where, as an historical matter, the imposed legal and political systems erased the political and legal systems of Indigenous peoples. The struggle against imposed Western systems of law and governance, which James Tully calls "strange multiplicity" (Tully 1995), is the subject of this chapter, with particular reference to the Australian context. We begin with a native title claim hearing by the Alyawarr, Kaytetye, Warumungu, and Wakay peoples at Alepeyewenh Homeland in the Northern Territory, Australia. As the scene unfolds, deeper constitutional tensions come to life.

* * *

The heat of the day subsides. Campfires flicker in the dusk light. Small groups on mattresses and blankets, or dirt, sit drinking tea, chewing tobacco and dining on kangaroo tails. Flames flare up occasionally, illuminating the scrub and Toyotas. Fifty metres away, the tent flaps in the warm evening breeze. Tomorrow, the judge's helicopter will plonk down beside the tent, and the hearing will commence. For now, around one campfire, women sing awely, *songs celebrating the* Kwerrimp (Spirit Women) *in the surrounding country. The songs are authorless, handed down from the spirit ancestors in ceremonies and dreams. The women practice songs they will perform for the court. Two days earlier, at the Sydney Olympics Opening Ceremony, the same women were watched by hundreds of millions. Painted up, they performed the Seven Sisters dance with countrywomen from across Central Australia. The dancers wore fluorescent security wristbands. Television commentators described the wristbands as sacred traditional costume. Now, a three-hour flight and seven hour drive later, the dancers are back with family in the dirt and heat, tired but chatty, ready to convince a judge that under Australian law, they are the owners of their traditional country.*

INTRODUCTION

This scene, describing the *Alyawarr* native title claim hearing at Alepeyewenh Homeland in the Northern Territory, Australia, typifies the clash of belief systems, cultural frameworks and foundational legal principles that arises when Indigenous Australians seek to make claims before the Australian legal system for recognition of their original rights to land. At the heart of this clash is the reality that Aboriginal people hold a "constitutional" imagination that differs from that underpinning the constitution of the Australian settler-colonial nation. In this unwritten constitution, neither law nor the ground of law is concentrated in a unified, quasi-linguistic structure. The Indigenous "constitution" is the *Dreaming*, a dynamic bequest grounded in and moving through the physical and cultural landscape, which does not place human agency at the center. This "constitutional" imagining is a fundamentally different understanding of the nature of truth and the form of inter-relationships: human to human; human to land; and human to spirit realm. Moreover, the expressive modalities through which Aboriginal people transmit these understandings, and the constitutional principles that they adopt to prove ownership of land, are radically different from those recognized and legitimated in the modern legal system of the settler-colonial nation state. Specifically, the expressive media that Aboriginal people adopt for these purposes are dramatically performative (ritual song, ceremonial dance and mythic narrative, for example) as distinct from forms such as documentation or even expert oral testimony.

Given these radical differences, some fundamental questions arise. Why should the Australian legal system deal with Indigenous claims to land that are based on profoundly different legal and cultural principles? And if we accept normative reasons for its so doing, how does it do so, given the differential modes of transmission or expressive forms at play? And what of the differential in power between these two constitutional and legal systems, and their accompanying media for communication? The author was present at the hearings for the *Alyawarr* and *De Rose* cases. Through an exploration of the conflict between the forms of expression assumed within the dominant legal system (documentation and oral testimony) and the performative forms that are expressive of Aboriginal law, these cases illustrate the conflict between divergent notions of sovereignty and law. Through exploring this conflict at the level of expressive media, the challenges involved in the law of the Australian state engaging with different sources and forms of law, are revealed. In its acts of recognition, the settler-colonial state recapitulates its legal hegemony and refuses to countenance a competing form of sovereignty.

The issues raised by the cases discussed here, and more generally the political and legal strategies that Australia's Indigenous peoples have deployed to seek recognition of their law and rights, while unique in their particular issues and inflections of difference, are indicative of one of the most important trends in the cultural history of law of the twentieth century. The latter part of the twentieth century in particular saw the emergence of a politics of difference, sometimes known as a *politics of recognition* (Taylor 1992b: 25–38) where various groups, including women, ethnic and religious minorities and Indigenous peoples, sought political and cultural recognition of their distinctive identities, ways of ordering the world, and in some cases, their systems of law (Tully 1995: 116–124; Young 1990). This form of political and legal contestation both drew on, and departed from earlier rights claims, which principally drew on the principle of equality and sought equal access to the basic rights available to all other citizens, but historically denied to these groups (to vote, to equal pay, to stand for office and so on). In the case of Indigenous peoples in settler-colonial nations such as Australia, Canada, New Zealand, or the United States, such claims to recognition, because they raised fundamental issues about the legitimacy of sovereign states, took on a particularly radical hue. These groups were not simply asking the sovereign nation to recognize that they were citizens for whom culture, or family, or work had a different meaning to that which had been assumed. Rather, at their outer limits, by propounding competing versions of history and law, they were challenging the legitimacy of the sovereignty of the settler-colonial state itself (Pearson 1994: 1–9; Simpson 1993: 195–210).

This trend was manifest in the activism of Indigenous peoples throughout the world to pressure nation-states to promulgate and accede to emergent international norms that recognized Indigenous peoples' political, economic, social and cultural rights, rights that they could then claim at home (Davis 2016: 74; Wiessner 2008: 1141). At the same time, in the domestic courts of many of these states, Indigenous peoples were making claims to land rights and various forms of cultural preservation and self-determination using whatever political leverage and limited legal mechanisms were available to them.[1] In New Zealand, Canada, the United States, and other states, the existence of treaties, or constitutional or statutory recognition of the sovereign status of at least some Indigenous peoples provided a foothold for such legal claims to be made (Wiessner 2011: 135).[2] Although, even then, there were many who had been excluded and needed to find creative ways of staking the legitimacy of their claims. In Australia, however, there was no recognition of Indigenous sovereignty in the Constitution nor were there treaties. Based on the colonial language of authority, the British sovereign claim over the Australian continent occurred on the basis of a claim that the land, and surrounding waters, was *terra nullius* ("land belonging to no one"). Subsequently, the constitutional foundation of the modern Australian nation in 1901 did not recognize the presence of the original inhabitants, let alone view them as subjects with a political system and property rights. Reflecting this ontological understanding of sovereignty and race, the Australian Constitution did not *see* Indigenous people as part of that which was to be ordered as a subject of law. Rather, Indigenous people were treated as extralegal objects. This has made claims to land rights based on prior and ongoing ownership far more difficult to make, and progress towards recognition slower to achieve than in some other jurisdictions.

The constitutional omission of Indigenous people raises deep questions. What does it mean to have, or be dispossessed of, sovereignty? How is sovereignty constituted? How does the Constitution reify colonial forms of expression coincident with local cultural archives of history and knowledge alongside institutions and processes that exercise power? Implicit in these questions are assumptions about the genealogy of authority, textuality, process, and institutional access. These elements—all of which helped to deliver the Australian colonial regime a sense of certainty about its claim to sovereignty—reflect the long history of "sovereignty's" evolving meanings. One of those meanings, stretching back to the Middle Ages, links sovereignty to land. In this respect, even if the king were deemed the primary sovereign, land owning barons were viewed as co-equal powers (Grimm 2015: 14). With the collapse of the medieval order, and the ensuing emergence of the modern state, a new concept of sovereignty arose. Following Jean Bodin's conceptualization, sovereignty became a unified concept centering on the "indivisibility" of supreme political power (Grimm 2015: 23). In the sixteenth century, such sovereign power could hardly be conceived apart from a supreme monarch. In the revolutionary times of the late seventeenth century, however, this notion of absolute, extralegal power would pass to the people. Popular sovereignty meant that even if the people transferred their sovereign power to a king, it was theirs to bestow, or withdraw (Grimm 2015: 27–28). Thus the debate around sovereignty readily shifts to questions concerning who exactly are the "people" whose original sovereign rights are at issue.

In Australia, constitutional exclusion meant that Indigenous people were not only *not* recognized as having preexisting sovereignty and property rights; they were not even recognized as Australian citizens until the mid-twentieth century. Yet, despite formal citizenship, the systematic inequality they still experience calls into question the robustness of their contemporary citizenship in a substantive sense.[3] Legislation giving Indigenous Australians the vote was only passed in the Commonwealth and various states from the early 1960s. They were not counted in the census (indeed, they were, evocatively, classified as flora and fauna) and they were treated as wards of the state until the mid-twentieth century. Moreover, Australian states adopted laws and policies expressly designed to bring about the destruction of Indigenous Australians as distinctive peoples with unique cultures, with the policy of forcibly removing Indigenous children from their families and communities and placing them in institutions or white foster or adoptive homes among the means for achieving this political and cultural "assimilation" (Human Rights and Equal Opportunity Commission 1997). Constitutional reform to (partially) remove discriminatory provisions occurred with the 1967 Referendum, which amended section 51(xxvi) of the Constitution and gave the Federal Parliament power to legislate in Aboriginal affairs. In reality, however, and despite the popular misconception that the 1967 referendum was the great Australian vote for racial equality, this constitutional change was modest, as was its substantive effect (Attwood and Markus 2007: 54–70).

MABO, NATIVE TITLE AND SOVEREIGNTY

In the decades following the 1967 Referendum, Indigenous people continued campaigning for justice and civil and political rights—seeking a treaty, recognition of sovereignty, constitutional amendment, reparation for non-payment of wages, and land rights. Partial success occurred in getting land rights recognized by statute in some states and, most significantly, in the Northern Territory with the enactment of the *Aboriginal Land Rights Act 1976 (Northern Territory)* (ALRA). Nevertheless, right up until 1992 and the successful High Court challenge in *Mabo*, the doctrine of *terra nullius* ("land belonging to no-one") was upheld in law.[4] This landmark case was named after Edward Koiki Mabo, a member of the Merriam people of the Murray Islands in the Torres Strait (between Australia and Papua New Guinea). The decision recognized that the Merriam people had enjoyed rights and interests in land based on traditional laws and customs, occupation and connection at the time of colonization and that this ownership persisted. The decision created a common law native title by recognizing that there had been preexisting title that had not been automatically extinguished when the Crown proclaimed sovereignty, and that this could continue where the Crown had not granted another form of title. That is, it recognized a form of preexisting land ownership, thereby overturning the doctrine of *terra nullius*, while simultaneously recognizing that the Crown had the power to extinguish such title.

The Crown thereby retained an affirmation of absolute sovereignty. The sovereignty of the Australian legal system over native title was confirmed because the former prevails where the two conflict; and native title can be wiped out by statutory and judicial instruments (Mantziaris and Martin 2000: 13–14). This assertion of primacy of the sovereignty and law of the modern nation state was fortified through the Commonwealth's passing the Native Title Act 1993 (NTA). The NTA encoded native title into a form of title under the umbrella of the Australian legal system and required that, to obtain recognition of such title, Aboriginal and Torres Strait Islander people needed to bring their claims before Australian courts, a process managed by the National Native Title Tribunal (NNTT).

As noted, while *Mabo* established a form of land title that was not derived from the Crown, neither *Mabo*, nor subsequent judicial decisions, nor the Commonwealth Parliament have countenanced a preexisting sovereignty. Indeed, the High Court has rejected efforts "to use native title as a vehicle" to push arguments for Aboriginal sovereignty (Mantziaris and Martin 2000: 28), stating in *Mabo*, for example that common law recognition of native title, "would be precluded if the recognition were to fracture a skeletal principle of our legal system."[5] That skeleton is sovereignty. In *Coe v Commonwealth*, the Court rejected a claim of "residual sovereignty" by members of the Wiradjuri people of New South Wales.[6] Similarly in *Walker v NSW*, the Court held: "*Mabo (No. 2)* is entirely at odds with the notion that sovereignty adverse to the Crown resides in the Aboriginal people of Australia."[7] In *Wik*, Kirby J. noted neither *Mabo* nor the *Native Title Act* created a "dual system of law," or even "a limited sovereignty."[8]

Nevertheless, many Aboriginal groups contend they never gave their rights as sovereign peoples to the British colonizers, and claim their own independence and cultural, legal and political continuities (Davis and Williams 2015: 120–121; Hookey 1984: 2). This is especially the case in parts of Australia where traditional land interests have not been subject to legislative or judicial extinguishment, or prolonged historical dislocation. In the Blue Mud Bay (north-east Arnhem Land) native title case,[9] for example, Morphy saw the successful Yolngu claimants as, "encapsulated … not colonised" (Morphy 2007: 33, also 56). According to Morphy, their claim was a "political act" (Morphy 2007: 32), asserting their sense of sovereignty, and the "incommensurability" of their own system of law as against the Australian legal system (Morphy 2007: 54).

Indeed, despite the courts' denial of "a dual legal system," or what might be termed formal legal pluralism (the simultaneous existence of more than one legal system) Aboriginal rules, customs and symbols do simultaneously exist and operate alongside the imposed legal order (Moore 1973: 720).[10] Sometimes Indigenous rules, such as dispute resolution processes, are granted broader legitimacy via acknowledgment of customary law. However, despite international precedents (Hookey 1984: 8–13), recognition of customary law in Australia has been limited and piecemeal (Williams 1987: 150, 160–163). At the same time, evidence that features of Indigenous normative ordering have been shaped by encounters and conflicts with colonial legal and political procedures and institutions challenges the ideology that Indigenous law and custom is ancient and immutable, and points to the existence of longstanding and informal, if unequal, legal pluralism (Williams 1987: 110, 149, 162). In some instances, such coexistence is managed through the existence of relatively distinct domains of the laws' application, or through pragmatic negotiation. In disputes over land ownership, however, conflict is far more likely, raising the question of what happens when two radically different legal systems and cultural forms of law meet and seek to communicate with each other.

THE *DREAMING* AS UNWRITTEN CONSTITUTION

Beyond the colonial and historical legacy, the difficulties of recognizing claims to preexisting sovereignty are exacerbated by the complexity of how Aboriginal people understand, transmit and represent their relationship with, and rights in, land, as well as by their incommensurability with the understanding and modes of representation and transmission of the modern Australian state. These differences point to substantially divergent sources of legal authority. Aboriginal people hold that ongoing traditional laws and customs provide their own *constitution* for ordering and observing interests in land. At the heart of this sense of "constitution"—or "*the Law*," as it is often called in Aboriginal English—are founding beliefs concerning the creation of country, cultural and linguistic identity, and the responsibility of humans (including ancestors) to connect with—and reproduce—the landscape, people, stories, and beliefs. As Mantziaris and Martin note:

> "Law" for traditionally oriented Indigenous people is not simply the system of rules, norms and sanctions through which society is ordered. It is the foundation of reality. The "law" or "the Dreaming" ... encompasses such domains as the relations between people, and relations between people and the landscape, as well as the metaphysical and moral underpinnings of those relations ... "The law" is viewed as ... essentially immutable and cannot be declared through institutions [courts, for example] that function by means of human agency. (2000: 35–36)

Reflecting the no-human-agency ideology, Aboriginal people say "white man got no Dreaming."[11] Or, signaling inconsistent human (political and legal) agency, that "whitefella law changes all the time." Constitutional change inevitably falls into this category as well. As a "constitution" orders and regulates laws, relationships, and behaviors, then in what is the Indigenous "constitution"—the Dreaming—grounded? How are cultural representations of the "constitution" as a foundational narrative made manifest with juridical authority?[12] The answer is through the land, and this answer marks the Aboriginal narrative as possessing fundamentally different epistemological norms. Langton has argued that Aboriginal property relations are embedded in and derive from "a spiritual bequest" or sacred ancestral past with its own cultural ontology (Langton 2010: 75–97). In Central Australia, where this chapter's case studies are located, it is believed the landscape, human society and the conditions for the survival of all were established by spiritual ancestors, or *Dreaming* beings, who travelled the land in a creative era long ago. The *spiritual* ancestors interacted with the early *human* ancestors, and the two are indistinguishable in oral memory. Reflecting this interaction, the physical and cultural landscape, celebrated in oral traditions, contains metamorphosed signs bequeathed by the spiritual beings to the first human ancestors. These signs (in the form of waterholes, rock outcrops, ochre deposits, mature trees, etc.) exist as visible form or subsurface essence in specific places and are synonymous with the land itself. The landscape is, in a celebrated description, "a humanized realm saturated with significations" (Stanner 1965/1984: 161). The signs also exist in songs, stories, designs, ceremonies, and sacred objects. Continuing adherence to these cultural elements reaffirms the human connection with the landscape's spiritual properties. Local terms describing these fundamental beliefs integrate several concepts: cosmogony, cosmology, spirit beings and their journeys (*Dreamings*), spiritual power, law, ritual, religious objects, designs, songs, and related "sacred" and "everyday" actions (Elliott 1999: 55–61).

These fundamental beliefs, with sometimes major regional and local differences, are held and transmitted through oral performance and emplaced enactment over generations.[13] That is, in danced rituals, in sung myths, in painted and worn designs, and in interactions with the landscape. "Performance of knowledge," as Rose notes, "(through song, dance, story, history, use of country) is a performance of ownership: it identifies the person as one with rights and responsibilities to that country" (Rose 1994: 2).[14] These (and related) forms of enacted knowledge, when transported into a land claim hearing, I have termed *performance evidence*.[15]

It is well documented that song is an integral part of Australian Indigenous ceremonial law, and assertions of interest in land.[16] In Central Australia, as Moyle observed of Alyawarr claims to land ownership, "songs and ceremonies are inseparable" (Moyle 1983: 90). Songs, "have the status of an ultimate authority" in matters of ceremonial detail, historical fact and land ownership (Moyle 1983: 91). Moyle found Alyawarr songs, "represent the earliest statements about land ownership—a kind of original land claim ... and without the songs which recount the Dreamtime activities, they [Agharringa people] have no claim to the land" (Moyle 1983: 91–93).[17] Parallel principles apply in Yankunytjatjara territory where the *De Rose* claim area is situated. For example, during the *De Rose* hearing, at the *Kalaya* (Emu) site KANTJA, senior claimant Peter Tjutatja was asked "why are you *nguraritja* [land owner] for here?" He replied: "Because we got *inma Kalaya*. *Inma*, songs, *kalaya* the emu, and we own that and I am *nguraritja* because of that" (*De Rose* Ts: 516).[18]

JUDICIAL PROCESS AND THE RECEPTION OF PERFORMANCE EVIDENCE

In fact, and despite the conceptual difficulties discussed, in practice, leading Australian land claim judgments have long construed evidence of traditional beliefs and customs, including songs and ceremonies, as constituting *law*. One hears this in some exemplary excerpts from judgments: "if ever a system could be called 'a government of laws, and not of men', it is that shown in the evidence before me"[19]; "a system of rules" (Toohey J. in *Mabo (No. 2)*); "law in Aboriginal terms is an aggregation of traditional values, rules, beliefs and practices derived from the Aboriginal past"[20]; and "any adequate description of ... interests in land needs to describe how such identification takes place as an orderly, but not necessarily predictable, political, legal and cultural process."[21] Evidence of laws and customs was heard in the three Australian land claim cases that have given rise to Federal Government legislative responses: *Milirrpum* led to the Aboriginal Land Rights (NT) Act (1976); *Mabo* led to the *Native Title Act* (1993); and *Wik* led to the 1997 amendments to the *Native Title Act*. Notably, each response addressed lawful Indigenous connection to land only, not broader claims to legal sovereignty.

Nevertheless, for Australian courts, forms of transmission such as performance evidence pose a challenge, and this remains the case, even where formal rules of evidence are introduced with the intention of accommodating "cultural concerns." So, for example, while native title litigation in the Australian judicial system is still subject to rules of evidence, at least formally, the Native Title Act provides that the Federal Court can take into account, "cultural and customary concerns."[22] Federal Court rules concerning native title proceedings (Division 34.7) recognize that some evidence may be of a "cultural or customary nature." This is defined as relating to the "culture, genealogy, customs or traditions of Aboriginal peoples or Torres Strait Islanders."[23] Subsequent clauses set out special rules applicable to "cultural or customary" evidence. These rules address provisions for confidentiality and secrecy restrictions;[24] where and when evidence is presented;[25] and group evidence.[26]

Nevertheless, the persistent assumption in the Federal Court rules is that most evidence will be delivered in oral or written form. One can, in other words, discern the persistence of an unexamined cultural and legal imagination even as the legislation seems to make space for another form. Thus for example, the Act provides that claimant evidence may be, "given by way of singing, dancing, storytelling or in any way other than ... *normal* ... evidence."[27] Where this is to occur, the court must be given reasonable notice and provision is made regarding the requirement of confidentiality orders due to gender-based restrictions or other customary concerns. No other guidance is given to a presiding judge on how to deal with this "other than normal evidence," although those hearing native title matters do have the liberty to make or vary practice and procedure rules of court they deem, "necessary or convenient."[28]

The depth of the problem posed for Australian courts by the form of such evidence is evident in the convention that, following performance evidence, the courts seek oral evidence that is understood as explaining the symbols present in the performance evidence (be they visual, sung, acted, or demonstrated). Judges prefer anthropological interpretations to make "intelligible and useful" (Mantziaris and Martin 2000: 34) the evidence of traditional laws and customs that Aboriginal people transmit according to their own systems of representation. They prefer to see laws and customs relating to land as "structures of fixity and predictability" and "systematic and definable" (Mantziaris and Martin 2000: 34). Accordingly, the judicial process favors the written word and accords authority to documents (reports, genealogies, maps, secondary sources, witness statements, points of claim) and declarations (such as oral evidence by witnesses) reduced to writing (Hausler 2012: 51). With performance evidence however, the presentation of the evidence can lack obvious sequence and literal meaning. Insisting that unwritten traditional art and beliefs be retransmitted in documentary form as a line-by-line transcript challenges (if not obliterates) the ontological framework and authoritative position of performance evidence in a land claim. From the perspective of courts, unfamiliar with these media and the epistemologies they represent, this makes the process of cultural analysis and interpretation difficult. What evidence is being analyzed: the content or form of the evidence, or both? How has the court's staging and location impacted the presentation of evidence? If there is a spontaneous aspect to the evidence—as was the case with performances in *Alyawarr* and *De Rose*—how can an anthropological interpretation validly find systematic predictability as preferred by the court?

As a form of evidentiary meaning-making through "bodily presence" (Sherwin 2013: 1) or "visual storytelling" (Sherwin 2013: 3),[29] performance evidence does not readily conform to formalities of oral testimony. Judicial reliance on the written record, at the cost of performance evidence, places major strictures on the ability of Indigenous claimants to present their knowledge as evidence *in the best way* known to themselves and, as such, raises procedural fairness issues. Typically, oral evidence takes the form of a question-and-answer format—itself a "non-Aboriginal way of eliciting information" (Sutton 1994: 23)—and produces a transcript of short answers or even mono-syllabic responses. This is often the case even from the most knowledgeable senior witnesses, who commonly refer this hearing format as "sit-down" evidence (Sutton 1994: 23). Due to the perils of converting unwritten, esoteric, and relational beliefs into conventional legal language, much oral evidence of traditional laws and customs is "incapable of reduction to writing" in a meaningful way. Moreover, such evidence presupposes specific background and cultural knowledge not held by those outside the local community (Mantziaris and Martin 2000: 42).[30] Performance evidence often references the religious significance of highly localized entities (site features, mythological events, local group ancestors, for example). While considered influential declarations of proprietary interests by Indigenous participants, this knowledge-based "intense localism" makes deriving "authoritative" accounts from that evidence elusive, and is subject to profound "hermeneutical problems" (Mantziaris and Martin 2000: 40–42).

Indeed, witnesses may choose to present their evidence through performance precisely to ensure that the content of their beliefs does not become fixed and static in writing, open to appropriation and interpretation by "specialist," or disputing, outsiders. In performance, beliefs, and practices remain experiential, dynamic and their ongoing enactment remains substantially within the control of the local community (Burke 2014: 6, par.14; Mantziaris and Martin 2000: 40–42).

PERFORMANCE EVIDENCE IN LAND CLAIMS

In land claim hearings, claimants' enactments and speech, quite intentionally, are locally situated and knowledge-based cultural performances. Legal argument during a hearing is another form of rarified cultural production, within known perimeters of formal procedure and role-relationships (Sherwin 2013: 1). For Aboriginal witnesses, courtroom procedures are often unknown and shifting, a challenging environment frequently compounded by linguistic differences, miscommunication and the judiciary's indifference or resistance to those acting as interpreters (Cooke 1995: 55–56).

Cultural performances in land claim hearings under the Aboriginal Land Rights Act have been accepted as evidence since the 1970s in the Northern Territory. Under the ALRA, an Aboriginal Land Commissioner assesses land claims against a statutory definition of traditional ownership,[31] and makes recommendations to the Federal Aboriginal Affairs Minister to grant Aboriginal freehold title.[32] Formally, claims under the ALRA are heard as part of an inquiry, a relatively informal process that has allowed Aboriginal Land Commissioners to afford Indigenous claimants significant latitude to present evidence in innovative ways. For example, ALRA claims have received evidence in the form of *sound* (singing, chanting, humming, clapping, slapping, instrumental accompaniment, silence and all of these mixed with storytelling narrative); *movement* (ceremonial dancing and related mimetic actions, swaying, jumping, walking, hopping, beating the ground, pointing[33] and gesturing [including non-verbal cues to singers and dancers]; approach and access protocols [during on-site evidence]; site cleaning and maintenance, use of country and foraging excursions); *imagery* (painted body designs, ground sculpture, ground paintings, designs on ceremonial objects, mud maps); and *material culture* (site features, ceremony grounds and objects [poles, feathers, etc.], clapsticks, boomerangs, paintings and environmental three-dimensional objects [bush medicine plants, bush tucker, wooden, gum and stone artifacts]).

Innovative ways of hearing evidence have also included group evidence and direct conversation between claimants and judge, without any legal intermediary (Sutton 1994: 22–23).[34] A striking example of "direct conversation" evidence, and of the flexibility of evidence elicitation in ALRA claims more generally, occurred in the Alcoota Land Claim in 1996. The claim was to the former Alcoota Pastoral Lease, located approximately 200 km north-east of Alice Springs, in a semi-arid part of Central Australia. At a rockhole site named ARLKARLARRWENHELEK,[35] senior claimant Ken Tilmouth Penangk, wearing a lapel mic, asked the Aboriginal Land Commissioner (Justice Gray) to point out where the rockhole was. (The two were walking around on a flat rock platform, with no obvious rockhole, or water, in sight.) The judge took Ken's request in good humor, "Oh, show you that rock hole, yes. Well, I'll try. You tell me which direction I should walk in" (*Alcoota Land Claim* Ts.684).[36] After looking without success the judge confessed, "Oh, I'd get perish, no doubt about it" (*Alcoota Land Claim* Ts.684). Eventually the judge noticed ants disappearing under a hand-sized stone, and exclaimed, "found it." Ken feigned relief, congratulated the judge, and told onlookers cheekily, "We couldn't see that rock hole. He [the judge] showed me" (*Alcoota Land Claim* Ts.685). Ken then picked up the stone, revealing it as a natural "plug," known locally as *inpekenh*, hiding a cavernous basin of freshwater underneath the rock platform. Having witnessed this direct claimant/Judge conversational evidence, I agree with Sutton that it results in the "richest, the most relevant and sincere evidence" possible (1994: 23).

In his *Alcoota Land Claim* report, which recommended a grant of freehold title, Gray J. noted performance of customary practices as evidence of Aboriginal law and connection to land. At one site alone (IRRPETYWENGKEN),[37] he documented the multifaceted layers of such practices:

> a group of men from the Atwel[38] group showed me a painting, representing the *Ntang Ngkwitek* [Edible Pigweed Seed] dreaming. The design depicted in the painting is secret to men. They also performed a secret men's song. Women who came to the site came according to a required ritual, which required them to approach in a line, carrying twigs. The importance of the site requires quiet behaviour. Throwing stones and spitting are prohibited. At the site itself, there is a spring. Women who take water from it must come and go by a particular path. There are marks on the rocks that represent the seeds of the dreaming, which were cooked by a woman or women in the public version of the dreaming story. There is a tree at the site that represents an old woman who ground the seeds, so that they could be eaten, in the dreaming. There are hunting restrictions in the vicinity of the site, based on the kinship categories. (Gray 2007: 143, par.4.6.7)

Gray J. summed up the importance of song and ceremonial evidence in the *Alcoota Land Claim*, as indicating a "very robust" connection to land and ceremonial life, and that:

> In my experience as Aboriginal Land Commissioner, I do not think I have seen more strongly manifested attachment [to land] than I witnessed among these claimants. (Gray 2007: 174–175)

Fifty-seven percent of ALRA Aboriginal Land Commissioner reports mention the significance of songs and ceremonies performed during the hearing (Koch 2013: 12). The meaning of such evidence in establishing connection to land was stated by Gray J. in the *Warlmanpa (Muckaty Pastoral Lease) Land Claim*:

> The connection between a group and a particular site of significance is provided by entities which are glossed as "dreamings" in the English language ... Their continued presence and influence is acknowledged and the connection between dreamings, people and country is maintained through ceremony and song. (Gray 1987: 38)

When land claims moved from the relatively informal enquiry of the ALRA to the hearings by the Federal Court, introducing and making space for the media whereby

Aboriginal people transmit evidence of ownership faced a new set of challenges. This was in part because of Federal Court requirements regarding rules of evidence, and in part because of the heavy contestation of early native title cases. Claims litigated in the first decade of the NTA, as *Alyawarr* and *De Rose* were, tended to be contested by opposing parties because the legal reach of native title was still being developed. Amid the stress of each hearings, presentation of performance evidence ideally requires considerable planning and effort by the claimant participants as well as cooperation, accommodation and a degree of hospitality from the court. In actuality, though, native title litigation is rarely ideal and a cooperative court atmosphere is not always forthcoming. This is the case even when, in theory, formal rules of evidence seek to make the court a reasonably accommodating space. Extrajudicial *variables*—the attitudes of the judge, hearing location and layout, and the degree of litigious tension in the hearing—have an impact upon the ability, willingness and confidence of claimants to present performance evidence.[39]

In *Performing Law*, for example, dealing with the Blue Mud Bay hearing that took place in 2005 under the NTA, Frances Morphy shows how the court's location on country and control of its own symbols and formalities within "a constructed ritual space" inhibited the Yolngu claimants' attempts to make "sacred power manifest" (Morphy 2007: 34, 44).[40] Morphy focuses on two "ritual performances" (Morphy 2007: 45–48). The first was an opening ceremony to welcome the Court (involving a courtroom procession, painted body designs, singing and chanting with clapstick accompaniment of ceremonial names for country, and display of ceremonial objects) (Morphy 2007: 44–46); the second was a visit to a men's ceremonial ground (consisting of men's body paint, men carrying spears, on-site gender separation and posture restrictions) (Morphy 2007: 46–47).[41] Both events occurred with Court permission, and court officials were invited to observe appropriate cultural protocols.

Revealingly, however, neither event became part of formal evidence in the Blue Mud Bay hearing. Morphy suggests that one reason for this was that "no one had suggested … [the performances] should be regarded as having evidential content" (Morphy 2007: 48). Without subsequent in-session oral evidence, the performances were regarded as "non-evidence" by the Court (Morphy 2007: 48). Concerned about the potential for appeal, the judge (Selway J.), treated the ritual performances as non-evidence, an out of session "view" by the Court, and therefore devoid of evidentiary meaning (Morphy 2007: 48).

One might see in the Blue Mud Bay performances the "double bind" (Morphy 2007: 54) faced by claimants when enacting meaningful evidence of land connection: to have native title recognized requires making *rom* (the Yolngu term for "laws and customs") commensurable with Australian native title law, but this requires doing the impossible—alienating themselves from their own laws and customs, and identity (Morphy 2007: 54). Perhaps though, from another perspective, drawing on Williams' "two laws" model (1987: 109), what is going on here is not so much Aboriginal people's capture in a double bind, as their strategically engaging with the Australian legal system, while remaining firmly within their own. Morphy implies precisely this. Because of the distinctiveness of continuing Yolngu laws and sovereignty, even though Yolngu law may now be "encapsulated" by the Anglo-Australian legal system, it is not "colonized" by it (2007: 33, 44, 54). Indeed, Yolngu see native title as "essentially irrelevant" (Morphy 2007: 56). One can see this conflict playing out in two earlier native title cases, *Alyawarr* and *De Rose*, to which I now turn.

ALYAWARR

The *Alyawarr*[42] native title application over land approximately 450 km north-east of Alice Springs (Northern Territory), within the Davenport/Murchison Ranges and formerly part of Kurundi Pastoral Lease and the township of Hatches Creek, was lodged in 1995.[43] The Northern Territory Government was the only other party to the application. At the hearing, government counsel tested the evidence of traditional connection, but did not strenuously oppose the claimants. The hearing of claimant evidence occurred in September 2000. In 2004, the Federal Court decision by Mansfield J. found for the claimants, including exclusive possession over the former township of Hatches Creek. In 2006, the full Federal Court upheld the original judgment. The application area is now jointly managed as *Eytwelepwenty National Park*.[44]

In *Alyawarr*, various forms of performance evidence were brought, including: conduct of site approach and site cleaning protocols, followed by oral explanations;[45] dancing, singing and ceremonial posture demonstrations by men and women;[46] displays and explanations of in-situ and canvas artworks depicting claim land mythologie;[47] displays of the uses of material culture, such as grinding stones;[48] gender restricted displays and exegeses of sacra (including sacred objects and ground paintings);[49] and food gathering trips in which claimants and the court participated, followed by displays and explanations of the bush foods and bush medicines collected (details below).

Each of these forms of performance evidence occurred with the cooperation of the Court and both parties (the claimants and Northern Territory Government).[50] Four examples highlight how the court facilitated this evidence (Figures 2.1–2.3).

First, a bush tucker trip was organized in which claimants, court officials and counsel for both parties participated. The next day (September 18, 2000), the collected bush foods, medicines and resources were displayed on a ground sheet in the hearing tent, and their uses explained by senior claimants Linda Dobbs Apwerl and Lucy Dobbs Apwerl.[51] Explanations stated how, when, and where to find each item; how it is used or processed; and what local name and story related to each. The display demonstrated the claimants' ongoing knowledge and traditional use of the land's resources. Anthropologist Susan Donaldson was present during the foraging trip. She recalled:

> The hunting trip was a classic. After the NTG [Northern Territory Government] got over the environment that they had to deal with (a lesson in itself in gaining respect for the people who lived there in the past) they were in awe at the hands-on information exchange. I recall one poignant moment when a claimant said, "this is the way we teach our young people, we don't put it in a book we show them, just like we are showing you." The claimants had full control of the lesson. The evidence. (Susan Donaldson, pers. comm. to author, May 31, 2013)

A memorable part of this *enacted* evidence was that, as opposition counsel took part in the trip, *they* had direct experience and observation of how the claimants' went about finding and collecting each of the items. They had a sense of "ownership" of *their* bush tucker experience. It also meant that claimants and opposition parties got to know each other. This circumstance produced a breakthrough moment (and it was only a moment) where opposition counsel, without prompting, contributed to the claimants' evidence by putting onto the court record their own direct observations from the trip. Their observations included who had spotted the goanna first, and which of the claimants wielded the ax best when chopping sugarbag.

Second, a week after this trip, a display of public *awely* (women's song and ceremony) occurred. Claimant women who went on the bush tucker trip also performed in the *awely* demonstration. The *awely* performance, representing *Kwerrimp* (Spirit Women) associated with Antarrengeny and Tyaw countries, was elaborate and required several hours' preparation. It consisted of preparation of a ceremonial ground, *wak* (humpy or shade), *walth* (ceremonial sticks), *tyaynarr* (mulga dancing sticks) with *arrkaylp* (cockatoo feathers); production of artwork using *tyepal* (snappy gum painting sticks); painted body designs; and group singing synchronized with dance movements (Donaldson 2000: 2–3). On completion, key participants gave oral evidence on the meanings of the various body paint designs, songs, objects, performance sequences, ritual movements and their responsibilities to the two countries depicted in the performance (*Alyawarr* Ts.1115–1136).

The *awely* demonstration formed a tight compliment to the bush tucker trip. One of the ceremonial and mythological emblems celebrated—the medicinal *kwerr-arr kwerr* plant—was one of the bush medicines collected earlier. The theme of maintaining cultural

FIGURE 2.1 Main tent and shade during the *Alyawarr* hearing at ALEPEYEWENH (Black Tank Outstation, Hatches Creek, site No. 32), September 2000. The judge (Mansfield J.), court staff and recordists, barristers, advisors, interpreters and those giving evidence sat at tables inside the tent. Observers listened to proceedings via a public address system (males under the yellow tarp, females in the shade left-hand side). All evidence at this location was oral. Performance evidence also occurred at locations near ALEPEYEWENH, and elsewhere throughout the claim land. On September 25, 2000, Tyaw and Antarrengeny *Awely* (women's ceremony) was performed for the Judge, with subsequent oral evidence (*Transcript of Evidence* pp. 1114–1136). On September 26, 2000 mens' singing and two *Rlamperety* (ground paintings) representing the *Rwaney* or *Kwelharr* (Black-footed Rock Wallaby) Dreaming at ATHETHEW (site No.16) were displayed for the court, followed by gender restricted evidence (*Transcript of Evidence* pp. 1335–1373). At the claimants' request, no photographs were taken of either. Reproduced with the permission of the Federal Court of Australia.

and ecological reproduction through ceremonial performance could not have been more immediately or effectively expressed.

Third, on-site evidence frequently involved spontaneous gestural enactment and observance of site approach protocols. While not formal ceremonial demonstrations, this form of customary observance typically references the mythic associations of a place (as ceremonies do also). At ILENTYARLEWERREPP-ARRERNELHEW,[52] a low whitish hill, senior claimant Frankie Holmes Akemarr enacted how the *Ilenty Atherr* (Two Galahs) Dreaming beings landed at the site "like a helicopter" to feed on wattle tree seed (*ntang alerrey*) and grass seeds (*Alyawarr* Ts.1513). Frankie's bodily gestures, watched carefully by Mansfield J. and Frankie's Antarrengeny countrymen, occurred midstream his oral evidence.

Fourth, the *Alyawarr* hearing received extensive evidence of localized traditions via exegesis of rock art motifs at several locations. This reflects the hilly claim landscape, with many rock shelters and walls with painted or engraved designs. So prevalent was the pointing out of visual iconography during the *Alyawarr* hearing, at one site this led to a fascinating piece of cross-cultural representational interpretation.[53] A senior male

FIGURE 2.2 Preparation for Women's Performance Evidence during the *Alyawarr* hearing, at site ATETYERRETYER (site No. 21), September 20, 2000. Hessian is placed between vehicles to provide shade and a screen for *Awely* (women's ceremonial dancing) that occurred in the space between the vehicles. The site ATETYERRETYER is a ceremonial ground where women perform *Awely* during *Apwelh* (male initiation) ceremonies nearby. Women's oral evidence related to the *Awely* demonstration formed part of a gender restricted transcript, by order of Mansfield J. (*Transcript of Evidence* pp. 471–512). Reproduced with the permission of the Federal Court of Australia.

FIGURE 2.3 Senior claimant Frankie Holmes Akemarr gives performance evidence during the *Alyawarr* hearing, at site ILENTYARLEWERREPP-ARRERNELHEW (site No. 37), September 27, 2000. The site is affiliated with the *Ilenty Atherr* (Two Galahs) Dreaming. Here Frankie shows the Court how the *Ilenty Atherr* (Two Galahs) Dreaming from Irrerlerr country landed at this site "like a helicopter." They were flying around looking for grass seed and *alerrey* (wattle tree seed), both found in this area. They then flew off to ATHETHERR (Battery Waterhole; site No. 85). (*Transcript of Evidence* pp. 1513). Reproduced with the permission of the Federal Court of Australia and Frankie Holmes Akemarr.

claimant was striving to explain his belief concerning the deep symbolic truths behind the painted motifs on the rockface behind him.[54] The witness stopped, gazing at a flat-ish wooden object placed prominently on the judge's table.[55] The old man pointed at the object, and said:

> We got to follow that one, one way. When I tell you, they do that way. I believe your side [*pointing at the wooden object*] well, you got to believe me again. We—you read and write it, but that Dreaming in here too [*pointing at the rockface behind him*]. We can tell you, we can't tell lie, we got to tell the true thing. Well that's the believing [*pointing at the wooden object again*], you got to believe [*pointing at the rockface again*]. (*Alyawarr* Ts.911)

The wooden object on the judge's desk was an oversize compass. The old man giving evidence, as he told me later, thought it was a Christian cross. This, he thought, meant the judge was a believer and, therefore, likely to appreciate the object's reference in his explanation of Alyawarr *Dreaming* truth.

DE ROSE

The *De Rose*[56] native title application over the De Rose Hill Pastoral Lease, located in the far north of South Australia approximately 400 km south of Alice Springs, was lodged in 1994. Other parties to the application were the South Australian Government and lessees to the pastoral lease. The trial lasted sixty-five days (Wooley 2006: 5). At the time of hearing on-country claimant evidence in June-July 2001, both these parties vigorously opposed the claimants, although in later proceedings the South Australian Government did not oppose the claim. In 2002, the Federal Court decision by O'Loughlin J. found against the claimants. In 2003 and 2005, the full Federal Court overturned the original judgment and found for the claimants.[57] This was on the grounds that O'Loughlin J. had made errors of law and fact relating to the claimants' continuous connection with the claimed land (Wooley 2006: 4–5).[58] The lessees' appeal to the High Court was refused in 2005.

In *De Rose*, performance evidence consisted of singing of *inma* (songs), with beat accompaniment to singing and dancing (*De Rose* Ts. 87–88, 90, 94, 129–130). Material culture items, such as stone artifacts, grinding grooves, remnants of shelters and constructed site elements, were shown and explained to the court. Further, bush food resources collected on site were displayed as the court was led on "show and tell" walks, such as by senior applicant Peter De Rose at the site KANTJA.[59]

FIGURE 2.4 Main tent during the *De Rose* hearing at ILINTJITJARA, June-July 2001. The judge (O'Loughlin J.), court staff and recordists, barristers, advisors, interpreters and those giving evidence sat at tables inside the tent. Observers sat on chairs outside trying to hear proceedings (there was no public address system). All evidence at this location was oral. On-site evidence, including performance evidence, occurred at locations on the claim land nearby. At the claimants' request, no photographs were taken of performance evidence during the hearing. Reproduced with the permission of the Federal Court of Australia.

FIGURE 2.5 On-country evidence at site KANTJA (site No. 29, southern De Rose Hill pastoral lease) during the *De Rose* hearing, July 6, 2001. Evidence was given this site is affiliated with *Kalaya* (Emu) from KIRARA (site No. 26), a *Tjukurrpa* (Dreaming) which then travels to ILPALKA (site No. 40). The claimants stated they knew the *inma* (songs) for the *Kalaya* (Emu) Dreaming but, given the mixed audience, they did not sing. The court is seated in the sandy bed of Kantja (or Agnes) Creek. (*Transcript of Evidence* pp. 506–558). Reproduced with the permission of the Federal Court of Australia.

One of the reasons De Rose Hill was chosen as the South Australian pastoral lease testcase for native title was the claimants' strong cultural links with the claim area, and their knowledge of ceremonial law connected with sites located there. For reasons that will be explained, during the hearing the court was "given a glimpse" only of the performance of these sacred stories (Wooley 2006: 5).

In contrast to the cooperative atmosphere in *Alyawarr*, in the *De Rose* hearing the meaning of the performance evidence was repeatedly contested and challenged by opposing counsel. The effects of this contestation were many. It significantly changed and reduced the frequency of presentation of performance evidence. Dislocation and disruption occurred on the occasions when this evidence was presented. The cogency of this evidence on the hearing's restricted transcript record was diminished to the point of elimination. The claimants' respect for the court and willingness to offer expansive answers, be they oral or performative, was eroded, due to the perception that members of the court were disrespectful, if not downright hostile, to their cultural traditions.

Both prior to and during the hearing, *De Rose* claimants had insisted they could not have their songs recorded because this would be, "in breach of their law and risk for them

FIGURE 2.6 Bush foods collected and displayed during evidence at site KANTJA (site No. 29) *De Rose* hearing, July 6, 2001. Shown are: *tjanmata* (bush onion) in red dish; *wangunu* (edible seed from naked woollybutt) in *wira* (wooden scoop) and *mai kalka* (edible grass seed) in white cup. The seeds are pounded and baked to make seed-cake (*Transcript of Evidence* pp. 538–541). *Kanti* (stone blades) and *kiti* (adhesive resin from spinifex grass) was also collected at this site and shown to the court (*Transcript of Evidence* pp. 555–557). Reproduced with the permission of the Federal Court of Australia.

severe penalties" (*De Rose* RTs.88). They were, however, keen to have the court visit and hear evidence at sites of cultural significance within the claim area during the hearing. Here emerges the "double bind" claimants confront in giving land claim evidence.

During on-site hearings within the claim area, claimants in *De Rose* were asked questions like: "How do you know he can still sing the songs for this place?" (*De Rose* RTs.84). Claimants also received confrontational questioning, such as: "But you can't sing the songs for this place?" (*De Rose* RTs.84).[60] Mere oral statements to the contrary were challenged. In response, the claimants' inclination, despite strong cultural prohibitions, was to meet counsel's "test" with action—including by breaking into group singing and chanting, more or less spontaneously. When claimants did so, opposing counsel objected on the following grounds: they had no prior notice; the song was not recorded by the court; they did not have a translation of the song; and could not adjudge the song's localized meaning or relevance. For example, at one site, a question by the claimants' counsel referring to an (unrecorded) song performance during the previous day's hearing (July 3, 2001) was objected to because, "the song that was sung yesterday wasn't taken down in any way" (*De Rose* RTs.40–41). This meant no one could verify, to the court's satisfaction, what the song was about (*De Rose* RTs.45). Eventually, testimony about the song did become evidence, but not before the fluency of the witness's site-sequence description of the song's creation, ownership and localized significance had been lost (*De Rose* RTs.41–45).

On a later hearing day (July 5, 2001), cross-examination of witnesses on their local knowledge produced impromptu dancing and "very vigorous singing," including by "manifestly frail" senior claimants (*De Rose* RTs.87–88). Because the singing occurred spontaneously and while walking between planned oral evidence sessions, the opportunity for the transcript to record and preserve the singing was missed.

The impromptu nature of the sung performances during the *De Rose* hearing led opposing counsel to raise five objections. First, whether everyone was actually singing was disputed. Second, objection was raised to anyone (judge, counsel or claimants) making transcript reference to the singing since, it was claimed, there was no audible evidence of the singing on the hearing recording. Third, objection was made that no court record of the singing (and therefore no translation) meant they would, "never be able to know or test" the site-specific content of the singing (*De Rose* RTs.87–88). A fourth objection was against explanatory talking among the singers during and between verses of the singing. This was on the grounds that it was "difficult" that "different people were saying different things at different times," and that unrecorded speaking among witnesses had "the capacity to influence the court" (*De Rose* RTs.87–88). This objection overlooked Federal Court rules that allow for sung and group evidence,[61] and ignores the long history of such evidence in ALRA claims. Fifth, building on each of the preceding objections, a generalized complaint was made that, "this whole process is fraught with great danger" (*De Rose* RTs.88).

In summary, the litigants' complaints targeted the claimants' ability to spontaneously introduce performance evidence into the hearing. The objections were summed up by opposing counsel in absolutist terms:

> We ... object and protest at demonstrations unless they are recorded but, if they are not to be recorded, in our submission they can *never ever* be put to any other use than a mere demonstration and they could have no evidentiary weight or purpose beyond that and certainly they could not be used to bolster *any* suggestion of *any* association with a particular person, place or event. (*De Rose* RTs.88; italics added)

At this point in the hearing the judge intervened. His Honor allowed the claimants to decline recording their singing, if they so wished. But added: "the *consequences* ... are theirs as to the value and weight that can be put on the songs" (*De Rose* RTs.89; italics added). The consequences were real, indeed. The judge then ruled inadmissible any questions or statements by witnesses that referred back to the (unrecorded) singing (*De Rose* RTs.90). By making this ruling, the judge allowed the objections, noting, "[here] is a good example of the dangers that we have fallen into" (*De Rose* RTs.90). Precisely what the "dangers" were was not explicated by His Honor. The inadmissible ruling was made despite His Honor noting that the rules of court provide for, "evidence to be taken as to songs and dance" (*De Rose* RTs.90). Federal Court rules also allow a judge to make any order considered appropriate in the interests of justice which, given the obstructive circumstances described here, seems a relevant consideration.[62]

With in-session performance evidence effectively blocked, claimants reluctantly reversed their opposition to their singing being recorded. The decision was made in direct response to a challenging and obstructive hearing environment, and is an illustration of the "double bind" they faced. However, the new course of action met complications when the difficulty of translating the songs was pointed out. The interpreter told the court:

it is very difficult to translate the words of songs because they are not everyday language words. They are hard and difficult from back in creation days when these ancestors travelled through and they made it like a map ... very old songs, very old. (*De Rose* RTs.91–92)

Further legal argument followed, without resolving this completely foreseeable, though complex, issue.[63]

Finally, the claimant group sang again. On this occasion the singing, with ground-beating accompaniment, was recorded.[64] The duration of the eight verses sung was three minutes and fourteen seconds. On the audio recording, the singing in the last four verses is noticeably louder and more vocal than in the first four—affirming the "very vigorous singing" observation by claimants' counsel. With singers mindful that the session was being recorded, the usual banter among participants between verses was truncated, carried out in whispered voices and via gesture.[65] The fact that singing occurred at all is noted by a mere two words in the court transcript: "song performed" (*De Rose* RTs.94).

In subsequent evidence it was observed by one of the singers, "We broke the law by singing to you for this purpose" (*De Rose* RTs.94). By "the law" the witness is referring to restrictions under local Yankunytjatjara law. Song exegesis followed. Addressing the earlier dismissal that their songs cannot connect "person, place or event," claimants gave evidence that, "We were singing this song, this place." Witnesses identified *tjukurrpa* (Dreaming) entities and site features with specific words sung in the song verses (*De Rose* RTs.94–97). As a demonstration of connection to land through a traditional artform, in this case singing, it is hard to imagine more credible people/place/Dreaming story triangulation. Or, in other words, knowledge/geography/mythology triangulation. This was a notable achievement given the litigious environment in which the singing occurred.

The effect of this episode on the *De Rose* hearing was profound and ongoing. Performance of sacred songs (and dances) as evidence of connection to country was recurrently and substantially curtailed by legal objections and rulings. Claimants gradually truncated or withheld presentation of performance evidence. Performance of a song occurred on just one further occasion during the hearing: it was identified as a public song sung by women and men (*De Rose* RTs.129–130). In evidence at a subsequent site, an elderly *De Rose* claimant repulsed questions, telling the judge: "that song [was] enough for your people" (*De Rose* RTs.111). In place of song and dance performance enacting the exploits of Dreaming beings, evidence of the continuity of these beliefs was reduced to verbal claims, for instance: "Yes, they can do the *inma* [singing] and the dance today" (*De Rose* RTs.170). The claimants' overall participation in, and engagement with, the hearing, declined: hats on heads hung lower; foot scribbling in the dirt increased; chairs were shuffled further away from the hearing tent; and audible gallery conversation during formal proceedings increased. As the days went on, claimants simply refused to demonstrate or speak about deeper aspects of their site-specific traditions (*De Rose* RTs.133).

In summary, the *De Rose* hearing (and transcript) is a vivid illustration of how an obstructive litigious environment can effectively undermine and inhibit a claimant groups' capacity, and inclination, to present evidence of interests in country through *performance*. A hostile litigious environment and a perception that the Court was disbelieving—rather than gaps in the claimants' knowledge—were the factors that derailed performance evidence in *De Rose*, to the detriment of the claim to native title. The De Rose Hill claimants won their native title in the end, with the full Federal Court finding that the primary judge had misinterpreted section 223 of the NTA which deals with continuous connection, and made errors of law and fact in the process.[66] But in getting there they encountered an adversarial judicial process that was deeply inhospitable, confusing, and disrespectful. The case illustrates how, even when the formal rules allow for performance evidence, it is presented within a context where it is, almost inevitably, understood as not normal, peripheral, eccentric and difficult, and therefore readily disputed. Formal rules may go some way in accommodating difference, but in the context of differences of this scale-differences about how we understand law, how we understand the sources of law, what we think counts as truth-formal rules can only go so far. Performative evidence occupies the place of the other—having to stake its claim for legitimacy. This is a particular problem when the claimant performers are also operating within strong protocols of authority and respect under Aboriginal law, albeit well alive to their marginal place within the dominant legal system.[67]

CONCLUSION

In Australia, the establishment of a judicial system and (later) constitutional arrangements was not only an assertion of sovereignty and the rule of law, but of colonial power and cultural hegemony (Kahn 1999: 108–113). Sovereignty not only conveys a claim to normative and metaphysical validity, but also makes culturally specific imaginative evaluations of institutions and the beliefs and behaviors of citizens, including in judicial processes (Kahn 1999: 39). In a court hearing, "meaning depends on context, and ... truth depends on the ways in which it is represented" (Sherwin 2012: 5). The formation and presentation of cultural knowledge and practices are always situated and constituted in beliefs and in intentional daily and ritualized individual and group (visual and aural) actions. For Indigenous claimants, their desire and capacity to represent the reality of their claim to land in a meaningful way are mediated by the courts' procedures and rules of evidence, as managed by the judge and legal practitioners, all of which are steeped in an alien system of meaning and representation. The Australian judicial system is working within a collective imaginary that constitutes what counts as proof, and unconventional performative communication forms do not readily fit this rubric.[68] Indeed, one might well describe the situation as what Bourdieu calls "doxic," where there is a "quasi-perfect correspondence between the objective order and the subjective principles of organization" (Bourdieu 1977: 164). For those citizen subjects whose subjectively held principles conform to these "objective" structures, the result is an unreflexive sense of naturalness or self-evidence. For those whose principles do not conform, the ensuing alienation goes beyond a situation of mere heterodoxy, for there is not even an awareness of the possibility of "different or antagonistic beliefs."

As a legal and cultural institution of the sovereign power, courts are disconcerting environments for Aboriginal people, including when presenting performance evidence. Indigenous litigants believe that their performance evidence, in contrast to oral testimony, has an inherent and "peculiar efficacy" that, once witnessed, ensures comprehension and belief will inevitably follow (Sherwin 2012: 3). This belief materializes when sacred objects (or sites, ceremonies or designs) are revealed during land claim proceedings. When disclosing such property, often seen as "title deeds" (Morphy 1983: 131) to land, claimants make statements like "now you understand" (Stanner 1979: 278), as a senior Rirratjingu man told Stanner during the Gove (Yirrkala) Land Rights Case, first litigated land claim in Australia.[69] While performative evidence holds evocative cultural and cognitive significance for its Aboriginal owners, the same reaction is not automatically shared by the court.

If one focuses on the particular problems that have arisen in native title hearings, one might conclude that greater flexibility in the rules of evidence allowing for the presentation of performance evidence in land claims would provide a way of addressing the inherent discrimination in a system that operates on the basis of a set of distinctive cultural assumptions. But practical or instrumental considerations are hardly a sturdy enough foundation to bear the weight of the epistemological and ontological issues this chapter has raised. Practical accommodations do not get to the deeper issue of the challenge for Australian law of encountering Indigenous peoples and Indigenous claims on their own terms. The inherent discrimination in the land claim processes described can only be addressed through social, political, and constitutional change and recognition. At issue here are universal human rights, universal dignity, the right to cultural integrity and diversity, the right to be heard, and the moral value and property rights of those who are vulnerable in the face of greater power.

The issues raised by the case studies in this chapter shine a light on broader considerations: how do divergent cultural systems communicate their foundational ideas and values? How, and why, should the dominant legal system recognize intra-nation legal claims to land that are based on substantially incompatible legal authorities and ontologies? How can the constitution of legal authority in such claims be conceived in a manner that does justice to sources derived from outside the operative legal system? What normative principles and values are consonant with the recognition of Indigenous claims to sovereignty? Constitutional recognition of Australia's Indigenous peoples' prior occupation and custodianship will not be resolved until these competing claims to cultural and legal authenticity and authority are confronted. Ongoing debates about constitutional recognition might provoke us to recognize that constitutions are cultural, legal, and political constructs that encode profound ontological and epistemological assumptions. Where these assumptions remain doxic, the possibility of authentically recognizing and allowing expression for difference in the living constitution of contemporary societies and states will remain impossible.

CHAPTER THREE

Codes

Judging the Rwandan Soundscape

JAMES E.K. PARKER

The English word "code" comes from the Latin *codex*, which derives in turn from *caudex*, meaning "wood" or "tree." To begin with, the term seems to have been used interchangeably with *tabulae* to refer to the wooden writing tablets covered in wax, held together by cords, and used for note-taking and the recording of ephemera since at least the time of Homer (Roberts and Skeat 1983: 12–13). But by the first century CE *codex* had begun to refer to something else: to complete works, *libri*, entire texts written on leaves of parchment or papyrus and bound together at the spine (Roberts and Skeat 1983: 24). Originally then, code wasn't a legal term at all. When it was used in legal contexts, the word referred only to a law's materiality and medium: its particular mode of inscription, the way it spoke and made itself authoritative, the means by which it circulated. It is striking, even symptomatic, that in its contemporary usage the word's mediological roots have been so decisively lost. In the modern age, law's textuality is too often taken for granted. Code: "a systematic collection or digest of the laws of a country, or of those relating to a particular subject" (*OED*). Codification: "the process of bringing together a legislative act and all its amendments in a single new act" (European Commission). To codify today is to collect and consolidate, to gather and rationalize. The medium is either simply assumed, ignored or, I am tempted to say, repressed.

Of the many casualties of modern law's obsessive textualism, one has undoubtedly been a concern for sound and listening. Contemporary legal thought and practice suffer from a kind of deafness. Testimony is given and judgment pronounced out loud, into microphones, for transmission via audio-video link and broadcast online, and yet you would hardly know it from the literature (Parker 2011). Law is deeply implicated in the fabrication of our sonic environments and experience, courts and legislatures claim to govern both the kinds of sounds we are permitted to make—what we can play, say, or sing, where and when—and who gets to listen, but the way in which sound is conceived for such purposes is barely ever reflected upon, let alone subjected to critique (Parker 2015a). For the most part, matters of acoustics are either ignored altogether or treated as if they were somehow self-evident, a matter of simple common sense, when they are nothing of the sort (Bull and Back 2003; Pinch and Bjisterveld 2012; Sterne 2012). Needless to say, this is a problem, even an ethical failure. Legal scholars and practitioners must cultivate a new sensitivity to questions of sound and listening. We must start holding legal institutions to account for how they think and work with sound, for the normative judgments they make, and for the diverse ways in which law is implicated in the coding of our sonic worlds.

This chapter takes up this imperative in relation to the Rwandan genocide and the work of the International Criminal Tribunal for Rwanda ("ICTR"). It is about the ICTR's *sonic imagination*: how the tribunal conceived of the Rwandan soundscape, its role in the genocide, why, and with what consequences (Sterne 2012). Much of the analysis is pursued in relation to one case in particular. As we will see, the trial of popular musician and singer Simon Bikindi offers a peculiarly rich opportunity to consider the tribunal's approach to sound.[1] Not just that. Many of the issues raised by the *Bikindi* case were also distinctly modern (though see Davis 2008). Substantively, the case was centrally concerned with sound reproduction technologies and broadcast media—two quintessentially twentieth-century phenomena (Sterne 2003)—and their roles in the perpetration of violence. Institutionally, the founding of the ICTR in 1994 was a crucial step in the expansion and normalization of international criminal law itself, having been born less than fifty years earlier at Nuremberg. So if the relationship between law and sound initially seems either marginal or trivial somehow, a matter of merely "academic" interest, the *Bikindi* case makes it abundantly clear that it shouldn't. Well over half a million people were killed in the course of the Rwandan genocide, and here was an extremely high-profile international legal institution—indeed, one concerned with articulating a still nascent form of legal order—alleging a *singer* to have been one of the ninety-two "most responsible."[2] It is not just that questions of sound were absolutely central in the Bikindi case. The stakes could hardly have been higher.

Even though the argument in this chapter is largely concerned with Bikindi, Rwanda and the ICTR, my hope is that its implications will resonate much further. Ultimately, the kind of inquiry I am both arguing for and attempting to exemplify here is just as relevant to the law of copyright, torts, contract and run-of-the-mill domestic procedural hearings as it is to high-profile international trials and the law of genocide. The gravity of the circumstances may be different, but many of the issues and challenges are the same.

LEGACY

We will get to Bikindi. Allow me to start elsewhere: with a film. A child is rolling a tire down an empty road, smiling as he runs towards the camera. But we know immediately that all is not as it seems. Because as we look, we also listen: to a low rumble and high violin which, together, undercut and render instantly precarious the innocence of the scene. This is the "audiovisual contract" Michel Chion has written about: the inevitable welding of a dialogue between sound and image in the experience of film, "a sort of symbolic pact," he calls it, to which the audio-spectator implicitly agrees on entering the filmic world (1994). And so, as the image cuts for a split second to what may be a portable radio (Figure 3.1), we know that it is, because we also hear the sound of frequencies scrambling, searching for a signal before the dial settles finally on a muffled voice and a caption appears. "These people are a dirty race." The signal scrambles again as another image of a radio flashes up. "We must exterminate them." More crackling and noise. "The Tutsis are evil. Extermination is the only solution." And then another voice: deep, serious, American this time. "It came from the radio", the narrator intones, and we see close-ups of machetes now over a bass note that is increasingly unnerving as it surges and thickens with fuzz. "At first it was possible to ignore," the voice continues, "but the sound would not go away. It only got louder." We see a brief shot of a politician mid-speech, his hand lifted emphatically in the air. A woman cries out. There are bodies limp and contorted on the ground. "And louder." A man raises his machete to the camera. "And louder." The shot pans towards another radio set at the foot of a pile of rubble as the caption reads: "We will kill them one by one!" And finally the narrator again, over plaintive chords on the piano and a solemn cello: "In the early hours of April 7, 1994, the call to kill got so loud it drowned out everything else. It swept across the country like a storm. For 100 bloody days, Rwanda experienced one of the worst atrocities in human history and the international community stood by" (ICTR 2014).

These are the opening moments of a short film produced by the ICTR in 2014 to commemorate its establishment by the UN twenty years earlier, a matter of months after the bloodshed had ended. Here, in just sixty seconds, is a complete theory of the genocide, an extremely potent distillation of the tribunal's findings, years of institutional labor gathered, rationalized, and condensed—codified—in film right on the front page of the tribunal's so-called "legacy website." And Rwanda's soundscape is absolutely central to it. The entire genocide, in fact, is presented as a hideous sound-effect: the irresistible consequence of radio's weaponization, a whole nation swept up in a tidal wave of hateful voices and bilious speech. Of the hundreds of thousands killed between April and July 1994, the vast majority were Tutsi: some estimates suggest as much as three-quarters of the total Tutsi population (Des Forges 1999: 6). Though it was conceived, and to a large extent coordinated, centrally by a small group within the majority Hutu government (MRND) in the context of a civil war, the genocide was carried out by a combination of the military, a government-backed militia group known as the *Interahamwe* and an apparently willing population. Hundreds of thousands of Rwandans played their part. Not only was this genocide, it was a genocide in which there were nearly as many perpetrators as there were victims.

FIGURE 3.1 Still from "20 Years Challenging Impunity" © ICTR.

BIKINDI

Many of those perpetrators were fans of Simon Bikindi. In the early 1990s, Bikindi was one of the country's best-known musicians and popular figures. He was both a politician and a celebrity, "probably the most talented artist of his generation,"[3] "Rwanda's Michael Jackson" (McNeil 2002). And by the end of 1994 his songs had soundtracked a genocide. Three songs in particular had featured regularly on the infamous *Radio Télévision Libre des Mille Collines* ("RTLM") and on the government station Radio Rwanda, but recordings were also readily available on cassette, and Bikindi had performed regularly at stadiums throughout the country. The result, one witness testified at trial, was that "members of the population knew [his songs] by heart, and when they perpetrated those crimes, they would sing the songs, they would say that they were furious and that they wanted to avenge the deaths of their relatives."[4] Although six separate charges were brought against Bikindi in total, at root he stood accused of inciting genocide with his songs.

The *Bikindi* case is particularly rich when it comes to the ICTR's approach to sound and its role in the genocide. Like the more famous *Media* case before it—which resulted in the conviction of two founding members and directors at RTLM for broadcasts intended to incite acts of genocide[5]—Bikindi's trial was centrally concerned with radio. And just like in the *Media* case, the way radio was depicted by the tribunal throughout proceedings is cause for serious concern. But because Bikindi was being tried primarily as a singer, the tribunal was forced to grapple with a number of related issues too. What exactly was the difference between a song and a speech, for instance, for the purposes of the law of genocide? Or between an audio recording and a live performance? Did it matter whether the audio was heard on the radio or over a loudspeaker, and if so why? As we will see, the ICTR's response to these sorts of questions often left a lot to be desired. But it would be a mistake to localize the blame in this respect. To the extent that the tribunal's account of the Rwandan soundscape was inadequate, this was partly symptomatic of the more general deafness with which I am arguing so much of contemporary legal thought and practice is afflicted (Parker 2015a, b).

Bikindi was eventually convicted of incitement to genocide. Crucially, however, it was not his songs that ultimately proved determinative. Instead, the trial Chamber relied on a number of statements he was found to have made over a loudspeaker by the side of the road one day in June 1994, which is to say, right in the middle of the Rwandan genocide. Bikindi had "used a public address system," the Chamber said, "to state that the majority population, the Hutu, should rise up to exterminate the minority, the Tutsi." And then later on that day he had "used the same system to ask if people had been killing Tutsi, who he referred to as snakes."[6] As for Bikindi's songs, they had clearly been intended to encourage hatred. Moreover, they had actually been *used* by presenters on RTLM and on the government station Radio Rwanda to incite genocidal killings. But it had not been established, the Chamber ruled, that this was also Bikindi's intention.[7] How did the tribunal conceive of Bikindi's songs and speech on the way to this decision? How did it situate them relative to the sonic world in which they were heard? What function did it envisage for the technologies and media apparatuses which it insisted were so important in this respect? What was their role when it came to contextualizing, shaping or otherwise framing the listening experience for Rwandan listeners? Such questions were never explicitly asked in the Bikindi case, but that does not mean they are unimportant. Indeed, the way in which the tribunal unwittingly responded to them was crucial to securing Bikindi's eventual conviction, as we will see.

The analysis begins by showing how the trial Chamber's depiction of Bikindi's songs and speech as emerging from a noisy backdrop tells a familiar story about sound's relation to the social and juridical. Rather than being something for which we *must* take responsibility, as in certain other legal contexts, noise appeared in the tribunal's account as precisely that part of the soundscape to which its jurisdiction did not extend. Noise was the name given to the lawless in sound, that which is both ungoverned and also, in this context, ungovernable. In the second section of the chapter I consider the tribunal's account of radio and this time I am more critical. The tribunal's approach, I suggest, was consistent with a very common narrative in relation to the Rwandan genocide which presents radio as a symbol of the genocide itself. And it was important, therefore, that it was also on the radio that Bikindi's songs had achieved their maximum diffusion. But the account of radio offered by the tribunal was extremely thin. It rendered a complex technical and social apparatus as little more than a means of extending and intensifying the speaking voice. This sort of instrumental thinking is quite common both in relation to radio, in particular, and broadcast media in general. And the tribunal's approach was clearly symptomatic to some extent of the broader impoverishment of its sonic imagination. In the particular circumstances of the Bikindi case, however, it was clearly also bound up with the doctrinal imperative to individualize responsibility: the institutional requirement to hold Bikindi and only Bikindi to account. The ICTR's deafness when it came to radio should concern us in its own right, as a matter of justice and good judgment. It is particularly worrying, I will suggest, when the tribunal plays such a key role in representing and memorializing the genocide it set out to judge. In the final section of the chapter, I consider the tribunal's approach to the related matters of audio recording and reproduction. Insofar as Bikindi's songs were heard throughout Rwanda, it was primarily by means of the recordings he had made prior to the genocide, which featured regularly on radio stations like RTLM and Radio Rwanda. This was a problem for the tribunal because the nature of audio recording vastly complicated the hermeneutic task and therefore also the task of judgment. By rupturing the apparent link between the presence of the singer and the listening public, the meaning of Bikindi's songs was displaced onto the radio announcers who framed them for their listeners. It was these radio announcers whose intent was truly genocidal, the Chamber said, not Bikindi. The chapter ends by suggesting that the Chamber failed to take the consequences of its own arguments as far as it might have, and that this failure may have been yet another symptom of a general institutional deafness.

NOISE

The following passage is taken from the trial Chamber's judgment in the *Bikindi* case just as it is elaborating the "factual findings" which would ultimately found Bikindi's conviction. It is exemplary of an approach which, though presented here in particularly clear and distilled form, was in evidence elsewhere in the *Bikindi* case as well as in other proceedings before the ICTR. "Witness AKK testified that he saw Bikindi in June 1994," the Chamber wrote, "in a vehicle, as part of a convoy heading towards Kayove."

> AKK lived close to the road and saw buses full of *Interahamwe*, blowing whistles and making lots of noise with clubs and firearms. Bikindi was in a vehicle outfitted with a loudspeaker, over which songs were being broadcast with intermittent statements made by Bikindi. Witness AKK stated that Bikindi was not singing that day, as cassettes

of his songs were being used. Witness AKK heard Bikindi say "You sons of *Sebahinzi*, who are the majority, I am speaking to you, you know that the Tutsi are minority. Rise up and look everywhere possible and do not spare anybody."[8]

What we have here is a soundscape divided, split in two. On the one hand, the noisy backdrop: hails of gunfire, piercing whistles, clubs on metal, the acoustic terrain of genocide's "invisible battlefield" (Goodman 2010: xvii). On the other hand, Bikindi's songs and speech: foregrounded, amplified, distinct, and amenable therefore to the tribunal's jurisdiction. "Based on the words he proffered and the manner he disseminated his message," the Chamber found that Bikindi had "deliberately, directly and publicly incited the commission of genocide."[9]

Noise is often depicted like this. It is constantly in the process of being defined and redefined by its opposite. This is why Chion calls noise "segregationist" (2011). In information theory, noise is "that which a signal has to overcome through reduction or redundancy in order to get across" (Steintrager 2011: 249). For Jacques Attali, noise is "a resonance that interferes with the audition of a message in the process of emission." It does not, therefore, "exist in itself, but only in relation to the system within which it is inscribed" (1985: 26). More than that, though, noise is often the name given to the specifically disorderly and ungovernable in the system in question. For Steve Goodman, it is "intrinsically radical" (2010: 7). For Chion again, that which "bothers," "disturbs" or "pollutes" (2011: 245). And in Hillel Schwartz's gargantuan audio-cultural history *Making Noise: From Babel to the Big Bang & Beyond*, noise by definition is "what breaks through," a confounding of order (2011: 28). It is no coincidence that the word has its etymological roots in the Latin *nausea* (Serres 1995: 13, 20). Well beyond the particular circumstances of Bikindi, Rwanda, or the ICTR, noise is frequently the name given to the element of disruption or dissonance in both sound and the social: a failure properly to harmonize, the breach of the peace, a kind of sickness.

Sure enough, many of those who testified at the ICTR identified noise with genocide itself. In the *Media* case, for instance, the trial Chamber reported that, "Witness ABC, a Hutu man from Kigali, testified that he was in Rugunga when RTLM radio announced at around 8:00 p.m. that President Habyarimana's plane had been shot at. After the announcement, the witness heard gunfire and grenade explosions which continued all night. The next morning, RTLM stated that some people who were opposed to the regime had been killed."[10] Here, gunfire and grenade explosions are the very first evidence—acoustic or otherwise—that everything is no longer as it was, that the fragility of the social order has been breached and that turmoil looms. The example is far from an isolated one. At Bikindi's trial, witnesses would often testify to even more specific examples of noise's alertive function. "Just as the Daihatsu passed," witness AHP explained, "I also heard a lot of people making noise from where the Daihatsu had come from, and I went there to find out what had happened. When I arrived at where the people were making noise, I learnt from the people who were there that the *conseiller*, Sibomana, had taken some Tutsis who had been hiding in a certain house."[11] This is witness Antoine Nyetera responding to a question from counsel for the defense. "Q. Mr. Nyetera, to whom would you attribute those attacks? Or better still, did you hear about those attacks over the radio, for instance? A. If people heard grenade explosions at night, the next morning I would pass by a house blown out—a house blown up."[12] And here is some testimony from Rwanda's own *Gacaca* courts read onto the record at one point in the *Bikindi* case: "We heard whistles being blown," the witness remembered, and immediately "we sought refuge in a—in the bamboo bush."[13]

Noise often arrives before visual confirmation: a sign or "signal" of imminent danger (Daughtry 2014; Schafer 1977: 10). That is both a fact of the phenomenology of conflict and a consequence of sound's peculiar disrespect for architectural and visual space. One witness put it particularly unambiguously in the *Karera* case. "I knew that Tutsi could not be making such noise," he testified, "only *Interahamwe* could make such noise. So I escaped after hearing that noise."[14] And in the *Bikindi* case we find an interesting inversion of this example in the transcript of an RTLM broadcast from April 1994 which was entered into evidence by the prosecution. Therein, Gaspard Gahigi, the presenter in question, makes explicit the link between noise and his community of listeners. The association between the two, he claims, was often exploited by the Tutsi-associated *Inkotanyi* rebel group as a kind of acoustic trick.

> Now, when Inkotanyi arrive at a place, for them to be able to kill people who are at roadblocks, they shout and blow whistles. So, the citizens rush up, thinking that it is their fellows and then, they fire at them. So, be careful about people who come blowing whistles ... be careful about that and know that soldiers are around. [15]

In Rwanda in 1994, evidently, noise and genocide were intimately related.

The juridical consequences were as follows. First, the presentation of Rwanda's sonic environment during the genocide as noisy—buses full of *Interahamwe* "blowing whistles and making lots of noise with clubs and firearms"[16]—helped both in evidentiary terms and rhetorically to establish a narrative of conflict. Noise registers in the *Bikindi* judgment both as a technique of intimidation and as sign and symptom of actual social dysfunction, the breakdown of civil order. Second, this sonic narrative conforms to a parallel and similarly familiar technological discourse. The particular *kinds* of noise depicted at the tribunal were all decidedly low-tech: whistles blowing, clubs banging on the metal of car doors, gunshots fired into the air: the acoustic manifestation of a famously low-tech conflict in which so-called "small arms" and "light weapons" rather than "heavier" munitions such as planes, tanks, rockets, and bombs were central (Figure 3.2). Indeed, in the standard historical accounts, a large part of the horror of 1994 derives precisely from this technological aspect, revealed here at the level of sonics: the grotesque proximity, the brutal lack of mediation, between perpetrator and victim, Hutu and Tutsi, which this technological dimension implies (Des Forges 1999: 9, 97; McNulty 2000: Verwimp 2006: 5). It is as if war in the West were somehow more civilized, and specifically by virtue of its technical "sophistication": the clinical, anesthetic distance of drone warfare and targeted aerial bombardment. So the particular forms of noise being depicted in the judgment in the *Bikindi* case—whistles, clubs on metal, handguns—map well onto a story about the supposedly "tribal" or even "primitive" nature of the Rwandan conflict which we also see reflected in the tribunal's discourse about radio.[17] The ICTR's endorsement of the phrase "Radio Machete" to describe RTLM in the *Media* case, for instance, its metaphorization of RTLM as "drumbeat" of the genocide:[18] these are all too overt echoes of media theorist Marshall McLuhan's dubious claims about the association between radio and Africanness, both replete with "tribal magic," as we will see (1964).

Third, and most importantly, noise is positioned by the tribunal as both counterpoint and backdrop to Bikindi's songs and speech. It is in this original act of segregation that the tribunal's peculiar doctrinal concerns begin to manifest themselves at the level of acoustics. Whereas in the law of nuisance, for instance, noise often appears as the object of juridical inquiry, here it is both the limit and other of responsibility in relation to sound (Bijsterveld 2008; Thompson 2004: 115–168). Noise maps to genocide itself. It is the acoustic manifestation of the social problem from which individual, criminal

FIGURE 3.2 Still from "20 Years Challenging Impunity" © ICTR.

responsibility must be distinguished. In doctrinal terms, noise is presented by the tribunal as precisely the *opposite* of legally relevant "expression," the *absence* of a "direct" and clearly articulated "idea" or "opinion" for the purposes of the law of freedom of expression and the doctrine of "direct and public incitement to genocide" (ICTR Statute). It is not just the ungoverned therefore, but, in doctrinal terms, also the ungovernable in sound: that part of the soundscape to which the tribunal's jurisdiction did not extend. For the ICTR, noise begins where responsibility ends. It is the disorderly backdrop from which Bikindi's voice must emerge—direct, public, and meaningful—into the realm of criminal accountability.

RADIO

By far the most predominant means by which it did so was on the radio. It was on the radio that Bikindi was alleged to have "participated in the campaign to defeat the enemy in the media."[19] The privately owned RTLM had been "created as a vehicle for anti-Tutsi propaganda," the prosecution alleged, "with a media programming objective of sensitizing and inciting the listening public to target and commit violent acts against Tutsi, extolling Hutu solidarity, and targeting the Tutsi as accomplices of the enemy."[20] Bikindi was said to have collaborated with a number of high-ranking officials, including President Habyarimana, in founding it for this purpose. Not only did RTLM feature his songs "several times a day," "usually during an early morning broadcast, at lunchtime and in the early evening,"[21] Bikindi had conspicuously failed to exercise his right under Rwandan law to "forbid or enjoin" their public broadcast.[22] In doing so he had "acquiesced," the prosecution claimed, "in the manner in which RTLM used his songs to promote death and destruction."[23]

Those were the allegations as far as radio was concerned. In its judgment, the Trial Chamber determined as follows. First, it was on the radio that Bikindi's songs had reached their maximum diffusion. The Chamber ruled that they had been played "repeatedly on

RTLM and Radio Rwanda in 1992, 1993 and the first half of 1994." Moreover, two songs in particular were played "even more frequently during the genocide,"[24] "over and over," according to one witness, "more than five times per day."[25] Another claimed to have heard them "continuously," "all day long."[26] Second, although RTLM had undoubtedly become a "vehicle for anti-Tutsi propaganda" as early as the end of 1993, which is to say only a few months after it began broadcasting,[27] it was not clear it had been created for such a purpose.[28] Furthermore, there was no evidence that either Bikindi's involvement in launching the station "with 49 other individuals" or his continued "minor shareholding" in it gave him any control over programming.[29] When Bikindi was interviewed on RTLM in December 1993 and January 1994, for instance, he had supported President Habyarimana and "vigorously criticized" Fuastin Twagiramungu, who had been designated Prime Minister of Rwanda by the Arusha Accords in July 1993, but "nothing in these interviews show(ed) that Bikindi had any kind of authority over the radio programming or over RTLM in general."[30] Finally, not only had the prosecution failed to prove that Bikindi had the right to prohibit the broadcasting of his songs under Rwandan legislation,[31] "mere acquiescence" was not sufficient to constitute criminal responsibility in international criminal law. The prosecution would have needed to establish a *duty* to stop the broadcast of his songs, which it failed to do.[32] How was radio itself presented on the way to these findings? What kind of account did the tribunal's juridical concerns enable or produce? Why? And with what consequences?

Scott Straus has argued that in the years since 1994 radio has become a "symbol" of the Rwandan genocide in the international imaginary (Straus 2006, 2007: 610). In his highly influential *Rwanda: Les Médias du Génocide*, Jean-Pierre Chrétien put it like this. "Two tools, one very modern, the other less so, were used particularly widely during the genocide of the Tutsis in Rwanda: the radio and the machete, the first to give and receive orders, the second to execute them" (1995: 191, translation my own). "Killers often carried a machete in one hand, and a transistor radio in the other," writes Samantha Power (2001: 89). And for Linda Melvern RTLM was a "propaganda weapon like no other," "radio murder" (2000: 71; 2005: 25). Even Alison Des Forges, in her renowned account of the genocide for Human Rights Watch, variously metaphorizes radio as the "voice of extremism," the "voice of the government," the "voice of the campaign" and simply the "voice of genocide" (1999: 58, 60, 190, 496). In a more recent collection, introduced and endorsed by none other than Kofi Annan, Allan Thompson called RTLM "the voice of Hutu Power" (2007: 2).

The approach we find throughout the *Bikindi* case is very similar. This was not a coincidence. Not only might we expect many of those involved in Bikindi's trial to have read and absorbed some of this literature, much of it was explicitly incorporated at the level of expertise. Excerpts from Chrétien's book were both admitted into evidence in the *Bikindi* case and cited on a number of occasions in the Chamber's judgment.[33] In fact, both Chrétien and Des Forges were key expert witnesses for the prosecution in the *Media* case in which two of RTLM's other more influential founders Ferdinand Nahimana and Jean-Busco Barayagwiza were prosecuted and eventually convicted of incitement to genocide,[34] and which bore a significant influence on the tribunal's thinking in relation to Bikindi.[35] Radio was both a privileged feature of the Rwandan soundscape for the ICTR and heavily instrumentalized by it, as we will see. The tribunal consistently rendered radio as a tool or technique of *amplification*, a means of preaching hate more widely and more effectively than the natural, untechnologized voice would allow.

In the *Bikindi* judgment, as in each of the prosecutor's indictments before it,[36] RTLM was constantly referred to as a "vehicle" for the "dissemination" of anti-Tutsi propaganda.[37] "The Chamber finds beyond reasonable doubt that RTLM was a vehicle for anti-Tutsi propaganda."[38] "Upon reading of the transcripts of RTLM broadcasts admitted into evidence," it wrote, "RTLM clearly and effectively disseminated anti-Tutsi propaganda as early as the end of 1993."[39] The role of radio here is clear. It is a method for the dispersal of incendiary political "expression," and a particularly efficient one at that. The Chamber cited the following testimony, for instance, without either comment or critique. "The Defence Expert testified that a radio broadcast throughout the entire territory would have a far more considerable impact than a public performance."[40] The same approach can be seen even more clearly in the *Media* case. Again, radio is constantly figured there as a "vehicle," "used" to "transmit," "convey," "spread" and "disseminate" "messages," "ideology" and "views": a technique, in other words, for the expression and distribution of intentional thought as manifested in the technologized voice.[41] To "disseminate," after all –from the Latin *seminare*, to sow—means to scatter one's seed widely. The roots of the word "broadcast" are similarly agricultural. It literally meant to cast broadly: to spread out or disperse (Peters 1999: 206–214). But radio also featured extensively in the *Media* case as an "object," a "tool" and a "weapon." According to one witness whose evidence was endorsed by the Chamber, "one would find little radios in offices, cafes, bars, and other public gathering places, even in taxis."[42] "Radios and weapons" were "the two key objects that would be found at roadblocks," the witness claimed.[43] According to another, "almost everyone had a radio and listened to RTLM."[44] Elsewhere, RTLM was described as "the crucial propaganda tool,"[45] a "tool for killing,"[46] the "*radio que tue*,"[47] "Radio Machete" (Figure 3.3).[48]

What made the radio *so* effective, *such* an ideal "vehicle" for the purposes of "disseminating" propaganda, even if RTLM had not originally been intended as such? In its judgment in the *Media* case, the trial Chamber explained:

FIGURE 3.3 Still from "20 Years Challenging Impunity" © ICTR.

The nature of radio transmission made RTLM particularly dangerous and harmful, as did the breadth of its reach. Unlike print media, radio is immediately present and active. The power of the human voice, heard by the Chamber when the broadcast tapes were played in Kinyarwanda, adds a quality and dimension beyond words to the message conveyed. In this setting, radio heightened the sense of fear, the sense of danger and the sense of urgency giving rise to the need for action by listeners. The denigration of Tutsi ethnicity was augmented by the visceral scorn coming out of the airwaves—the ridiculing laugh and the nasty sneer. These elements greatly amplified the impact of RTLM broadcasts.[49]

Two qualities made RTLM "particularly dangerous and harmful" as far as the ICTR was concerned. First, the "breadth" of its "reach," the precise extent of which, interestingly, was never actually addressed in detail by the tribunal.[50] Second, the potency of its effects, which are glossed immediately as essential to radio's "nature." This natural potency derives, apparently, from the peculiar immediacy of the radio voice which, unlike the text-oriented "print media," is imagined as being both particularly "present and active."[51]

The depiction of radio naturalized at the ICTR conforms closely to ancient and deeply held theological and metaphysical attitudes or commitments, whereby vision maps to distance, disengagement, reason and intellect, and sound is immersive, present, embodied, affective, even divine (Derrida 1976; Sterne 2003: 15). Here, they have simply been technologized, translated into the field of radio. Radio on this account is an extension of the speaking body in exactly the same way that the machete might be thought of as merely an extension of the arm or hand. Both are figured as prosthetics: one acoustic, the other haptic. Where one improves the reach and power of the voice in the "expression" of incendiary "ideas" and "opinions," the other does the same for the arm in the infliction of pain. Radio, thus, like some supercharged version of the voice, is rendered as intrinsically "powerful" and "visceral." It "heightens," "augments," and, finally, "amplifies the impact" of the "messages" being broadcast. In his award-winning account of the genocide *Shake Hands with the Devil*, General Roméo Dallaire, who led the UN's peace-keeping force to Rwanda between 1993 and 1994 and who also testified a number of times at the tribunal,[52] famously wrote that in Rwanda "radio was akin to the voice of God" (2003: 272). There is very little in either the *Bikindi* or the *Media* cases to suggest that the ICTR would disagree.

One suspects that a number of related racial and cultural prejudices may have been in play here too. In the *Bikindi* case the Chamber was happy to endorse witness BHH's testimony, for instance, that "the African population, and the Rwandan population in particular, has the tendency to respect what is broadcast on government radio stations which stand as official sources. He added that people tend to think that what is broadcast on the national radio station has a legal force or some kind of authority."[53] The sentiment is very similar to one expressed by renowned media theorist Marshall McLuhan, for whom radio's potency in totalitarian regimes was related directly to its supposed Africanness. Hitler's Germany "danced entranced to the tribal drum of radio" he wrote in 1964's *Understanding Media*, the clear implication being: if only Germany had been less aural, more literate, less African, more European (1964: 260). For McLuhan:

Radio affects most people intimately, person-to-person … That is the immediate aspect of radio. A private experience. The subliminal depths of radio are charged with the resonating echoes of tribal horns and antique drums. This is inherent in the very nature of the medium, with its power to turn the psyche and society into a single echo chamber. (1964: 261)

Notice how similar McLuhan's language is here to that of the tribunal above, and how in both cases the account of radio is presented as "natural." Consider too just how little agency is granted to the listeners in both accounts. In its presence and its intimacy, radio does things to you, whether you like it or not. "RTLM broadcasting was a drumbeat," the Chamber wrote in the *Media* case, "calling on listeners to take action against the enemy and enemy accomplices."[54] The association between rhythm and the compulsive African body is an old one. There is a long history, Simon Frith writes, "of defining black culture, specifically African culture, as the body, the other of the bourgeois mind." "The primitive in music (rhythm), the primitive in social evolution (the medieval, the African), and the primitive in human development (the infantile) are thus reflections of each other" (1996: 127, 130). Similarly familiar is the elision between so-called "oral traditions"—in the *Bikindi* case, the Rwandan tradition was repeatedly referred to in these terms[55]—and either critical or intellectual deficit. In her influential study *Oral Literature in Africa*, for instance, Ruth Finnegan writes that "in the popular view [the concept of an *oral* literature] seems to convey on the one hand the idea of mystery, on the other that of crude and artistically undeveloped formulations" (1970: 1). Indeed, the entire book can be read as an attempt to reconfigure the deep association between orality and the "primitive," to revalorize oral traditions, in other words, for the Western reader. The ICTR's portrayal of the Rwandan radio listener is consistent with such stereotypes about both Rwandans and Africans more generally: that "they obey orders blindly, that they are poorly educated and thus easily manipulated, and that they are immersed in a culture of prejudice" (Straus 2007: 617). This time, the prejudice simply comes with a technological gloss, which also operates as an obfuscation. As Richard Carver puts it, "the notion that people could be incited to acts of extreme violence merely by listening to the radio is only tenable if it is accepted that RTLM propaganda unlocked profound or even primordial hatreds" (2000: 190).

So far we have identified two main features of the tribunal's account of radio in the *Bikindi* case. First, a real consistency with the broader discourse in relation to the medium's role in the Rwandan genocide, inherited by the tribunal partly in the form of expert evidence. Second, the work of certain familiar but unfounded attitudes regarding the relations between sight and sound, reason and unreason, the West and Africa, playing out this time at the level of technology. I now want to identify two further elements to the tribunal's approach, both of which were the result of a specifically juridical orientation. On the one hand, a tendency towards *reification*. On the other, an entrenched *instrumentalism*.

In the work of Georg Lukács, "reification" refers to the objectification of social relations, and particularly of commodity structures (1971: 83). As taken up by Jonathan Sterne, the term names the same process in relation to media. It refers to the tendency to mistake the historical conditions of a medium for its fundamental nature, to understand the complex constellation of technical and social practices embodied in a medium like radio or television as if they were somehow inevitable or intrinsic to the technology itself (Sterne 1999: 503–504). This is precisely the logic we find in relation to radio at the ICTR.

Technologically, analogue—as opposed to the more recent digital—radio depends on the bringing together of microphones, amplifiers and loudspeakers as well as the ability to send and receive electroacoustic signals by way of electromagnetic radiation with minimal noise or interference. At the level of infrastructure, it requires the alignment of these technologies in a very particular way. A whole host of decisions needs to be made and then carefully implemented, regulated, and maintained in relation to how they are networked. If radio was predominantly centralized and uni-directional in Rwanda, therefore, which is to say, truly a broadcast medium rather than modular and dialogical like the telephone, neither of these characteristics were inherent to the technologies themselves (on the telephone's brief history as a broadcast medium, see Sterne 2003: 192–194). They had to be designed. Transmitters with a significant range had first to be funded and then built. In order to establish an audience, receivers needed to have been distributed and the network "heavily promoted by UNESCO and other international aid agencies" as a method of "modernization" and "development," as indeed it was throughout much of Africa in the twentieth century (Kellow and Steeves 1998: 115; Larkin 2008). To give some idea of the numbers in this respect, whereas in 1970 there was one radio receiver for every 120 Rwandans, by 1989—just five years before the genocide—the ratio was more like one for every thirteen (Chrétien 1995: 57). Then there are the crucial related questions of programming and listenership: the particular ways in which radio programs present themselves to the ear and are integrated into the lives of their listeners, none of which are either necessary or stable; the specific forms of attention and affect a broadcaster both nurtures and produces; the way in which the audience is addressed and encouraged to interact (or not to); the specific modes of listening facilitated, whether individual or communal, concentrated or distracted (Douglas 1987; Larkin 2008; Smulyan 1994). Darryl Li has argued, for instance, that if RTLM exerted a certain "intangible power" in the run up to and during the genocide, this had nothing to do with radio's essence or "nature," nor its ability to simply compel or manipulate a peculiarly gullible audience. Rather, the station's success in this respect was a function of its ability to "implicate listeners in the project of the genocide," to inveigle its way into the routines of everyday life by means of news, debates, music, talk-back, and a generally informal and jocular style (Li 2004: 16). If RTLM was authoritative, in other words, this wasn't because it assumed the voice of God, but precisely the opposite: because of its ability to co-opt "normality itself in the service of violence," which is to say something much more subtle and complex (Li 2004: 23). All this nuance was simply elided at the crucial moments in the *Bikindi* case. Once radio had been reified as a "tool," "object" or "vehicle" for the "dissemination" of propaganda, it was presented by the tribunal as ready and waiting to be put to inflammatory use: an instrument of genocide.

As critical media theorist Andrew Feenberg explains, "instrumentalism" refers to the "common sense idea that technologies are 'tools' standing ready to serve the purposes of their users" (1991: 5). Not only do technologies have an "essence" on such an account, that essence, by definition, "distinguishes it from the human (essence) that, as its efficient cause, makes and uses technology" (Coonfield 2006: 287). This is why for Martin Heidegger instrumental thinking is necessarily anthropological too (1977). Presupposed in the separateness of the (reified) tool is a theory of man capable of "mastering" it, of wielding it at will (Heidegger 1977). This same anthropocentrism is also why for Félix Guattari the instrumentalist conception of technology tends to depict such mastery in terms of "the extension and the projection of the living being" (2009: 92). "With every tool man is perfecting his own organs," wrote Sigmund Freud (2001: 101). Even if that perfection is sometimes to insidious ends.

But instrumental thinking is not just anthropological. In this context it is thoroughly juridical too: entailed in the very project of international criminal law itself. As an entire media apparatus—which is to say an historically specific network of technologies, affects, people and practices—radio is a social problem, and responsibility in relation to it is therefore necessarily diffuse. It falls to a station's owners, programmers, and announcers, but also to its many listeners and interlocutors, to the technology itself, to Rwanda's colonizers, to the postcolonial governments and NGOs who installed, maintained and promoted the necessary infrastructure, even to the international bodies who failed to intervene and "jam" the station's signal once it had become clear what was happening on the ground (Metzl 1997). As a simple tool for the extension of the voice, by contrast, responsibility is individualized. Of necessity, it resolves back to the speaker, singer, or whoever it was who allowed or encouraged their voice to be broadcast in the first place.

It is often pointed out that because of its commitment to a "strong idea of individual responsibility" (Mégret 2014), international criminal justice can tend to erase or at least marginalize the role played by social structures and systemic factors in the commission of mass atrocities in the stories it tells about them (Drumbl 2005; Gevers 2014; Mégret 2014; Simpson 2014). The same point is made less often about media. And yet as the *Bikindi* case clearly shows, straining accounts of the Rwandan genocide through the filter of international criminal law had a major distorting effect on how radio's role in the genocide was understood. If the ICTR consistently presented radio as a "tool" that could be wielded at will, just like a machete, this wasn't just a result of the expert witnesses it called, or the conventional wisdom it absorbed, but also partly a function of the law itself. In international criminal law, in other words, the attribution of responsibility actually *depends* on the accused's mastery of their tools. And the result has been the institutionalization of an account of radio that is not just over-determined, reductionist or racist, but also—by virtue of the ICTR's profound influence on public discourse on the genocide—increasingly central to how the genocide is remembered. Indeed, as Gerry Simpson points out when the Rwandan genocide is remembered today, the proceedings of the ICTR have become a ubiquitous reference point, even to the extent that the two may now be "ineluctably linked" (Simpson 2014: 159). So it isn't just that history has just been "judicialized," as Simpson succinctly puts it (2014: 159). At least where the Rwandan genocide is concerned, history has been *criminalized*: made to depend on international criminal law's commitment to individual responsibility and the twin concepts of human agency and media required to sustain that commitment.

AUDIO RECORDING

When Bikindi's songs were featured on RTLM and Radio Rwanda, it was only ever in the form of recordings which the Chamber found had been made at a private studio in Kigali in early 1993, and then distributed on tape.[56] Two of the songs recorded, it said, had clearly been intended to "disseminate pro-Hutu ideology and anti-Tutsi propaganda, and thus to encourage ethnic hatred."[57] This fell short, however, of a specific intention to incite genocide, and it was not until the recordings were subsequently "deployed" on the radio in 1994 that the provocative "commentary" by radio announcers would lead to their re-branding for explicitly genocidal purposes.[58] "A month into the genocide," the Chamber wrote, the "interpretations" on RTLM were becoming increasingly "inflammatory."[59] On May 17, 1994, for instance, the RTLM journalist Kantano Habimana had the following to say by way of introduction to one of Bikindi's songs:

Now, let us allow Bikindi to predict the future of the *Inkotanyi* and to tell them the fact awaiting them once the sons of Sebahinzi unite and fight them ... They are vanishing, gradually, as the bombs land on them, as they continue to be killed like rats ... Bikindi will in a short while tell you what will happen in future [*sic*] ... Please listen to Bikindi's advice to the *Inkotanyi*. He is warning them that they will all be wiped out, come what may, because all the sons of Sebahinzi are closely watching whatever has to do with the *Inkotanyi*, fighting them and hunting them down. That is what is happening now, and the *Inkotanyi* are on the verge of extinction.[60]

It was this sort of framing, the Chamber said, that manifested a truly genocidal intent. Recordings of Bikindi's songs were *used* for genocidal purposes, but that purpose was not Bikindi's. Because he had neither any "control or influence over the programming of RTLM or Radio Rwanda", nor any positive duty in law to attempt to stop them from being broadcast, Bikindi could not be held responsible for any such use.[61]

Gregory Gordon has argued, therefore, that "an implied 'instrumentality' criterion" can be gleaned from the *Bikindi* judgment: that "when recordings are involved, the recorded would-be inciter must be responsible for actual contemporaneous dissemination of the criminal speech (i.e., the playing of the recording) that is charged" (2010: 622). Gordon is right in one respect. The tribunal's logic here *was* "instrumental." It also involved the projection of a "complex assemblage of human and tool, machines and meanings, codes and connections" onto a singular object, ready and waiting to be deployed at will (Coonfield 2006: 288). This time, however, the object or tool in question was a tape recording as opposed to the radio. But Gordon goes too far in suggesting that the *Bikindi* case can be read as authority for the claim that the would-be inciter *must* be involved in the act of dissemination—of pressing play, as it were—for responsibility to ensue. There is nothing in the Chamber's judgment to suggest that if Bikindi's songs had been more overtly incendiary—if it had been possible to find in them a "specific intention to incite genocide" in addition to the mere "encouragement of ethnic hatred"—that the Chamber would in principle have required his involvement in their "deployment" too. Composition and recording may well have been enough on their own. Nevertheless, audio recording did present a problem for the tribunal.

In R. Murray Schafer's account, the electroacoustic transmission and reproduction of sound is referred to as "schizophonia" (1977: 88). The psychiatric connotations are quite deliberate. "Related to schizophrenia," Schafer writes, the term was intended "to convey the same sense of aberration and drama" (1977: 91). Schizophonia, from the Greek *schizo* meaning split and *phone* meaning voice, refers to the dislocation between an original sound and its electroacoustic reproduction louder, later and elsewhere. It was precisely this split that caused the ICTR so much trouble. Whereas radio, in its supposed proximity to the loudspeaker and therefore to the natural voice, seemed to allow for the expressive chain, as it were, between the present intention of the speaker/singer and the listener's ear to remain intact, recording dramatically interrupted it. In doing so, it enabled the intervention of another intentionality, another voice, and along with it another layer in the construction of any given recording's meaning and effects. As a result, it vastly complicated the hermeneutic project and therefore the task of judgment. And yet the tribunal never quite took this insight as far as it might have. It recognized that electroacoustic reproduction is never simply a matter of repetition, that it always also involves a difference, and that to reproduce is by its very nature to reframe: to change. But it failed to apply this same logic to the one moment where Bikindi himself *was* involved in the act of reproduction.

When the Chamber wrote that there was "no evidence that Bikindi played a role in the dissemination or deployment of his three songs in 1994," that was not entirely accurate.[62] Bikindi may not have played a decisive role in his songs' diffusion throughout the Rwandan radioscape, but there was at least one occasion in 1994 when he was undoubtedly involved in their "broadcasting" nevertheless. The Chamber even said as much in the very passage that would ultimately found his conviction. To repeat:

> Witness AKK testified that he saw Bikindi in June 1994, in a vehicle, as part of a convoy heading towards Kayove. AKK lived close to the road and saw buses full of *Interahamwe*, blowing whistles and making lots of noise with clubs and firearms. Bikindi was in a vehicle outfitted with a loudspeaker, over which songs were being broadcast with intermittent statements made by Bikindi. Witness AKK stated that Bikindi was not singing that day, as cassettes of his songs were being used. Witness AKK heard Bikindi say "You sons of *Sebahinzi*, who are the majority, I am speaking to you, you know that the Tutsi are minority. Rise up and look everywhere possible and do not spare anybody."[63]

When Witness AKJ, "heard Bikindi ask over a loudspeaker 'Have you killed the Tutsi here?' and whether they had killed the 'snakes'," he also "heard Bikindi's songs being played as the vehicles moved on."[64]

What is this if not the very same sort of restaging which in the case of RTLM the tribunal was happy to deem genocidal? If a journalist at RTLM was capable of "deploying" Bikindi's songs for genocidal purposes by broadcasting them along with inflammatory commentary, why not the man himself? Even if the Chamber was right and Bikindi had not intended his songs to incite genocide at the time of their composition, it was entirely open to the Chamber, and moreover precisely by virtue of its own logic, to find that Bikindi's own commentary—which in the Chamber's *own* analysis was intended to incite the killing of Tutsi—also constituted a reframing to genocidal ends. How else was Bikindi's audience meant to understand the performance of his songs in this context, backed by the noisy spectacle of an armed militia and punctuated by the rest of Bikindi's genocidal rhetoric? What purpose did the broadcasting of his songs play here if not to bolster the authority and effect of his statements? How could they fail to be colored by the context of their performance, by all the shouts and gunfire and noise? How could they *not* be imbued with a renewed salience or gravitas?

I am not suggesting that the Chamber ought necessarily to have found Bikindi culpable in this respect. That the tribunal failed even to *explore* this possibility, however, is revealing. Here was a man accused of inciting genocide with his songs and who was playing those very songs at precisely the moment he spoke the words which would ultimately lead to his imprisonment. Yet somehow this performance was deemed unworthy of consideration. It is as if, from an institutional perspective, the songs are totally beside the point here: as if, as far as the tribunal is concerned, they have more in common with the noisy backdrop than with Bikindi's own utterances. Indeed, it is hard not to wonder if this wasn't always the case to some extent: if Bikindi's songs weren't *always* conceived by the tribunal as being partly non-justiciable, *always* more noise than signal from a juridical perspective, *always* somehow secondary to the relative transparency of the word or text as expressive of the speaker's intentions: yet more evidence, in other words, of the deafness with which so much legal thought and practice is afflicted.

CONCLUSION

The account of the Rwandan soundscape produced by the ICTR in the *Bikindi* case was both the product of familiar narratives, themes, prejudices, and traditions from outside an overtly juridical context and the result of certain very specific juridical concerns. To begin with, the doctrine of "direct and public incitement to genocide" necessitated the segregation of the soundscape. On the one hand, the acoustic backdrop—noisy, social and, most importantly, ungovernable—marked the limit of the tribunal's jurisdiction in relation to sound. On the other hand, the acoustic foreground was occupied by Bikindi's songs and speech, both of which invariably distinguished themselves by means of technology: the radio, a loudspeaker, an audio recording. Radio, we saw, was in many respects the most important of these. It was radio, in the end, that gave Bikindi's songs their maximum diffusion both before and during the genocide and which, in doing so, worked to cement his popularity and fame. The tribunal's representation of radio was highly instrumental. Radio was not a network, but a tool, and specifically for the amplification of intentional human action; in this case, the vocalization of anti-Tutsi propaganda. Radio both flooded the Rwandan soundscape with such voices and intensified their effects on an apparently naïve listenership. The consonance with the commemorative film narrated briefly at the outset of this chapter is striking. There too radio is a tool, an instrument of atrocity, just like the machetes that feature so prominently beside it. The narrator could hardly have put it more succinctly: "It came," he says, "from the radio" (ICTR 2014). Even though Bikindi's songs were in fact deployed to genocidal ends on Rwanda's airwaves, the fact that Bikindi was not himself involved in this deployment meant that he could not be deemed responsible to the extent that they were. Responsibility resolved instead to the journalists who, in the act of broadcasting and contextualization, also reframed them: were able to inject some of their own intentionality into the mix. Not so where Bikindi's own restaging was concerned. Just at the crucial moment, on the road to Kayove that day in June 1994, his songs simply receded into the noisy background.

For an institution whose depiction of the Rwandan soundscape, and especially radio, left so much to be desired, the ICTR's faith in its ability to rehabilitate that soundscape is disconcerting. This is how the tribunal's "legacy" film ends. "Those that survived the genocide asked the United Nations to help rebuild a trust that had been lost," the narrator explains, "and, through justice, put the country they remembered back together. The mandate was clear. The way forward was not. Hundreds of thousands of victims, tens of thousands in jail, but the courtrooms were empty, with rumours of only five judges and a handful of lawyers left alive" (ICTR 2014). The camera looks up to towering buildings, gleaming white, their antennas reaching yet further into the clear blue sky. This is the International Conference Centre in Arusha, Tanzania: home to the ICTR since November 1995, and, despite the narrator's insistence on the clarity of its mandate, against the express wishes of the Rwandan Government.[65] As we hear of the tribunal's many achievements over the years, especially its key convictions—the directors of RTLM and Bikindi all among them—the camera lingers on shots of courtrooms decked out with microphones and computer monitors, witnesses, barristers, judges in headphones, and we see a series of close-ups of various diagrams, photographs, and other items of evidence with their exhibit numbers and other bureaucratic symbols featured prominently. Clearly, this is an institution that prides itself on its technical sophistication, which maybe even understands this as a marker of modernity and of the authority and prestige of international criminal justice itself (but this was already palpable in the film's production values from the very

FIGURE 3.4 Still from "20 Years Challenging Impunity" © ICTR.

first frame). Now we see images of children dancing (Figure 3.4). The soundtrack is nondiegetic (Chion 1994: 73), so we cannot tell for sure, but it is safe to assume that the music they are listening to is not Bikindi's. "Today in Rwanda it's safe to listen to the radio again," the narrator promises, as if that were somehow a result of the ICTR's labors: the instrumentalization now of justice itself. "The sound is of a nation rebuilding and a world pushing forward despite great imperfection, each day closer to a time when international law offers justice to all people, everywhere." And a single note on the piano rings out.

CHAPTER FOUR

Agreements

Truth, Politics, and the Value of Performing Impersonations

DIANA TAYLOR

The wavering line between truth and fiction has been a staple of late modern culture. Performance in this context is a particularly telling form: the supposed authenticity of face-to-face encounter is written into its medium, while it is also simultaneously premised on simulation. This chapter explores *impersonation* as a practice of masquerading that troubles the boundaries between "performance" and the "law." While it may be fine to pretend to be a police officer on-stage, it's against the law to do so in "real" life. *Impersonation* encompasses both theatrical and fraudulent behaviors—everything from actors to con men to criminal acts. Performance and theater, by definition, enact identities, critical positions, situations, and emotions that do not coincide with the actor's. "There is a gap at the heart of the mimetic continuity" as Jacques Rancière put it.[1] Audiences recognize and participate in the "gap," the as-ifness, or the deception. As Coleridge put it, people willingly participate in the "suspension of disbelief" when the story is infused with "human interest and a semblance of truth."[2]

The law, however, has trouble with semblance when it comes to impersonations. Perhaps this is because of an underlying ambiguity regarding what it is exactly that impersonations are asking us to agree to. Must the impersonation succeed as an intended fiction? Of course, it might be thought that the law has trouble with semblance precisely because of its fictive aspect. Yet, the law has little difficulty with fiction in other respects. Consider, for example, that a legal contract is typically defined as "a meeting of minds with the understanding and acceptance of reciprocal legal rights and duties as to particular actions or obligations, which the parties intend to exchange; a mutual assent to do or refrain from doing something; a contract."[3] Such terms as "meeting of minds" and "intent" and "assent" are fictions that suggest that people clearly understand what they are agreeing to.[4] What do people assent to when they witness an impersonation, and what do they intend when they participate in one? As we shall see, effective political performances may risk legal censure as the price to be paid for exploiting the slippery terrain of impersonation.

Orson Welles' 1938 radio broadcast "War of the Worlds" terrified his audience. He pretended to be a newscaster giving live bulletins about an invasion from Mars. He found it shocking, he said afterwards, that listeners would believe in Martians.[5] Should there be a law, a critic asked him, against such enactments? And what would that legislation be?

Sophie Calle, a French artist, dressed in a wig and stalked a stranger photographing even the most banal aspects of his existence (*Suite Venitienne*, 1980). In 1981, she pretended to be a maid to enter hotel rooms and photograph strangers' belongings. At least one of her subjects sued her for invasion of privacy.[6] Bill Talen, aka Reverend Billy, of the Church of Stop Shopping, is an actor pretending to be an evangelical preacher. He has been arrested repeatedly throughout the United States for taking on corporate interests by reciting the First Amendment and 'exorcizing' cash registers.

Are these art works "true" or "false"? Is their intent to deceive their subjects and audiences, or even to harm them? Or do these artists intend to make visible deep-seated assumptions (about national paranoia, privacy, and savage capitalism) that go unexamined? Do we agree on what the artist intended to achieve? Who is the authority? Does "freedom of speech" trump accusations against "false" even malicious speech?[7] Who gets to decide? The judge? The art world? A legal definition of "agreement" as "specify[ing] the minimum acceptable standard of performance" only further complicates the issue.[8] Define performance.[9]

The usual definitions of impersonation cite the intention to deceive, to profit, or to harm behind the act that makes it a criminal offense.[10] The issue is actually not that straightforward. Theater aims to deceive and reaps financial benefits at the box office from doing so. People going to the theater, however, know they will be deceived; they participate in and enjoy the deception. Yet certain performances might well start before the audience realizes it. A Chicano director, Daniel Martinez, staged his play in an old theater in a rundown part of downtown Los Angeles. The well-off theater-going audience had to stand in line in front of the people who lived on the streets. The homeless folks looked on at the audience with great curiosity. The theatergoers did not know that the performance was about them until they walked inside the theater and saw projections of audience members coming in from the street and from the lobby.[11] The Brazilian theater director, Augusto Boal, developed "invisible theater."[12] Two actors, pretending to be ordinary citizens, stood at a bus stop and started an argument about the ongoing war. Was war justifiable? Soon a group of people started to congregate and join in the argument.

So when is impersonation unlawful? A Legal Dictionary tells us that false impersonation is by definition a crime: "The crime of false impersonation is defined by federal statutes and by state statutes that differ from jurisdiction to jurisdiction."[13] These definitions reflect a lack of agreement on what impersonation means. One might say that impersonation is always "false" if by false we mean the pretend nature of taking on a persona or role that differs with the actor's. Under Federal law (18 US Code 912) those pretending to act as a US officer or employee "as such, or in such pretended character demands or obtains any money, paper, document, or thing of value, shall be fined under this title or imprisoned not more than three years, or both."[14] Under the New York penal code, 190. 25, criminal impersonation applies to those impersonating police officers or physicians while subsections 1 and 2 classify as a misdemeanor an act whereby a person "pretends to be a representative of some person or organization and does an act in such pretended capacity with intent to obtain a benefit or to injure or defraud another."[15] What about a political performance that parodies a corporate website?

In what follows, I want to describe a specific instance in which an activist performance I was involved with impersonated Monsanto Corporation. This example enables me to examine the ambiguity inherent in impersonation and what it means to impersonate a corporation. Etymologically linked to *corporare*, Latin for embody, the word came to refer to a "legally authorized entity" in the 1620s.[16] "Corporations" have had "bodies" and been considered "persons" for a long time, it seems, and pretending to be that body or person can have adverse effects. Here, then, I examine the ways in which impersonation led to conundrums about which kinds of impersonation are naturalized and which seem to trespass beyond the limits of the law.

Over the years, the Hemispheric Institute of Performance and Politics ('Hemi'), which I founded and direct, has offered a number of courses on *Art and Resistance* in Chiapas, Mexico. Hemi, located at New York University, offers graduate-level courses through the department of performance studies where I teach, and accepts students from NYU and from universities throughout the Americas. That year, as usual, the goal was to create an immersive, multilingual environment in which collaborative learning could take place through *doing* as well as through traditional text and discussion based seminars. In addition to researching the topic of resistance as a series of acts—from armed resistance to civil disobedience, revolt, refusal, protest, foot-dragging and so on—we always offer a workshop that ends in a public performance directed by Mexico's foremost performance artist and activist, Jesusa Rodríguez.[17]

During this third iteration of the course, we focused on the health, social, and economic problems caused by genetically modified corn. Monsanto had asked permission from SAGARPA, the Mexican Secretariat of Agriculture, to plant genetically modified ("GM") corn commercially in Mexico. They had planted it experimentally since 2009. Although there had been a moratorium on planting GM corn issued by Mexico's National Biosecurity Commission in 1998, President Felipe Calderón lifted it in 2009 after a meeting with Monsanto.[18] Activists throughout Mexico were mobilized to intervene against further invasion of GM corn. Genetically modified organisms ("GMOS"), they agree, impoverish local farmers and pose serious health dangers. They also threaten the diversity of the crop, the environment, and the cultures that developed in connection to agricultural practices. Monsanto, like other corporations, funds scholars to contest the evidence against them. Its goal is not to prove that GMOs are safe or beneficial to society, but to create enough doubt in people's minds so that safety and economic issues become a matter of opinion rather than a matter of fact.[19] Mesoamericans have been developing corn for the past 10,000 years. They think of themselves, by extension, as the "people of corn." Hundreds of countries have condemned planting GM crops, and understand them as especially threatening to countries of origin, those places where the crops were first grown and developed.[20]

In July 2013, as usual, the thirty-five participants from throughout the Americas (and beyond) staged a fabulous street performance of the *People of Corn* (Figure 4.1). Its target was the corporate giant Monsanto. As is typical of both theatrical and legal fictions, the mammoth agricultural complex was reduced to one representable character, Monsanto. For this performance, Monsanto wore a tuxedo, a top hat, and a pig's face. On his arm, a glorious drag performer dressed in a variation of the national flag pranced around as the adoring Motherland, eager to pick up the pennies that fell from Monsanto's wallet (Figure 4.2). The performer could not wear the actual flag as that is against the law in Mexico. The People of Corn, covered in beautiful body paint, sang and danced to the God of Corn. The performance moved towards the Zócalo, or city center of San Cristóbal, gathering more spectators as it moved along. The performance ended with a public volleyball game in front of the town's main cathedral between Monsanto's evildoers and the People of Corn (Figure 4.3). Everyone was invited to participate on either side, though almost everyone took the side of the People of Corn. A young Mayan girl threw the ball that defeated the Monsanto team, to great applause and shouts of joy. The group carried the beaming girl on their shoulders in triumph.

FIGURE 4.1 Lorie Novak Sin Maíz. Source: Photo by Diana Taylor.

FIGURE 4.2 Monsanto and Motherland. Source: Photo by Diana Taylor.

FIGURE 4.3 Beating Monsanto. Source: Photo by Diana Taylor.

But this year, as in past years, we invited artists, scholars, and activists to participate in the course. Lorie Novak, a photographer and professor of 'Photo and Imaging' at NYU joined us for the second time. Jacques Servin of the Yes Men, who was a visiting professor in performance studies, also participated. Andy Bichlbaum (Jacques Servin) and Mike Bonanno (Igor Vamos) are the Yes Men, artivists who parody powerful corporate leaders and spokesmen through what they call *identity correction,* that is, "impersonating big-time criminals in order to publicly humiliate them, and otherwise giving journalists excuses to cover important issues."[21] So while the Yes Men use the media, they do not target the media. Rather, as they say, they give journalists the excuse to talk about serious and ongoing issues that do not necessarily qualify as newsworthy. As Servin (as Bichlbaum) writes in *Beautiful Trouble*:

> When trying to understand how a machine works, it helps to expose its guts. The same can be said of powerful people or corporations who enrich themselves at the expense of everyone else. By catching powerful entities off-guard—say, by speaking on their behalf about wonderful things they should do (but in reality won't)—you can momentarily expose them to public scrutiny. In this way, everyone gets to see how they work and can figure out how better to oppose them ... This is identity correction ... Instead of speaking truth to power, as the Quakers suggest, you assume the mask of power to speak a little lie that tells a greater truth.[22]

Since 1999, the Yes Men have been getting into all sorts of mischief, impersonating a spokesperson from Dow Chemical on the BBC NewsHour, another from Halliburton, yet another claiming to be from the US Chamber of Commerce in a live forum, and so on

(Figure 4.4). During these impersonations, the two often build false hope that companies will finally do the right thing (recompense the victims of the Bhopal disaster in Dow's case) or that the US Chamber of Commerce would support environmental legislation.[23] When the organizations rushed to declare that in fact the announcements were a hoax, that they had no intention of doing the right thing, they fell into what is known as a "decision dilemma"—the "damned if you do and damned if you don't" gold standard for activists. The "target" looks ridiculous no matter what it does.[24]

Typically, a Yes Men action starts with a fake website. Andy and Mike create nearly identical sites and simply change the url slightly. Their fake Dow Chemical site drew some criticism from Dow, but nothing else. When the BBC was looking for a Dow Chemical representative to speak to on the twentieth anniversary of the Bhopal disaster, they found Jude Finisterra (the saint of lost causes positioned at the end of the world) happy to comply. On the air, Finisterra was all concern and thoughtfulness, the very picture of the well-meaning executive. At moments, as often with Servin's various personas, he looked slightly baffled and even silly.[25] The complexity of it all often throws his characters slightly off kilter, giving them a somewhat lost feel. The film, *The Yes Men Fix the World* (2009), shows a very nervous Servin almost running out of the BBC studios before he gets caught as the stock prices of Dow in Europe drop precipitously. Dow was too savvy to sue the Yes Men, but they did send "spies," as Servin calls them, to keep track of their doings.[26]

The US Chamber of Commerce, on the other hand, demonstrated less caution. It was so incensed at the Yes Men fake site that they issued a takedown notice in 2009 demanding they take down the "infringing material."[27] The Electronic Frontier Foundation (EFF), defending the Yes Men, argued that the "Parodic Site is obviously designed for purposes of criticism and comment and protected by the fair use doctrine."[28]

FIGURE 4.4 Jacques Servin's BBC Dow Announcement. Source: Photo by Diana Taylor.

As with the Dow case, the Yes Men decided to impersonate a Chamber spokesperson to push the hoax further. In 2010, Andy gave a press conference pretending to be a representative of the US Chamber of Commerce, announcing the Chamber had reversed its plans to derail responsible Congressional legislation on climate change.[29] The Chamber, which presents itself *as if* it were a government agency, sued the Yes Men for "fraudulent acts ... [that] deceived the press and the public and caused injury to the Chamber." "These acts" the Complaint continued, "are nothing less than commercial identity theft masquerading as social activism."[30] The Chamber insisted that these "conducts" are "destructive of public discourse" because they "disguise the true motives of the persons who took that property." The defendants, Servin and Vamos, the lawsuit states, are "engaged in a business [they] call 'identity correction.'" The Complaint repeated that the acts were fraud, not "hoaxes," used to promote the Yes Men's films and increase the sale of T-shirts. The Chamber's Complaint quotes Servin as telling the New York Times: "We're comedians, basically. It's all theater." As the lawsuit dragged on and on, the Chamber finally gave up its suit. The Yes Men then sued them back, for dropping the suit. The legal framework ironically enabled the Yes Men to develop even more theater. "Sometimes it takes a lie to expose the truth," the Yes Men say. All the brouhaha provoked by the hoaxes proved invaluable in keeping the companies' wrongdoings in the public eye.

Impersonating corporations leads to a fun house world of mirroring and masking that troubles perception, making it look as if power always resides elsewhere, impossible to locate. Corporations are hard to pin down. They may buy and brand real estate but their interests lie elsewhere. Bureaucrats wear suits and ties to incarnate financial interests of the mega rich who hide behind corporate labels. Ventriloquists reiterate faux facts, little and big lies that emanate from who knows where. Meanwhile actors are called "fakes."

In 2013, when Servin was with us in Chiapas, activists were anxiously waiting for the news of whether SAGARPA would grant Monsanto's bid to plant GM corn commercially. Jesusa Rodríguez communicated with activists from throughout the country, coordinating events and efforts to intercede. For years she had led nationwide protests through her *Resistencia creativa* project that inform Mexicans about the dangers posed by GMOs. As we sat drinking a beer in the Zapatista restaurant on Real de Guadalupe, an upscale walking street in San Cristóbal de las Casas, the idea came to us—we would create a Yes Men action against Monsanto. Some local activists and some participants in the class wanted to join in. In a few days we had prepared our digital action. In true Yes Men fashion, we launched a fake website claiming to be Monsanto's. Our press release, on the fake Monsanto website, announced that the request had been granted by SAGARPA and thanked all those people in government for their invaluable help in moving Monsanto's interests along to fruition. We, of course, thanked them by name and cc'd them in our communiqué.

> [MEXICO CITY (August 14, 2013): The planting of genetically modified (GM) cornfields on a large commercial scale has been approved by the Mexican Secretariat of Agriculture (SAGARPA). The permit allows the planting of 250,000 hectares of three varieties of GM corn (MON-89034-3, MON-00603-6 and MON-88017-3) in the states of Chihuahua, Coahuila and Durango. This is the first time GM corn will have been planted on a large commercial scale in Mexico.[31]

Our release went on to add that Monsanto, aware that critics would decry the threat to the diversity of corn in Mexico, contaminated or displaced by the GM crops, would enact certain measures. "One such initiative is the National Seed Vault (Bóveda Nacional de

Semillas, BNS), whose charter is to safeguard the 246 native Mexican corn strains from ever being fully lost." The "fully" lost, we felt, was a nice touch. Researchers and celebrity chefs could come and examine the native seeds in the vault.

Another initiative, we claimed, was the creation of the Codex México ("Codice México"), a digital archive preserving the vast wealth of Mexican culture for centuries to come. The five hundred year old *amatl* (bark) manuscripts that contain much of what we know about pre-conquest Mexico are called "codexes." Our "'Codex México' is a visionary initiative that will allow future generations of children to know far more about our lives today than we know of our pre-Columbian ancestors," noted forensic anthropologist Marcelo Rodríguez Gutiérrez. "Never again will the wealth of this region's culture be lost as social conditions change." This new conquest, we suggested, would be kinder and less devastating than the last. To illustrate the contribution of the Codex, Lorie Novak included corny photographs and empty captions: "Native woman eating corn."

Monsanto, faced with the decision dilemma of responding to or ignoring the prank, did not take long to respond. Within twenty minutes they had us on the phone demanding that we take our hoax site down. They insisted we issue a retraction immediately. We agreed, of course. Another press release, again seemingly from Monsanto, "denounced the release as a hoax, crediting a group of students and activists called *Sin Maíz No Hay Vida* (Without Corn There Is No Life)."[32] There we fully explained what Monsanto was up to. The "reveal," the Yes Men's revelation of the hoax, always happens within twenty-four hours of the act, if it hasn't been uncovered before. The lie may be useful in illuminating a larger egregious act, but it is not allowed to stand.[33] A few news outlets knew that both our press release and our denouncement were a prank—no one familiar with Monsanto's strategies could believe that the corporation would issue such declarations—but they took advantage of the excuse to throw light on the corruption shrouding Monsanto and SAGARPA. Given the widespread activism around the GMO issue, we were leaked a confidential email that Monsanto had just sent to SAGARPA, apologizing for the confusion that our announcements had caused and promising to get things under control.[34] Monsanto reiterated the need for confidentiality. Monsanto, imposters too, had to perform their role as responsible and efficacious collaborators for the authorities. We of course published that as well.

On September 13, 2013, Monsanto contacted the president of NYU to complain about the street and digital action. They wanted to know about the course, see the syllabus, and understand the relationship of these actions to NYU. They also demanded an apology from NYU.

This created a new drama, one that dominated our fall semester 2013 at NYU. This drama was complex. In Victor Turner's language of social drama, it could be characterized as consisting of a *breach* or rupture caused by a transgressive act (launching the fake website?), a *crisis* (which spanned the Fall semester), the *reparative* acts (involving Monsanto lawyers, NYU, and myself), and the *resolution* (hopefully to come).[35] The series of acts that comprised the drama shifted between overt and covert, play and "dark play" in Richard Schechner's words.[36] Play, like the law perhaps, is usually regulated by rules and agreements, but it was not quite clear during that time what we all thought we were agreeing to. Had we even agreed to agree? More in the realm of dark play, we did not all know who all were playing. The law structured its performance of authority and consensus, agreeing that we were in violation. We defended different rules based on freedom of speech that included the right to parody and critique.

In several ways, Monsanto started to appear as a "person" and "persona" invested with personality before my eyes. "Persona" in classical Greek theater, is literally the mask through which the actor speaks the words. No one ever saw the face of the being that uttered the words, only the mask or persona transmitting them. Monsanto's spokespeople were literally mouthpieces, ventriloquists conveying language. I never knew who, if anybody, was behind the mask. The mask of Monsanto removed the "object from our grasp" to paraphrase Brecht.[37] But contrary to Brecht's "alienation effect" that builds on dialectical materialism "to unearth society's laws of motion ... [and] treats social situations as processes, and traces out all their inconsistencies,"[38] this form of alienation made the powers more inaccessible and potent, unlocatable yet ubiquitous. Monsanto's spokespeople impersonated and embodied a corporation (*corporare*) that itself impersonated being a "person."

On a different level, Monsanto seemed to be a "person" with feelings. It (he? she?) claimed to have been hurt, embarrassed, and needed an apology. Corporations legally count as "persons" after all; they have rights and, apparently, they have emotions that get hurt. "Monsanto" had complained of this to NYU. But who exactly *is* Monsanto? Where were the people behind the masks the company wore? Its hurt was clearly a legal fiction, a useful form of impersonation in its own right. Apparently, the fiction of the corporation as a person was a permissible impersonation, while impersonating a corporate impersonation was not. But where do we find consensus regarding which impersonation ought to count most under color of law? What part of the social contract has been breached here, launching this drama as a *legal* crisis in the first place? Who says this gets to play out as legal drama rather than as a cultural or political one?

NYU lawyers repeatedly questioned Servin and me. Phrases such as "code of ethics," "academic freedom," and "conflict of interest" came up. Apparently, our action had placed us on the wrong side of each.

We stressed that the digital action had nothing to do with NYU. It was not on the syllabus or part of the course. We forwarded the materials, syllabus included, requested by Monsanto. NYU, we reiterated, had no reason to issue an apology.

We had a few questions of our own for Monsanto. What did Monsanto object to—the street action or the digital action? Is impersonation on the street different from impersonation online? It could not be that simple. We had impersonated Monsanto before in a street action, comparing the insatiable agribusiness to the insatiable mouth of Tlaltecuhtli, the Aztec god/dess of the Earth who devours her creations. It would seem that this kind of embodied action did not resonate much. Yet, Servin had been sued for impersonating a Chamber of Commerce representative in the flesh. The difference, Servin and I concluded, was not about the online/off line nature of the impersonation; it was about the reach of the prank. It is as if the greater the visibility of the performance, the greater the imperative to stop it. And that, rather than implicating an act of social wrongdoing, seems to highlight the significance of expressive freedom.

We also wanted to know exactly how our action had harmed Monsanto? After all, it was just play. This kind of street performance is a form of representation. Monsanto in a pig's mask was a representation. A performative, on the other hand, can be considered a speech act, a form of incitement.[39] We, like Yes Men before, claimed ours was intended as an art project—a performance rather than a performative. And arguably, if readers had actually believed the fake website, it might be said that we were trying to make Monsanto look good, as if it cared about bio and cultural diversity.[40] Again, how do we know what social or legal agreement, if any, had been breached?

As for our purported violations, we also had questions for NYU. "Conflict of interest? Really?" I asked, looking at an officer from NYU who had herself enjoyed an important position at Monsanto. She straightened herself uncomfortably in her chair and scratched the accusation off her list of our infractions.

Violation of an ethical code? What ethical code do you have in mind? Polluting the environment, destroying local economies, and harming humans? You can't establish violations until you've clarified what underlying agreement has been breached. On what basis, then, does the law legitimate certain performances, turning away from the harms they cause, while negatively sanctioning other performances, like street plays, because of the harm they are said to cause?

Monsanto had seemingly infinite resources and multiple strategies to counter any critiques or evidence of wrongdoing against them. All we (professors) had to protect us was academic freedom.[41] As I put in an email to members of the administration who continued to question whether or not my actions were covered by academic freedom: "For me, as a performance studies scholar, the hoax and writing and acting are all ways to express ourselves in the face of enormous corporate interests that do very real harm."

The logic of the situation we found ourselves in was paradoxical: if my use of a hoax were part of an NYU course, it would be covered by academic freedom. If it were not covered, because it took place outside the limits of my institutional commitments, then why would NYU have to weigh in? To make matters more uncertain, it wasn't clear what academic freedom might mean, or what it covers. Greg Lukianoff defines it in *Fire's Guide to Free Speech on Campus* "as a general recognition that the academy must be free to research, teach, and debate ideas without censorship or outside interference". Following that definition, those who study and teach there must be able to pursue knowledge without corporations impeding and subverting academic work.[42] Monsanto and other corporations and military entities fund research at all of our universities. There is a rotating-door hiring process between these industries and universities, as the role of my ex-Monsanto, now current administrative officer makes clear. These businesses influence what areas of inquiry are important, prioritized, and funded. And yet I am not allowed to critique them? Is that academic freedom?

If we must make a choice, as the law apparently requires, then we will need to agree on an underlying value. Which performance is more important to society: a band of concerned artists and academics impersonating a hurtful corporation, or a corporation intent on impersonating hurt feelings? When it comes to impersonations, I for one hope that the law will embrace the value of maximizing expressive and political freedom.

EPILOGUE

After many back-and-forths, it seemed that the street action, which was officially related to our course, did not really bother Monsanto. I gathered from the NYU lawyers that a few bodies on the street in Chiapas did not worry the corporation. While the actor wore a pig's mask to impersonate Monsanto, no one actually believed it was Monsanto—it was a performance; the joke was clear. An internet action, on the other hand, reached a far broader audience (including the people who were considering granting permission to Monsanto).

It might be argued that some people at least for a short period of time actually thought the fake announcement came from Monsanto. If that misunderstanding got them activated then wasn't that, like the misunderstanding Orson Welles inspired back in 1938, about a

Martian invasion, also couched within the domain of creative expression? And doesn't the importance of such speech increase when its political stakes rise? In any case, Monsanto was taking this level of exposure very seriously indeed, operating behind closed doors as usual to intimidate their critics.

As the fall semester wore on, it seemed that Monsanto no longer insisted on a formal public apology from NYU. A confidential apology, available only to "persons who need to know," as an email put it, would be sufficient. As before, I argued strongly against this, stating that Monsanto would use the (confidential) apology to justify itself and discredit critique before Mexican lawmakers.

Civil liberties lawyers have expressed concern that the ambiguity around the legal understandings of impersonation could clamp down on free speech. As Matt Zimmerman, the lawyer with the Electronic Frontier Foundation that defended the Yes Men from the Chamber of Commerce, notes

> the concern is it gives a lot of discretion to law enforcement to go after First Amendment activity ... The resulting consequence of that is that people will feel chilled and intimidated and hence decide to not engage in perfectly legitimate forms of social protest because they're worried that not only might they be sued, but they could actually go to jail. [43]

Political speech, is after all, what the First Amendment goes to lengths to protect, according to Christopher Dunn of the New York Civil Liberties Union: "Political, religious and other speech often is intended to be annoying. But that is precisely the type of speech the First Amendment was designed to protect."[44]

In October 2013, a Mexico City judge, Marroquin Zaleta, issued a temporary halt that prohibited SAGARPA from granting Monsanto permission to plant GM corn in Mexico, either on an experimental, pilot, or commercial basis.[45] A December 2013 ruling upheld that position.[46] Subsequent court rulings have prohibited the planting of GM corn in Central America. Until August 25, 2015 it has been illegal to plant GM corn in most of Mexico and Central America. But AgroBIO and other firms have lobbied to overturn Judge Marroquin Zaleta's 2013 ruling and demand he be taken off the case.[47] The struggle continues.

Did our digital action prove efficacious? Did we help to derail or at least postpone Monsanto's plans? Although we would love to think so, this hoax was one of thousands of interventions that artists and activists constantly carry out to keep GMOs out of Mexico and other countries. We were happy to be among people who use their talents to keep bad things from happening.

But the action did place many in a "decision dilemma." Would NYU tell Monsanto to go away, and reiterate that NYU had nothing to do with the digital action (my suggestion)? What would happen to Jesusa Rodríguez, to Jacques Servin, and to me? Would the Hemispheric Institute have to distance itself even further from direct actions such as this one?

As of this writing, the Hemi, NYU, Monsanto conundrum seems to have been dropped, if not exactly resolved. Monsanto, of course, is too smart to go after the Yes Men. Monsanto "just" wanted a letter from NYU that declared our action unethical. They were even willing to accept a confidential letter, read by only a few key people. I could not find out if NYU ever issued the letter of apology.

Happily, in any case, we were history.

But I too had been caught up in identity correction. I told the NYU lawyer that I would write the incident up in an essay. "If they [Monsanto] come after me for that,

I'll write more." But again, it's not that simple. I too have been forced to confront my mask of power and recognize how risk is unevenly distributed throughout society. Jesusa Rodríguez risks her life (which has been threatened more than once). Visiting and adjunct faculty face more risks of losing jobs than do tenured, full, and distinguished professors. Organizations such as Hemi also run risks of losing support and funding. In short, the prank had repercussions for all of us, in different ways.

Have I changed tactics in regard to truth and power?

YES MA'AM!![48]

CHAPTER FIVE

Arguments

*Should Videos of Trees Have Standing?
An Inquiry into the Legal Rites of Unnatural Objects
at the ICTY*

SUSAN SCHUPPLI

Arguments, or the rhetorical construction of truth about historical events, have always lain at the heart of legal trials. In this sense, it is not bare facts in themselves but how they can be assembled into a coherent and convincing narrative that provides the foundation for law's findings on the truth. However, through the course of the twentieth century, the materials upon which arguments could be built have radically altered. This chapter sets out to explore mediated evidence, the role of scientific expertise, and the ways in which they combine to create new legal assemblages. More specifically, it considers how visual media, especially videos and photographs, are increasingly engaged in the construction of the arguments that legal practitioners deploy and that courts are called upon to adjudicate. As visual images proliferate in courts, visual rhetoric and visual argumentation unfold alongside the traditional rhetoric of words alone (Sherwin 2007). This broadening of the rhetorical spectrum within legal practice calls for new forms of expertise and eloquence based on an expanded capacity to decode, in order to meaningfully examine, visual evidence and visual advocacy.

The title of this chapter is both an invocation of and homage to a now landmark legal essay written in 1972: Christopher D. Stone's *Should Trees Have Standing?—Towards Legal Rights for Natural Objects* (Stone 1972). In adapting Stone's title and leading question, the chapter aims to unfold some of the ways in which the procedural arrangements of international criminal courts such as the International Tribunal for the former Yugoslavia (ICTY) manage, and are challenged by, the non-human witnesses or "unnatural objects" that enter into its vast legal machinery. Despite the primacy of human testimony within the majority of the war crimes allegations prosecuted by the tribunal, in a number of instances, non-human witnesses and media forensics have played a significant role in the argument and resolution of cases. Using the trial of Slavko Dokmanović as my primary case study (Figure 5.1) along with supplementary references to other ICTY prosecutions, this chapter considers the role of non-human witnesses in the production of contemporary legal truths.

FIGURE 5.1 IT-95-13a: Dokmanovic [JPG] Video still of Exhibit D2 at 15:42 Document Type: Exhibit 217 • Date: 17/06/1998 • By: Prosecution. Source: ICTY Court Records.

<u>Witness Paul Tabbush examined by Mr. Clint Williamson[1]</u>
[International Tribunal for the former Yugoslavia, Thursday, 18th June 1998]:

```
   Q. As you travelled this route, were you also able to
recognize any of the trees which you believe might have been
depicted in the video segment marked 15.42?
   A. Yes.
   Q. What kind of tree did you initially recognize there?
   A. Well, the original one was a Lombardy poplar I had seen on
the video still, segment 15.42, what appeared to be the outline
of a Lombardy poplar or a tree of similar appearance.
   Q. Is there something distinctive about this Lombardy poplar?
   A. Yes. It's a very distinctive tree with upswept branches.
   Q. I would like for you at this time to view Prosecutor's
Exhibit 222, and if this can be displayed on the ELMO as well,
and if you would point out the tree you're talking about?
   A. I'm referring to the very upswept branches of this
tree here with a very straight central stem and then upswept
branches with a very tight angle between those branches and the
main stem.
   Q. Now, after spotting the Lombardy poplar, did you recognise
another tree in that immediate area?
```

A. Yes, I did.

Q. How did you recognise this tree?

A. This tree bears a certain spatial relationship with the building behind it.

Q. Did you have an opportunity to examine the tree more closely?

A. Yes. In fact, I had a video still with me of the building and of this particular tree, and I examined the branch angles and the arrangement of the main branches of that tree in relation to the image on the video.

Q. What did you look for in trying to determine if this tree that you were examining was the same one depicted in the videotape at 15.42?

A. Firstly, there is the spatial relationship with the Lombardy poplar. It had to be some distance from it because of the way in which it appears in the video. Also, it bears a relationship with a building which has its gable close to and facing the road.

Q. At this time, I would like for you to look at Prosecutor's Exhibit 218.

Is this the tree that we're talking about?

A. Yes, indeed. This is the tree I inspected.

Q. What kind of tree is this?

A. It's a walnut tree.

Q. What was your conclusion after examining this tree as to whether it was the same one seen in the video segment at 15.42?

A. Yes, I recognised this tree immediately.

Q. Now, after you located these various trees from the videotape, did you document their locations on this map which we have marked as Prosecutor's Exhibit 241?

A. Yes, that's correct....

Q. Mr. Tabbush, are there certain characteristics unique and distinctive to a particular tree which would differentiate it from other trees and allow you to positively identify it?

A. Yes. The arrangement of the major branches on a tree are caused by a combination of genetic and environmental factors so that no two trees will be exactly the same.

Q. In this regard, trees are somewhat like people, are they not, except perhaps even more unique, since environment also affects their appearance?

A. That's right. Not only environment, of course, but they are—people are symmetrical about a central access. Trees aren't symmetrical about any access. So if two identical trees were rotated through ten degrees, you would see a different image of branching.

Q. If you have two trees that are genetically identical planted next to each other, would their appearance be the same?

A. It would be extremely unlikely. Even if there were no environmental factors, it would be extremely unlikely that

they were both planted in the same radial orientation. In other
words, one is more likely to be rotated around its vertical
access with respect to the other one. It would be very unlikely
that they would both be planted in the same orientation.
   Q. Is there any doubt in your mind that this walnut tree that
you examined and on which you have done these comparisons is
the same one that is depicted in the videotape at 15.42?
   A. None at all. (ICTY 1998c: Paras 3380-3397)

This exchange between expert witness Professor Paul Tabbush and Prosecutor Mr. Clint Williamson takes places during the war crimes prosecutions of the ICTY, specifically the trial of Slavko Dokmanović. The ICTY was established by United Nations Security Council Resolution 827 on May 25, 1993, in response to reports of grave wrongdoing in Bosnia as well as in reaction to mounting pressure from the international community.[2] As a temporary ad hoc institution, the ICTY was granted prosecutorial jurisdiction over allegations of crimes against humanity committed across the territories of the former Yugoslavia. From January 19 to June 25, 1998, the ICTY heard the trial against Dokmanović, who was charged with participating in the mass execution of more than 200 people at the Ovčara farm southeast of Vukovar, Croatia on November 20, 1991. What makes this exchange particularly noteworthy is that the videotape alibi provided by Dokmanović and his defense counsel (Toma Fila and Vladimir Petrović) was proven to be false, based upon a detailed media reconstruction documenting the route that Dokmanović claimed to have traveled and filmed on the day of the massacre.

Although this investigation was conducted in February 1998, more than six years later and at a different time of year, it allowed for a comparative mathematical analysis of various trees that appeared in the videotape alibi as well as in its subsequent reenactment. Dokmanović maintained that he could not have been at the Ovčara farm during the time of the massacre since he was travelling far south of Vukovar and had shot video footage with a time code and date stamp along the way that matched the exact date and time of the mass killings. His defense team duly entered this tape into evidence as defense Exhibit 2 (ICTY 1998b, Court Transcript 980617IT: Para 3768). However, the prosecution was skeptical, not least because two survivors, Berghofer and Čakalić, had provided eyewitness testimony placing Dokmanović at the scene. "Two witnesses confirmed that they personally saw Slavko Dokmanović for a short while two to five minutes in the hangar at the Ovčara farm in the interval between 2 and 4 p.m" (ICTY 1998a, Court Transcript 98041: Para 1878). Perhaps not surprisingly the fortuitous existence of the video alibi raised considerable doubts, prompting the prosecution to enlist the aid of one of the ICTY's investigators—Vladimir Dzuro—in reconstructing Dokmanović's movements on the afternoon in question. "With camera in hand, Dzuro hopped in a vehicle and retraced the route Dokmanović claimed he took on the afternoon of Nov. 20, 1991, recording the drive in the same way the Defence claimed Dokmanović had done" (Matheson 2015). Ultimately a Lombardy poplar, mulberry, and walnut tree would come to stand as crucial material witnesses in the prosecution of an alleged war criminal.

According to the indictment issued by the ICTY on April 3, 1996, and amended on December 2, 1997, Slavko Dokmanović "aided and abetted" JNA and Serbian paramilitary, under the command of Mile Mrkšić, Miroslav Radić, and Veselin Šljivančanin, in the forced removal and transport of approximately 260 non-Serbs who had taken refuge from the siege of Vukovar in the local hospital. "Among those removed in this way were wounded patients, hospital staff, soldiers who had been defending the city, Croatian political activists, and other civilians. By the time the medical staff meeting with Major Šljivančanin concluded, the soldiers had removed almost all of the men who were at the hospital" (Goldstone 1995). From the Vukovar Hospital the captives were taken to a farm in Ovčara where they were beaten at great length and eventually moved to a location between the farm and Grabovo, where they were shot and killed. Dokmanović was charged with personal criminal responsibility for various events that took place that day, each of which was subject to areas of jurisdiction granted to the ICTY under Resolution 827: grave breaches of the Geneva Conventions, violations of the laws or customs of war, and crimes against humanity.[3]

A frame-by-frame video analysis conducted by British silviculturist and "tree expert" Paul Tabbush, detailing the unique growth pattern of several trees pictured along the route that Dokmanović had purportedly taken (Figures 5.2–5.3), overturned his alibi and confirmed that he had in fact made a U-turn returning back to the vicinity of the farm. When OTP Investigator Dzuro reconstructed and recorded the exact route taken by Dokmanović, according to specifications provided by his defense counsel as well in statements he gave when interviewed in Scheveningen prison, the well-established trees that appeared at the end of the alibi videotape, which also designated the endpoint of Dokmanović's journey, were nowhere in sight. In their place grew an entirely different grouping of mature trees. Unfortunately, or perhaps deliberately, the original recording was shot out of a car window and all that is visible at the end of tape are buses, the roof gable of a house, and the tops of trees. While the architecture of buildings that were still standing years later would have provided easy points of cross-reference had they been filmed, in their absence the intricate lacework of branches growing over a period of six seasons required an unusual form of expertise for a war crimes tribunal: a specialist in the taxonomic classification and identification of wooded plants—a dendrologist. Dendrology is a specialized field of botany situated within the broader domain of silviculture, which is itself concerned with the growth, establishment, and managements of forests.

Since no two trees ever grow in a precisely identical manner, the complex geometry generated by their branch structure functions as a kind of arboreal signature that is considered more distinctive than the whorls of human fingerprints. Although the disputed video with its mute bystanders could not prove Dokmanović's specific involvement in the perpetration of a war crime, it did offer corroborating evidence in support of testimony given by the two surviving eyewitnesses, who insisted that Dokmanović was indeed present at the time of the mass execution, something he had vehemently denied. The trial thus turned upon a remarkable conjunction between disparate forms of evidence and multiple modes of testimony, from eyewitness accounts, investigative reports, and media documentation, to the geometrical expression of natural objects and the analytic observations of an expert who could decode the fingerprints of trees. On June 29, 1998, Dokmanović committed suicide while in the ICTY Detention Unit. Consequently, the Trial Chamber terminated all proceedings against him two weeks later.

In his well-known text, Stone (1972) raised the provocation, by way of his title—*Should Trees Have Standing? Towards Legal Rights for Natural Objects*—as to whether nature should be entitled to a form of legal recognition independent of the humans who might make use of it for commerce or pleasure. He posed this question in order to advance the possibility that natural objects such as a forest be taken seriously as legal actors and thus accorded certain rights, privileges, and obligations under the law. To stand before the law means to be recognized and treated as an equal in the eyes of the judiciary regardless of one's station in life or wealth. Historically, this condition of equal

FIGURES 5.2–5.3 IT-95-13a: Dokmanovic [MPG] Video segment of alleged locations depicted on exhibit D2 at 15:36 and 15:42 Document Type: Exhibit 231 • Date: 18/06/1998 • By: Prosecution. Source: ICTY Court Records.

legal recognition effectively designated white men and not women or slaves as the sole holders of rights, but the point was that "to stand before the law," meant to be recognized by the judiciary as a rights-bearing agent. While a nature reserve may be a protected entity whose stewardship is governed and protected by environmental legislation and even enforced by law, such a natural object does not in and of itself have any recourse to the law except in so far as its destruction or misuse might impact upon the humans who avail themselves of it as a source of respite and space of leisure. The nature reserve, like forests, rivers or mountains are therefore legally "rightless," that is to say, subject to the law but not the bearer of rights themselves.

Environmental policies may protect an old growth forest such as Cathedral Grove on Vancouver Island in so far as it is conserved for our continued enjoyment and use, but these regulatory controls have not been drafted with a view towards granting such ancient trees their own legal rights independent of their specific use-value to humans (Stone 1972: 463). There are few exceptions to this global legal framework, apart from the recent adoptions of the Pachamama Constitution or Law of Mother Earth in Bolivia and Ecuador (Tavares 2014: 553). These new legal arrangements have transformed nature into a subject and bearer of rights rather than a mere object upon which the actions of other rights-bearing agents are performed. Many of the entities long engaged in the willful destruction of nature are themselves non-human actors such as mining companies or oil and gas refineries, whose legal rights have been historically enshrined within the concept of corporate legal personhood (Dewey 1926). Indeed, Stone reminds us that the legal world has long been "peopled with in-animate rights-holders: trusts, corporations, joint ventures, municipalities, Subchapter R partnerships, and nations states, to mention just a few" (Stone 1972: 452). These lifeless rights-bearers do not necessarily have the capacity to speak directly to the court and must rely upon lawyers as mediators much like most people who find themselves subject to the law. Today the notion that non-human entities such as corporations can operate as fully recognized legal persons that can own property, sue for damages, or be found liable for their deeds may not seem as counter-intuitive as it once did.

Stone's innovation was to propose a further extension of the concept of legal personhood to a new group of non-human agents, namely natural objects. The ontological condition of the human as *the* proper body that could stand before the law was replaced by the legal condition of personhood established in the late nineteenth century in which rights and obligations could accrue to non-humans. Trees are ontologically given as "standing" in terms of their vertical orientation towards the sun and soil from which they derive their nourishment and strength of purpose, but their capacity to stand legally before the law as rights-bearing and obliging agents does not proceed from any such a priori natural "bearing" or physiological comportment. The ironic demand invoked by Stone, that trees should have standing when they are obviously already literally standing, serves to highlight the degree to which the "laws of nature" and the "legal rights of nature" remain largely incommensurate categories of assembly despite their suggestive semantic borrowings.

I propose to continue his wordplay in this chapter in order to reflect upon the legal status of another group of non-human objects—namely media—specifically photographic and videotaped images of trees. But not with a view towards advancing their legal agency as rights-bearing entities, rather with the intention of asserting their considerable agency to bear witness to "legal rites," specifically those evidentiary practices and protocols that governed the war crimes prosecutions of the International Criminal Tribunal for the former Yugoslavia (Figure 5.4), which are at the time of writing in their final stages with only the Trial of Ratko Mladić still in session. In doing so, I advance a notion of visual evidence as constituting a new kind of witness that emerged already in the late nineteenth century when a US judge asked the rhetorical question "Can the sun lie?" in querying the veracity of photographs as they began to enter into legal proceedings (Thurston (online)). By assigning an animistic capacity for deception to the sun, he inferred that non-human entities (and by extension, perhaps even technical processes) could play a crucial role in the production of evidence. Namely that the mode of appearance of the media object—the technicity of the photograph put before a jury—was equal in consideration to the epistemic claims that could be made on behalf of its pictorial value. But when faced with the improbable prospect of cross-examining the sun directly, he also opened the proceedings of the court to the influence of specific forms of "expert" knowledge that would increasingly be called upon to ventriloquize the object-world. The judge continued: "Perhaps we may say that though the sun does not lie, the liar may use the sun as a tool. Let us, then, beware of the liar who lies in the name of the sun" (Thurston (online)).

As a quasi-historic body with its cases largely completed and sentencing rendered, thousands of ICTY Court Records have been made public and are accessible online or by written request. These artifacts represent a comprehensive legal record of the first international criminal law court—a process of war crimes prosecution and archival reckoning that began with the Nuremberg and Tokyo Trials in the 1940s, and continued with the creation of the International Criminal Tribunal for Rwanda (UNICTR) in 1994. These materials also provide extraordinary insight into the complex inner workings of an international court. In particular, they disclose the procedures and practices that convert testimony and artifacts into matters of legal evidence capable of presiding over questions of public truth.

Although the ICTY Court Records represent its unrestricted public offerings, they are but a small fraction of the actual materials gathered and records produced by the tribunal since its inception in 1993. Full disclosure of all its legal materials with provisions for protected witnesses remains one of the tribunal's core ambitions, though there has been much dispute as to where and how such a permanent facility should be located and

FIGURE 5.4 Courtroom of the International Criminal Tribunal, during a swearing-in ceremony of judges. Source: Photograph provided courtesy of the ICTY.

administered. The issue of future appeals and the late arrest of its final fugitive, Goran Hadžić on July 20, 2011, have also meant that its "Completion Strategy" will need to transfer cases to local judiciaries for prosecution. As a United Nations court, conventionally all materials from its tribunals return to UN Headquarters in New York, where they are sequestered away at some considerable distance from their primary stakeholders. However, the decision has now been made to keep the archives in The Hague as a legacy project, where access can be made more readily available to those directly affected by the Balkan Wars, or where they can be used as a tool for reconciliation and legal pedagogy.[4] "By transferring evidentiary materials as well as making electronic databases and archives available to national institutions, the Tribunal will ensure an effective transition from an international court to domestic judiciaries."[5]

Today the vast archival holdings of the ICTY's Office of the Prosecutor (OTP) exceeds 9.3 million entries and includes photographs, diaries, maps, diagrams, exhumation records, X-rays, radio intercepts, audio recordings, and videotapes, as well as physical objects such as scale models, computer hard drives, personal effects, munitions, and even remnants of charred timber and stone (Figures 5.5–5.6). All is here, save bio-hazardous materials such as blood-soaked clothing, which would have been documented and then disposed of. By 2010, the ICTY Court Records required 3,704 meters of storage shelving alone. In addition to OTP exhibits, transcripts of the cases and procedural documents are also scanned and entered into the e-court database of the Records of the Trial and Appeals Chambers. Over the course of many years, I have been conducting research into the evidential holdings of the ICTY, focusing my examination upon the various issues that arise when media and other non-textual forms of evidence enter into legal proceedings as a "material witness" entrusted with the task of testifying before the tribunals of history. Through my creative practice as an artist and researcher, I have investigated the ways in which the injustices of war are being managed by judicial instruments through the presentation and production of evidence (Schuppli 2014). At every juncture in the administrative circuits of the tribunal and its prosecutions, there is much "evidence" to suggest that evidential materials are not only carrying information related to a potential war crime (photographs of destroyed buildings, videos of hate speech, maps of military strategy, models of concentration camps, X-rays of bullet-ravaged bodies), but are themselves also registering and aggregating the protocols of the court.

I have come across many examples where materials entered into one trial re-appear in another, but in a somewhat altered or modified form. While the vast majority of ICTY Court Records consist of paper documents (99 percent) followed in number by maps and then photographs, visual material is often duplicated and re-used in different cases. "Judges will accept copies in place of originals; if originals have been introduced, judges may decide that a copy can be substituted in the case file and the original returned to the evidence control office" (Peterson 2008: 18). It is important to bear in mind that in the ICTY, with its preponderance of paper records, all exhibits enter the court as digitized screen images through the e-court system and ELMO visualizer[6] unless the judiciary requests that an original piece of evidence be sourced from the vault, which happens very infrequently.[7] Indeed, throughout my years of research, during which time I followed hundreds of evidential objects through the various trials in which they appeared and re-appeared, I was rather surprised to note only one instance in which actual material evidence was requested by the prosecution, brought into Chambers, unsealed and re-examined by an expert witness. The incident concerned the remains of a destroyed structure during the cross-examination of fire inspector Benjamin Dimas on Tuesday

FIGURES 5.5–5.6 Evidence vault of the Office of the Prosecutor OTP. Source: Reuters/Damir Sagolj.

March 24, 2009.[8] Although the charred remains were initially presented inside their sealed evidence bag and placed on the ELMO so that they could be viewed on everyone's desktop monitor, it was determined that the dirty plastic didn't permit sufficient visual access to the material for purposes of reassessment, thus requiring the unsealing of the bag and removal of evidence (Figures 5.7–5.8).

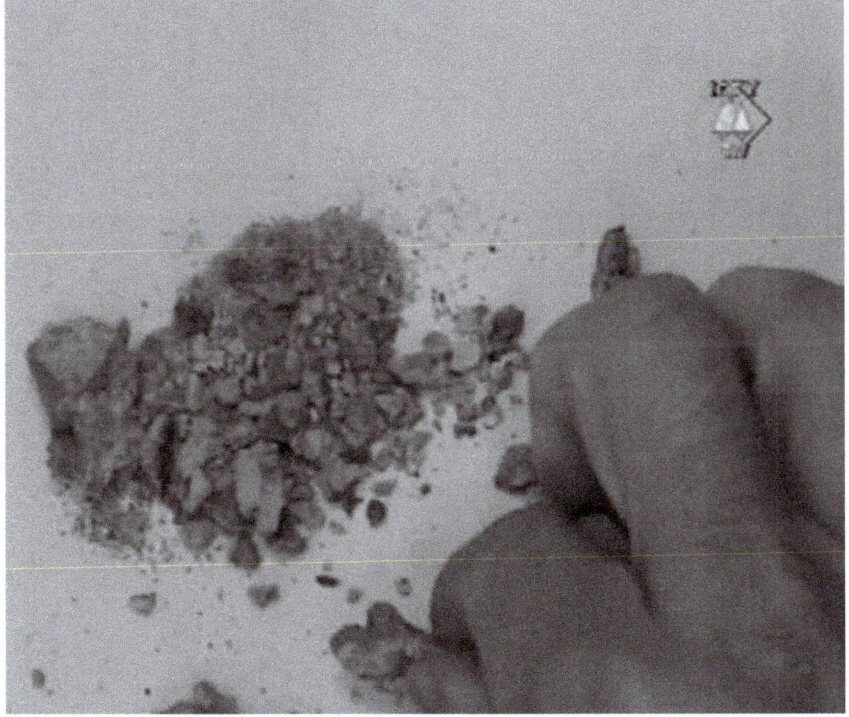

FIGURES 5.7–5.8 IT-98–32/1: Lukic et al. [MPG] Expert Witness Fire Inspector Benjamin Dimas opening an examined sealed evidence bag. March 24, 2009. Source: ICTY Press Office.

Expert Witness Benjamin Dimas cross-examined by Mr. Dermot Groome
[International Tribunal for the former Yugoslavia, Tuesday, 24 March 2009]

Q. Okay. I'm going to ask that you—with the usher's assistance that you take a look at a bag. It's an evidence bag, and if it could be placed on the ELMO.

Mr.Alarid: And, Your Honour, we would object to this form of tendering the materials to the witness. One, the witness has been already accepted by the Court as an expert in fire investigation. I looked at the bag and Mr. Groome refused to open the bags for me. The reason being is—and the objection is that if you're going to put questions of this nature to this witness as an expert, he should be allowed to inspect the contents. The fact of the matter is that the bags from whatever dirt, they're almost opaque at this point in time, so it makes it very suggestive without a real opportunity to examine the contents of the bag. I would object to a simple ELMO presentation.

Mr.Groome: Your Honour, I fully agree with Mr. Alarid, so I'm going to ask the witness to open the bag, pour the contents on a tray, and examine it here before us …

Q. I'm going to ask that you take a scissor, and I'm sure you're familiar with opening evidence bags, but I'm going to ask you to cut it at the bottom, not near seal, so we always have a record of the seal, and I'm going to ask you to pour the contents onto the white tray.

Judge Robinson: Mr. Groome, what's the provenance of this bag and its contents?

Mr.Groome: Your Honour, if Your Honours will recall from the video, this was the bag that was—and we can see the same writing on the bag. Again, I'm not tendering it at this time, but it's obvious from the video that this was the material taken out of the electric box and placed in the bag. I can call up that portion of the video if Your Honour wants to compare the writing on this bag with the writing on the video.

Trial Chamber confers]

Judge Robinson: No, that's not necessary.

Mr.Groome:

Q. Okay. Sir, can you please open the bag and just put the contents on the tray.

A. [Witness opens bag] (ICTY 2009: 6032-6034).

As the expert witness carefully cut open the plastic evidence bag and poured out its contents, a court camera zoomed in and began following an ant that had inadvertently been sealed inside the bag along with its charred debris. During the ensuing period of cross-examination the ant explores the material recovered from the scene, freed from its own incarceration from within the evidence bag. That a court camera lingers upon this diminutive intruder is perhaps not surprising given the general tedium that must surely set in when documenting the proceedings of a tribunal that has now been running for over thirty years, in which personnel such as interpreters and technicians are specifically required to channel the events of the court without registering its horrific content. Failure to do so might result in staff supplementing the translation of its proceedings with their own affective residue, which would trouble the ideal of impartiality that governs its procedures and legacy.[9]

When I requested video footage of this particular cross-examination from the ICTY, I didn't realize that I would stumble upon this extra-diegetic event. One in which the intercession of an ant becomes a poignant reminder that even the strict guidelines for documenting and recording the high-stakes procedures of a war crimes tribunal can be momentarily subverted by the distractions induced by an unexpected agent, regardless of how legally insignificant. It is, after all, administrative personnel, such as this cameraman charged with documenting the historic proceedings of the ICTY, who are actively shaping its legal legacy and posthumous image. Both the Nuremberg and Eichmann trials were clearly undertaken with a well-defined sense of their mandate to produce an historical archive and an image of retributive justice. In this sense, these were not, strictly speaking, legal proceedings in which determinations of guilt and innocence were still to be settled. By contrast, the documentation of legal processes in the trial Chambers of the ICTY seems to be rather less stage-managed as a "legacy project," even though recording and transmission technologies are thoroughly integrated into the architecture of its three Trial Chambers and are central to their modes of operation.[10]

But what really astonished me throughout my explorations of the Court Records was the degree to which evidentiary materials carried the seemingly incongruous imprint of the tribunal, often being modified to accommodate their presentation in court (Figures 5.9–5.10). While originals are safeguarded within the relatively stable environmental conditions of the OTP evidence vault, when they interface with the court as digital displays they undergo all manner of adaptation. Color photographs are marked by witnesses, duplicated, cropped, and photocopied, oftentimes re-appearing as degraded B&W images in another prosecution. Lengthy videos might be edited and spliced with inter-titles to assist with prosecutorial narration, or to clarify a complex sequence of events for a witness. While such modifications do not necessarily impinge upon the probative value of evidentiary materials, they do function as a kind of palimpsest that allows me to read the history of their transit through the court.

Moreover, I would argue that through such processes of modification, a kind of violence is also done to the evidential object or courtroom exhibit that is akin to the processes of cross-examination experienced by human witnesses when the force of their trauma is confronted by the blunt force bureaucracy of the law. While some jurists might disagree with this characterization, it is certainly not erroneous to suggest that the nature of legal dramaturgy within the criminal court produces highly unnatural and circumscribed encounters in which the affective dimensions of testimony are often disarticulated and flattened through repeated and at times intensely personal questioning and cross-examination, as well as by virtue of the selective presentation of exhibits. One of the most paradigmatic examples is certainly the now historic case of Rodney King, in which amateur camcorder footage documenting his roadside beating by the LAPD was re-edited when it was entered into court to downplay the racialized violence directed towards King, while intensifying the "black" menace of his body as a confrontational form in which violence was "naturally" inscribed. The vicious assault towards King, an African-American motorist stopped during a routine traffic check on March 3, 1991, by one Hispanic and three white officers, was fortuitously captured on tape by local resident George Holliday, inaugurating what has since become known as citizen journalism. When the analogue footage was professionally digitized for its presentation in trial —the officers were accused of assault with a deadly weapon and use of excessive force—much of the ferocity directed towards King was selectively removed, thus shifting the affective

FIGURES 5.9–5.10 Audio-visual technology used in the Trial Chamber. Source: Photographs provided courtesy of the ICTY.

narrative from a savage attack upon King to a perceived threat of violence towards the officers. By virtue of conducting a frame-by-frame analysis and stripping the video of sound, the jury was spared its visceral violence. An acquittal ensued and riots erupted throughout Los Angeles (Sherwin 2007). To undergo the proceedings of the court is, on some level, to endure a certain kind of socially acceptable violence, albeit one whose operations are in principle oriented towards the production of justice. The same can be said to hold true for material artifacts that enter into its prosecutorial machinery and are submitted to its legal rites of passage (Figures 5.11–5.21 and Figures 5.22–5.23).

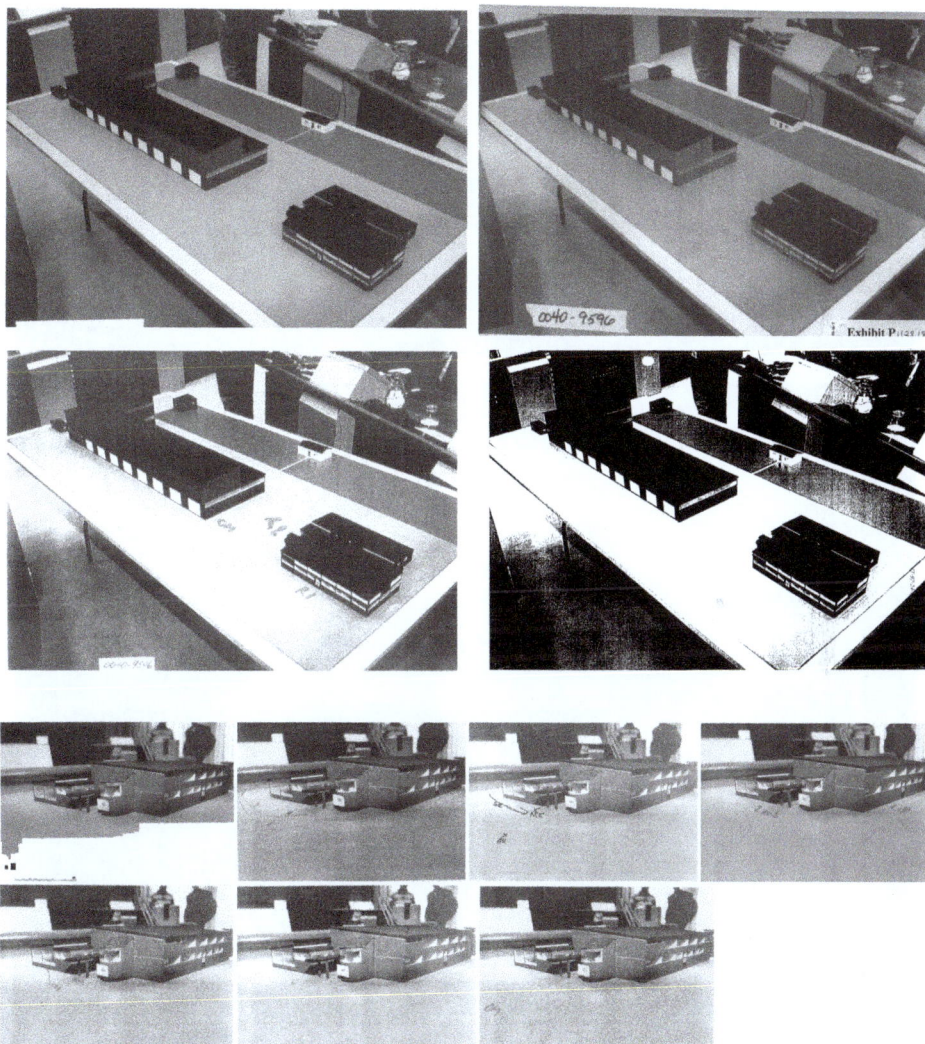

FIGURES 5.11–5.21 IT-99-36: Brdjanin [JPG] Multiple versions of the same picture of the Omarska model, considered the most notorious concentration camp of the Bosnian war, that have been variously copied, cropped and/or marked by witnesses. Document Type: Exhibit P1128.18. Source: ICTY Court Records.

FIGURES 5.22–5.23 IT-95–14/2: Kordic and Cerkez [PPT] Set of 54 photographs of destroyed buildings in Han Ploca. Document Type: Exhibit 1837. Source: ICTY Court Records. Note also the increase in hole-punch marks. Source: ICTY Court Records.

These operations of registration designate a condition of "material witnessing" that I continue to elaborate upon in my wider practice as an artist-researcher. Within a legal context, the material witness is a person who is deemed to have information germane to the subject matter of a lawsuit or criminal prosecution that is significant enough to affect the outcome of the trial. In other words, the witness, by means of the information they may possess, is considered sufficiently *pertinent* to the legal proceedings such that every effort must be made to procure their testimony. Humans become witnesses when their knowledge or experience positions them as semantically "material" to a case. My particular usage, in contrast, takes the concept quite literally: material *as* witness, and refers to the double agency of matter as both harboring direct evidence of events as well as providing circumstantial evidence of the interlocutory methods and epistemic frameworks whereby such matter comes to be consequential. Material witness is, in effect, a Mobius-like concept that continually twists (as I have expressed elsewhere) between divulging "evidence of the event" and exposing "the event of evidence" (Schuppli forthcoming). In pursuing this research, I have examined a wide range of materials that archive their complex interactions with the world, producing ontological transformations and informatic dispositions that can be forensically decoded and reassembled back into an alternate or parallel history of an event.

The ICTY Court Records in particular have offered a significant opportunity for exploring the evidential role of matter as both registering external events, as well as exposing the partisan practices and procedures that enable such materials to publicly testify and bear witness. Because legal practices within a criminal case are heavily reliant upon the rhetorical potential of objects to assist the judiciary in making or disputing truth claims, it is easy to render transparent the very methods which enable such forms of narration to take place. In as much as witnesses and experts do play a central role in testifying to events, the power of objects to act as visual aids, to help shape testimony, to confer authority and substantiate the claims of specialists, in short to help build a case, is noteworthy and should be elaborated and reflected upon. For example, Robert H. Jackson, Chief US Prosecutor at Nuremberg (1945–1946), made the controversial decision to base the Trials entirely upon the administrative archive of the Nazi regime rather than upon the testimony of survivors, thus eschewing living witnesses in favor of the rhetorical capacity of documentary evidence. Jackson's decision emphasized both the sober impartiality he attributed to such material artifacts—the paper trails that would corroborate the systematic planning and implementation that went into exterminating six million European Jews—but also the implicit belief that the sheer scale and transparent ambitions of the Third Reich evidenced in these records (Figure 5.24) would convert mute witnesses into fully realized agents of legal speech. Through the assumed transparency of the legal object-world of Nuremberg, the material record would be made to speak for itself.

While Nuremberg made enormous contributions to jurisprudence in "setting up a binding legal precedent of crimes against humanity," it was the Eichmann Trial in Jerusalem (1961) that returned the living witness to the stands, inaugurating what Thomas Keenan and Eyal Weizman call the "era of the witness" (2012: 12) in deference to Shoshana Felman and Dori Laub's claim that the twentieth century was the "era of testimony" (Felman 2002; Wieviorka 2006). Felman maintains that the two trials—Nuremberg and Eichmann—staged the fundamental differences between non-human and human forms of evidence (something I will return to shortly with respect to the Dokmanović trial). However, as Hannah Arendt has argued in her critique of the latter, the Eichmann Trial also shifted legal attention towards the victim and away from the perpetrator (Arendt 1963; Felman 2001: 244). Although legal forums, especially the ICTY, offer a useful

FIGURE 5.24 US Army staffers organize stacks of German documents collected by war crimes investigators as evidence for the International Military Tribunal. Nuremberg, Germany. November 20, 1945—October 1, 1946. Source: National Archives and Records Administration.

context for working through the notion of the "material witness," the concept is not pursued as an exclusively legal one, nor do I dwell upon questions of judgment in relationship to the injustices that they mediate. But I do examine the intertwined relations between human and non-human forms of testimony and the capacity of each to bear witness to powerful events as they enter into public discourse as agents of dispute.

As was the situation with many of the media artifacts that were entered into evidence during the prosecutions of the ICTY, the burden of evidential proof concerning allegations of serious crimes or evidence of tragic events fell, oftentimes, upon the documentary claims of poor images and defective media. That is to say, media shot or recorded under hazardous conditions or at great personal risk during times of war. In another project, I have reflected upon a videotape shot by Liri Loshi in the aftermath of the 1999 massacre at Izbica, a rural village in Kosovo. In that work, I argued that the material state of the videotape (Exhibit P232) also serves to diffract the violence done to the bodies he recorded on tape. Appearing initially as an energetic field of interference patterns, eventually they break apart to expose a pictorial field, a meadow, in which the mute horror of dead bodies begins to reveal itself. These visual artifacts further emphasize the material violations of the body-proper that would ultimately emerge out of the depths of the image (Schuppli 2015).

Such impoverished visuals can of course also refer to the "soft" or low-res images produced by security cameras and remote sensing systems whose outputs are disadvantaged by their own technical limitations or by restrictions put in place by state intelligence agencies that downgrade commercial satellite resolution to maintain their military advantage. Nor are the shortcomings of visual media necessarily always a consequence of their diminished quality. Hi-res images that have been subject to various forms of post-production editing may also be considered poor because their probative value as unadulterated evidence is reduced. My usage of the terms "poor image" and "defective media" refers therefore not only to their aesthetic attributes and technical drawbacks, but also to their incapacitated juridical condition as convincing agents of truth, which in turn may necessitate further investigation on the part of the prosecutors and defense counsel.[11] It is also important to bear in mind that the diverse ways in which observers of media respond to and/or interpret the significance of particular images is itself conditioned by many external factors such as their social standing, political frameworks, formal education, cultural background and so on. The truth status of an image or video recording is thus not only a consequence of its formal attributes and material properties, but is arrived at through a complex series of negotiations between various forms of knowledge, technologies, and subjectivities (Kahan 2009).

In the case of the Dokmanović videotape, which required the wholesale reconstruction of the tendered evidence many years after the alleged time of the crime, its probative value was contingent upon a level of accuracy and clarity sufficient to allow Tabbush to conduct his comparative analysis and render his expert opinion. However, the numerous constraints encountered by Czech Investigator Dzuro in making a precise copy of the Dokmanović journey and his alleged alibi recording led, at times, to the production of a rather poor-quality videotape and substandard photographic images, as is revealed by his testimony in court.

Investigator Vladimir Dzuro examined by Mr. Clint Williamson
(International Tribunal for the former Yugoslavia, Thursday, 18th June 1998)

[Videotape played]:

A. Here I turn left towards Ovčara. It's very difficult to film it because the quality of the road is very bad.
Q. Has the condition of this road deteriorated since you have been travelling to Vukovar?
A. Yes. As I said yesterday, for the first time, it was August 1996 when we did the exhumation, and it's clear to see that the quality of the road is—there's no maintenance and the quality of the road is worse than it was in 1996.
Mr.Williamson:
Q. In viewing these videotapes, Mr. Dzuro, the times to go between the various locations are not identical to the travel times that you talked about a few moments ago when you went through your measurements to the court. Why is that?
A. Yes, you're right, the time is not the same. But for the purpose of making the video, I really had to drive very slow. You can see even with the slow driving, the quality of the video is not what I want it to be, but you just need more time to travel at a very slow speed; and the measurements I did for my report, there I was driving about 50 kilometres an hour. It was much, much faster than the one I did when I filmed the video.
A. Mr. Fila, we did our best to enhance the quality of this video as much as we could. But unfortunately, the tape itself doesn't give us any more option, yes. (ICTY 1998c: Paras 3806, 3817, 3849)

The contingency of image quality does at times seem to assume the character of a moral agent that is able to confer or withhold a determination of truth unless experts intervene to establish the status of images. While the presumed veracity of blurry, real-time footage functions convincingly within popular culture, in legal domains jurists cannot read such semiotics as a sufficient index of fact. In court, the truth claims of evidence must be produced. Dzuro's painstaking reconstruction, in which he measured distances between roof angles, roads, and trees in order to retrace Dokmanović's steps, combined with the detailed arboreal analysis of Professor Tabbush, were able to establish both the deceit of the original footage and the credibility of the investigative reproduction. The moral order of the image was, in this case, arrived at retroactively through the manufacture of *new* evidence. Dzuro's investigative media-work and especially the insights provided by Tabbush signal the expanding role that technical knowledge and scientific expertise will play in establishing where received knowledge about the truth in images resides.

Unlike the Balkan Wars, which ran during the transition from analogue to digital media and still generated substantial analogue materials as demonstrated by the ICTY's archival holdings, the preponderance of online media streaming out of conflict zones today requires juridical attention that is progressively directed towards the testimonials encoded in pixels and code. That is to say, the truth claims of metadata, which carries extraneous information about the image-event, such as date, time, and GPS coordinates. Together these are capable of substantiating, but also overturning, the self-evident claims of images as representations of events. Troubling the aesthetic fallacies of "naive realism" demands cross-examination not only of people—witnesses and experts—but also images themselves (Kahan 2009; Sherwin 2007).

Within legal proceedings such as those of the ICTY, evidential truths are generally corroborated by eyewitness testimony, expert reports, and reinforced by the broader context of the conflict, foregoing the need for scientific testing of evidence. However, the option remains for the judiciary, public prosecutors, and defense counsel to request further scientific analysis of evidence, and the Netherlands Forensic Institute was on standby to provide these services. Outside of the courtroom, within the domains of journalism and popular culture, degraded image quality has become a standard and widely used signifier of real-time, to the extent that the graininess of a surveillance image has attained an aesthetic value equivalent to that of indexical-truth. Not despite its visual deficiencies, but precisely because of them (Gates 2013; Scheeres 2002). Media theorist Thomas Y. Levin argues that the aesthetics of real-time image capture have reinvented the photographic index as a predominately temporal rather than spatial attribute. "By adopting the rhetorics of real-time broadcast so characteristic of television and a certain economy of CCTV—not to mention that of webcam culture—cinema has displaced an impoverished spatial rhetoric of photo-chemical indexicality with a thoroughly contemporary, and equally semiotically 'motivated' rhetoric of *temporal indexicality*" (Levin 2002: 592). Yet the visual poverty of media evidence presented during the war crimes prosecutions of the ICTY was more often than not a direct consequence of the limited availability of recording technology and haste with which footage was shot. In the case of Dzuro's reenactment video, its shortcomings are not an index of its having been obtained under perilous conditions of political duress, but rather a consequence of the passage of time in which some of the physical features of the landscape had changed. Transformations in the postwar landscape around Vukovar would ultimately require that videos of trees be called to the witness stand to testify before the judiciary as material witnesses to a crime.

ARGUMENTS

The technical witnesses and media artifacts that result from times of war, too, can struggle to meet the court's demand for coherent accounts of history. Rather than reducing their capacity to stand convincingly before the tribunals of history as witnesses to a crime, the degraded quality of such evidential material should, in fact, enhance their capacity for testimony. This is because the epistemic demands for a stable and ordered image-field that can be called upon to account for historical violence through explicative narration is undone by a sensate field of magnetic defects, or is troubled by poorly recorded imagery that serves to register the radical incomprehensibility of what has taken place. History saturates objects with temporal information, but for the forensic investigator who must extrude legal and ideally empirical evidence out of the past, overcoming the transformations induced by time poses significant obstacles. Such obstacles cannot be met by aesthetic strategies of inference or the mnemonic techniques of recall. Throughout his extended testimony in court, Dzuro recounts the many difficulties he faced in his objective to produce an exact temporal and spatial replica of the journey as it was undertaken in 1991, including the position of a traffic sign which had long since disappeared, save its concrete base. Dzuro was attempting to recreate the video stills that the FBI laboratories at Quantico in Virginia had extracted from the Dokmanović alibi video. In the exchange that follows we are able to gain some insight into the methods employed by Dzuro (Figure 5.25) in his determination to produce video evidence with the highest possible probative value despite the passage of many years.

FIGURE 5.25 IT-95-13a: Dokmanovic [JPG] Photograph taken by witness on February 12, 1998, depicting house at the alleged location recorded on Exhibit D2 at 15:42 • Document Type: Exhibit 226 • Date: 18/06/1998 • By: Prosecution. Source: ICTY Court Records.

Witness Vladimir Dzuro examined by Mr. Williamson, Thursday, 18th June 1998
[International Tribunal for the former Yugoslavia, Thursday, 18th June 1998]:

Q. Mr. Dzuro, at the point where we left off yesterday, we were talking about this trip that you had gone on to Vukovar in February of this year to investigate scenes that were depicted in the videotape. When you were on this visit to Vukovar, did you take any photographs of locations that you visited?

A. Yes, I did.

Q. At this time, I would like for you to view the first photograph, which I will mark as Prosecutor's Exhibit 224, and if you can explain to us what is depicted in this photograph? I would ask you, Mr. Dzuro, if you could display this on the ELMO, please? Can you explain what is depicted in this photograph, please?

A. I photographed this area. This is the spot I depicted on the map as well, which I marked as the location at 15.42. This is the house with the gable facing the road, the tree in front of it, the branches. Also, the electric post, the grass area on the right side of the road, the shed, and then in the background here is this tree with the very specific top (indicated). I will talk about that later …

This the area right here in front of the shed (indicated). If you look on this photograph and the still I took from the video, it is obvious there is something missing. There is a traffic sign in this area—there is a traffic sign in this area on the still which is not on this photograph, so I did an investigation into this, and I thoroughly walked in that area around, and I discovered the concrete base with the metal bar which is the same one which is used in that area for the traffic signs. So I took a photograph of that and the exact location where I discovered that, and this is the photograph.

Q. Now I am going to show you the next photograph which we will mark as Prosecutor's Exhibit 228, and if you can indicate what is depicted in this photograph, please?

A. So what I did afterwards, I—I wanted to reconstruct the scene. For that reason, first I took the picture of the scene the way it looked, which is the photograph—the first one I presented …

Q. Which was marked as Prosecutor's Exhibit 224; correct?

A. That's correct. And then I went to the UNTAES and asked for their assistance because I needed to obtain a traffic sign, this traffic sign which shows to the drivers that you are driving on the main road. The UNTAES, they weren't able to provide me with that, but they were happy to assist, so we went to the local police and asked them to provide a traffic sign, but unfortunately, the conditions in Vukovar the way they are, they also were not able to assist us with the traffic sign. So I asked

for the police, traffic police car, the patrol car, and we went
together back to the scene. What I didn't want to do, I didn't
want to remove the traffic sign from the other direction because
it could cause some traffic problems, so I asked the Croatian
police for their assistance … I wanted to have the traffic sign
here. There is a particular reason for that. But if I can
explain a little bit later?
Q. Perhaps that would make more sense, yes. Now, as I
understand it, just to make this absolutely clear, this
photograph is identical to the one that has been presented as
Prosecutor's Exhibit 224 except for the fact that you have
attempted to reconstruct what was seen in the videotape by
putting the sign back in place; is that correct?
A. Yes, that's correct. I wouldn't call it identical because
I'm not sure I managed to take the same angle because it is
very difficult to find the same angle if you do two photographs.
But this is the photograph of the same location. The only
difference is that on this one, I put the traffic sign back. (ICTY
2009: Paras 3791-3797)

Pragmatically, the forensic investigator must "work" evidence in the pursuit of legal objectivity, whereas the task of the "material witness" is to unveil the production of objectivity as a techno-discursive set of operations involving agreed-upon methods and accepted rhetorical frameworks. With respect to the ICTY, its juridical structure and evidential protocols were determined through "Rules of Procedure and Evidence" adopted by the United Nations on February 11, 1994. This document, crafted by the first judges who arrived in The Hague, lays down the 125 rules that direct the tribunal, from its organizational structure, prosecutorial operations, witness management and evidentiary processes, to its technical and media requirements.[12] Despite the fact that it has been amended forty-nine times over the lifetime of the tribunal, its codes established the "legal rites" referred to in my title, that govern the conventions of legal speech and regulate the production of evidence according to existing networks of power and domains of knowledge.[13]

In bringing this chapter to a close, I would like to return to the scene of evidence-making with which I began, namely the examination and cross-examination of Professor Paul Tabbush around the growth pattern of trees featured in the Dokmanović videotape alibi, as well as in the investigative video and photos produced by Vladimir Dzuro some years later. In this final act of the trial proceeding, nature emerges as a bearer of legal truths, one whose testimony will repudiate even that of the human witness whose lies it unearths (Figures 5.26–5.29). Through Tabbush's detailed account of the cartographic constancy retained by the branch structure of trees as they mature and grow; the tree is transformed into an irreproachable and unbending material witness that can be mapped onto its erstwhile video doppelganger. Its wooden features secure its singular identity and act as temporal indices that allow us to travel back in time to the day of the crime. "Q. Is there any doubt in your mind that this [mulberry] tree is the same one as depicted in the video segment marked 15.36? A. None at all" (ICTY 1998c: Para 3880). But what is fundamentally distinctive about these particular species of trees is that they are "unnatural" in the extreme. That is to say, they are vegetative-matter encoded within the image-matter of technical media. To gain access to the informational quotient that such mediated trees can yield requires not only expertise in the natural sciences,

FIGURE 5.26–5.29 IT-95-13a: Dokmanovic [MPG] Expert witness Paul Tabbush describing the manner in which trees grow and comparing a photograph from February 12, 1998 and a video still of the same tree from November 20, 1991 on the ELMO Source: ICTY Press Office.

but also skills in media analysis and production. Together these competencies combine to create new categories of legal evidence in which unnatural objects—videos of trees—can bear upon questions of legal truth and even determinations of war crimes.

> Q. Are you affiliated with any professional organisations?
> A. I'm a member of the UK Institute of Chartered Foresters. I am also a member of the International Poplar Commission, which is a United Nations organisation. (ICTY 1998c: Paras 3874-3875)

At the time of the trial, Tabbush was himself a member of the International Poplar Commission, one of the oldest statutory bodies created by the Food and Agriculture Organisation of the United Nations. Founded in the ruinous wake of the war, it designated the cultivation, conservation, and utilization of poplar and willow trees as key factors in efforts to repair the countryside and rebuild the industrial economies of Europe.[14] Thus, already in 1947, there was recognition that the environmental devastation wrought by the war would require the establishment of new legislative frameworks for ensuring the productive agency and protection of nature. In response, the fast-growing poplar was strategically enlisted by the UN to participate in the rehabilitation of Europe's degraded lands and diminished rural livelihoods. An entanglement between nature, military violence and an international body that prophetically gestures towards the very same tree that will make an appearance within the UN's prosecution of Slavko Dokmanović some fifty year later. While Christopher D. Stone's 1972 provocation that nature becomes a rights-bearing agent has yet to be fully realized, the crucial role that non-human forms of testimony and new forms of evidence, such as videos of trees, have played in resolving questions of legal truth does position them as active agents in the production of jurisprudence.

In the Dokmanović trial much was made by defense counsel as to the unreliability of eyewitness testimony advanced in support of his alibi. Two statements that placed him at the scene were refuted. This was done by way of reference to two entirely unrelated cases prosecuted by the ICTY, in which prior acts of witnessing were cited as representative of the vagaries of eyewitness testimony.[15] Given criminal law's foundational reliance upon legal precedent, is it not possible that trees will also come to be regarded as much more than mere background features of crime scene imagery, but may serve as valuable "natural" resources for the production of new legal axioms? Since its establishment on May 25, 1993, the operations of the ICTY have generated millions of procedural records and processed a staggering number of exhibits. Out of this vast archive of evidential holdings, a videotape of a mulberry, walnut, and poplar tree have emerged to stand as steadfast material witnesses before the law.

Witness Paul Tabbush examined by Mr. Clint Williamson
[International Tribunal for the former Yugoslavia, Thursday, 18th June 1998]

Mr. Williamson:

> Q. During the course of the initial consultation with the Prosecution in April, did you have an opportunity to view some photo stills which had been made from a videotape?
> A. Yes, I did.
> Q. Did you also have an opportunity to view portions of that videotape that had time displays of 15.36 and 15.42?
> A. Yes, that's correct.

Q. Based on what you saw, did you feel that there was sufficient material available which would allow you to positively identify the trees which were depicted?

A. Yes. Some of the video stills were of sufficient quality to make out major branch angles and the positions of major branches.

Q. Now, subsequent to that time, in May of this year, did you have occasion to travel to the Vukovar area in order to personally examine the trees that were in question?

A. Yes. …

Q. I would like for you at this time to view Prosecutor's Exhibit 215, and also I'll ask him to view 232 …

Q. What is different, if anything, between the two photographs?

A. Based on the time line on the video, six growing seasons have passed between these two images, and therefore, the fine branch tracery has extended and become thicker …

Q. Did you use these photographs to create a set of photographic overlays?

A. Yes, I did.

Q. How did you go about doing this?

A. I used imaging software and a flatbed scanner to scan the images and the photographs in such a way that I was able to scale them to the same scale. And then I cropped the image taken from the photograph so that it was small enough to fit over the video still image. This then, because it's at the same scale, allows you to see whether the branches coincide. […

Mr.Tabbush

[Cross-examined by Mr. Fila]:

Q. But I want to ask: Professor, if I understood you correctly, you were in Vukovar at the time of full vegetation whereas your compilations and analysis were based on the photographs and the video stills made by Mr. Dzuro; did I understand that correctly?

A. Yes. Yes, that's correct.

Q. Then my second question would be: Does this tree which we see in front, Prosecutor's Exhibit 218, you said that after a certain time, it grows wider, not—it doesn't grow upwards. I mean the walnut.

A. Yes. Can I explain?

Q. Yes. That's what I would like you to explain.

A. Trees extend from their tips, they don't grow, as it were, in the middle of branches, so they leave behind them the major branch angles which represent where buds were set as the tree grew.

Q. Not there, on the other one. Please show that.

A. For instance, this major branch angle here would remain once it was formed by the terminal bud, as it grew upwards, it would remain behind as a major branch position and would not change its height with time (indicated).

Q. Well, in which—so I understand you correctly, in which period of growth does the tree reach its maximum height above which it doesn't grow any longer? How many years does it take?

A. Yes. I'm sorry, I don't think I've made myself clear. The tree grows in height throughout its life, but as it grows, it leaves behind it the significant pattern of branching which doesn't change with time, but, of course, the height of the tree changes continuously throughout its life.

Q. So am I correct in my understanding that, for instance, relative to this roof or the bus, the widening of the angle is not the same, but in the course of growth, this changes?

A. The angles remain as they are. What changes as the tree grows is that the branches get fatter, they increase in girth, but the bud positions remain as they were when they were laid down throughout the life of the tree.

Q. But the height, but the height growths, so this bud is not always in the same position relative to a fixed point?

A. As this—if I may point at this branch here? At the end of a certain year, the tree was at this height. It then produced two buds. One bud produced a side branch and the other one produced a more vertical branch. At the end of the next year, this branch was here and this branch was somewhere around here (indicated). I can't see exactly. So the tip is extending, but the position left behind remains as it was at the time that this node, i.e. this branching position was formed during the development of the tree.

Q. I understand that. I understand that much, yes. But this part of the tree which you've just shown us, this branching position, does it grow relative to the ground? Do I make myself clear?

A. Yes.

Q. Does it grow in height like a person grows? A person, for instance, has a big nose, but he grows in height. Is it the same with trees?

A. No. No, it's not the same. It's not the same with trees. Trees—this point here does not progress up the tree as the tree grows; it's left behind. The bud then extends from here for a year, sets another bud, and then continues to extend, but this angle will always be at the same height above the ground as it was when it was formed (indicated).

Q. I see. Look, for instance, at the edge of the bus and then look at this lower part, the first branching position, above the bus. That's it. And a bit to the right. That's it. Up to which year did this grow and when did it stop growing relative to the roof? I don't know which way to explain it better. Does it always have the same parallel or does it grow, because the house doesn't grow. At least that much we can assume.

A. I can't tell exactly in which year this fork formed, but let us say—

Q. That's exactly what I'm asking.

A. Yes. But when it was formed, which was several years ago, you can tell that from the growth rate of the tree, it formed in this exact position above the ground and then remained there as the tree grew above that point.

MR.FILA: I apologize, Your Honour. I feel a little stupid, like a parent explaining something to a child and then starting with butterflies, but I'll try to make myself as clear as possible.

Q. In the eight or seven years since the event and the pictures made by Mr. Dzuro, did this ratio change between the tree and the house, just in terms of height, not in terms of angles, not in terms of anything else?

A. The height—this is six—

Q. That's exactly this part which I'm interested in, relative to the house. Please draw a line to the house, to the left. Did that remain the same for the past seven or eight years, or is it lower or higher than it used to be at the time of the event?

A. The same.

Mr.Fila: It remained the same for the past seven years. That's what I wanted to know. Thank you. No more questions. (ICTY 1998c: Paras 3879-3901)

United Nations
Nations Unies

International Criminal Tribunal for the Former Yugoslavia

Tribunal Pénal International pour l'ex-Yougoslavie

Office of the Prosecutor

Bureau du Procureur

INTERNAL REPORT

Thursday, 11 June, 1998

I am Vladimir DZURO, I am an investigator for the Office of the Prosecutor (OTP) of the ICTY in The Hague.

On 26 and 27 November 1997, Investigator Dennis Milner and I interviewed Slavko Dokmanović in the Scheveningen prison in The Hague. During the course of the interview, Mr. Dokmanović mentioned that he was in possession of video recordings, which he intended to produce to support his alibi. This was the first indication that an alibi video existed.

On 19 January 1998, I was informed by Legal Advisor Clint Williamson that Mr. Fila had supplied the mentioned video tape to the Court and that the OTP would get access to it soon afterwards.

As soon as the OTP obtained a copy of the tape, my colleagues and I had the opportunity to view it. I was tasked by the Prosecutor to identify places shown on the video in Vukovar.

At that time, I began the process of attempting to determine various locations depicted on the videotape, particularly those in relative proximity to Ovčara.

I started my task at the ICTY Video Unit where I printed a number of stills out of the video tape. I also studied the city plan of Vukovar, a map of the Vukovar region, and the statement given to us by Mr. Dokmanović in the Scheveningen prison.

Relying on the above sources, I tentatively established the route that Mr. Dokmanović is alleged to have taken on 20 November 1991.

In February 1998, I travelled on a mission to Vukovar. My primary task at that time was to positively identify locations shown on the videotape and also to determine if the times displayed on the videotape were consistent with actual travel times between the apparent locations.

Based on my on-scene investigations, I was able to establish that at the indicated times the following actions were depicted on the videotape at the locations described below:

15.17 - The group with the cameraman appears to depart from Velepromet
15.26 - The group with the cameraman appears to arrive in the centre of Vukovar
15.30 - The vehicle passes through Sajmište Street travelling in the direction of the southern outskirts of Vukovar towards Negoslavci
15.36 - The vehicle passes the last houses on the southern side of Vukovar as it travels in a southerly direction (on the Vukovar-Negoslavci road).
15.42 - Buses travelling in a southerly direction are filmed at a location approximately 370 meters north of the scene depicted at 15.36 (i.e., approximately 370 meters back toward the centre of Vukovar.

FIGURE 5.30 Internal report

CHAPTER SIX

Property and Possession

On the Illegality of Situational Art

ALISON YOUNG

In the latter half of the twentieth century, an illicit activity became both a significant art movement and a prevalent cultural practice. Street art and graffiti have in recent years come to signify urban creativity, while remaining firmly criminalized: although street art is increasingly present within mainstream cultural institutions as much as in city spaces, it remains an illicit activity that can lead to criminal sanctions against its practitioners. Street art and graffiti are thus currently positioned at a threshold of legitimacy: their histories derive from the illicit or semi-licit activities of protest movements, youth cultures, and punk, but their recent incorporation into the mainstream art world means that the divide between their status as art practices and their categorization as crimes becomes evermore stark. This chapter, in addressing the subject of property and possession, examines the role law plays in helping to determine what is "public" and what is "private" space in society. In so doing, it engages with the ways in which law responds to the urban images generated by street artists and graffiti writers, considering the interconnections of criminal law and property law as a means of *framing* words and images placed in city spaces without permission.[1]

One morning, as I left my house in the inner-city neighborhood of Fitzroy in Melbourne, I noticed that the letters "DN" had been written in violet paint on the outer wall that forms part of the entryway to my front door (Figure 6.1). I knew that DN were the initials of "Dick Nose," the moniker or alias of a well-known street personality in Melbourne, an individual infamous for his prolific tagging of surfaces, meaning that he wrote DN, DN, Dick Nose, DN, and on and on, in marker pen or spray paint, on any surface that appealed to him. I assumed that Dick Nose himself had written the letters DN on my front wall; when I saw that they appeared on each and every house I imagined him walking along the street, late in the previous night, initiating the entire street with his tag.

But I was wrong about this. I later learned that Dick Nose had died from an overdose, and the profusion of DNs along my street and elsewhere in the neighborhood was the product of *memorial* tagging, carried out by those who knew him and wanted to commemorate his existence. When I got back from work, I looked again at the letters, and recalled how I had imagined Dick Nose writing his name on every wall in our street—an effective memorialization, indeed, and one that I was content to retain on my wall.

FIGURE 6.1 Memorial tag for Dick Nose. Source: Photograph by Alison Young, 2012.

Not every resident shared my affection for the DNs in our street. A neighbor took me aside, saying that he was happy to give me a couple of his council-issued repainting vouchers, which we are supposed to use for walls that have been tagged. When I explained that I was happy to keep the tag, he looked bemused; for him, the lettering was out of place, or perhaps, to put it more strongly, *the lettering had no place in the street at all*.

DN is not the only text deemed "out of place" in my street. As in most urban centers, images simply "appear," and words are added to the walls. Street artists and graffiti writers regularly add to the surfaces of my street as throughout so much of Melbourne. Graffiti writers usually write their graffiti name or "tag" with permanent markers or aerosol cans (less frequently they use paint rollers or even fire extinguishers). A tag can appear as a "throw-up," involving rapidly written "bubble" letters in two colors, painted quickly on a wall. Graffiti writers also create what is known as a "piece"; that is, a complex, larger, mural-like design in which a range of colors and complex techniques create the writer's tag name (Figure 6.2). A recent innovation is the use of a high-pressure hose to remove dirt, paint or other layers from a surface to create a "reverse" tag. Others use water and mops to write upon the pavement or lasers to project tags onto buildings. Some have even written their tag in three dimensions, carving letters into a metal or concrete shape, which is then bolted onto a wall or street sign.

As is clear from the above, graffiti, since it centers on letters, is a kind of calligraphy (Chastanet 2007; see also generally on graffiti Castleman 1984; Ferrell 1996; Macdonald 2001; MacDowall 2006; Snyder 2009) (Figure 6.3). While the unauthorized additions of graffiti writers to the streetscape tend to be dictated by the centrality of the tag name in graffiti culture, street art has no limit as to content. Street artists use many different media (paper, paint, objects, the built environment itself) and often place artworks to contrast with the surface on which it has been applied (Figure 6.4). While stencilled images have long been associated with street art, artists have also hand drawn, painted and glued artworks onto walls (see further McGaw 2008; Schacter 2008, 2013; Young 2014) (Figure 6.5).

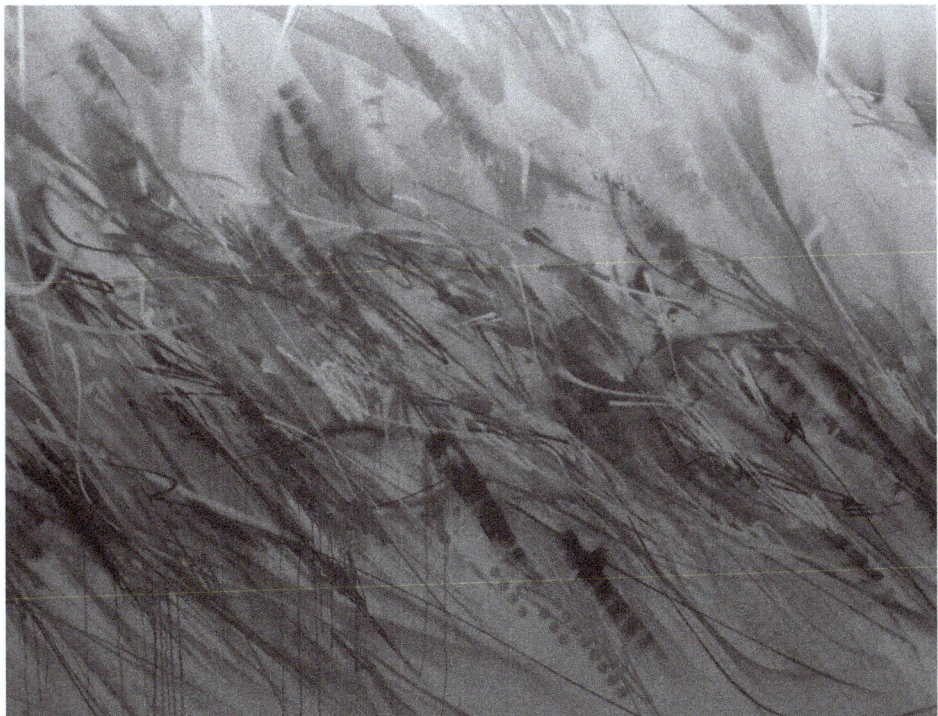

FIGURE 6.2 Piece by Slicer. Source: Photograph by Alison Young, 2013.

FIGURE 6.3 Tag by Fray. Source: Photograph by Alison Young, 2008.

PROPERTY AND POSSESSION   133

FIGURE 6.4 Piece by Urban Cake Lady. Source: Photograph by Alison Young, 2011.

A number of factors determine which surfaces are selected by street artists and graffiti writers. For graffiti writers, locations are often chosen by virtue of their visibility, so as to ensure that their tag is seen by as many other writers as possible. Other sites will command respect through the audacity or athleticism required to write there, if it is high above the ground, on a moving train, or on a rooftop (on the selection of "spots" see Ferrell and Weide 2010). Street artists often wish to maximize their audience, but other considerations equally apply. For example, urban surfaces vary in their suitability for the application of street art: stickers tend to adhere well to metal surfaces such as lampposts, utility hole covers, shutters, and street signs, but not to stone or concrete, while paint will sink into stone and achieve greater durability than when it is added to laminated materials. Many artists choose a location according to aesthetic criteria: a warehouse doorway might offer a framed recess; the peeling paint on a wall can form an appealing backdrop for a pasted-on painting or drawing. The artist Morcky, in Amsterdam, explained:

> I like my work to fit around what we can call "structurals": things which are part of that place. I like to play a lot with perspective and to adapt my work to certain surfaces. You always have to have … a vision of how you can fit into a certain area or certain spot—how you can *use* a place when you paint there.[2]

The artist and gallerist Emess said: "I try to put my work in a space where it fits with the environment," and the artist Various agreed: "working in the streets showed how important it is to work *with* the space in your art."

FIGURE 6.5 Piece by Be Free. Source: Photograph by Alison Young, 2012.

Contemporary cities are full of what I call "situational art." A situational artwork exists within a nexus of characteristics including:

> [The artwork's] placement in public space such that this placement becomes an integral aspect of the work and of viewing the work; second, the aims of the artist as primarily

being the creation of an image such that commercial or informational concerns are secondary or absent; and, third, the illegality of the work existing either as a result of its placement without permission or through the assumptions about the work brought by the spectator. (Young 2014: 8)

Situational artworks can be found on street furniture, walls, signs, billboards, pavements and fences. As such, they appear on the surfaces of the city; they attach to its component parts. Every city block contains a succession of shapes, signs, and populations. As an assemblage, a city's built qualities are initially the most readily apparent, and these manifest to the citizen both as tangible objects and things (concrete roads, bluestone foundations, glass windows, advertising billboards, sandstone buildings, and so on) and as a kaleidoscope of images, which jointly and singly communicate the identity of the space as "urban." Cities, then, are made from metal, stone glass, concrete, and brick. But in order to enable various essential functions—the circulation of traffic and pedestrians, the clustering of individuals in homes, workplaces, and centers of consumption—cities require architecture and infrastructure, the surfaces of which become part of the *situation* in which graffiti writers or street artists place words and images. Such urban architecture and infrastructures have an entrenched legal status as property whose propriety is disturbed by the challenges of situational art.

SITUATIONAL ART AND THE COMMONSENSE OF URBAN SPACE

Jacques Rancière proposes that "[art] reframe[s] the way in which practices, manners of being and modes of feeling and saying are interwoven in a commonsense" (2004: 100). A "commonsense" must locate itself; and situational art always *takes place somewhere*; it can be seen on walls, along train lines, on the rear of fences, high up on buildings, on street signs, on the pavement, in short, on almost any urban surface. The unavoidable facts that a situational artwork is both uncommissioned and *takes place* present a challenge to the commonsense regimes of property and propriety that govern urban spaces.

Of course, artworks are commodities, assets that can be bought, sold, and gifted. When an artwork is bought by an individual, a corporation or a public entity like a museum, the right to display it transfers to the purchaser. A spectator in a museum will assume that the art on display is either owned by the museum or on loan from its owner (an intuition which is no doubt correct most of the time).[3] Similarly, when visiting a private house, I assume that any artwork on display is legitimately owned (even though there is a thriving market in stolen art and plenty of thorny problems with provenance). Despite these potential fault lines, artworks held or displayed either at home or at work, in museums or in galleries, are assumed to be legally owned and to constitute property in and of themselves.

A very different set of assumptions comes into play when an artwork is placed in the street. There are plenty of commissioned images in public space: public artworks, the building-as-image that arises from architecture, official street signage and other everyday images. The act of commissioning is an exercise of the rights of a propertied individual or entity. This may be a unilateral act by a sovereign actor (such as when an individual paints the outside of their house or a patriot hangs a flag from their window on a national holiday). Commissioning may also involve a network of constraints and contributions: as in the fraught enterprise of redesigning the World Trade Center in New York City, and the many reviews and public consultations that were required. Even the humble street sign may find itself altered if it is reviewed by a government department and found to be lacking sufficient visibility or communicative efficacy.

The artist, architect or sign-maker acts as the agent of the commissioner (property owner, resident, corporation, government) and with varying degrees of autonomy. The municipal sign-maker is unable to exercise aesthetic autonomy and is usually required to follow conventions and regulations as to the size, color, and shape of signs. Some artists working on a commissioned piece may have complete creative autonomy over the resulting work, others have to follow clear prescriptive dictates.

Street artists and graffiti writers create *uncommissioned* words and images in public space. They may have a great deal more autonomy than the humble sign-maker; yet, at the same time, their artwork is also the result of a complicated collaborative process. Consider the factors that need to be taken into account: location; nature of the location; ease of installing the work; ability to see the work; ability to see (if installing after darkness); manifold risks (injury from falling, arrest, assault); the vagaries of the weather. Artists and graffiti writers also pay heed to a range of conventions regarding placement. These include the nature of the surface; the presence of other preexisting artworks (in order to follow the unwritten laws of the street); the nature of the property (residential dwelling, public thoroughfare, train station) and the specific rules governing its ownership and use.

The vast majority of situational artworks are done without permission. Thinking about them as "uncommissioned" helps us to see how they challenge conventional conceptualizations of space and ownership by virtue of a lack of *authorization*. Since the fifteenth century, commissioning (closely tied to patronage) has been central to the very idea of art, and has connoted the authority to carry out a particular artistic enterprise (see Hollingsworth 1994). It has also, importantly, connoted a situation of *contract*; that is, an exchange of mutual consideration so as to bring each party under the authority of a shared set of terms (it also acquired particular associations such as the notion that a prime minister or president might authorize the actions of judicial, military, or naval officers). When an individual, a corporation or a branch of the state commissions an artist, the commission passes authority from the property owner (controller, regulator, manager) to the artist. This authorization is only temporary and expires (according to the terms of the explicit or implicit contract) upon completion of the work or, alternatively, if the terms of the contract are breached (e.g., if the work is installed somewhere other than the agreed location).

The street artwork, as an uncommissioned work, lacks such authorization. It is a text lacking authority or, indeed, an author. It may have a maker, but that is not the same, in law, as an author. The commission (and relatedly the contract, such as exists between an artist and her gallerist or art dealer) *authorizes* the creation of works; a situational artwork lacks any such authorization. A work of art created spontaneously in a studio by an artist is authorized by the artist's signature. Her signature acts not merely as an identifier—her biography and reputation—but also, as Jacques Derrida points out in *Signsponge/Signéponge* (1984), as an integral textual component of the work and one that is unable to exist outside of that artist's body of work. Neither can the signature exist outside of law, since authorization requires an author to self-endow themselves with value. It is often said of street artworks that they simply "appear" as if by magic in the night; as if no one had agency in their creation and installation. This common response is symptomatic of the artwork's position outside the conventions of authority and authorization. Since all artworks owe their existence to the law (in which case it makes sense to claim that the law itself writes or paints all texts and images) it follows that graffiti and street art (being uncommissioned) cannot properly be said, in law, to be art at all.

This lack of authorization constitutes the first of two key ways in which the situational artwork challenges conventional regimes of authority and ownership. The second relates to the fact that an artwork is illicit when it is located on property belonging to another, and without the permission of the property owner. "Permission" attests to the dimension discussed above, since it derives from the authority of commissioning: the owner commissions or consents to an artwork and thus authorizes the artist's actions. However, ownership (or the lack of it) is as important as the permission or commission in defining the legitimacy (or the lack of it) for a situational artwork. Situational art often arises as a result of an act of *trespass* (Dew 2007; McCormick et al. 2010). Trespass, as noted by McCormick et al., derives its semantic origins from ideas of "offense" and "sin" (from the Old French, *trespasser*, "to pass beyond or across," with a contemporary gloss to be found in the modern French idiom, *trépasser*, meaning "to die" as in to euphemistically "pass over to the other side").

The illicit use of another's property creates for the trespasser—as they cross that boundary—a sense of ownership in that property. As José Parlá puts it: "Kids are seeing [trains] and they're like, 'A perfect place to put my art because it will travel from the Bronx to Coney Island and then everyone will see it' ... Now it becomes *your* train, you have *ownership* in something. You're thinking *politically*. You're thinking like a *pirate*" (my emphases). As long as there have been property boundaries, there have been individuals seeking to push up against them, cross them, contest them, whether in the form of burglars, poachers, pirates, or situational artists.[4] Penalver and Katyal point out that the prohibition of the illicit use of property through trespass has always been as much about status, profit, value and social hierarchy as land: "Laws of criminal trespass protect the boundaries around real property, established through market transactions" (2010: 11).

Trespass also derives meaning from a number of other important associations. First, it connotes encroaching upon land belonging to another so that, even if an individual does not *physically enter* another's land, their actions or possessions may still be seen to have an impact upon that other person's property. Situational art attached to another's wall can thus be understood as trespass long after the artist has gone. Second, it connotes someone who does not respect boundaries and thus aligns the trespasser with those who, like tramps, vagabonds, and nomads, have no fixed abode and hence no respect for the normative dimensions of private property.[5]

Trespass is almost inevitable. Cities, as I will go on to explain, are criss-crossed with lines of ownership and exclusion; very few spaces are made available to artists. While a legal work, such as a commissioned mural on a council-authorized wall, brings street-based images into the everyday experience of citizens, it is not a "situational artwork" in that its existence is contingent upon permission granted by a property owner or a commission issued to an artist.

The assumption that an artist should seek legal permission if they wish to place work in the street points to the ways in which graffiti and street art are classified as a crime against property (I will return presently to the nexus between criminal and property law). So-called "legal walls" are still objects owned by another. The artist is only temporarily permitted to carry out the activity of creating an artwork. It is an exceptional moment within a matrix constituted by criminal and property law, outside of which lies situational art, a practice that is not only criminalized but also *unauthorized*. Graffiti writers and street artists thus exist without a voice, without standing, without sensibility.

THE SENSIBILITY OF THE SITUATIONAL ARTIST

Although discounted by the law, the sensibility of situational artists and writers is complex, encompassing theorizations of city, citizenship, place, and image. Many individuals who create such words and images do so because these surfaces are highly visible within the cityscape. Some graffiti writers intend their work for a general audience: tags are generally thought to communicate only to other writers, whereas characters and figurative pieces have a much broader appeal. But most write for the personal satisfaction that derives from completing a skillful or challenging piece—and for the approval of other writers. The graffiti writer Disturbanity, in Berlin, commented that "we want to produce something beautiful, sure, but it's in competition with other writers."[6]

For the street artist, the imagined or intended audience is broader, and so is the motivation. Street artists often assert a desire to enchant the spectator. The New York artists Ad Deville of Skewville told me that he aims to "do something funny or cool for people who see it, and to add to the space, not take something away from it." Elbow-Tow, also in New York, explained that he pastes his drawings in the street with a "hope that people who see them appreciate it, that they like it." Alice Pasquini, in Rome, places work in the street "for you, for the people who live here ... to give something to this place." Likewise Chaz, who makes street art under the name The London Police, uses the street in order to provide "a little smidgin of entertainment," while Waleska Nomura, in Sao Paulo, believes that when people see street art "it makes them happy."

Pleasure is not only an aspect of spectatorship; it is also an attribute of the *practice* of situational art. Just as graffiti writers derive pleasure from a well-executed tag or piece, street artists get it from placing work in the street. The Belgian artist Roa spoke of experiencing "a feeling of accomplishment, that you came to a place and made something, left something behind." Making art in the street, for Morcky, simply brings him happiness: "the strongest feeling I get is from painting outside." Artists often use the words "joy" and "happiness" in describing their experiences of painting in the street, and the resulting artwork is something that they see themselves, in turn, as giving to the spectator: it is "a gift to the city," said the artist Miso, and according to the veteran street artist John Fekner in New York, "the spirit of giving is an inherent trait in all street artists." Corporeal pleasure is another marked feature of street art for artists: many spoke of heightened sensations when working in the street. The artist Just, in Berlin, said that when he paints "[his] senses are very clear," an experience shared by CDH in Melbourne, who described having "a sense of being awake. Truly awake, like everything is heightened, you're more attuned ... The texture of the surface, the texture of the brick, the cold air on your skin, the feeling of the can in your hand ... It's like everything is turned up."

In order to experience such intensity, writers and artists move through city spaces in ways that are different from those of us who do not make uncommissioned art. Zedz, in Amsterdam, told me that "writers look at cities differently, every surface is for writing." Locations that others might regard as unattractive can be enormously appealing to street artists. Many find that decaying buildings or peeling paint on stone walls provide surfaces that work well as backdrops to street artworks. Erris said that while non-artists might find some places "pretty scary," he and his partner "will be like children, we are really happy."

Morcky was also quick to distinguish his relationship with city spaces from that of the non-artist: "I've got a totally different relationship with the city—the way you interpret everything. I know the way to interpret objects, places, walls, surfaces, if a surface is going to keep the paint for long because the surface is good enough or from which distance [the artwork] is visible."

The graffiti writers interviewed by Mark Halsey and I reported similar modes of engagement with urban space: one said that when he looked at a train carriage, he "saw a potential panel," and when he was "driving down the street, [he was] imagining like where [his] tag would be … and, yeah, imagining how cool it would look" (2006: 288). For these writers, walls that have no graffiti on them are "canvasses permanently in waiting," and they invariably spend a lot of time thinking about how a given wall will "look when it's done" (288). Such spaces are replete with imaginative possibility. As Halsey and I wrote at the time, such an attitude effects a "levelling of the terrains … of the city … normally taken to be replete with the signs of wealth, status and ownership" (296). The streetscape is commonly assumed to be the product of private and public interests: municipal regulation and private controls combine to produce a compromise around the look, feel, sound, and smell of city spaces. That such spaces are owned is taken for granted by most individuals, whether by virtue of being property owners themselves, or through habituation to property's pervasive normativity.

According to David Delaney, "[The] social world in which private property is a fundamental feature … is also territorialized with reference to public and private spaces" (2005: 5). However, public and private space are now thoroughly intertwined. Although we can readily point to private space (houses, office buildings) many places that seem public are in fact privately owned, even though they are accessible to some or all of the public (shopping malls, train stations, cafes, bars, and so on). The number of PROPSs (privately owned public spaces) in major cities around the world has increased such that there are now significantly fewer publicly owned spaces. Instead, communal spaces are usually licensed for public use, so as long as that use does not transgress the owner's expectations of what is permissible. As street artist Lister commented: "Public spaces aren't for people. Everything's so regimented and controlled" and Emess noted, "When you start working outside in the 'public' space, you realize that it isn't public at all. You're not allowed to do this; you're not allowed to do that. So you ask yourself, 'what's it for?'."[7]

Situational art is unlikely to bring about circumstances in which public space exists as a zone free of governmental or proprietorial control, and, despite the nostalgic or romantic idealization animating some artists' comments, there has never been a "public space" that existed, in some remote past, free of governmental control. Nevertheless, since public space is a patchwork of privately owned places, the placing of an illicit word or image in urban space constitutes a contestation of the system of property ownership. For Tom Civil, in Melbourne, placing work on urban surfaces is the result of thinking about the lack of "public space in the city and the privatization of the city." Meggs says that street art is about people reclaiming space; for Brad Downey, "street art shows people the city is theirs," and Emess says, "Whenever I see some tags on a wall … it gives me the feeling like, here's somebody who's taking back the space." CDH categorizes street art as a way of reminding people of other ways of relating to urban space: "If it's public space, any member of the public has the right to modify it in any way that they see fit. It's not council space, it's not private space, if it's public space, it belongs to the public, it belongs to the community." Phoenix puts this even more strongly: "It's the property owner who actually owns a wall, but as soon as someone tag[s] it, [they] own it."

PROPRIETORSHIP AND CRIMINAL IMPROPRIETY

That situational art challenges conventional notions of proprietorship is evident from the ways that criminal and property law combine to condemn unauthorized words and images in urban space. Graffiti and street art, when placed without permission on another's property, can be categorized as criminal in a range of ways (often depending on the jurisdiction). The shifting terrain of legislated criminality provides a backdrop against which to consider the criminal status of illicit words and images in public space. When words or images are written or painted on property belonging to another, without the owner's consent, this can constitute any one of a number of criminal offenses.

Under Article 145 of the New York Penal Law, for example, one aspect of "criminal mischief" is "making graffiti," defined as "etching, painting, covering, drawing upon or otherwise placing of a mark upon public or private property with intent to damage such property." Express permission of the property owner or operator is required to avoid prosecution with this Class A misdemeanor offense. A separate offense criminalizes "possession of graffiti instruments," meaning "any tool, instrument, article, substance, solution or other compound designed or commonly used to etch, paint, cover, draw upon or otherwise place a mark upon a piece of property which that person has no permission or authority to etch, paint, cover, draw upon or otherwise mark, under circumstances evincing an intent to use same in order to damage such property."

In some jurisdictions, generic prohibitions on property damage ensure that graffiti and street art are illegal; in others, such general provisions have come to be regarded as inadequate and further legislation enacted. In England and Wales, an individual can be prosecuted for the offense of "criminal damage" under the Criminal Damage Act 1971, but the Clean Neighbourhoods and Environment Act 2005 also creates a specific power for police officers to issue a £75 on-the-spot penalty notice for graffiti. Graffiti was an oft-cited justification for the social utility of Anti-Social Behaviour Orders in Britain throughout the 2000s, and many individuals caught by the authorities for graffiti-related activities found themselves issued with ASBOs prohibiting them from not only doing graffiti, but also travelling on public transport and even photographing graffiti.[8]

Many Australian states enacted similar legislation criminalizing graffiti even though it was already an offense under existing legislation. Thus the Graffiti Prevention Act appeared in Victoria, in 2007, complete with enhanced police powers despite the fact that graffiti had been prosecuted for years (entirely adequately it would seem) under the Crimes Act 1958 and the Summary Offences Act 1966. Debates in the Victorian Parliament show that a specific piece of legislation was seen as necessary to provide police officers with additional powers so that the perceived flood-tide of graffiti could be stemmed. This legislation created new offenses for police to prosecute and expressed disapproval of graffiti per se.

Comments by Dr. Denis Napthine, future Premier of Victoria, were typical of the mood of the debates:

> Anybody who tries to describe graffiti as something that is acceptable art or witty is just encouraging this form of irresponsible vandalism. Graffiti is not art; it is vandalism. It is irresponsible and illegal damage to public and private property, and it is offensive to the community ... [T]he bill proposes increased penalties. That is all very well and good, and we support that, but those increased penalties must be backed up by the courts ... We have to have tougher sentences, and we have to have courts that actually administer those tougher sentences.[9]

The prior legal approach—of prosecuting graffiti as criminal damage—is widely thought to have failed to communicate social disapproval of graffiti to both offenders and to the wider community. The creation of harsher graffiti-related offenses would, it was thought, convey both the unacceptability of the activity and society's censure of it. The activity of illicit mark-making was thus *recriminalized* through the new statutory prohibition.

Whichever offense is used to prosecute graffiti writers and street artists, the idea that placing words or images in public space without permission constitutes "damage" appears to be beyond question or doubt. Such self-evidence is either a tautological effect of its being named as such in the statutory provision or as the unspoken explanation for the need for the existence of a graffiti-specific offense. In the language of the legislation, "damage" tends to be a noun; meaning that it names an effect of the activity of graffiti; however, "damage" is also a verb that requires an agent, one who damages property, and the criminal law is thus positing the existence of *an individual who damages*.

Such a construction is profoundly limited. In my research with Mark Halsey, it emerged in interviews that graffiti writers wrote on urban surfaces for a range of reasons. These included pride in their ability to write skillfully, a desire to belong to a network of graffiti writers, enjoyment of the sociality of shared peer behavior, boredom in a particular location or situation, and pleasure in the corporeal experience of writing on walls. Street artists report a similarly diverse range of reasons for making situational art. These might include an interest in street art as a cultural form; a desire to join an identifiable community of artists; the belief that street art can beautify a location; public space as a means of displaying artwork; a decision to work with the surfaces and settings of the street as a component of an artwork, as well as factors to do with adrenaline, politicized opposition to social norms, or rebelliousness.

The artist and activist Jordan Seiler, who has organized takeovers of billboards and other advertising spaces in New York City, comments:

> Laws in themselves aren't preventing people from going out and writing on walls. There is some ingrained need to write on the space in which you live for some people. Not for everybody, but for some people, because they're going out and doing it, despite these very serious criminal prohibitions. Why do people want to go out and write on these walls? Well, because there's some sort of problem with how public space is cordoned off. You're not allowed to use it. So let's attack that issue.

Situational artworks can help us to think differently about property, place, and possession. As Tom Civil asserts, "When you have graffiti in a space, it's like it has become people's spaces, a reminder that we created these urban spaces *for people*." Graffiti writers and street artists often assume that placement of an artwork in "the street" means it is located in public space, rather than on private property; even when a wall might clearly be part of the outer boundary of a house, its exterior wall will frequently be regarded as *public* (such as when it abuts the thoroughfare). As Chaz, of The London Police, put it, "the streets belong to everyone." For graffiti writers and street artists, "public space" tends to be defined through a sense of publicness deriving from its *function* rather than its ownership.

Conventional legal definitions of property and place in the city are focused on ownership and on the boundaries between public and private (including corporate) legal persons. Commuters travel along roads to get from home to work and back again. Consumers move from one shop to another. And certainly all of the thoroughfares required for such movement are owned and regulated. There is no conceptualization of movement *through* urban space as a source of authority over property (instead, it is seen to generate a right to unimpeded passage and the responsibility to conduct oneself in various ways *en route*). Little attention is paid to notions of the *space-between* or the *space-through*.

For situational artists, however, through-passage gives rise to the potential to alter a streetscape in a range of ways. Knitted objects may be hung from street signs; words or images painted on a wall. Debates about ownership of surfaces do not have purchase because the very idea of entitlement arises through *proximity* to a surface and aesthetic reaction to what is already there. Thus, a doorway may become a suitable frame for an image, and a drab gray wall seem to be inviting the addition of colorful words or images. These artists do not consider their actions damaging, deviant, criminal, or troublesome. They do what they do so as to "have a connection to the city" (Just, Berlin); to "take part in a conversation" (Ghostpatrol, Melbourne), to make the city "better than it is right now" (Jordan, New York City), and to show that "the walls are the commons" (Swoon, New York).

PUBLIC SPACE AND THE COMMONS

In recent years, the concept of "the commons" has been a rallying-point for critical thinking in economics, law, and political theory.[10] In its original formulation, the commons referred to land customarily held in common, giving rise to a range of common law rights enforceable against landowners. According to Carol Rose, the extent of these rights developed to the point that "customary claims did resemble the doctrines vesting property-like rights in the general public: custom too was said to bestow rights on people whose precise identity was unknown and indefinite" (1994: 122).

To be recognized, customary rights in the commons needed to be long-lasting (preferably since "time immemorial"), reasonable, uncontentious, and relatively uncontested. Many land usages were protected through the notions of custom and commons including grazing, access to materials and through-passage. Under common law, custom provided a different means through which to manage and negotiate property rights; "a means different from ownership by either individuals or by organized governments" (Rose 1994: 124). Given these wide-ranging implications, we can see why scholars such as Holder and Flessas declare the commons "a powerful polemical tool, as well as a legal or descriptive term" (2008: 305).

Within contemporary commons research, a number of different paradigms can be identified. There is much scholarship rethinking approaches to resources such as air, water, food, and land as commons that are being encroached upon by private interests (see especially Ostrom 1990, 2000, 2008). Others focus upon ways in which the commons—denoting a space in which all citizens share rights of enjoyment, use, and ownership—provides an alternative way of thinking about urban space (Blomley 2008, 2011; Mitchell 2008; Chatterton 2010; Foster 2011; Harvey 2011). For some, the commons appears to offer a means through which to acquire the rights of ownership: Holder and Flessas argue that "the subject-position of the 'owner', although privileged in law and society, is being appropriated by flexible groupings of actors that would not formerly have been understood as being capable of supporting a claim to this position" (2008: 299). For others, drawing on Lefebvre, the commons reorganizes the meaning of ownership by valorizing use and action so as to constitute an obstacle to exclusion from the enjoyment of property or land (see, for example, Blomley 2008; Mitchell 2008).

Some accounts verge on a reiteration of the dichotomy between ownership and use, others position use as a means by which to wield the power of an owner. Such approaches either diminish the interests of a city's "others" as minoritarian exceptions awaiting authorization by the majority, or else reauthorize the dominant paradigm of property that underpins urban space. Is it possible, I wonder, to think of street artists and graffiti writers as pointing to another kind of commons? In following this line of thought, I tread a similar path to that of Davina Cooper, who argues for a "social commons" or a "space that constitutes, recognizes, and permits multiple, overlapping uses" (2007: 649; see also Cooper 2006). Kurt Iveson (2013) draws upon Jacques Rancière and Henri Lefebvre to think through the "do-it-yourself urbanisms" of graffiti, skateboarding and parkour in relation to the "right to the city." And Kafui Attoh argues for a general "right to the city" following Lefebvre's "notion of the city as an oeuvre, or as a work produced through the labor and the daily actions of those who live in [it]" (2011: 674). Attoh's formulation is particularly pertinent for present purposes:

> If anti-panhandling laws prevent the homeless from asserting their right to the city ... then the rights of the homeless are rights that stand *against a possible majority* who might believe that such laws are just and appropriate. When we argue that the homeless have a right to occupy a public park, it is a right that we would argue exists *despite the desire of a majority* (homeowners, renters, store keepers, developers) to deem otherwise. When we argue that protesters have a right to picket or occupy a street, it is a right that exists *despite a democratic majority* that may view such protests as nuisances, or disturbances. (2011: 677, emphases mine)[11]

SITUATIONAL ART, UNCOMMISSIONED IMAGE, PUBLIC SPACES

Understanding the sensibility of situational art allows us to conceptualize place, property and propriety in new ways. If a "right to the city" exists, it must relate not only to places found in the interstices of urban space, or in partitioned-off minoritarian spaces. It cannot be dependent upon the permission granted by proprietors to those without property or power. The commons adverted to by street artists and graffiti writers is not an exception, a custom to be asserted if and when permitted by the dominant paradigm of property rights. They see the city as an assemblage of surfaces, shapes, and textures that can be adapted and colored, a vision which derives from an innate sense of an extensive commons that runs through the entire urban landscape, is available to any citizen in any place, and is contingent only on one's ability to peer below the surface of the cityscape. Their persistent acts of illicit image-making paradoxically constitute a legality in which citizens are authorized by adaptation and proximity rather than use or ownership. In each act of installing a situational artwork, artists demonstrate a way of thinking not only about images and surfaces, but also about property and the city itself.

When such a commons is activated, a street is more than a thoroughfare for commuters on their way to work; it is also a space in which residents can set up communal gardens. A public park may facilitate recreation, but it can also be occupied by political protesters. A doorway provides entry to a warehouse or an office, but it can also frame a drawing or become the surface to which a poster is glued. A set of stairs, meant for climbing and access, may become a launch site for skateboarders. If the city is a commons, the possibilities for such activities are always present: not exceptions, but integral to the infrastructure and architecture of urban space. Let us return for a moment to Rancière's claim that "[art] reframe[s] the way in which practices, manners of being and modes of feeling and saying are interwoven in a commonsense" (2004: 100). Situational art asks us to imagine a new commonsense for *images*. Graffiti and street art may simply "appear" in urban space, but their apparent lack of (legal) authorship need not provoke anxiety. The defaults of image-making that require an artist, a commission, and an authorized mode of display or exhibition are merely habits; they seem natural but they need no longer go unquestioned. In cities around the world, the pervasiveness and popularity of street art and graffiti reminds us that images need not require a commission in order to be considered art. So-called "legal walls" and murals play a beneficial role in accustoming citizens to the presence of certain aesthetic genres. Yet the space they accord to street artists and graffiti writers is limited and fractional. And these sites are controlled by authorities (property owners, police, councils, governments) who refuse to recognize situational artwork as legal.

Despite such restrictions, innumerable graffiti writers and street artists create illicit work every day, and thus demonstrate their agency and ability to self-commission. Street art thus *makes its own space*, not as a partitioned, permitted, semi-tolerated activity, but as an emergent, self-reflexive practice, a de-territorializing tactic that exposes the multiple boundaries and borders of the propertied cityscape. Instead of a territorialized city dependent upon boundaries and exclusions, situational artists point to the possibility of a public city founded on "communication"; that is, a space founded through the urban imagination and the circulation of signs (see Nancy 1991). The "urban inscription" created by street artists and graffiti writers gives such a space the possibility of becoming known and experienced, as Dickens puts it, "through the bodily, rhythmic writing and re-writing of it" (Dickens 2008: 27). For in each encounter with a situational artwork, property and propriety are called into question, and the possibility of a public city is reiterated.

CHAPTER SEVEN

Wrongs

A Conversation with Filmmaker Joshua Oppenheimer

RICHARD SHERWIN, JOSHUA OPPENHEIMER,
AND DANIELLE CELERMAJER

In the aftermath of the Second World War, the horror of the Holocaust helped to inaugurate a "memory imperative" (Levy and Sznaider 2010). In the Nuremberg trials documentaries like *The Nazi Plan* and *Nazi Concentration Camps* were presented as visual evidence of the atrocities committed. Photographs, film documentaries and written testimonies bearing witness to atrocities came to be seen as critical components of the work of ethico-political transformation and reconstruction (Brink and Oppenheimer 2012; Gregory 2006; Hirsch 1997; McLagan 2003; Zelizer 1999). This was particularly evident in the course of political transitions when institutions struggled to deal with past violations by the state.

The collective sense of being a witness to history was facilitated by the rapid advance of visual mass media, which seemed capable of instantly capturing and transmitting the experiences of victims and survivors. At the same time, potent images engineered by state-sponsored films—from Leni Riefenstahl's *Triumph of the Will* (1935) to Frank Capra's *Prelude to War* (1942)—also made clear that the visual record is capable of serving many masters, reflecting widely divergent claims to truth. Little wonder that Joseph Goebbels, upon becoming Hitler's Minister of Propaganda, moved swiftly to take control of the German film industry as the most scientific means of influencing the masses (Rentschler 1996). To be sure, fictionalized film accounts of history, like their documentary counterparts, have served as didactic devices through which the viewing public may bear witness to the horrors of political violence—perhaps in an effort to overcome it (as in Roland Joffe's *The Killing Fields* [1984]), perhaps to receive rationales and affective cues that justify and perhaps even stoke it (as in Kathryn Bigelow's *Zero Dark Thirty* [2012]).

The intermingling of various film genres and techniques of visual persuasion—in the service of diverse interests, beliefs, and strategic objectives—has complicated the transmission process. From Truman Capote's literary scheme of telling true stories with the tools of fiction (as evidenced in his "nonfiction novel" *In Cold Blood: A True Account of a Multiple Murder and Its Consequences* [1965]), to Orson Welles' prescient exploration of forgery and simulation in his pseudo-documentary *F for Fake* (1975), the lines between documentary and dramatic feature have continued to blur. Yet, even a docudrama, such as Errol Morris's remarkable film, *The Thin Blue Line* (1988), was able to alter the outcome of a real criminal case, facilitating Randall Dale Adam's strange exodus from death row (as a convicted cop killer) to freedom (Sherwin 2000).

It has been said that "every epoch is defined by its own practices of knowledge and strategies of power, which are composed from regimes of visibility and procedures of expression" (Rodowick 2001: xi). The way we mind the world and others around us changes along with significant changes in our tools of perception and mass communication. Over time, we become the tools we use (Turkle 196:26, 46). The camera is already inside our head, so to speak, along with the stream of digital programs and cultural codes that we commonly use to recognize patterns on the screen before us. In a visual age like ours, visual storytelling asserts its own measure of content, craft, and efficacy along with its own sense of expectation, interpretation, and critique. Indeed, the matrix of reality-based and synthetic visual representations in which we now dwell has produced a growing sense that the distinction between digital simulation and live experience may be fading from memory. The domains of law and politics are hardly immune to these developments (Sherwin 2000, 2011).

In the film work of Joshua Oppenheimer, the clash and merging of diverse film genres together with their respective ways of knowing—from the surrealism of dramatized imaginings to the cinema verité of presently unfolding truths—achieve a startling culmination. For if it is one thing to explore the power (and limits) of film to capture or alter truth as a matter of art, it is something else again to do so in an effort to come to grips with state-sponsored genocidal violence. Yet it is precisely that species of violence, which erupted in Indonesia in 1965–1966, claiming the lives of at least 500,000 victims (and perhaps twice that number), that is the subject of Oppenheimer's films.

It began on the night of September 30, 1965, when six of Indonesia's top army generals were abducted and murdered in an aborted coup attempt. The actors and motivations behind the action remain unclear. In response, General Suharto seized the reins of government. To consolidate his power, he initiated a nationwide purge in which enemies of the state (alleged "Communists," trade unionists, organized peasants, and anyone else deemed a threat to the state) were rounded up and slaughtered (Brink and Oppenheimer 2012: 287). Violence on such a massive scale exceeded the army's capacity. Civilian militias on the local level had to be enlisted to help "cleanse" the state of "evil" so that a "New Order" might be established (Brink and Oppenheimer 2012: 288).

Suharto remained in power for over four decades thereafter. As co-agents of that political and military triumph, the civilian killers were subsequently praised as heroes of the state. The failure to hold the perpetrators to account abetted ongoing harassment of the survivors, their families, and friends. It also ensured that the victims' stories were silenced or marginalized. A culture of impunity developed, underpinning broader criminal practices (from crude shakedowns in the marketplace to fraudulent land schemes) targeting vulnerable minorities—often at the hands of the thugs, gangsters, and neofascist militias that continued to serve the state's needs.

Confronting this state of affairs, filmmaker Joshua Oppenheimer poses two questions: What is it like to live with the knowledge that you have murdered in cold blood scores, perhaps even hundreds of innocent people? And what is it like for the victims to live within a regime of such repressive silence? *The Act of Killing* asks the first question. *The Look of Silence* asks the second.

Oppenheimer found that the aging civilian killers, when approached, were only too happy to recount the brutal torture and mass murder that they had committed in their youth (Figure 7.1). And so the filmmaker enters a strange state of play, providing the killers both the opportunity and the technical means to make a film of their violent and sadistic exploits. Anwar Congo is the chief protagonist in this creative venture: white-haired now, rail thin, charismatic and, despite the apparent comfort and prestige of his current social status, tortured by his violent past. As he moves from scene to scene, we are thrust into his interior, visual world. Culturally immersed in the westerns and crime noirs of Hollywood, Congo's visual vocabulary is rich and astute. He uses his film knowledge to play out fantasies of denial together with recollections of violence and death that incessantly fill his mind (Figure 7.2).

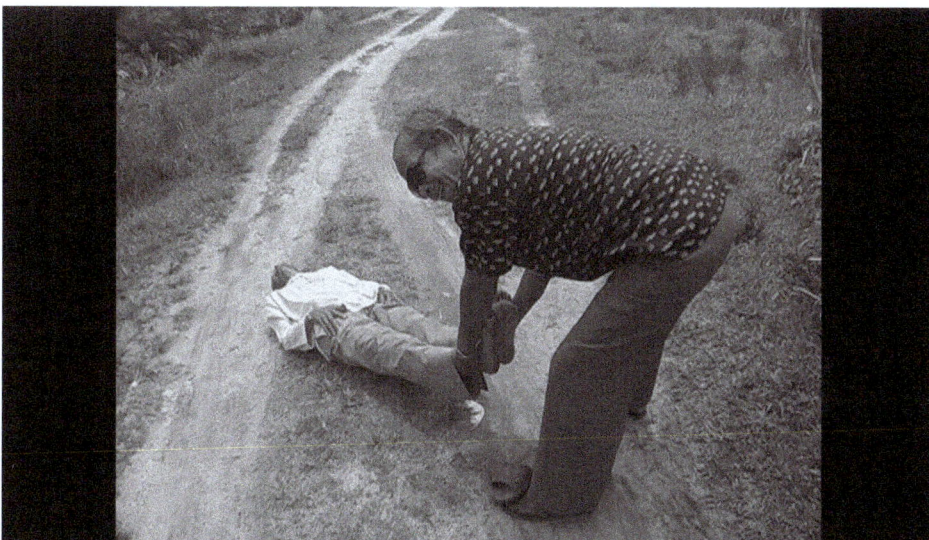

FIGURE 7.1 Dramatization scene from *The Act of Killing*. Source: The Act of Killing, Carlos Arango de Montis and Joshua Oppenheimer.

FIGURE 7.2 Dramatization scene from *The Act of Killing*. Source: The Act of Killing, Carlos Arango de Montis and Joshua Oppenheimer.

FIGURE 7.3 Fantasy scene from *The Act of Killing*. Source: The Act of Killing, Carlos Arango de Montis and Joshua Oppenheimer.

As it turns out, nightmares disturb Congo's sleep. He can't stop seeing the open eyes of the decapitated head of a random victim that he left like litter on the killing ground. As if to purge his demons, Congo stages his worst deeds, one after another. Brutal scenes of sadistic torture and killing by strangulation with a wire, in which Congo sometimes is the killer, sometimes the victim, are interspersed with majestic waterfalls, beautiful dancing girls, and carnivalesque cross-dressing (for Congo, the would-be film director, is well aware that an audience must also have beauty and humor if their attention is to be held) (Figure 7.3).

Bizarre, surreal, perverse: the film moves from one scene to the next, accelerating into the terrible fever dream that we come to recognize as Congo's anguished internal state. As if the impossible cognitive dissonance in which he lives, oscillating between "state hero" and "murderous beast," cannot hold. One image follows another, dizzying in their mad profusion. Nothing adds up. Congo's baroque world of proliferating spectacles of extreme violence and sensual delight remains unstable at its core. Perhaps that is what animates the profusion in the first place. The nothingness at the center must be avoided at all costs, for fear of total collapse.

The folly of Congo's visual staging is soon evident. The cumulative details of self-deceptive denial and self-lacerating violence (as in the scene where a crazed perpetrator forces Congo's decapitated head to swallow his own liver) know no resolution. They can only quicken. And as they quicken, the fever dream intensifies, until it finally reaches a culmination—and the house of cards that is Anwar Congo's mental world falls apart. That collapse appears in the final scene in *The Act of Killing*. We see Congo standing on the same rooftop where he killed so many of his victims in cold blood decades ago. He is silent, seemingly reflective. And then he begins to heave, again and again convulsive retching overtakes his frail, wracked body. It is the body's unconscious knowledge enacting what Congo's tortured mind lacks the power to utter. An internal catastrophe that mirrors the external catastrophe in which Congo all too willingly participated, has finally come to dominate the world in which he lives (Sherwin 2014) (Figure 7.4).

FIGURE 7.4 Scene of Anwar Congo retching, from *The Act of Killing*. Source: The Act of Killing, Carlos Arango de Montis and Joshua Oppenheimer.

In his second film, Oppenheimer shifts from the perpetrator's mindset to that of the victim. Adi "Rukun" (not his real name) is now the main protagonist. His brother, Ramli, was brutally tortured, mutilated, and killed during the Indonesian genocide, a year before Adi was born. Working as an optometrist, while living amidst his brother's killers, Adi's life mission is to speak truth to power. But it is not vengeance that motivates him. Rather, it is the need to pierce the veil of oppressive silence, to confront the killers with their feckless denials, their empty fantasies, their perverse bravado. Do you not see it was wrong? Have you no remorse, no regret? Such is Adi's refrain as (in no idle metaphor) he calmly fits lenses on the eyes of the killers around him, or sits across from them, including those in positions of significant political power. Forced to hide his identity, resisting threats of renewed violence if he continues to speak the unspeakable about the past, Adi persists in his questioning.

The vertiginous, unstable images of Congo's fever dream have now given way to something calm and steady. Adi's gaze is stable, securely rooted (Figure 7.5). The silence of the dead, and the dignity of the living who survive them, pervades every scene in *The Look of Silence*, scenes that are graced by Adi's capacity for love: love of his elderly, long-suffering parents, for whom he must now care, love of his lost brother, who so many years ago set in motion the ethical demand of Adi's life mission, and love for his children who will inherit a legacy of suffering and injustice. We see this in simple scenes of everyday life: Adi washing his blind and nearly deaf and demented father—unable now to escape the prison of his grief; Adi speaking in close intimacy with his careworn mother as she cracks nuts on a stone; Adi playing with his young daughter, jumping delightedly on her bed as she humorously mimics her father's sales pitch for new glasses, and Adi walking with his older son, solemnly explaining the lies his teachers are telling him at school.

Two films, two different interventions in the history of mass murder. One, a fever dream of incessantly shifting personas, disguises, oscillating wildly from self-deceit to self-conviction, showing us what it is like to look in the mirror of a perpetrator's life—a life

FIGURE 7.5 Image of Adi from *The Look of Silence*. Source: The Act of Killing, Carlos Arango de Montis and Joshua Oppenheimer.

lived in the homeless terror of unacknowledged guilt and shame. The second, almost an idyll—but for the background of violence and death, and the exquisite, almost unbearable suffering left in their wake. We see what it is like to look in the mirror of a victim condemned to live beneath a veil of oppressive silence, but who refuses to succumb—not with violence or cries for retribution, but with dignity and moral conviction vouchsafed by the silent authority of the dead.

Two different gazes, two different image worlds—reflecting key dimensions of the visual economy of contemporary Indonesia. But this is not simply an allegory of a society internally riven by a history of unspeakable violence and oppressive silence. It is also a symbolic visualization of the way law confronts (or fails to confront) violence. It places before us, in corporeal images of almost unbearable intensity, the mute knowledge of the body: its fevers, its fantasies, its wretchedness, as well as its dignity, its sweetness, its moral rightness, and its capacity to empathize and to love.

That the representation of state violence and its aftermath might lead to political transformation has served as something of an article of faith in contemporary human rights discourse, as is evident in the dramatic rise of truth and reconciliation commissions in the latter half of the twentieth century (Hayner 2002; Mendeloff 2004; Minow 1998). It is as though the right to truth, and the right of victims to have their experiences reflected in official, public, and national histories, has increasingly come to be understood as a form of justice (Henderson 2000; Phelps 2004; Villa-Vicencio et al. 2003).[1] On this view, with truth and reconciliation comes the end of impunity, establishing peace and the possibility of constructing a new national identity.[2]

The centrality of exposing the truth of atrocities is also evident in the human rights movement more generally, whose principal methodology consists of documenting violations ("naming") in order to spark public outrage and political responsiveness ("shaming") (Roth 2004). Indeed, the failure to say and to show what actually occurred is understood as the basis for impunity in a formal sense (Roht-Arriaza 1995), and a "culture of impunity" more broadly (Zalaquett 1991). Understood in this way, the failure to account for the past implicitly sanctions the narratives of the wrongdoers. This not only lays the foundation for the commission of future crimes, but it also impedes the establishment of a culture of democracy and a state premised on respect for human rights and the rule of law (Huyse 2003).

For the victims of past wrongs this means being condemned to a future of unreality, where the truths that they know cannot be spoken. Like the ghost of Prince Hamlet's murdered father, the state's unacknowledged wrongful violence exerts a spectral force over the lives of victims and perpetrators alike. As Marie-Louise Knott writes (and as the lives of Anwar Congo and Adi Rukun attest): "A world in which the facts are unreal is a nightmare. 'Being'—living in a world that faces up to the present—is confronted by 'nonbeing'—a world that pretends to have assimilated with the false reality created by the murderers" (Knott 2014). Embedded in this emphasis on ensuring that wrongs are exposed and officially condemned is an understanding that the work of justice is not simply backward looking, but is, critically, about the present and the future (Teitel 2000).

Still, the situation remains complex, both unsettled and unsettling. For notwithstanding the proliferation of institutions and social movements committed to exorcizing such specters of the unredeemed past, political cultures of impunity persist around the globe. It was only in the latter part of the twentieth century that Indigenous rights movements received international and national attention as they sought to bring to awareness the sedimentation of the wrongs committed against them in the founding of modern states such as the United States, Canada, Australia, and New Zealand (Anaya 2004; Barsh 1986; Ivison et al. 2000).[3] While high-profile trials or truth commissions in countries such as Argentina, South Africa, and Cambodia invite hope for the future, many states have yet to accede to calls for justice. And so the exemplary work of Joshua Oppenheimer, together with other artists and activists committed to heeding that call, remains vital.

* * *

On July 6, 2015, in a small café in the Chelsea neighborhood of New York City, we sat down with Joshua Oppenheimer to discuss cinema, memory, truth, fantasy, human rights, genocide, and the possibility of redemptive justice in Indonesia:

> Dany Celermajer ["DC"]: As you know, this book is about the culture of law in the twentieth century, and one of the distinct shifts that we've observed during this period is the way that we experience law through narrative. The narratives through which we imagine right and wrong help to shape our experience of law— what it ought to do, how it ought to work under a given set of circumstances, and so on. This narrative turn has gained momentum as a result of the human rights and transitional justice movements, and film has played an increasingly significant role in those movements. How would you locate yourself in regard to that narrative turn, particularly with respect to wrongdoing and conceptions of right and justice?
>
> Joshua Oppenheimer ["JO"]: I think that I'd start by saying that my two films are interventions in precisely that: you have a place where there was a genocide, where perpetrators have been in power ever since and have written a narrative and have been able to cling to and impose upon the society a narrative that justifies the whole complex of narratives, indeed you may call it a culture that justifies and normalizes and naturalizes what they've done. This is of course fraught with danger for the future in that when atrocities are naturalized, the ground is thus prepared for them to happen again. What you can say *The Act of Killing* did was to enter that space, like the child in *The Emperor's New Clothes*, and make it impossible for people to continue repeating those lies.

Anyone who's seen it or even talked extensively about it finds, in the words of Adi Zulkadry, one of the death squad members in the film, that it is impossible not to admit what they've always suspected to be true, namely: that the genocide was wrong, and that all of the government propaganda is a lie. It made it impossible not to admit, not to acknowledge those suspicions. Like the child in *The Emperor's New Clothes*, *The Act of Killing* is an intervention in cognitive dissonance. Because the individual private morality, which I think takes different forms in different cultures, but invariably because of the way we as human beings are nurtured from such a long time as babies through a sixteen, seventeen, eighteen-year childhood—however long in different cultures, for so many years, private morality invariably protects life and invariably treats murder (in general terms) as taboo. So you have this cognitive dissonance between a private morality, where everybody knows what happened is wrong, and a public culture of form, that is to say, these complex narratives, which assert that what happened was justified and even to be celebrated.

People have been forced to live in this cognitive dissonance. And so, just like the child in *The Emperor's New Clothes* intervenes, people are forced to now say that the king is naked when they always knew the king was naked, but have been too afraid to say it. So, too, *The Act of Killing* makes it impossible to continue inhabiting that cognitive dissonance, to continue lying to oneself. And *The Look of Silence* I think did something similar where it comes in also like the child in *The Emperor's New Clothes* not exposing anything that people did not already know to be true, mainly this time forcing people to acknowledge this abyss of fear and guilt, and for the perpetrators' fear of their own guilt that divides everybody in this society, including everyone from themselves in a sense because it divides people from their own pasts. They're unable to talk about their pasts, and once that's intervened in, then the discourse of law—despite what Adi also says in *The Act of Killing*, "War crimes are defined by winners, and I'm a winner so I ought to be able to make my own definitions"—despite that, the discourse of law provides this alternative frame where people are now talking about having thus intervened in the cognitive dissonance that prevented people from acknowledging what was wrong and from talking about it. Now people *have* to talk about it and there is this ready language from the human rights community, from the international community, from the sense in Indonesia that now the world is aware of this, that means people now talk about this in terms of "crimes against humanity," in terms of "genocide," in terms of "gross violation of human rights" and other legal concepts that have this specific history.

Richard Sherwin ["RS"]: Reframing it?

JO: Yes, there's a fundamental reframing, and you can see that in the impact of the two films in Indonesia, where before the mainstream media (with very few exceptions) was silent about the killings or invariably repeated the government narratives saying this was either "a necessary bloodletting," "painful but heroic," or simply part of the "heroic extermination of the Indonesian communists." *Now* the mainstream society talks about "crimes against humanity" and "genocide." Even the government—when *The Act of Killing* was nominated for an Academy award in late January, early February 2014—the president's spokesman said, "Look we know what happened in 1965 was a crime against humanity and we know we need reconciliation, but we'll have it in our own time." That radically shifts the field of struggle that needs to take place going forward. Now the question is: will the truth and reconciliation process that's been introduced by the government (in part maybe in response to these two films, and the change in discourse that the two films have helped bring about) be adequate—will it be credible?

DC: What do you think it was about the film that helped bring about that change in discourse? Because there were novels and other forms of narrative ...

JO: I think it's because the film is about the lies themselves. Both films are about the lies and the conditions of silence themselves. I was actually just struggling to write an introduction to one of the more well known novels about this, Leila Chudori's *Pulang* or "Home," which is being translated into English. Most of the books dealing with this are trying to imagine the past from behind multiple veils of silence and multiple forms of blindness. There's the silence and blindness that come from the fact that the victims are dead and the survivors (most of them) have been intimidated into silence. There's the blindness that comes from historical records being radically redacted through state censorship and secrecy. There's the blindness that comes from indoctrination in these narratives that we've already talked about to justify what happened and created all sorts of stereotypes about who the victims were, thereby erasing any sense of what they were really struggling for, what values they were about, what solidarities brought them together. What was exterminated has been banished into silence and darkness. So many of the attempts in the past try to imagine what happened and what the conflict was about have been exactly that: attempts to imagine from behind a veil of secrecy and silence. And I think what I've tried to do is make films about the silence itself—

DC: And about the veils ...

JO: And about the present, about the present day workings of that veil. So people who say to me, "Look, you've pulled back the curtain and unveiled the nightmare," I say no. If my films have made an impact inside Indonesia and internationally, it's because they show that the curtain itself is the nightmare, because the films are about the present and not the past. They're films about two fundamentally complimentary but different aspects of impunity today: first the lies, the fantasies, the stories that the perpetrators tell themselves, the persona that they inhabit so that they can live with themselves, and the terrible corrupting effects of those fictions that have been imposed on the whole society: the thuggery, the fear, and the corruption. And the second film is similarly dealing with present day impunity, but this time: what does it do to human beings that have to live for fifty years in that regime, particularly survivors surrounded by the still powerful perpetrators? What does it do to a human being to have to live afraid for half a century?

RS: Picking up on that, but shifting gears just a little bit towards the poetic quality of these films: it seems as if you've created two complementary image-worlds with these films, and I see them as co-essential. The image-world of the perpetrator in a sense is very unreliable, it's unstable. Fantasy and reality intermingle freely, we're not really sure where we are, and then ultimately it just seems to break down. We see Anwar reduced in the end to this mute, retching body which one might describe as bare life—this is like the state of exception, the zero point of politics. And by contrast, in *The Look of Silence*, it's a totally different aesthetic. The moral gaze is so clear and so steady, and that silent strength of Adi holds us and draws us in. So I wanted to ask you about these two image-worlds in terms of the aesthetic choices that you've made. First, is it fair to describe the "image-worlds" in the way that I just did, and second, how does one make choices using different film codes that convey these different types of reality?

JO: First of all, I think your description of *The Act of Killing* and of both films is very beautiful and apt. I think that *The Act of Killing*, because it is ultimately a film about escapism and guilt, and precisely therefore the cognitive dissonance that implies—the sort of guilt which one constantly is running away from, and the escapist fantasies to run away from that guilt—it becomes this kind of inevitably flamboyant fever-dream of a film, that's inevitable. It's about the construction of reality itself through those fantasies, but it's an inherently unstable reality which you also suggested, which I love because I would say every perpetrator I filmed lives their life in manic flight from a kind of pall of guilt and shame that follows them everywhere they go, that wakes them in the middle of their sleep with horrific nightmares, but because they have not been removed from power, they still have available to them this victor's history which celebrates what they've done. And so they do what anybody would do, which is if they're tormented by something—because again, this private morality I talked about earlier, out of which they had to be incited to join the group which was doing something that was contradicting their private morality—they would do what any of us would do, which is to cling to the stories of the group. So the sort of surreal boasting of the perpetrators, in both films, I think can be understood as an attempt to take these rotten, bitter memories that haunt them and that follow them and to try to sugarcoat them, in the sweet language of a victor's history that would celebrate what they did. But it's slightly more complicated than that, because maybe it's more like alchemy, right? Whether there's a rotten core there always, or not, that's simply covered with the sweet coating of lie, is questionable. Maybe, rather, the horror that motivates the need to wrap what they've done, to encrypt what they've done in heroic language of the victor's history, is not there as a rotten core but as a kind of destabilizing presence that forces the shell to continuously transmute and transmogrify.

RS: And how do you see yourself? You're facilitating that?

JO: So precisely in *The Act of Killing*, what happens is Anwar—and you see this much more clearly in the uncut version of the film, is Anwar watching footage of himself and proposing the next scene. He would always feel disturbed and feel doubt when watching the footage of himself, but instead of admitting what was bothering him—which would be tantamount to admitting what he did was wrong in some way—instead, he always proposed what he considered to be an improvement, as though if he fixed the scene aesthetically he could fix his past morally. And so you have this transmogrification, this transmutation of the wrapper, this sugar coating. It changes. It's not consistent. It's not stable.

So you get this kind of succession of self-states. You see, we would just keep repeating that same process recursively, but we would shoot one scene, Anwar would watch it and propose the next scene, shoot the next scene, Anwar would watch it and propose the next scene … And so Anwar moves through this succession of fantasies, lies, personas—because sometimes they're not even justifying what he's done, sometimes when he can no longer run away from his guilt he throws himself almost despairingly into a film noir persona, which is certainly evil but at least it's glamorous, which maybe makes it bearable. Or maybe it's just simply that by performing the gangster of a film that he might have liked, he simply distances himself enough so that he can live with that guilt. So there's this succession of personas that Anwar moves through, and it's a slow-motion unpacking of what he might do in any given afternoon in his life in a much less intense way ... He's enacting for the film over the course of months and years this movement through multiple, conflicting, different stories that he inhabits so that he can live with himself.

RS: And what about your role? You're making choices. For example, you chose a cut from that horrific scene with Herman and Anwar with a decapitated head to a banal, urban shopping mall ...

JO: So having explained that aspect of how it's a shifting reality and an unstable reality, it's not lies that cover a reality but the reality itself is shifting. I had two feelings: I felt that I should make the scenes—in the shooting and in the editing—as powerfully and as beautifully as Anwar would wish them to be, so that the audience is transported with Anwar, and immersed and lost with Anwar. In the uncut version of the film, the audience is immersed with Anwar and lost with Anwar in this evolving, shifting nightmare and I think that turns the film, particularly maybe in the second half, into something that isn't even a documentary but truly a fever dream—not as metaphor but truly, it's like Anwar's fever dream. And I just want to say I love what you said about where it leaves him at the end because I had felt in the past that that ending, first of all, we're seeing what guilt does to a human body in a way that I'm not sure I've seen before, but also that by that point in the film, he's constructed through his relationship to Herman, through his relationship to the political interludes about elections, about corruption, about the paramilitary movement that punctuates the film, he's constructed by the end when he's retching as much more than an individual confronting his guilt but as a vessel for this whole society. So it takes us from the human body to this, as you put it, "degree zero" of what politics is about, insofar as politics is about collective decisions about who should hold the monopoly on violence and how that power should be executed.

And at the end of the day, violence has victims and has its toll on us. Once we're swept into this world, *The Act of Killing* is punctuated by these abrupt cuts to silence. These silences, these haunted landscapes, often derelict buildings with one figure in the middle, or a cityscape or a shopping mall with one figure kind of lost in a kind of haze—these are abrupt shifts in the perspective of the film: First of all, to the absent dead, who I hope haunt every frame of the film; and in the shopping mall to some serious moral questions about what was all of this for, what was it *really* for? And was it worth it, actually? Because we are immersed over the two hours and forty minutes in a culture that's saying this was worth it. And then if this is what it's for, that question is thrown to the audience and we're somehow implicated.

But there's a kind of visual language of those fixed landscape shots that punctate the director's cut of *The Act of Killing* that develops over the course of the film. They have a dramaturgy and that whole language, that whole idea of making the city a character but not filming it through conventional reportage, hand-held footage in the streets that you might see in most documentaries, particularly about a city in a country that you've never been to and know little about. That grammar evolved in response to one of the very first of those shots that I filmed with one of the very last that comes in the film which is this mysterious shot of an airplane crash in the middle of a street that comes near the end of the film, and there's lightning overhead and there are crowds of people snapping pictures on their smartphones of the wreckage. And that's the second to last of those tableaus, if you like. The final one is the very final shot in the uncut version of the film, and the sort of key, iconic image of the film: it's the fish with the dancing girls and the storm (Figure 7.6). So what begins initially as a kind of counterpoint to Anwar, as the world—as the space of the absent dead—grows as Anwar grows, from being an individual to being a kind of vessel for this whole society, they somehow merge. As the film becomes a kind of fever dream, those landscape shots develop into something that's indistinguishable from the internal nightmare of this regime and, therefore, of Anwar, because the regime and Anwar have merged. And so the final shot is from the realm of Anwar's fantasy, and it's the culmination of that line of tableaus that punctuates the whole film.

So there's even a shifting quality in the reality that punctuates *The Act of Killing* as a kind of counterpoint to the fiction. And in *The Look of Silence*, I had a sense—you said they were very different—but I had a sense that the two films should be precisely complementary, and that for *The Look of Silence*, I wanted the viewer to feel as though they entered any of those silent spaces that punctuate *The Act of Killing* and feel what it would be like to have to live there as a survivor, surrounded by the cacophony—the unstable cacophony of

FIGURE 7.6 Fantasy scene from *The Act of Killing*. Source: The Act of Killing, Carlos Arango de Montis and Joshua Oppenheimer.

the perpetrators. What is it like to have to rebuild a life in the ruin to which they have condemned you? And what is it like to have to spend your life there, and what does it do to a human body? Whereas *The Act of Killing*, at the end of every sequence there are these hard cuts to silences I have described, at the end of every sequence except in the end the tableaus and the fictional universe of Anwar starts to merge … In *The Look of Silence*, in the sequencing there are very few hard cuts because you are in that silent space almost the whole time except when we cut in and out of the boasting and the threatening of the perpetrators. So *The Look of Silence* is almost like the mirror image or the invert of *The Act of Killing*. *The Act of Killing* is this realm of fantasy that's interrupted by the silent spaces of the dead, and *The Look of Silence* is the silent space of the dead, occasionally punctuated by the boasting and threats of the perpetrators.

RS: So is it fair to say, then, that it's like moving from that zero point of politics, crossing a threshold to the second film, to the possibility of some moral hope, moral strength, moral courage, recreating the possibility of politics. Is that a fair statement?

JO: It's maybe a little more hopeful than I would say because when you talk about it this way, the two films are really one work, because I think in the first film—to go back to your last question about why it has this impact—in the first film, we hear an account of the atrocities from the perspective of the perpetrators. So first of all, unlike the fictions that you mentioned, it's undeniable. And we're hearing it from the very men that have been celebrated as heroes, who therefore should be enjoying their status as heroes in their old age, and you see even they—although they've escaped justice, they have not escaped punishment, and by the end of the film, because of the way Anwar is constructed as a kind of vessel for the whole society in the dramaturgy, in the editing of the film, when the moral lie collapses for Anwar, the moral lie for Indonesians watching the film, the whole society's or regime's moral lie also collapses. This is not to say that reality is a lie—the reality is *built* on that moral lie, so therefore it becomes visible for what it is. Then into the space opened by that, where now people cannot help but acknowledge that moral lie, into that space comes the second film. And you're absolutely right, that it shows that through Adi's dignified example, and I would also say in a smaller but also important way, especially for relatives of perpetrators who have seen the film in Indonesia, for the daughter who apologizes on behalf of her father, that it is a kind of model (Figure 7.7); but because Adi's project, which is the level of his own community, fails, it takes place in this overwhelming, sort of haunted space of silence and fear—because it fails, there's also this appeal about the possibility of politics, where we say, "Ok, this is the kind of discussion we *ought* to be able to have," and we can't, and Adi can't. And it fails. And so what do we now so it can succeed? So anyone seeing the film in Indonesia is forced almost to acknowledge this abyss of fear and guilt that divides people, but also forced to acknowledge this prison of fear—even if it's a prison of internalized self-censorship—that no longer feels particularly frightening, but manifests itself as apathy, because apathy is a way of coping with powerlessness. Be that as it may, it forces people to acknowledge that, so anyone seeing the film then has to support a struggle for some kind of truth,

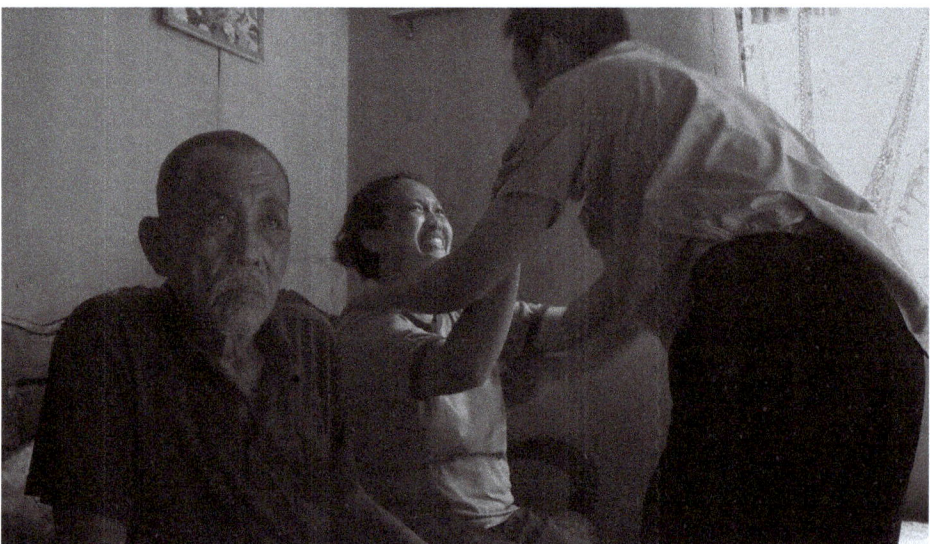

FIGURE 7.7 Daughter of perpetrator (in foreground) asks Adi for forgiveness in a scene from *The Look of Silence*. Source: The Look of Silence, Joshua Oppenheimer and Lars Skree.

        reconciliation, and some form of justice. So I would say, the possibility of politics is something the second film in particular issues into and takes one forward into the future.

DC: In *The Look of Silence* there are scenes in which Adi is in conversation with perpetrators who, as you say, are constructing their reality through narrative. But then what the films *shows* is something like a truth of the body, where there's a shudder of recognition, and then the person quickly rights himself back to his constructed reality. So you were talking with Richard about "Reality breaking through." Reality is always constructed through narrative. But it's as if there's this truth of the body that then comes back at certain moments and intervenes.

JO: I think that's right. I think both films catalyze, trigger, and document confrontations with the body. So through Anwar, I mean he's performing. I'm not saying at the end when he's retching, but I'm saying when Anwar's proposing a dramatization—and I use that word instead of reenactment, because "dramatization" is about the lies and the fantasies of the present, whereas reenactment would be somehow about illustrating the past, which is not what the film is engaged with at all. That's almost precisely the opposite of what the film is dealing with. Anyway, when Anwar is forced to not just envision a fantasy but then to embody it, and gradually over the course of the film, the fantasies, the lies, through this confrontation with his own performance—while watching it, but also his own *experience* of performing— mean that over the course of the film the lies, the fantasies, these personas no longer somehow protect him from his own guilt, which (and I spoke earlier about private morality) maybe that does, when there's no culture to justify it, maybe the last preserve of that private morality is in one's own body.

And I think in *The Look of Silence*, we're documenting also these confrontations because the perpetrators are forced to attempt to reassert the kind of justification of what they've done, that they were at ease with when confronting me years earlier, they're forced to assert it defensively in front of Adi and in front of his gentle but very steady gaze—and of course, when you're defending something, you're aware of the attack ... you're aware of the indictment, otherwise you don't need to defend, and being aware of the indictment opens a crack through which this manifestation of disgust, guilt, I think, becomes visible. When Adi proposed to me that he wanted to confront the perpetrators and *why*—that he thought somehow he would find peace with his neighbors and that would allow his family to live in peace—I thought that we would fail to get that, because I had spent five years working with Anwar and at the end of that process we never got to that. At the end of five years, we never got to a conscious, *verbal* acknowledgment of what he did was wrong, which is what Adi would need to be able to forgive. Even in the uncut version of *The Act of Killing*, when Anwar is retching he's still saying my conscience told me they had to be killed. So he's still trying to repeat the lie, it's just no longer protecting him from his own feelings ... I guess I intuited, being asked to take moral responsibility by Adi would open the kind of fissure in their performance, where the body would slip through and the guilt would slip through, and if I could film their reactions sensitively enough and precisely enough, I would be able to show the shame and the guilt ...

DC: In a previous interview which Richard and I read, you talk about this inevitable or inescapable gap between the narrative or mediated construction of the self and some more primary experience of the self. Jacques Lacan, for example, speaks about the mirror stage and that at a certain point we have a primary experience of reality but then, after that, our experience of ourselves is always mediated through narratives and images. I'm wondering about the way in which you use radical ruptures and the *affective* dimension of your films to point to that inescapable gap, and also perhaps to reorganize that relationship between an array of fantasy selves and some more primary experience (not only for perpetrators, but for all of us).

JO: Lacan is difficult enough to read that I don't feel confident in talking about these thoughts in terms of Lacan, but I do think that what we're talking about is related to what I said earlier about it's not that there's this stable reservoir of guilt and then there's a kind of sugar-coating. That's a very simple metaphor, but the truth is that there's this unspeakable primal kind of horror or mystery that fuels a kind of inevitable transmogrification of the myths and the representations and the performances that make us what we are. And I think the role of cinema, for me—and certainly what I try to do in my filmmaking—is to create these kinds of confrontations with that mystery ...

I know the word that Lacan would use here is "Real," but because I am so uncertain as to whether I'm using that term correctly I'll just say something erupts through the tissue of the images between the scenes, and of course that's why there's no narration, there's not my narrative of how I went through this, because that is very often about *containing* those ruptures ... and distracting one's attention from them. Because they're always there—even in the nightly news, they're there. Right? If one turns off the sound and just looks at the kind of strange ... It's there, it's just that we're being distracted from it. It's there always. It's there now. I mean ... the very fact that we exist, that there's something rather than nothing, this profound mystery ... Like what the hell is this? I spend all my days trying to think about that. Every time I walk to the movie theater, I'm sitting there ... I feel the great tragedy of my existence, because it also gives me my fear of death. The great tragedy of my existence is that I cannot feel that strange kind of almost electrically pulsing mystery of the presence of anything in front of my eyes all the time, and I'm trying to always get back to it.

RS: But that's the poetic genius of your work, because you *do* have access and you can make us experience it.

JO: Maybe when I'm editing ... because I was thinking about the experience of editing *The Look of Silence*, but also both my films, you know, instantly. People sometimes ask, "Couldn't you consider using a score, or couldn't you consider making the film this way, or couldn't you consider the film doing" I couldn't, because if I make a wrong turn in the editing, it feels like a knife in the stomach. It just, as you watch it, you go "No." I'm not saying there aren't moments when I become blind, and therefore I think that this doesn't work in the overall structure. But if I have a cut that's too easy, when that mystery should be all around us, it feels just simply wrong. I can't do it. I'm *incapable* of doing it. And I wonder whether this ability to find that mystery, if I succeed in that—and I take that as a compliment, but I'm not sure—I wonder if it has to do with the fact that these decisions are, as my mentor, Dusan Makavejev told me, they are like decisions of *all* your senses: your tastes, your feeling, your ears, your stomach, your smell ... I'm working in a space that's not about words.

RS: Okay, I'm going to nudge you a little bit on that one. Because you refer to editing, and you seem to give pride of position to *affect*, the gut reality that eludes articulation—it's a presence that you're molding. And yet, these editorial decisions have to be made. So what about the relationship between affect and narrative: which one controls? Listening to what you just said, it sounds as if affect is driving what feels right, and yet, we have a film, for example, in *The Act of Killing*, where Anwar's scene at the end plays a profound *narrative* role—you're narrating what comes as close as the film will come to a kind of moment of redemptive possibility, of acknowledgement, at least from the body, at least unconsciously ... But it's a narrative choice, isn't it? For us to read everything that went before as leading to that scene. That's a narrative choice, no?

JO: I think the question about the meaning of Anwar's scene at the end, or what it does for people narratively, is very much about the viewer. I think in the uncut *The Act of Killing*, that scene where Anwar butchers the teddy bear sort of places him in a space psychologically that's beyond repair. And we know it as we go into the final downward spiral. For me, I think at the end, a man totally destroyed, we see this degree zero of the human body in its relationship to politics and violence ... and it's the possibility of redemption therefore in a *precise* way, because it suggests that if all of us, or even Anwar, knows that this is wrong then surely we ought to construct a society where we practice empathy, we practice doubt, particularly vis-à-vis the stories told by authority, which would incite us to commit violence and therefore should be able to live a way where this kind of violence, which should be unthinkable, actually becomes unimaginable. And that, of course, taking up that project, questioning its possibilities in the context of impunity, is then, in a way, the political project of the second film, right? So, this is a kind of aside, because I think some people who have seen the shorter version of the film really expect redemption at the end and they therefore see, "Well Anwar is starting to be redeemed," and I would say that this is an image of a man destroyed, not redeemed.

But, leaving that aside, I think the question of narrative and affect in editing, at best in the experience of editing, go hand in hand: they're one thing. Because to feel the beautiful cut is to be at the place where you understand, and not just intellectually but in your body, in your sense of what it would be like to be in that space. You understand everything I, or my characters, understand by that point in the shooting.

So if you think that you're not telling a story to somebody but you're *translating* an experience of shooting and the first part of the editing, where you're also kind of working your way through the layers of material and meaning—you're still exploring, you're still excavating the meaning that you found in the shooting—if you think about that period where you're constructing the film as a kind of translation, a kind of physical, embodied knowledge, an insight that you develop while shooting the film, for somebody who has no knowledge of this place or this story, then what you are doing is trying to bring people who are just like you—you have to assume that they're just like you, you can't make films for others who are different. I mean you can, it's a journalistic documentary, but I can't, I have to assume my viewers everywhere in the world are just like me, and yet they know nothing of this situation—and then I have to bring them to a place where they're able to feel those things, otherwise the sequence motivated by affect won't feel right.

Now, I'm not entirely being honest if I say there's no tension between these two processes. I think that it's one of the reasons why I work with an editor. It's because I'm working with very experienced editors, and I think Niels Pagh Andersen is one of the great editors in the history of cinema, but I also think he's very experienced in the construction of narrative. He's done this dozen and dozens and dozens of times, whereas I've only done this twice. So what do I know? There is a kind of intellectual division of labor, artistic division of labor, where he's also looking out for that. But we're doing everything together—it's the interesting thing about our process: we're in the editing room from the first day to the last day of editing, all day together, and it's not because I'm monitoring him or I don't trust him. It's because we're doing something together that neither of us could do on our own. And it's a different thing from what we can do on our own. It's a kind of dance that we have. And editing *The Look of Silence* was very interesting because it was while we were still releasing *The Act of Killing* and we had just finished *The Act of Killing* and we already understood what it meant as a work. So we started editing *The Look of Silence* in the most strange way: we put down the first shot, then the second shot, then the third shot and we built the opening, and I don't think we changed a single frame in the opening. And that's not how you should normally edit a film—it's not how we edited *The Act of Killing* at all, but it was like we were dancing partners who really knew how to dance together at that point.

RS: I think people have this urgency to get narrative closure, and so you're fighting that, it seems to me, in what you're describing as a kind of false closure regarding the perception of Anwar's "redemption" at the end of *The Act of Killing*. And yet, at the same time, we need to feel as if we're being held in some kind of unified structure.

JO: I think you're right … I feel like the reason I do what I do is to explore some of the most basic mysteries of what it means to be human. I mean I said I'm sitting here trying to think about the strange mystery of the fact that any of this exists. When I get my driver's license renewed, I'm thinking, "Here I am, engaging with this enormous bureaucracy, thousands of strangers are working together on the basis of some multiple, interlocking fictions to get this piece of processed hydrocarbon with recognizably my image printed on it that will allow me to drive a car."

It's like [the German philosopher Arthur Schopenhauer's] "world as will and representation." When you think of the world as just pure will, everything becomes—every object, every process, every project—becomes a fiction. It's just pure flux and flow, and we are all part of the same thing. I'm trying to encounter this mystery, certainly in my daily life and in my film work, and then I'm trying to make that available for you and to immerse you in that, so I'm of course suspicious of any move in the editing and it feels false to me, it feels false to the whole motivation that led me to make the film if I make a move that feels like I'm explaining or closing. The sections of *The Look of Silence* that are most were difficult for me—and same in *The Act of Killing*—are the sections where I'm just setting things up so people can appreciate what comes next. Like there's a sequence where in *The Look of Silence* we're in the classroom, with the kid, Igbal, Adi's son is in class, and being taught propaganda. And Adi's telling him that this is a lie. I know it's a powerful moment for people, but it is also one of the most explanatory and clear moves that I make, and I do it because I need to get past that so we can start the film really. And so I have this skepticism—this almost physical revulsion—to closure.

But one way you can make the audience feel held, as you put it, and safe at least in terms of not lost, without giving them closure, and what Niels [Andersen] would call "overtelling," one way of doing that is to just make sure that the viewer as rarely as possible is behind you. It's great when the viewer is ahead, expecting something, hoping for something, so that they're awaiting every image with anticipation. And in non-fiction film it's almost unavoidable that there are moments when the viewer is behind because you don't have exactly the moment you need in a conversation to explain something. It's very rare that that's a good thing, that the viewer's behind. And in fiction, you'll know at once it's obnoxious when you're behind, as a strategy, because you feel like the filmmaker knows the story, the filmmaker can put whatever she wants here, so why doesn't she bring me? It's like a false suspense—what's going to happen next, what's going on? It's like, well, just tell me what's going on so I can actually read the situation because cinema is not about plot, it's about all of these embodied experiences.

RS: But, following up your reference to Schopenhauer [*The World As Will And Representation*], the trouble I have with that—like the trouble one might have with Buddhism without compassion or Deleuzian immanence without a moral vision—is that *you have a moral vision*. It isn't just one thing after another. When we experience your films, we are anchored in your moral vision. So the affective rupture isn't the thing in itself for you, right? The narrative has to orchestrate, or constellate, that rupture so that it's consistent with this gut sense of justice, the sense that something needs to be corrected here, no?

JO: You're right—about me, about my instincts. And maybe why I moved from philosophy as a kind of hobby—because it was never a major or a real field of study—but moved from that into filmmaking was I couldn't find a suitable metaphysical basis for the moral anguish that motivates all of my work. People say your work is angry.

DC: Angry?

JO: Yeah, that there's an anger to it, to me. And I think they're right that there's a kind of vision of something that's utterly corrupt, and I hope and I trust that if we would just recognize the kind of fundamental mystery that actually unites us, everybody would know that it's corrupt. I think you're right, there's a contradiction there. You're more learned in this than I, so if you can give me a little basis for why I …

RS: You have it. You have the vision that's orchestrating the affect. So that's another way of putting my question: *Who's in charge of the image?* Is the narrative organizing? You're answer, initially, was: "Well the affect is what's driving my gut." But this vision—something to do with justice—ought not to be underestimated, no?

JO: That's what I meant when I said there's this driving anger or outrage. Right? There's this kind of sense of …

RS: It's an ethically inflected aesthetic.

JO: It is … This is very interesting … I see cinema and the purpose of cinema, and the purpose of art in general perhaps, is holding up a mirror, where we confront aspects of ourselves that we recognize immediately as true, but we've been too afraid to talk about. And they can be difficult to talk about because they implicate us, we feel guilty if we think about them. The things we see in that mirror of art and cinema can be too frightening to talk about because we're actually threatened and intimidated into ignoring them. Could be because we feel powerless in the face of them and that's shameful. And it could also be that there's simply this enduring mystery about what we are that we encounter, that I have a feeling the purpose of cinema is to force, invite, control the audience into confronting some fundamental truth that viewers already know. They already know. It's the shock of the familiar, not the shock of the new.

Maybe journalism is the shock of the new, but I'm trying to provoke this show of the familiar, of the *uncanny* almost. But that moment of truth, I believe—and I don't have a philosophical argument for why this is so—but I believe that encounter with the truth has to embody a moral truth too. Otherwise, it's a moral lie. This is not an argument that cinema should always be serious and didactic. On the contrary, it implies that cinema must be entertaining, at least in the sense that it must be *absorbing*, because it has a run time, a duration, a beginning, a middle, and an end, and if you want to involve the viewer in looking in that mirror and contemplating what she is seeing in the mirror over the course of the runtime of the film, you have to absorb them. So this is not an argument against entertainment, it's an argument against escapism. There's a basic sense here that an escapist fantasy might be effective—it might be an effective story, but it's not a *good* story in the sense that it's a moral lie.

DC: It's interesting because when you talk about the way in which film intoxicates Anwar, and then they go and kill, it's almost like you're trying to absorb, then actually open and fragment rather than intoxicate, but you don't want to just leave the viewer cold, you want to absorb, but then not seduce …

RS: Perhaps that's the difference between spectacle and non-spectacle …

JO: Yeah, but implicit in my approach is the sense that the intoxication itself—Anwar's own intoxication with cinema, all the perpetrators and their own intoxication with their own fictions, fantasies, lies—that this *is* the reality of contemporary Indonesia. So one has to start by making a film about that intoxication, and for the viewer to understand that, they have to be drawn into feeling what it's like and to understanding its emotional currents, it's eddies and flows, that also lead to this kind of transmutation, from one fantasy, one lie into another that might contradict the previous, and to yet another … I mean there's an obvious contradiction between Anwar at the waterfall receiving a medal from his own victims, people he's killed, who are now in heaven, and Anwar butchering the teddy bear. These are contradictory fantasies, so there's no consistency. So the viewer needs to ride the rapids and see where it takes them from one fantasy to another. It's a kind of bumpy, crazy ride.

So I certainly don't want to just invite the viewer to enjoy and to be seduced by the spectacle of Anwar's fantasy, but at the same time, I could have approached the film from a much more Brechtian perspective and, for example, had Anwar—well I actually think Brecht, even though he would interrupt his fictions with these moments of alienation, I think that they were also seductive—but, for example, the waterfall scene could have been filmed like a cheap, Southeast Asian karaoke video where we would have a distance on it. We'd be sneering at Anwar. But as I said earlier, it was important for me that the viewer be absorbed by and drawn into the beauty and horror of Anwar's dramatizations, so that the waterfall scene is of course kitsch, but it is also hopefully, undeniably majestic, and the viewer has her breath taken by that.

DC: One thing that struck both of us about your films is that in *The Look of Silence* there's such empathy and such intimacy—and you'd expect that with a survivor—but it is there in *The Act of Killing* as well. It's almost love. And I just wanted you to reflect on the role that intimacy—and love—plays in the work that the films are doing in creating some possibility of justice, or rupture in the viewer.

JO: Well, for the whole project of both films having the viewer feel the physical consequences of guilt and the physical consequences of a politics built on fear and impunity, and in the second film, for the viewer to feel what does it do to human beings to have to live half a century in fear and silence—*we have to feel* with the people in the film.

So in *The Act of Killing* I'm inviting the viewer to become very intimate with Anwar through my intimacy with him, and because I don't believe we can understand human beings from a distance and I think the role of an artist, and the role certainly of a filmmaker, is not to be a court. Our job is not to assemble facts and lay out the details of crimes and then either condemn or exonerate. That's not our role, and in fact, I think often human rights documentaries unfortunately often create this illusion. That's something that unfortunately many human rights documentaries *do*: creating a false sense that we have dealt with this. Well that may be how a court may deal with it, as part of a mechanism of justice, but art and film should bring us to place of understanding. And that doesn't mean sympathy and that doesn't mean excuse—it means empathy. So I take as a starting point that if I have a man who killed a thousand people who were unarmed, not in the context of a war, that this is obviously wrong. And there is a kind of moral outrage and a distance at the same time as there's intimacy in the film.

In *The Act of Killing* with some distance—especially in the first two-thirds of the film—we watch with horror the evolving dramatization that Anwar and his friends are putting together. I take it for granted that my viewers will understand that what they've done forty-five years ago was wrong, and if they can't see that then there's something wrong with the viewer. But I take it also as axiomatic that if we want to have any hope and understanding of how human beings do this, but more importantly—because that's not really what *The Act of Killing* is about—how as human beings we live with the devastating guilt that comes with doing this to each other (and how in fact we *avoid* feeling that devastating guilt) and the terrible, distorting, corrupting consequences of that very human avoidance of guilt, motivated in part by the fact that every perpetrator is a human being and therefore is haunted by what they've done, just as you or I would be if we'd done that. If we want to understand that, and therefore have any chance of righting our moral compass so we can find the way of addressing these things, we need to feel that as a human experience—and that involves understanding, not in the sense of exculpation or excusing, but in the sense of feeling a true sense of empathy.

So through my closeness with Anwar, viewers are invited to get very close to him too, and empathize, not sympathize, but empathize. And, ultimately, for viewers inside Indonesia to ask very important questions about, "Okay, what is this society that we're all a part of?" And for viewers abroad to ask: "How are we all closer to perpetrators than we'd like to think?"

DC: And how are we complicit?

JO: Yes, exactly, that precisely, how we are complicit? And in *The Look of Silence*, there's a kind of paradox where one might expect that I would film ten—three, four five ten—families to show, so that the viewer could sort of understand and extract a general sense of what are the victims' and survivors' experiences of this genocide. But that of course would be an abstraction, and that would therefore be from a distance. And I realize that actually, no, my task is to make you feel like you are Adi, or your brother is Adi, and Adi's parents are your parents, your grandparents, Adi's children are your children, and what would it be like to be this family?

So, paradoxically, by going very, very close, and by honing in almost microscopically on one family, I hope the film becomes much bigger and universal, because it becomes about all of us. So in that sense, I think this principle of empathy and intimacy and indeed love, because I love Anwar—it's a complicated kind of love, of course, and I think Anwar actually loves me, and it's a complicated kind of love—but this principle of empathy and intimacy and even love is what makes these two films not a kind of journalistic window onto a far-off country that people knew nothing about before they saw it. And I'm quite sure if that's what the films were, no one would care. People would see them and they'd say, "That's terrible what happened there, I didn't know about that. But, of course, there's also ISIS, and there was a virtual world war in the Congo just ten years ago. Why should we care about this *now*?" That intimacy, that love, that closeness is what makes these films not windows onto a far off place, but *mirrors* in which we see ourselves.

RS: So when modeling this relationship that's so palpable in both films, this intimacy, this love, is it fair to say that that's maybe part of the vision of justice that we talked about earlier?

JO: Yes, I think so. That's a beautifully made point. I haven't said that or thought that before. But certainly, if every perpetrator of every act of evil in our history has been a human being like us—and I'm reminded of Primo Levi's wonderful comment that there may be monsters among us, but there are too few to worry about[4]—if every perpetrator in our history is a human being like us, at first that's a terrifying thought because it means, well then maybe we could be those, we could do that too. And while all of us would hope that if we grew up in Anwar Congo's family in 1950s Indonesia, that come 1965, we would make different decisions, we all know that we are extremely lucky never to have to find out.

So at first it's a terrifying truth that every perpetrator is human, but it's also the *only* hopeful understanding of political evil. It's the only hopeful poise through which we can view these kinds of events. Because if there are just bad guys among us, which is unfortunately the story that almost all of our media tells us again and again and again, what our politicians tell us—it was the folly of the Blair years in Britain, for example, and certainly the Bush years in the US, to divide the world, to put good guys against bad guys—forget Blair and Bush, it's been the folly of our politics forever. It's the fundamental escapist fantasy that serves mainly to exculpate ourselves. But if that's the case, if that were true, then all we could do is identify the bad guys, neutralize them, by either imprisoning them or killing them or somehow fundamentally disempowering them and monitoring them. And then we of course start doing exactly the same thing that those bad guys are supposed to have done.

The hopeful response, to answer your question, I mean the only hopeful understanding, is that everybody who has ever done this is human and, therefore, we ought to be able to come up with ways of living together where we empathize with each other more deeply. And maybe yes, the empathy through which I try to make my films can be a kind of model, or a hint at that for viewers, that we can empathize with each other more deeply, that we can practice the widest possible human empathy, which is the only way to achieve the widest possible human dignity. And also—and I think these two things are slightly distinct—encourage a collective discussion that fosters the questioning of authority. Our education systems everywhere in the world, to differing degrees, are about teaching our children to respect authority and not to think. But actually that's dangerous. We ought to be teaching our children to question everything that we're taught.

EPILOGUE

Our conversation ended there, and we exchanged farewells. Having moved toward the door of the cafe, Joshua suddenly turned around and walked back to say this:

JO: And if you have thoughts about where comes our morality, I would love to know.

RS: I think you told us. It's in the relationship. This is an ethical phenomenology, as we see in [French philosopher Emmanuel] Levinas's work (Levinas 1969, 1989): "Your face is my responsibility."

JO: So it's our mutual connectedness.

RS: Yes.

With a smile, Joshua nodded, turned, and walked back into "the strange, almost electrically pulsing mystery" of the present.

CHAPTER EIGHT

Legal Profession

Beaten Black and Blue—Lessons from Watching the Rodney King Case

CHRISTIAN DELAGE

On February 26, 2012, Trayvon Martin, a seventeen-year-old unarmed African-American walking through a gated community in Sanford, Florida, was fatally shot by a neighborhood watch volunteer who found his behavior suspicious. The police detained and questioned the gunman, George Zimmerman, but released him without charges. Trayvon's parents considered the shooting a racist act that the police refused to acknowledge as such. Their campaign to have Zimmerman brought to justice gathered enough steam to have him charged with second-degree murder on April 11. The trial started a year later in Sanford and ended on July 13, 2013, with the jury finding Zimmerman not guilty, accepting his claim that he was acting in self-defense. In Florida and many other states, "stand-your-ground" laws authorize people to use force to defend themselves against real or perceived threats.[1] The acquittal sparked a public outcry that was widely covered in the media. Without commenting on the jury's decision, President Obama made a very explicit statement on racism past and present in the United States:

> You know, when Trayvon Martin was first shot I said that this could have been my son. Another way of saying that is Trayvon Martin could have been me thirty-five years ago. And when you think about why, in the African-American community at least, there's a lot of pain around what happened here, I think it's important to recognize that the African-American community is looking at this issue through a set of experiences and a history that doesn't go away. ("Remarks by the President on Trayvon Martin," The White House, James S. Brady Press Briefing Room, July 19, 2013.)

It did not take long for that history to repeat itself. On August 9, 2014, Michael Brown, an eighteen-year-old African-American, was fatally shot by Darren Wilson, a white police officer, in Ferguson, Missouri. Three months later, a St. Louis County grand jury decided not to indict Wilson. Then came the deaths of Kajieme Powell, Ezell Ford, John Crawford III, and Eric Garner. All were killed by police officers.

In most of the cases, images were filmed by surveillance cameras (John Crawford III) or cellphones showing the shooting itself (Kajieme Powell) or the immediate aftermath (Trayvon Martin's uncle walking up to his nephew's bloody body and being pushed away by a police officer as the witness's growing anger can be heard in the background). These images—which had gone viral on social networks and been regularly featured on network television—left viewers aghast at the fatal chain of events. Nevertheless, the images have not modified the course of justice.

It is often said that we are now living in a society dominated by the instant dissemination and immediate power of images. But in fact, like other documentary sources or incriminating evidence that historians or judges use, pictures often acquire meaning based on a process of comparison with other documents in an effort to establish the truth. This raises important questions, such as what evidentiary parameters will regulate the parties' use of such images in court, and after analyzing the video's content, can the court exercise adequate control over its effects on viewers (i.e., members of the jury)? Moreover, if police departments mandate body-worn cameras, would such routine visual monitoring of a police officer's behavior in the performance of his duties help to change his ingrained perception that African-Americans are (more than others) a potential threat to his and the community's safety? That perception should be countered by standard police operating procedures, but such systems of control and monitoring currently appear to be inadequate.

To give this tragic chain of events some historical background, thereby questioning a picture's ability to provide decisive objective proof, it would be helpful to look back at the first major case in which video evidence, and visual jurisprudence more generally, was crucial in determining the outcome.[2]

If ever a court case shook up the American legal system, it was the 1992 state criminal trial of the four Los Angeles police officers serendipitously captured on videotape in the act of ferociously beating an African-American motorist named Rodney King. The officers' initial acquittal triggered unprecedented social and political upheaval, first in Los Angeles, where some of the most violent riots ever seen in the United States erupted, then across the nation, provoking direct presidential commentary on the case. Indeed, if the violent arrest of a speeding motorist upgraded a local news item to global status, this was due to the unprecedented media exposure of events surrounding his arrest. The notoriety of this case highlights not only serious ethical lapses in the Los Angeles Police Department (LAPD) practices, but also the jarring impact of new visual technologies operating within the legal system. Indeed, the violence inflicted on King acted as the catalyst precisely because it was but one chapter in an ongoing history of racial animus against African-American citizens, only this time it could not be concealed beneath internal investigations and invalidation of African-American's testimony.

By 2016, at the time this chapter was written, the combination of persistent and systematic police violence against African-Americans, with its now regular exposure through mobile phone technology, had reached an apex in the "Black Lives Matter" campaign (Keeanga-Yamahtta 2016), born of frustration that even apparently incontrovertible evidence of abuse was not sufficient to ensure that the legal system protected the rights of black Americans.

What the King case made plain was the difficulty that the law had adjusting to this new technological environment in its search for truth and justice inside the courtroom and in society at large. When lawyers and judges are not familiar with the polysemy of the image, the truth-testing process of adversarial justice can find itself in great difficulty. This is what the public saw in the criminal case against the officers who beat Rodney King. The trial depended a lot on visual evidence. Certainly for the prosecutor, who repeatedly told the jurors in his summation, "You have the videotape. Watch it, ladies and gentlemen. What more do we need?" And watch it they did. But did each member of the jury see the same things? And how did the efforts of the defense to cast them as spectators in a very particular kind of drama shape their understandings?

THE ROUTINE

At first glance, the description of a car traveling too fast at night on one of the urban Los Angeles freeways was nothing but routine for Tim and Melanie Singer, two officers of the California Highway Patrol (CHP). The fact that the driver failed to stop when summoned, while also not unusual, aggravated the offense. On the evening of March 3, 1991, Rodney King was driving, without a specific destination, on Interstate 210 (the Foothill Freeway) in the San Fernando Valley of Los Angeles. He was travelling west, with two friends, Bryant Allen and Freddie Helms, after having watched a baseball game together on television. "After ten, eleven PM in LA," he would recount later:

> the highways are usually more open, and the flow of traffic easily gets into the high seventies to eighties. Trouble is, after a few miles at that speed, ninety starts to feel like eighty, and I must have been in the passing lane where cars hit those speeds pretty easily. All of sudden, a California Highway Patrol (CHP) officer, Melanie Singer, started chasing me because she said she clocked me going 115 mph on the Foothill Freeway and 80 mph on city Streets. Singer wasn't the only one after me. The L.A. police were on my tail too. (King 2012)

The chase lasted a good fifteen minutes, and King was eventually blocked by a truck that forced him to stop the vehicle.

King's initial failure upon being stopped by police to comply with their command to get out of his car and lie prone on the pavement may have been understandable. King knew that a new criminal charge would put him back in prison for violating parole for a grocery robbery in Monterey Park two years earlier, for which he had served a one-year prison sentence. Unemployed, he was scheduled to show up the following Monday at a labor office. The LAPD, however, was unaware of these circumstances at the time of his arrest for speeding.

Allen and Helms immediately obeyed the officers' orders to get out of the car and lie down on their bellies, but King was slower and acting erratically. Surprised by his unusual behavior, and fearing he might have a weapon, Melanie Singer approached him with her gun drawn. At that point, Sergeant Koon stepped in between them and tasered King twice, sending 100,000 volts of electricity through his body each time.[3]

An independent investigating commission described the arrest's aftermath in a report written four months later, but before the first judicial investigation:

> King is on the ground. He rose and moved toward Powell. Solano termed it a "lunge," and said it was in the direction of Koon. It is not possible to tell from the videotape if King's movement is intended as an attack or simply an effort to get away. Taser wires can be seen coming from King's body. As King moved forward, Powell struck King with his baton. The blow hit King several additional times with his baton. The videotape shows Briseno moving in to try to stop Powell from swinging, and Powell then backing up. Koon reportedly yelled "that's enough." King then rose to his knees; Powell and Wind continued to hit King with their batons while he was on the ground. King was struck again and again, [and] apparently continued to try to get

up … Finally, after fifty-six baton blows and six kicks, five or six officers swarmed in and placed King in both handcuffs and cordcuffs restraining his arms and legs. King was dragged on his stomach to the side of the road to await arrival of a rescue ambulance.[4]

The investigators were referring to a video showing in detail the blows King received. An apartment building stands just opposite the parking lot where his car had been pulled over. Wanting to see what all the commotion was about, a resident, George Holliday, had stepped out onto his balcony. Seeing what was happening a bit farther away, Holliday went back inside to get a Sony Handycam camera he had just received as a gift and started filming the scene shortly after the arrest began. Sony amateur video cameras were considered the best in the world at the time. The electronics company had started selling them to the general public at affordable prices in the mid-1980s. For the first time, the audiovisual recording of brutality at the hands of the LAPD might qualify as apparently irrefutable evidence in a court of law.

Did the police officers subduing King abide by the rules they were supposed to follow in such a situation, that is, when they consider a suspect's behavior threatening during a traffic stop? In fact, there was a pattern of LAPD mistreatment of African-Americans. Representatives of California's African-American and Latino community organizations denounced it on a regular basis, but the police hierarchy never condemned or publicly called for an end to the use of unreasonable force. In some cases, ordinary, habitual, almost internalized racism seems to be a normal part of routine freeway stops.[5]

Police indifference is obvious in the conversations recorded between Officers Koon and Powell and the watch commander on the night of March 3, 1991:

12:56 a.m.	From Sgt. Stacy C. Koon to Foothill watch commander's office: "…*You just had a big time use of force … tased and beat the suspect of CHP pursuit, Big Time.*"
12:57 a.m.	From watch commander's office to Koon: "*Oh well … I'm sure the lizard didn't deserve it … Ha, ha. I'll let them know O.K.*"
1:11 a.m.	From Koon to watch commander's office: " *… I'm gonna drop by the station for a fresh taser and darts … please have desk have one ready.*'
1:11 a.m.	From watch commander's office to Koon: "*Okey doke on the ACC desk … You want extra darts??? It's got two.*"
1:12 a.m.	From Powell and Wind to the foot patrol officer: "*… ooops.*"
1:12 a.m.	From the foot patrol to Powell and Wind: "*oops, what?*"
1:13 a.m.	From Powell and Wind to the foot patrol: "*I haven't beaten anyone this bad in a long time.*"
1:15 a.m.	From the foot patrol to Powell and Winds: "*Oh not again … Why for you do that … I thought you agreed to chill out for awhile ….What did he do?*"
1:16 a.m.	From Powell and Wind to the foot patrol: "*I think he was Dusted … many broken bones later … After the pursuit …*"
1:17 a.m.	From the foot patrol to Powell and Wind: "*What pursuit?*" (Linder 2001)

Police brutality seems to have been discussed internally: the watch commander complains that Powell and Winds are at it again after promising to "chill." They refer to the individual stopped as a "lizard," and to their encounter with him as a scene out of *Gorillas in the Mist* (1988), reflecting a form of dehumanization deeply rooted in American racism. At the same time, the exchange attests to a kind of tacit permission or consent from the upper ranks, so much is the violence cloaked in the ordinary daily routine of a traffic stop.

What do the rules say about these circumstances? The LAPD's Use of Force Policy provides that: "While the use of reasonable physical force may be necessary in situations which cannot be otherwise controlled, force may not be resorted to unless other reasonable alternatives have been exhausted or would clearly be ineffective under the particular circumstances. Officers are permitted to use whatever force that is reasonable and necessary to protect others or themselves from bodily harm."[6]

For the investigating commission, there is no doubt: Holliday's video helped not only to reconstruct King's arrest, but also to focus attention on the need to better control police behavior: "The videotaped beating of Rodney G. King ... galvanized public demand for evaluation and reform of police procedure involving the use of force."[7]

PROOF BY THE IMAGE

A famous precedent occurred in 1963, when Dallas clothing manufacturer Abraham Zapruder filmed President Kennedy's motorcade driving through Dealey Plaza with his 8mm camera (Motyl 1998; Zavada 1998). The legal and media impact of this 26.7-seconds-long footage documenting Kennedy's assassination is well known. Less well known, though of great interest when comparing it to Holliday's video, is that the first public use of Zapruder's footage, which had already been viewed by the Secret Service, the FBI, and the White House, consisted of several black and white frames published by *Life* magazine and, later, *Time*.[8] From the beginning of its investigation, the Warren Commission deemed the original positive print of the Zapruder film to be of the best possible quality, but also requested a reenactment not of the murder itself, but of its filming with Zapruder's camera on Dealey Plaza. The goal was to check the filming conditions to ensure they were adequate, which was unnecessary in the King case, as Holliday was in his apartment.[9]

There are nonetheless three notable differences. On the one hand, Zapruder's Bell & Howell camera left him little time for filming. On the other, he had prepared for the film and chosen the location: a turn at a right angle. Zapruder recorded the assassination because he was well, though unexpectedly, positioned. But he could not be sure of what he had recorded until after the film was developed. In contrast, Holliday's video camcorder could run for several minutes and the images it recorded could be viewed immediately afterwards. (Of course, the protagonists were unaware of being filmed and behaved as if no third party were present.) However, Holliday lacked experience in filming and mishandled the camera: the zoom increases distant vibrations, while the site, though lit by the helicopters' spotlights, is left in semi-darkness. So, because the video does not record the full event, and because the brightness is low, the images are hard to make out.

After the police refused to take the videotape into consideration, the day after King's arrest Holliday brought it to local television station KTLA, which gave it to the LAPD—and broadcast it on the evening news. Had it only been seen locally, its impact, though already considerable, would have been limited. However, a news network that had just significantly boosted its ratings with live coverage of the first Gulf War immediately picked up this particular local news item. (This ultimately lends the news credibility never garnered thus far.) In turn, Cable News Network (CNN) got hold of the video and broadcast it non-stop as "Breaking News". On March 6, additional networks followed suit, prompting LAPD Police Chief Daryl Gates to announce that the officers involved could be criminally prosecuted for their assault upon King. On March 11, after the tape was viewed together with other evidence that had already been collected, a grand jury indicted the four police officers.

FROM INVESTIGATION TO TRIAL

While Daryl Gates was dragging his feet on conducting an investigation, and the judicial process was ongoing, Los Angeles Mayor Tom Bradley set up a commission. Chaired by Senator Warren Christopher, its task was to impartially and exhaustively examine the LAPD's structure and operations, including recruitment, management, training practices, internal discipline, and police responsiveness to citizen complaints. In a compilation of messages that police officers exchanged during 182 days from November 1989 to March 1991, the commission found hundreds of them about beatings of African-Americans, such as this one: "Capture him, beat him and treat him like dirt ... "[10] It also cited an LAPD survey of 960 officers showing that nearly 25 percent of them agreed that "Racial bias (prejudice) on the part of officers toward minority citizens currently exists and contributes to a negative interaction between police and community"[11] In the King case, not all the police officers on the scene beat him, but nor did they intervene to prevent their colleagues from doing so.[12]

The trial, then in a preparatory stage, was delayed due to a decision to move it to Simi Valley, which is in a predominantly white conservative county, ensuring that the jury would have a similar make-up. The primary reason given for the decision was that the videotape might cause unrest in the court of public opinion, and therefore among the jurors.

"In that decision," Louis-Georges Schwartz wrote, "Judges Klein, Danielson, Crowsley, and Heinz of California's Second District Court of Appeals use a prophetic figure of speech when they wrote that after the tape was broadcast 'a firestorm immediately developed in the Los Angeles area, so intense and pervasive was the reaction to the videotape'" (*Powell v. Superior Court*) (Schwartz 2009). So the idea that the media capitalized on the video's emotional power is what seems to have bothered the judges most. They probably, and rightly, feared the graphic power of moving images screened in the courtroom, a situation Fritz Lang showed in his 1936 film *Fury* [13]

The hearings started in early March 1992.[14] The prosecutor, Terry White, an African-American, made the Holliday videotape the crux of his opening statement, showing it in full. With scant precedent, a jury now faced the communication impact of evidence in the form of a video in an introductory and powerful way. Is it harder to form an opinion based on the cross-examination of witnesses, or on moving images? The prosecution seemed to give the footage great prominence, but the defense would not be outdone. The parsing of images was often interrupted and frozen on still frames. Similarly to what is done for statements and other documents presented as evidence, the images were cross-examined, providing valuable material for radically different interpretations.

The event narrative then returned to King's behavior when he was stopped. He did not testify at the four LAPD officers' trial. That prevented his cross-examination by the defense, which could dwell on his criminal record or his blood-alcohol level at the time of the events. Nevertheless, it seemed necessary to clarify King's first reaction. In this context, Melanie Singer's testimony was particularly important to the prosecution. Prosecutor White was well aware of the fact that, having asked King to get out of the car, turn around and put his hands on the roof, Singer could neither see his eyes nor anticipate his actions. King only partially obeyed the order: he appeared to be saying something to the officers, waving at the helicopter flying overhead and smiling. Singer testified that her partner ordered him to lie prone on the ground and put his hands where he could see them. At this point in Singer's narrative of events, Officer Powell apparently stepped in:

> SINGER: Officer Powell came up to the right of him and in a matter of seconds, he took out his baton, he had it in a power swing, and he struck the driver across the top of his cheekbone, splitting the face from the top of his ear to his chin.
> WHITE: Prior to Officer Powell hitting him with a baton, did anyone give the driver any type of commands after this second Taser shot that you described?
> SINGER: No, sir.
> WHITE: Was there any reason for the strike to the head by Officer Powell at the time he struck him?
> SINGER: In my opinion, no sir, there was no reason for it. (Linder 2001)

Referring to testimony already given by Melanie Singer before the trial, Michael Stone, Officer Powell's attorney, considered her assessment of the situation unchanged. He then

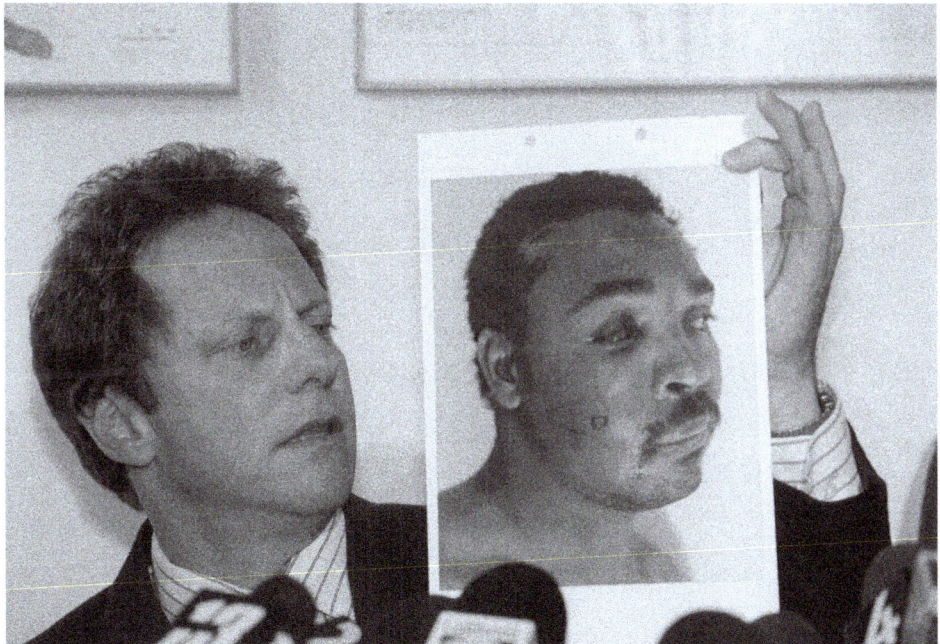

FIGURE 8.1 Rodney King, photo taken three days after his March 3, 1991 videotaped beating, one of three introduced into evidence by the prosecution in the trial of four LAPD officers in Simi Valley, Calif. Source: Nick Ut/© Associated Press, 1991.

tried to destabilize her testimony by resorting to a photograph of Rodney King taken at the hospital just after his arrest (Figure 8.1):

> MICHAEL STONE: Well, you described in your earlier testimony, and you just reiterated, the skin was split from the ear to the chin, was that right?
> SINGER: Yes.
> STONE: Does that [pointing to a hospital photo of King's face] appear to be sutured in that photograph?
> SINGER: Pardon me sir? No, sir.
> STONE: Does that appear to be split in that photograph?
> SINGER: No, sir.
> STONE: Do you have any explanation for that?
> SINGER: I saw what I saw, sir. (Linder 2001)[15]

Interestingly, Melanie Singer did not discuss the photograph, giving an opposite view of the facts to Stone's interpretation, as if responding to its "objectivity" with her own subjectivity in the performance of her duties ("I saw what I saw"). Stone's tactic might have paid off later on in the hearings if a discrepancy could have been created between the protagonists' perception of events at the time and how the scene was documented by the image. Even if one key prosecution witness opened up the possibility of such a distortion, it would have paved the way for the defense to cast doubt on Holliday's video.

A further, more classic difficulty compounded the first: when weighed against the LAPD officers' symbolic authority vis-à-vis a popular jury, a witness's performance needs to be convincing, starting with body language and oral expression. And it could hardly be said that the first of the two passengers called to testify impressed anyone either with his eloquence or his appearance:

> WHITE: How long had you known Mr. King?
> ALLEN: Know King about all my youth's [sic] life.
> JUDGE WEISBURG: How long?
> ALLEN: my youth's life, about 12 ... years.
> JUDGE WEISBURG: Could you speak up a little, move a little closer to the microphone.
> WHITE: And on the evening of March 2, 1991 did you see Mr. King?
> ALLEN: Say that again.
> WHITE: Alright, on the evening of March 2, 1991, did you and Mr. King get together?
> ALLEN: Say March 1991? March 3rd, 1991, yeah ... (Linder 2001)

THE CONFLICTING USES OF VIDEO AS EVIDENCE

While preparing for the Nuremberg trial, Telford Taylor, Counsel for the Prosecution, wrote a memo to the attention of Attorney General Robert H. Jackson on the question of testimony: for the first time, at this level at least, images were to be shown as evidence against the defendants:

> To be sure, the testimony of a witness is subject to attack, but so is the testimony of a document. A document cannot talk, and therefore cannot be cross-examined, but it can, of course, be attacked other ways—it can be explained away or contradicted by witnesses, by other documents, or by any other kind of evidence. (Taylor 1945)

That is just what happened in Simi Valley, when, surprisingly, counsel for the police officers decided to use the Holliday video to illustrate and supplement the main defense narrative that their clients were to set in motion on direct examination. Prosecutor White showed the video in full and without interruptions. The defense chose to proceed by showing excerpts, mostly freeze frames. While reading segments of a document seems to be a legitimate procedure that does not alter the document itself, the same does not hold true for a movie. Indeed, in American jurisprudence, photographs are often considered potential evidence. The moving image is resorted to at a later stage and, most importantly, if and only if the photograph is insufficient, and motion brings about specific elements to the understanding of the fact under judgment.[16] It is then that the moving image, not a frozen still frame, ought to be taken into account. Incidentally, the image in question was in fact frozen and not fixed, as it was actually a 1/30th segment, i.e., generally a subliminal image, which, for example, in terms of copyright, has no clear legal status.[17]

Nonetheless, right from the start, defendant Stacey Koon's attorney, Darryl Mounger, emphasized the officers' perception of King's physical appearance and body language by resorting to video evidence (Figure 8.2). His first aim was to clarify a number of words the police officers used in their verbal exchange with King. Koon was asked to explain what he meant by "buffed out" when describing King: "Buffed out is jargon that I have come to associate with very muscular, in other words an individual that is very pumped up as far as muscles ... My initial response is that he is probably an ex-con." He was then asked to explain the expression "Thrown off" ("The next thing I saw was Officer Powell is thrown off of Mr. King and Officer Briseno is struggling to get away."). He replied:

> Mr. King's left arm was behind him and Officer Powell was on his back and Officer Briseno was trying to force the arm up to meet so the wrist would match behind the cuff and all of a sudden Mr. King's arm just came out from him and they swayed to the left and swayed to the right and Officer Powell was thrown off and Office Briseno kinda of landed on his behind. I ordered them to back off and then I tased the suspect, Mr. King. (Linder 2001)

The defense attorney's goal was tactical: police officers knew exactly how to interpret King's behavior and reacted according to the procedure. They are professionals, while the jury is not familiar with their language and standards of operation. Slowing things down and breaking up the flow of images into stills allows ordinary lay people, like jurors, to see what the police have been trained to do. However, Koon's words then took a slightly different turn. He stated that King let out a kind of roar leaving them perplexed about his attitude and, at any rate, suggesting that force should be used. It is precisely then, as the animal metaphor is not too far from the deliberately racist one mentioned in the exchange at the police station, that Koon's lawyer put the videotape on, as if to illustrate his client's words, allowing him to make his point again:

> WITNESS KOON: He repeated this ah this ah groan similar to like a wounded animal and then he ah I could see the vibrations on him but he seem to be overcoming it ... This time I thought the suspect was under the influence of PCP. PCP is a dangerous drug, it's a kinda like a policeman's nightmare that the individual that's under this is super strong ah they have more or less a one track mind they exhibit super strength, they equate it with a monster is what they equate it with ...

FIGURE 8.2 An attorney points to still copies of a video of the Rodney King beating as the video is displayed on television monitor in a Simi Valley courtroom. Source: © Joe Kennedy/*Los Angeles Times*, 1992.

> MOUNGER: You see the officers [on the videotape, being shown in the courtroom] giving a torrent of blows to his body.
> WITNESS KOON: Yes, to his arms, to his torso, to his legs ... This was a managed and controlled use of force. It followed the policy and procedures of the Los Angeles Police Department and the training. (Linder 2001)

Thus, the Defense attorney slowly advanced in his demonstration, using the video as if it were based on King's arrest report. Still, Mounger was well aware of the fact that the images showed a continuously exerted violence, and that this could only impress the jury, stamping it more firmly on their memories than the police officers' explanations. He then decided to question Koon on these images:

> MOUNGER: How do you view looking at this videotape sir?
> DEFENSE ATTORNEY: Objection, irrelevant.
> JUDGE WEISBURG: Overruled, you can answer the question.
> WITNESS KOON: It's violent and it's brutal.
> MOUNGER: Was this anything that you enjoyed?
> WITNESS KOON: No.
> MOUNGER: Why was it done?
> WITNESS KOON: It was done to control an aggressive combative suspect and sometimes police work is brutal. That's just a fact of life. (Linder 2001)

Officer Powell gave another statement during the trial: "I was completely in fear for my life, scared to death."[18] But the most interesting thing is how Koon reacted to his own image. Commenting on the video at the same time as it was being shown in fragments, he became a distanced viewer of his own action: he conceded it was violent, but said he did not enjoy it and acted out of duty. The video helped him react differently compared to the time of the beating, to convince himself that he had acted reasonably, which was not the case. It played in his favor, and the defense could repeat the process with other witnesses called to the stand. For example, Charles L. Duke, the expert chosen by the officers' attorney, feigned skepticism about the video's veracity before concluding that it failed to demonstrate the defendants' guilt:

> PROSECUTOR TERRY WHITE: Sgt. Duke when you first saw this videotape you were shocked by what you saw, weren't you?
> WITNESS DUKE: I wasn't shocked, no.
> PROSECUTOR WHITE: Um … when you first saw this videotape did you believe that ah … it possibly contained excessive force by these officers?
> WITNESS DUKE: I never form an opinion until I get all the facts.
> PROSECUTOR WHITE: Sgt. Duke, when you first looked at this videotape did you possibly believe that it contained excessive force? Yes or no.
> WITNESS DUKE: I'd have to say no. (Linder 2001)

Generally speaking, the video was mainly used to investigate whether King's apparent behavior or the potential risk he might represent warranted the blows against him. Under those circumstances, the focus is not so much on police brutality per se, but on the time-course of the arrest, and the second-by-second segmentation of the facts the moving picture affords. As Telford Taylor correctly anticipated, the video became a bone of contention between the parties, whose interpretations conflicted. Towards the end of the trial, Chief Prosecutor White feared that the police officers might have turned the video to their advantage by superimposing their biased commentary on its obvious meaning. Chafing at their denials, he attempted to make the video sufficient evidence of their abuses, iron-clad evidence that would be superior to all the various arguments, capable of absolutely prevailing on a third party beyond the shadow of a doubt.

> PROSECUTOR WHITE: You are the impartial judges of the facts in this case. And just as the judge is the judge of the law, you are the judges of the fact. And as judges you should remain impartial and not be an advocate for one side or the other. It is your job to call the evidence as you see it, to decide the case on the evidence and let the chips fall where they may no matter where they may fall.
>
> This videotape is the central piece of evidence in this case. We don't need to rely on Stacy Koon's words. We don't need to rely on Lawrence Powell's words. We don't need to rely on what they say happen that night. We don't need to rely on what Mr. King says that night. We have the videotape and the videotape shows conclusively what occurred that night and it's something that can't be rebutted. It's there for everyone to see. It is the most objective piece of evidence you can have. You have to determine what a reasonable person, acting as a police office, would have done in this particular situation. (Linder 2001).

There is no doubt in the prosecutor's mind: Powell's brutality was unnecessary, unreasonable and continued even as King was on the ground "not doing anything." Koon was responsible for his orders, and his guilt lay first and foremost at this level.[19] Then he personally used the taser and delivered a baton blow. So did Wind. As for Briseno, even if he only dealt one blow, he was also guilty.[20] At this point, Prosecutor White, once again addressing the jury, said this about the video:

PROSECUTOR WHITE: … The thing you have to look at is at the point and time where Officer Briseno delivers this stomp to Mr. King. What is Mr. King doing at that p.oint in time? We want you to look at this entire video. We want you to do what the defense doesn't want you to do. They don't want you to look at this entire video …

I issue a challenge to Mr. Stone, to Mr. Depasquel, to Mr. Mounger, to play this videotape for you and to point out things in this tape that justify the continued use of the baton. I don't think they'll do it. I think they are going to get their little frames out. They're gonna to show 3:23:14. They're going to show you 3:24:27. They're gonna show you a frame here; they're gonna show you a frame there. They're not gonna show you the entire videotape. They probably won't even play the entire videotape for you. Cause they are afraid of the videotape. They're afraid because they know what that videotape shows … You don't need to be an expert to look at that video and say that is wrong. That is bad. That is criminal. (Linder 2001)[21]

Did White believe the video would speak for itself and that there was no need to justify its scope? According to Richard Sherwin, there is no doubt: "The prosecution … never challenged and perhaps never even realized how the defense narrative had captured and altered what the video images showed" (Sherwin 2011). In fact, if the prosecutor's assessment of the video was quite positivist, it was mainly because, for him, the document was part of a whole. There is a history of police brutality against African-Americans, and the Holliday video reveals—at last—what had not been recorded and shown until then.

BETWEEN EVIDENCE AND TESTIMONY

In a conversation with Bernard Stiegler, taking the example of the video showing police brutality against King, Jacques Derrida proposed the following line of reasoning:

In any case, the law did not consider the video to be a *testimony*, in the strict and traditional sense of the term. It was an exhibit to be interpreted, but the testimony could only be that of the cameraman, this young man who had the camera and who came to the witness stand, saying aloud after he had stated his name and speaking, without representative, in the first person: "I swear to tell the truth." He then testified (at least, he was supposed to have) to what he in good faith thought he saw, *himself*—a camera, an impersonal technical device, being unable to serve as a witness … (Derrida 2002).

Derrida's point is interesting in that it combines two concerns that are in fact distinct. The first, of a strictly legal nature, aims to ensure the authenticity of the document handed to the judges with a view to its being presented at the hearing and its possible qualification as evidence. The jurisprudence shows that this capacity is acquired when the person confirms under oath that he or she is the author of the film and that what is filmed corresponds in a just and truthful manner to that of which he or she was the eyewitness, actor or victim of. Judges are more at ease when dealing with a professional, the bearer of an ethical code and, better yet, if he or she is working for, or has been commissioned by, an institution or professional society whose employees benefit from its good reputation. However, if the author of the film cannot physically attend the trial, a certificate or an affidavit is acceptable.[22]

Derrida's second point has to do with the very definition of a visual document. Insofar as it originates from a recording technique, a visual document should bear an objective truth:

> People like to believe that, when a witness comes to the stand and speaks in his name, he is himself! He speaks ... Even if he lies, or even if he forgets, or even if his testimony is insufficient or finite, at least it can be truthful ... I pledge not to bear false witness, to say sincerely what I saw and heard. This is the truth I pledge to tell. It is therefore something true. It is not the objective truth. (Derrida and Stiegler: 98)

Images are a construct and their status as truth can only partially hinge on the recording technique. Can there be a situation in which a single image would summarize the entirety of an event, at least in its factual dimension? This is the question filmmaker Pier Paolo Pasolini asked himself about the Zapruder film. Suppose, he wrote:

> that we had not a single short movie of Kennedy's death, but a dozen such movies, as if we had as many long takes as subjectively reproduce the present of the President's death ... In fact this multiplication of "presents" abolishes the present, renders it vain, each present postulating the relativity of all others, their groundlessness, imprecision, and ambiguity. But what is crucial in the filmed representation of an event is its dual strength as present and historical past. The present belongs to the document itself, which can only show what is presented to the viewer at the moment in which the event took place. But to constitute it as past, that is to say, as a completed event, it must be accompanied by some type of interpretation or narrative closure, and thereby placed at a distance. (Pasolini 1976)

Pasolini proposed the idea of a narrator who could effectively coordinate the various subjective views of the same event, and give meaning to the ubiquity of his recordings: "Intuiting the truth—from careful analysis of the various naturalistic fragments constituted by the many small movies—he could reconstruct it ... This narrator transforms present into past ... a past that, not out of aesthetic choice, but for reasons inherent to the very nature of cinema, is always in the present mode (*it is therefore a historic present*)" (Pasolini 1976).

The idea of reconstructing a scene by putting its pieces together is interesting, especially in police and legal terms, but fails to settle the issue of the subjectivity inherent to any filming.

Despite White's long indictment against the LAPD officers, the verdict came on April 29, 1992: three of the four were acquitted of all charges. The jury declared its lack of jurisdiction to determine a charge against the fourth, Officer Briseno.

THE VERDICT PARADOXICALLY REINFORCES THE POWER OF IMAGES

Scarcely two hours later, riots of unprecedented violence erupted in Los Angeles. By the time they were over, fifty-three people were dead and over 7,000 arrested. Property damage amounted to more than $1 billion. The King video's viral nature was compounded by that of the riots, broadcast on all television stations, convincing—or compelling—President George H. W. Bush to make a televised address. On April 30, 1992, the president announced that he had ordered the Justice Department to rule on the possibility of filing a complaint against the LAPD officers for violating King's federal civil rights. Unable to intervene in the judgment handed down by the court, while condemning the violence that occurred after the verdict, Bush brought the case up to the federal level, thus publicly acknowledging persistent discrimination against African-Americans.

In his statement, President Bush stuck to an immediate reading of the event, out of any historical context. The television media provided some historical background: KNBC showed images of the 1965 Watts riots.[23] King's lawyer advised his client to make a statement and asked him to read a two-page text written for him. Completely overwhelmed by the dimension taken by his case, all he managed to say and repeat was: "Can we all get along?"

The significance of the Holliday video for the president of the United States should be stressed. This is what he said:

> Let's talk about the beating of Rodney King, because beyond the urgent need to restore order is the second issue, the question of justice: Whether Rodney King's Federal civil rights were violated. What you saw and what I saw on the TV video was revolting. I felt anger. I felt pain. I thought: How can I explain this to my grandchildren? Civil rights leaders and just plain citizens fearful of and sometimes victimized by police brutality were deeply hurt. And I know good and decent policemen who were equally appalled. I spoke this morning to many leaders of the civil rights community. And they saw the video, as we all did. For fourteen months they waited patiently, hopefully. They waited for the system to work. And when the verdict came in, they felt betrayed. Viewed from outside the trial, it was hard to understand how the verdict could possibly square with the video. Those civil rights leaders with whom I met were stunned. And so was I, and so was Barbara, and so were my kids. But the verdict Wednesday was not the end of the process. The Department of Justice had started its own investigation immediately after the Rodney King incident and was monitoring the State investigation and trial. (Bush 1992)

It is therefore owing to the images' power of conviction and to the fact that the trial somehow negated it, and not to the court hearing process, the LAPD officers' behavior or the jury's final attitude, that the US president admitted his shock at the verdict. That reaction probably would have remained within the family circle, to which the president alluded when accounting for his personal reaction, had there not been riots in Los Angeles. Seeing the video on the news is what ultimately convinced him to justify his decision. If images can serve justice, destabilizing its current practices, this usually occurs by opening the trial to public life, breaking down the courtroom walls and putting an end to closed-door trials.[24]

The subsequent federal trial found two of the LAPD officers guilty. The prosecutor, Allan Tieger, said:

> The significance with the Rodney King case, I think, is that it represented a kind of breakthrough in public awareness of the ways in which, and to some extent the legal ways in which, video can be used. Now those who might consider crimes have to know that, surprisingly, what they do can be preserved. And it can be preserved and can be used essentially in a way that is beyond dispute. (http://www.coursehero.com/file/7536626/The-Rodney-King-trials/)

Once again, over and above the acknowledgment of the LAPD officers' responsibility, what is highlighted is the video's legal relevance. However, use of the video is not confined to the legal sphere. The images have inspired artists. A number of films—documentaries (Fecske 1993; Lemon 1992; Pack 1999; Palumbo 1992), as well as fiction—have been based on or produced in memory of them, which helped to increase the presence and activate the memory of the Holliday video. In Spike Lee's *Malcolm X* (1992), it appears from the opening credits, with a superimposed American flag consumed by fire, featuring not in connection with the King case but as the general symbol of anti-black racism in the United States. Oliver Stone's *Natural Born Killers* (1994) closes with three successive excerpts from the O.J. Simpson trial (1994–1995), the Waco tragedy (1993), and the Holliday video. After a fleeting quotation in *Three Kings* (David O. Russell, 1999), the King case plays a central role in *Dark Blue* (Ron Shelton, 2002). That film opens with Holliday's images and closes with a scene of the riots in the wake of the first trial, thereby enclosing its own fiction in this historical context, where two police officers investigate a quadruple murder in a grocery store.

Whether abundantly broadcast and highlighted by the media, or by the prosecution or, conversely, cut up into still images, subject to the twisted rhetoric of the defense's interpretation, the Holliday video could not possibly have dispensed with a narrative that granted it its place, and cross-referenced it with other documents, ultimately turning it into something that Mark Osiel terms a "narrative transaction" (Osiel 1997). Knowledge of its discussion in the courtroom may even turn out to be instructive for those who may have based their opinion solely on the video, or on the trial transcripts. Thus, on the eve of the opening of the second trial, a *Baltimore Sun* reporter was rightly concerned that the trial would not be filmed:

> Federal courts are behind their state counterparts in recognizing the need for the public to see what goes on in courtrooms. It is unfortunate that this trial will not be televised. All people are going to see—over and over, no doubt—is the sickening videotape of the beating, with none of the accompanying attempts to put it into the context that the jurors of last year rightly or wrongly found persuasive of innocence. (*The Baltimore Sun* 1993)

The presence of images in court should be matched with the filming of court hearings where videos are shown. Indeed, in addition to its archival value, the filming process ensures better transmission of the public debate mediated by the judges, both during and after the fact. This would make disinformation attempts less resistant to image decryption, regardless of the manipulation's level of sophistication. Justice may then take on a new role, when the television media are not vigilant enough to avoid leaving their viewers defenseless (Galligan 1994).

That is why, in order to avoid the risk of new trials, and thus to forestall any inappropriate behavior, the LAPD tried out a preventive measure, drawing a lesson from the King case. Putting cameras in patrol cars, recall Joel Rubin, Andrew Blankstein and Scott Gold, was a key reform proposed by the Christopher Commission, which studied the LAPD after the King beating. After years of delays, the department recently installed cameras in a quarter of its cars and plans to outfit the rest of its fleet in coming years. In addition to deterring misconduct, police officials believe that cameras can help exonerate officers from false accusations (Rubin et al. 2011).

CONCLUSION

Let us return to Prosecutor White's positivism. His mistake seems to have been an excess of confidence in believing in the Holliday video's unambiguous meaning. As Frank P. Tomasulo recalls, not without malice, media history specialists had the same reaction at the annual Society for Cinema Studies congress in 1992 when they were informed of the

LAPD officers' acquittal. They circulated a petition rejecting the verdict on the grounds that it "contradicts powerful visual evidence—video evidence of excessive police brutality seen globally" (Rabinowitz 1994).

In fact, the image's value in attesting to the event was at stake and perceived as such. This time, police officers could not ignore or destabilize the witnesses because the evidence was material, and broadcasting it on television ensured it would leave a trace. It could sow dissent without calling its content into question: it triggered debate. What the defense lawyers and their experts did, after trying to cast doubt on the value of the moving image, was something quite different. They used the video, and eventually entirely covered it with their commentary. This not only allowed them to remove the sight and sound of violence in the impact of multiple police blows. They actually re-choreographed the images. What the jury now saw was that every time Rodney King rose up off the ground the police batons came down, and every time King lay prone the police batons rose up. More generally, when speech continuously intrudes on the viewers' watching of a film, their capacity for interpretation, which requires time after the relative passivity of the screening, is somewhat impaired. The riots after the verdict quickly deflated that arrogance and their television coverage compelled the American president himself to step in, partly because of the effect that the Holliday video had on him and his wife, long-distance spectators of the event. The government then sent the ball back into the court of the police, suggesting that they equip themselves with self-surveillance cameras. Has this technical gear, which has yet to produce incriminating evidence in a police brutality case, at least changed how officers work on an everyday basis?

We need to know more about what visual images are actually doing inside the courtroom and how they are doing it, using what visual codes, producing what reality effects, based on what emotional and other unconscious associations. The judgments we make are better ones when we know more about how and why we make them. In order to decode visual images, lawyers need to be visually literate. And in order to fulfill their gatekeeping function, judges need to understand with greater sophistication what makes visual evidence reliable or unduly prejudicial. Social scientists can help jurists and educators deal with this new challenge by adding to our knowledge of how visual meaning making works, particularly by laying out in closer detail its efficacies and pitfalls inside the courtroom. The search for truth and justice in contemporary, intermediated legal practice requires no less.

Since 2012, the deaths of African-Americans at the hands of police officers have gone legally unpunished, even though killings are much more serious than the blows inflicted on Rodney King. Those tragic events indicate a failure to prevent as well as to manage such acts. And yet one of the measures President Obama put forward is based on something the Christopher commission had already suggested twenty years earlier: outfitting police officers with body-worn cameras.[25] That includes purchasing video equipment of course, but also fostering closer ties between the police and civil rights organizations and community representatives to monitor the effects. Then, the image would act neither as evidence nor attestation, but as a type of "third party" between the police and citizens, ensuring respect of the contract of good governance without needing to resort to traditional classic media (Myers 2011). This tool, which opens up the possibility of sharing, could prove useful if the right to privacy and social relations at work are safeguarded at the same time, and if the virtual space of new social media is regulated.[26] These are not the least of the legal consequences of cases that, from Rodney King to Trayvon Martin, have brought to light facts which, if not elucidated by the truthfulness of the image alone, have nevertheless benefited from the power of its effect on viewers.

ACKNOWLEDGMENT

This text is based on a course I gave at the Cardozo Law School in 2012, when I asked my students to re-enact and film in the classroom, set up as a moot courtroom, some of the key moments of the first Rodney King trial, including the moment when a video was screened as evidence. I would like to thank Naïma Ghermani and Caroline Michel d'Annoville for inviting me to present an analysis of the Rodney King case during a 2014 symposium at the École française de Rome, "Image and Law II. Using Images in the Courtroom." I would also like to thank Richard Sherwin and Danielle Celermajer for reading and commenting on this text's first version, and Glenn Naumovitz for the work done on the translation of the text.

NOTES

Preface

1 Laurence Rosen, *Law as Culture: An Invitation* (Princeton: Princeton University Press, 2006), 199–200.
2 Pierre Legrand, *Fragments on Law-as-Culture* (Deventer: W E J Tjeenk Willink, Schoordijk Institute, 1999), 5.
3 Malcolm Andrews, *Landscape and Western Art* (Oxford History of Art) (Oxford: Oxford University Press, 1999), 53.

Introduction

1 In *Visualizing Law* I describe "eloquence" as just such an integrated ideal (Sherwin 2011).

Justice

1 "Leviathan the piercing serpent, even leviathan that crooked serpent ... the dragon that [is] in the sea," Isaiah 27: 1; "his scales are his pride ... Out of his mouth go burning lamps and sparks of fire leap out," Job 41: 19. See Melville (2007).
2 Google-Ngram analysis indicates several references in German newspapers and literature in the target period.
3 The specifically legal analysis of *Jurisprudence* is patchy, and sometimes inaccurate. Apart from the extended analysis in Schorske, see also Bohler-Muller (2007), Minkkinen (1999: 183–187), Van Marle (2010), Likhovski (2009), Douglas-Scott (2013).
4 While the date given on the final painting is 1903–1907, it was first exhibited in 1903 and few changes seem to have been made after that: see Nebehay 1994: Plates 10–11. The transition between the original sketch and Klimt's final work is discussed in Schorske (1982: 44). See Roth (1994: 733).
5 Unless indicated, in-text citations are to Aeschylus, *Oresteia* 1953; references are to line numbers in *Agamemnon* (A), *The Libation Bearers* (LB) or *Eumenides* (E). A range of other translations were consulted and compared, including Aeschylus, *Oresteia* 2003; Aeschylus, *Oresteia* 1977; Aeschylus, *Oresteia* 2000; Aeschylus, *Oresteia* 2009; and the National Theatre Production, Aeschylus, *The Orestia* 1981.
6 The production was influential in the modern Greek revival of the plays: George Mikhalis, *Modern Greek Theatre and National Cultural identity 1901–3*; Hardwick (n 43). See *Neue Freie Presse* (Leo Unglaub and Logan Kennedy tr, Vienna, December 8, 1900) 1–2.
7 Compare Klimt's version of *Nuda Veritas* for *Ver Sacrum*; and *Nuda Veritas* (1899); see Schorske (1980: 215–217).
8 The literature is vast and not to be cited, but the theme of recognition is a critical component of all these dimensions of critical legal theory: for further surveys of the theme, see Neuhouser (2009), Taylor (1992a, 1992b), Cooke (1997), Fraser (1997).
9 Agamben (1998: 151) quotes Emmanuel Levinas: "This feeling of identity between self and body ... will therefore never allow those who wish to begin with it to rediscover, in the

depths of this unity, the duality of a free spirit that struggles against the body to which it is chained. On the contrary, for such people, the whole of the spirit's essence lies in the fact that it is chained to the body."

10 See Manderson (2016). For additional discussions, see Douzinas and Gearey (2005: 113–115), Gewirtz (1988), Kuhns (1962), White (1989: chapter 8), Wagner (1999–2000). Perhaps the most sustained reading is that by Aristodemou (1999, 2000: chapter 1).

11 Klimt's provides this third position, which is the position not of objectivity or of subjectivity but of *judgment*, throughout the faculty paintings.

Constitution

1 In Canada, for example *R v Sparrow*, [1990] 1 SCR 1075 saw the common law upholding and applying the inherent Aboriginal rights set out in section 35(1) of the Constitution of Canada.

2 The Treaty of Waitangi in New Zealand, for example. On constitutional recognition and guarantees for Indigenous peoples and lands in the Canadian Constitution see Keon-Cohen (1984: 82–83, 85–86).

3 Drawing on T.H. Marshall's (1950) notion that whereas in the eighteenth century citizenship required recognition of civil rights and in the nineteenth political rights, in the twentieth century, full citizenship entailed social and economic rights.

4 Mabo v Queensland (No. 2) (1992) HCA 23; 175 CLR 1.

5 Mabo v Queensland (No. 2) (1992) 175 CLR 1 at 43.

6 *Coe v Commonwealth* (1993) 118 ALR 193 at 198–200.

7 *Walker v New South Wales* (1994) 182 CLR 45 at 48–49.

8 *Wik Peoples v Queensland* (1996) 187 CLR 1 at 214.

9 *Gawirrin Gumana v Northern Territory of Australia (No. 2)* [2005] FCA 1425.

10 Moore describes symbolic legal pluralism as existing in a "semiautonomous social field."

11 This expression is the title of a collection of essays by Australianist anthropologist W.E.H. Stanner (1979).

12 In referring to "constitution" as a foundational *narrative* I invoke Cover's interpretation of "law" as *nomos*, in which legal rules and institutions interact with cultural beliefs and practices in the production of legal meaning (1993: 95).

13 In the Timber Creek native title claim (*Griffiths v Northern Territory of Australia* [2006] FCA 903), orally based knowledge systems, and claims to land based upon them, were critiqued as inherently unreliable and extremely variable (see Koch 2013: 35–36). In my experience, assertions to land interest based on oral knowledge are not highly variable but remarkably consistent and subject to group regulation, corroboration and correction, if necessary. Nor should it be assumed that colonial methods of land appropriation were purely documentary: certain medieval land transfer rituals in England (livery of seisin and "beating the bounds," for example) survived into the nineteenth century, and in some forms survive today.

14 Painting should be added to Rose's list of media. As Morphy notes, "rights in land and rights in paintings ... are inextricably interwoven ... [I]t was the Ancestral Beings who handed over the land to particular human groups on condition that those groups continued to perform the ceremonies and produce the paintings and ceremonial objects that commemorate their creative acts" (1983: 131).

15 By employing the term "performance evidence" I am mindful that it may appear to re-instantiate the colonial power's preconceptions and terminological categories. Ultimately, I use the term *performance evidence* to connote ancestral and spiritual knowledge and

history, implicating, in its mode of expression, alternative sources of authority, including ontological and epistemological differences.

16 See in particular Koch (2013), surveying song and ceremonial evidence in Australian land claims.
17 Moyle made identical statements during expert evidence in the *Alyawarra and Kaititja Land Claim*. Moyle's views met with judicial approval and were quoted by Toohey J. in his report for that claim (1979: 22).
18 *Inma* is the Yankunytjatjara term for singing and traditional songs (Goddard 1992: 19). The underlining of l as in Ka*l*aya denotes a retroflex sound, pronounced by curling the tongue back slightly in the mouth.
19 *Milirrpum v Nabalco Pty Ltd* (1971) 17 FLR 141 at 267 (Blackburn J.). This case, also known as the Gove Land Rights Case, is commonly cited as the first litigation on Aboriginal land title in Australia.
20 *Ward v Western Australia* [1998] FCA 1478; 159 ALR 483 at 504 (Lee J.).
21 *Hayes v Northern Territory* [1999] FCA 1248 at 12 (Olney J.).
22 *Native Title Act* 1993 Cth s. 82(2).
23 Federal Court Rules—rule 34.119 at page 323. http://www.comlaw.gov.au/Details/F2011L01551.
24 Federal Court Rules—rule 34.120 at page 323; and rule 34.124 at page 325.
25 Federal Court Rules—rule 34.120 at page 323; rule 34.126 and rule 34.127 at page 326.
26 Federal Court Rules—rule 34.125 at page 325.
27 Federal Court Rules—rule 34.123 at page 325.
28 *Federal Court of Australia Act* 1976 Section 59(2)(zj). In fact, there are many non-verbal modes of communication that are part of Australian Aboriginal routine cultural discourse, and not only in religious domains. Documented non-verbal modes of traditional communication include gesture and pointing (Green 2009a: 237–251); non-language vocal gesture (Liberman 1985: 40–41); hand sign language (Green 2010: xxi); silence (Liberman 1985: 207–209); whispering (Green 2009b: 236–237) and mumbling (Liberman 1985: 231).
29 As Sherwin suggests in an earlier paper, "law without storytelling is like having rules without human conflict" (2012/13: 4).
30 Notwithstanding, judges in two litigated native title claims, Yorta Yorta and Blue Mud Bay, "displayed a judicial preference" for written documentation (including witness statements and secondary sources) on laws and customs over oral accounts provided directly by members of the respective claimant groups (Mantziaris and Martin 2000: 43).
31 Section 3(1) of the *Aboriginal Land Right Act 1976* defines "traditional Aboriginal owners" as, "*a local descent group of Aboriginals who: (a) have common spiritual affiliations to a site on the land, being affiliations that place the group under a primary spiritual responsibility for that site and for the land; and (b) are entitled by Aboriginal tradition to forage as of right over that land.*"
32 Approximately 40 percent of the Northern Territory of Australia is now held by traditional owners with Aboriginal freehold title, a much stronger form of title than *native* title.
33 "Pointing" was specifically and approvingly referred to by Toohey J. in the *Borroloola Land Claim* report (1979: 3).
34 Sutton makes the point that *group evidence* not only allows witnesses to "feel emotionally comfortable," but accords with Aboriginal customary land law in that expressing "collectively held laws and facts" is not a private matter, and requires "the proper witnesses" to be present and supportive (1994: 22–23).
35 *Alcoota Land Claim* site No. 116.

36 Date evidence given—May 22, 1996.
37 *Alcoota Land Claim* site No. 115.
38 *Atwel* is the name of a local descent group, Ken Tilmouth Penangk's father's father's (*arrengey*) group.
39 See F. Morphy "Performing Law: the Yolngu of Blue Mud Bay meet the native title process" (2007); and Grace Koch "We have the Song, so we have the Land: song and ceremony as proof of ownership in Aboriginal and Torres Strait Islander land claims" (2013). The impacts of court procedure and extrajudicial variables on land claim performance evidence in Australia has drawn limited scholarly consideration. The analyzes that do exist correct the spurious impression that courts hear and adjudicate performance evidence in an identical *legal* way to all other evidence.
40 Courts as sites of ritualized social and political practice is an obvious comparison to make. Ritter (2009: 166) notes Federal Court "ceremonial sittings" on country following a native title determination by consent exhibit "explicitly ritualistic" elements including "a dance or other cultural activities" by the successful claimants, and communal barbeque. Invoking another form of ritual—sorcery—Liberman (1985: 228) observes the accoutrement of Anglo-Australian courtrooms (use of symbols, costumes, oaths, extralegal rituals, etc.) "seems like sorcery to Aboriginals" in Central Australia.
41 An additional on-sea site visit—or "view"—was attempted but aborted due to bad weather. Yolngu claimants accounted for the rough seas, saying they were due to the ancestral forces at *Mungurru* (the deep saltwater area involved) being, "offended by the presence of so many strangers" (Morphy 2007: 52). Morphy notes that while not evidence, the aborted visit allowed the Court to experience "the believability of the belief" that humans do not have sovereignty over the ancestral beings and forces in the Yolngu land and seascape (Morphy 2007: 52).
42 The full case name is *Alyawarr, Kaytetye, Warumungu, Wakay Native Title Claim Group v Northern Territory of Australia* [2004] FCA 472. Cited as "*Alyawarr*."
43 The township of Hatches Creek was gazetted, but never built. It lies adjacent to the former Hatches Creek wolfram mining areas.
44 The park's name, *Eytwelepwenty*, literally means "where the Rwaney run." *Rwaney* is the Alyawarr name for the Black-footed Rock Wallaby found in the local ranges country. *Rwaney* are a major *Altyerr* (Dreaming) in the area.
45 *Alyawarr* Restricted ts.867–868 (September 23, 2000). The *amek-amek* (restricted) sites where this occurred are not named here in accordance with claimants' instructions.
46 *Alyawarr* ts.471–528 (September 20, 2000—women at ATETYERRETYER); ts.1115–1136 (September 25, 2000 following *awely* demonstration).
47 For example, *Alyawarr* Restricted ts.532–575, 930–977.
48 For example, *Alyawarr* Ts.580–582 re Linda Dobbs Apwerl demonstrating grinding stone use.
49 Specific details withheld in accordance with claimants' instructions and Court orders.
50 It is relevant to note that, eleven years earlier than the *Alyawarr* hearing, some of the same male and female claimants participants in "a number of ceremonial performances" during the *Wakaya/Alyawarre Land Claim*, an adjoining ALRA claim (see Olney J., 1990: par.2.14). On that occasion an expert report describing the performance evidence witnessed by the Land Commissioner was also submitted.
51 *Alyawarr* Ts.82–102. Resources displayed (and photographed by the court) were: *alkwarrey* (bush banana), *ntywey* (corkwood tree bark), *ntang antywerleny* and *ntang ampwey* (edible seed from wattle tree species), *atywerety* (bean tree seeds), *antwerl pantayerr* (bush

medicine from Native pine species), *inteng-inteng* (strong-smelling bush medicine plants), *kanakety* (bush tomato), *ngkwarl* (native honey, sugarbag), *anker* (spinifex wax), *arnernp* (edible medicinal resin) *arlewatyerr* (sand goanna) and *kwerr-arr kwerr* (bush medicine plant).

52 *Alyawarr*, Site No. 37.
53 The site in question is considered *amek-amek* (restricted) by local land owners and is therefore not named.
54 Now deceased and thus he is not named here.
55 The judge put this object on his table at every site visited during the hearing.
56 The full case name is: *Peter De Rose & Others v State of South Australia & Others* (No SG 6001 of 1996). Cited as "*De Rose*." This analysis of performance evidence in the *De Rose* hearing draws on both open and restricted transcripts. In consulting the restricted transcript, the author has taken care, in accordance with claimant wishes, to exclude restricted site-specific information, restricted song subject referents and names of claimants involved in restricted evidence sessions.
57 *De Rose v State of South Australia* [2003] FCAFC 286 (16 December 2003); *De Rose v State of South Australia (No. 2)* [2005] FCAFC 110 (8 June 2005), par.8; *De Rose v State of South Australia (No. 3)* [2005] FCAFC 137 (July 28, 2005).
58 Specifically, the full Federal Court (comprising Wilcox J., Sackville J., and Merkel J.) said O'Loughlin J. had misconstrued section 223(1) (a) and (b) of the NTA, which states connection to land exists "under" acknowledged and observed *laws and customs*, as distinct from connection through *physical occupation*, or lack of, which was the subjective and erroneous criteria O'Loughlin J. had applied.
59 The displays consisted of *tjanmata* (bush onions), *wanguṉu* (edible seed from naked woollybutt), *maku* (edible grubs), *wirny wirinypa* (bush tomato), *mai kalka* (edible grass seed), *tjala* (honey ants) and various medicinal bush plants. See *De Rose* Ts. 94, 538–541, 555–557.
60 In his judgment (2002: pars. 254–259), O'Loughlin J. made comment on the potential for miscommunication and misunderstanding with certain categories of (leading, optional, either/or, temporal) questions heard during the *De Rose* evidence, but had no issue with confrontational questioning. Without proffering explanation why Indigenous witnesses find questions difficult to understand, O'Loughlin J. (par. 254) concluded: "Witnesses cannot be blamed for evidence that is ambiguous or uncertain if they are required to answer questions that they find difficult to understand or analyse."
61 Rules 34.123 and 34.125 at page 325. www.comlaw.gov.au/Details/F2011L01551.
62 Federal Court Rules—Division 1.3, rule 1.32 at page 36.
63 The issue was foreseeable because the untranslatability of words in sung traditions is a widely documented phenomenon—see Merriam (1964: 189), (Hiatt and Hiatt 1966: 2), Strehlow (1971: 67), Clunies Ross (1978: 134), Moyle (1979: 93), Moyle (1983: 91–92), Moyle (1986: 135–136), Clunies Ross (1987: 5, 8) and Koch (2013: 33). In Central Australia Moyle, for example, notes Alyawarr song words are regarded as the words spoken by the spiritual ancestors in antiquity, contain "a combination of everyday and specialised words" (1983: 91–92). They can be transmitted to an individual singer via dreams (1986: 135–136).
64 The audio of the singing is preserved on cassette tape in the *Federal Court of Australia* Registry. In preparation of this chapter the author consulted the recording, with permission of the Deputy Registrar of the Federal Court, at the Court's NSW Registry, Sydney, on 31

July 2015. To the author's knowledge, to date the sung verses have not been translated or transcribed.
65 As observed by the author at the time (July 5, 2001).
66 Full Federal Court of Australia *De Rose v State of South Australia (No. 2)* [2005] FCAFC 110 (June 8, 2005) (Wilcox, Sackville, and Merkel JJ.), par.8. See original judgment *De Rose v State of South Australia* (2002) FCA 1342 (November 1, 2002) O'Loughlin J., pars. 905–911. See also Keen (2003: 322).
67 Anthropological commentary on *De Rose* has failed to fully consider the impacts of the hearing context on the presentation mediums of Aboriginal evidence. For example, in *Law's Anthropology*, Burke offers an account of ethnographic and expert evidence in *De Rose*. It is regrettable that the circumstances this chapter has discussed, which are part of the documented court record, were seen as too "complex" for Burke's attention (2011: 215). Burke's omission to critically examine the undermining and fragmentation of the claimants' performance evidence in *De Rose* is a significant defect, and renders his analysis "incomplete" (2011: 215), a point he concedes but does not address.
68 On the notion of social imaginaries see Taylor (2004).
69 *Milirrpum v Nabalco Pty Ltd* (1971) 17 FLR 141.

Codes

1 *Prosecutor v Bikindi* (Judgment) ICTR-01–72-T, T Ch III (December 2, 2008) ("*Bikindi* judgment") para. 422.
2 First Annual Report of the International Criminal Tribunal for the Prosecution of Persons Responsible for Genocide and Other Serious Violations of International Humanitarian Law Committed in the Territory of Rwanda (September 24, 1996) UN Doc A/51/399-S/1996/778, annex.
3 *Prosecutor v Bikindi* (Transcript) ICTR-01–72-T, T Ch III (Various dates) ("*Bikindi* transcript") February 13, 2007, 11.
4 *Bikindi* transcript, October 2, 2006, 37.
5 *Prosecutor v Nahimana* (Judgment and Sentence) ICTR-99–52-T, T Ch I (December 3, 2003) ("*Media* judgment").
6 *Bikindi* judgment, 422.
7 *Bikindi* judgment, para. 254.
8 *Bikindi* judgment, para. 268.
9 *Bikindi* judgment, para. 424.
10 *Media* judgment, para. 439.
11 *Bikindi* transcript, October 19, 2006, 37.
12 *Bikindi* transcript, October 5, 2007, 13.
13 *Bikindi* transcript, September 26, 2006, 28.
14 *Prosecutor v Karera* (Judgment and Sentence) ICTR-01–74-T, T Ch I (December 7, 2007) ("*Karera* judgment") n 324.
15 Exhibit No P11(E), "Transcript of RTLM Broadcast of 15 April 1994," *Prosecutor v Bikindi*, ICTR-01-72-0070 (June 2, 1997), 7.
16 *Bikindi* judgment, para. 268.
17 US President Bill Clinton, for instance, referred to the conflict as the product of "tribal resentments." And one advisor to French President François Mitterrand suggested that brutal slaughter was a usual practice among Africans and could not be easily eradicated (Des Forges 1999: 21).
18 *Media* judgment, para. 1031.

19 *Prosecutor v Bikindi* (Indictment) ICTR-01–72-I (July 4, 2001) ("Bikindi indictment") para. 9.
20 *Bikindi* judgment, para. 112.
21 *Bikindi* indictment, paras 9, 14.
22 *Bikindi* judgment, para. 116.
23 *Bikindi* transcript, May 26, 2008.
24 *Bikindi* judgment, para. 257.
25 *Bikindi* transcript, October 4, 2006, 15.
26 *Bikindi* transcript, October 2, 2006, 36.
27 RTLM began broadcasting in July 1993. See *Media* judgment, para. 342.
28 *Bikindi* judgment, para. 122.
29 *Bikindi* judgment, paras 122, 404–407.
30 *Bikindi* judgment, para. 119.
31 *Bikindi* judgment, para. 122.
32 *Bikindi* judgment, para. 439.
33 Exhibit No. P72, "Excerpts from Jean-Pierre Chrétien, *Rwanda: Les Médias du Génocide* (Karthala, 1999)," *Prosecutor v Bikindi*, ICTR-01–72; *Bikindi judgment*, paras 195, 249, 257.
34 *Media* judgment, para. 53. Alison Des Forges testified at the ICTR on eleven separate occasions.
35 The *Media* case was cited constantly throughout the *Bikindi* judgment.
36 *Bikindi* indictment, para. 10.
37 *Bikindi* judgment, especially paras 115, 122.
38 *Bikindi* judgment, para. 122.
39 *Bikindi* judgment, para. 114.
40 *Bikindi* judgment, para. 258.
41 See *Media* judgment, paras 428, 449, 455, 478, 487, 488, 509, 516, 574, 606, 668, 672, 754, 837, 957, 971, 1028.
42 *Media* judgment, para. 343.
43 *Media* judgment, para. 343.
44 *Media* judgment, para. 342.
45 *Media* judgment, para. 457.
46 *Media* judgment, para. 538.
47 *Media* judgment, para. 457.
48 *Media* judgment, para. 1031.
49 *Media* judgment, para. 1031.
50 The prosecution did call a Rwandan radio technician to testify at trial. He claimed that RTLM had a 100-watt transmitter that could reach the whole of the capital Kigali and a few areas south and east of Kigali as well as a less powerful transmitter on Mount Muhe in western Rwanda that could reach some areas in that part of the country. Scott Straus notes that, "if true, then RTLM would not have reached large segments of the country, including northern, northeastern, southern, and southwest area, where genocide occurred." Radio Rwanda, by contrast, did have national reach (Straus 2007: 617); *Prosecutor v Nahimana* (Transcript) ICTR-99–52-T, T Ch I (Various dates) July 4, 2001.
51 *Media* judgment, para. 1031. In this instance, the text in question is Kangura, the Rwandan newspaper also under consideration in the *Media* case.
52 *Prosecutor v Akayesu* (Judgment) ICTR-96–4-T, T Ch I (September 2, 1998); *Prosecutor v Bagosora* (Judgment and Sentence) ICTR-98–41-T, T Ch I (December 18, 2008);

Prosecutor v Bizimungu (Judgment and Sentence) ICTR-99–50-T, T Ch II (September 30, 2011).
53 *Bikindi* judgment, para. 258. The citations are to Bikindi transcript: October 25, 2007, 26; February 20, 2007, 13.
54 *Media* judgment, para. 1031.
55 *Bikindi* transcript: October 4, 2006, 12; February 12, 2007, 7; February 13, 2007, 33, 42; February 14, 2007, 8; February 16, 2007, 6.
56 *Bikindi* judgment, para. 121; *Bikindi* transcript: October 31, 2007, 31–2; October 16, 2007, 20.
57 *Bikindi* judgment, para. 254.
58 *Bikindi* judgment, paras 261, 264.
59 *Bikindi* judgment, para. 239.
60 *Bikindi* judgment, para. 239; Exhibit No. P3, 'Transcript of RTLM Broadcast of May 17, 1994', *Prosecutor v Bikindi*, ICTR-01-72-0207 (May 17, 1994) 19–20, 22.
61 *Bikindi* judgment, paras 262–263, 439.
62 *Bikindi* judgment, para. 263.
63 *Bikindi* judgment, para. 268.
64 *Bikindi* judgment, para. 269.
65 Statement of Rwanda (November 8, 1994) UN Doc S/PV.3453.

Agreements

1 Jacques Rancière, "Aesthetic Separation, Aesthetic Continuity," in *The Emancipated Spectator*, p. 62.
2 Samuel Taylor Coleridge, *The Collected Works of Samuel Taylor Coleridge: Biographia Literaria*, chapter 14. Princeton: Princeton University Press, 1983.
3 "Legal Dictionary" in the *Free Dictionary*, http://legal-dictionary.thefreedictionary.com/agreement.
4 Clearly there are some attempts at definition coming from the legal system, such as the "Definitions; generally" section of the US Code 21/321. www.law.cornell.edu/uscode/text/21/321. Nonetheless many terms, such a "hate" speech and crimes remain elusive.
5 George Orson Welles apologizes for the "The War of the Worlds" broadcast (October 31, 1938), www.youtube.com/watch?v=uuEGiruAFSw.
6 Sophie Calle's "The Address Book," An Excerpt, *The New Yorker*, October 8, 2012. www.newyorker.com/books/page-turner/sophie-calles-the-address-book-an-excerpt.
7 See www.law.cornell.edu/wex/libel.
8 See www.businessdictionary.com/definition/agreement.html.
9 I outline the many challenges of defining performance in my book *Performance*. Durham, NC: Duke University Press, 2016.
10 See the Free Dictionary, www.thefreedictionary.com/impersonation.
11 See Maria Teresa Marrero's "Public Art, Performance Art, and the Politics of Site," in Diana Taylor and Juan Villegas (eds.), *Negotiating Performance: Gender, Sexuality, and Theatricality in Latin/o America*. Durham, NC: Duke University Press, 1994, p. 111.
12 Augusto Boal, *Theatre of the Oppressed*. New York: Theatre Communications Group, 1979.
13 See http://legal-dictionary.thefreedictionary.com/Impersonation.
14 June 25, 1948, ch. 645, 62 Stat. 742; Pub. L. 103–322, title XXXIII, § 330016(1)(H), September 13, 1994, 108 Stat. 2147. www.law.cornell.edu/uscode/text/18/912.

15 See http://codes.lp.findlaw.com/nycode/PEN/THREE/K/190/190.25#sthash.3YcoLANi.dpuf.
16 See www.etymonline.com/index.php?term=corporation.
17 The Pulitzer prize winning journalist Tim Weiner described Jesusa Rodríguez as possibly "the most powerful woman in Mexico" in his piece, "Mexico City Journal; Pummeling the Powerful, with Comedy as Cudgel," *The New York Times*, June 15, 2001. www.nytimes.com/2001/06/15/world/mexico-city-journal-pummeling-the-powerful-with-comedy-as-cudgel.html.
18 "Restrictions on Genetically Modified Organisms: Mexico" www.loc.gov/law/help/restrictions-on-gmos/mexico.php.
19 See the pro-GMO report, "GM crops: global social-economic and environmental impacts," 1996–2011 by Graham Brookes and Peter Barfoot, who acknowledge that the study was partially funded by Monsanto. There are many more, but it is important to note as Jill Richardson does that Monsanto funds research, endows chairs, and interferes with research at top universities in the United States (www.cornucopia.org/2012/09/stanfords-spin-on-organics-allegedly-tainted-by-biotechnology-funding/). This funding of US universities is common practice, as is the revolving-door policy whereby officials from corporations serve as administrators at universities and vice versa. In *Merchants of Doubt*, Naomi Oreskes and Erik M. Conway explain how the tobacco industry kept regulation at bay, and customers hooked, long after it was known that smoking causes cancers by hiring scientists to muddy the picture by producing doubt. The same Oreskes says has been done by Exxon in the climate debate catastrophe: Naomi Oreskes, "Exxon's Climate Concealment," NYT op. ed., p. A21, October 10, 2015. The same has happened with other industries.
20 Convention on Biological Diversity (CBD) "adopted in 1992, the 190 ratifying countries agreed on the importance of establishing adequate safety measures for the environment and human health to address the possible risks posed by GMOs (genetically modified organisms). Intense negotiations started in 1995 and resulted in the adoption of the final text of the Cartagena Protocol on Biosafety (thereafter referred to as the Biosafety Protocol or BSP) in 2000." www.google.com.mx/url?sa=t&rct=j&q=&esrc=s&source=web&cd=1&ved=0CCYQFjAA&url=http%3A%2F%2Fwww.greenpeace.org%2Finternational%2FPageFiles%2F24242%2FGeneralbackgrounderMOP.doc&ei=jjThUtniKvfLsASF-4CIDQ&usg=AFQjCNHlDqZE_Lqbhy9j1sGF6ZQX1Rzbgg&sig2=Cr_S16Zs8FE3TqQ0TtPZ7A&bvm=bv.59568121,d.cWc (accessed January 15, 2014).
21 The Yes Men, http://theyesmen.org/. Last Accessed April 14, 2015.
22 Andrew Boyd (ed.), *Beautiful Trouble*. New York: O/R Books, 2012, p. 60. *Beautiful Trouble* is also available online, http://explore.beautifultrouble.org/#-1:00000.
23 The Bhopal Disaster, BBC_ The Yes Men. December 2004. www.youtube.com/watch?v=LiWlvBro9eI for the fake Dow Chemical announcement on the bbc and www.democracynow.org/2009/10/20/yes_men_pull_off_prank_claiming for the Chamber of Commerce hoax.
24 See "Bhopal Disaster, BBC, Yes Men," www.bing.com/videos/search?q=yes+men+bhopal&FORM=VIRE1#view=detail&mid=4CB49E368F869A60939E4CB49E368F869A60939E.
25 For the video of the BBC coverage of Dow Chemical accepting responsibility for the Bhopal disaster starring Servin of the Yes Men see www.youtube.com/watch?v=LiWlvBro9eI.
26 "In February 2012, it was widely reported in the 2012 Stratfor email leak that Dow Chemical Company hired private intelligence firm Stratfor to monitor the Yes Men."

The source for this is listed *as "'Stratfor was Dow's Bhopal spy: WikiLeaks.' The Times of India. February 28, 2012. Retrieved February 28, 2012."* The Yes Men, Wikipedia, https://en.wikipedia.org/wiki/The_Yes_Men#Dow_Chemical.

27 Chamber of Commerce vs Servin, www.eff.org/cases/chamber-commerce-v-servin, accessed October 2, 2015.
28 Ibid. In *Campbell v Acuff-Rose Music Inc.*, the Supreme Court recognized parody to be fair use, even when it is done for profit.
29 The Yes Men's newest film, *The Yes Men are Revolting*, shows their impersonation of the Chamber of Commerce and its aftermath: bing.com/videos/search?q=yes men chamber of commerce&qs=n&form=QBVR&pq=yes men chamber of commerce&sc=1–27&sp=-1&sk=#view=detail&mid=67690EDF58C70EB1E7BD67690EDF58C70EB1E7BD.
30 "Chamber of Commerce v. Servin: Complaint." EFF, www.eff.org/node/56749. Last accessed October 2, 2015.
31 For the full announcement see http://monsantoglobal.com.yeslab.org/mexico-grants-mexico-approval-to.html. For the fake website, go to http://monsantoglobal.com.yeslab.org/mexico-grants-mexico-approval-to.html. April 14, 2015.
32 See the Yes Lab website (yeslab.org) for a full description of the digital action, http://yeslab.org/monsanto.
33 The Yes Men do not seek to perpetuate a lie, as opposed to the case in which a man lied about receiving the Medal of Honor (www.law.cornell.edu/supremecourt/text/11–210). The point, rather, is to reveal the lie perpetrated on the public by corporations such as Dow Chemical and Monsanto.
34 To read the leaked letter, go to http://yeslab.org/monsanto-leak.
35 Victor Turner, *From Ritual to Theatre*. New York: Performing Arts Journal, 1982, p. 10.
36 Richard Schechner, *The Future of Ritual*. London and New York: Routledge, 1993, p. 27.
37 Bertolt Brecht, *Brecht on Theatre* (ed.) and translated by John Willett. New York: Hill and Wang, 1964, p. 192.
38 Ibid., p. 193.
39 See J.L. Austin, *How to Do Things with Words*. Cambridge, MA: Harvard University Press, 1962 and Judith Butler's *Excitable Speech: A Politics of the Performative*, New York: Routledge, 1997. Thanks to Anurima Banerji for pointing out this connection.
40 Thanks to Grace McLaughlin for her research assistance tracking down the cases and to Professor Amy Adler (NYU Law) for her help with this chapter.
41 Greg Lukianoff, *Fire's Guide to Free Speech on Campus*, includes a chapter on academic freedom which it defines "as a general recognition that the academy must be free to research, teach, and debate ideas without censorship or outside interference …" It notes that "however fuzzy its definition or uncertain its actual legal application [it] is still a powerful concept, crucial to our understanding of the university as a true marketplace of ideas" (p. 1510) www.thefire.org/fire-guides/fires-guide-to-free-speech-on-campus-3/read-online/
42 Ibid.
43 Victor Luckerstan, "Can You Go to Jail for Impersonating Someone Online?" *Time*, January 22, 2013. http://business.time.com/2013/01/22/can-you-go-to-jail-for-impersonating-someone-online/.
44 John Leland, "Top Court Champions Freedom to Annoy." *New York Times*, May 13, 2014. www.nytimes.com/2014/05/14/nyregion/top-court-champions-freedom-to-annoy.html?smid=pl-share&_r=1.

45 See www.nationofchange.org/mexico-bans-gmo-corn-effective-immediately-1382022349 and www.sinembargo.mx/10–10–2013/781011. April 14, 2015. For more information about the situation in Mexico in regard to Monsanto, and the activists who are working to keep the transnational corporation out, see www.semillasdevida.org.mx/index.php/component/content/article/91-categ-analisis-de-coyuntura-2013/145–10–13 April 14, 2015.
46 Angélica Enciso L. "Firme, la suspensión de permisos para cultivo de maíz transgénico." www.jornada.unam.mx/2013/12/24/politica/020n1pol Last accessed April 14, 2015.
47 See Don Quijones, "Mexican Judge Departs from Script, Turns Monsanto's Mexican Dream into Legal Nightmare." *Wolf Street*, September 1, 2014. http://wolfstreet.com/2014/09/01/mexican-judge-departs-from-script-turns-monsantos-mexican-dream-into-legal-nightmare/.
48 Thanks to Mary Notari, the original YES MA'AM, and Jacques Servin, for conferring this title on me. An earlier and much shorter version of this piece appeared in *Performance*. Diana Taylor, Durham, NC: Duke University Press, 2016.

Arguments

1 As they are being treated as artifacts in this chapter, the transcripts have been reproduced in their original form without correcting typographical or spelling errors. It is also noted that all transcripts are available on the public record.
2 "As conflict rages across the former Yugoslavia, the Security Council, spurred to action by reports of atrocities and pressure from international public opinion, unanimously adopts Resolution 827, formally establishing the International Criminal Tribunal for the former Yugoslavia." 3217th meeting of the Security Council, May 25, 1993, New York. *Source*: ICTY.
3 Slavko Dokmanović was charged on the basis of his individual criminal responsibility (Article 7(1)) and, or alternatively, superior criminal responsibility (Article 7(3) of the Statute)) with: Wilfully causing great suffering; willful killing (Grave breaches of the Geneva Conventions, Article 2(c)); Murder; cruel treatment (violations of the laws or customs of war, Article 3); Murder; inhumane acts (crimes against humanity, Article 5 (a) and (i)). He pleaded "not guilty" to all charges on July 4, 1997.
4 For a discussion of the memorial function of the ICTY archive, see Campbell (2012: 22, 24).
5 ICTY, "Completion Strategy," www.icty.org/en/about/tribunal/completion-strategy. Accessed 10.01.16.
6 ELMO visualizers have replaced the classic overhead projector and are used extensively in the ICTY. They allow in particular 3D objects that are brought into the court to be projected in real-time without the need for prior scanning and digitization. For example, a witness or expert may use the ELMO to point out features of a scale-model enabling all in the court to see this interaction on their own desktop monitors and screens.
7 Interview conducted with Bob Reid, ICTY Chief of Operations, in August 2013.
8 IT-98-32/1: Lukic et al. CD-ROM containing a video recording showing recovery of materials from the house in Pionirska street by an OTP investigator. Document Type: Exhibit P00307, Date: April 24, 2009, By: Prosecution.
9 Nuremberg translator Henry Lea explains the time lapse of speechlessness that passed until interpreters finally began to register and speak about what they had heard and translated. "It seems inscrutable that about eight years have passed, until the trials seemed to begin to have an decisive impact on Wolfgang Hildesheimer's works. This delay can be explained through the method of interpretation. The work of the interpreters demands an extremely

intensified concentration—the highest grade that I have ever experienced ... the interpreter (has to) concentrate on syntax only and deactivate everything else. One gets so attached to the wording that one does not notice the content. Only years later one awakes gradually and realizes the content, that had been registered somewhere subconsciously" (Vismann 2004: 11).

10 However, the ICTY & ICC too have been accused of prosecutorial bias (Human rightsWatch 2004).
11 Two authors who address related aspects of degraded images are Steyerl (2009) and Takahashi (2006).
12 ICTY, Rules of Procedure and Evidence, UN Doc. IT/32/Rev.49 (May 22, 2013), *entered into force* March 14, 1994, www.icty.org/sid/136.
13 See N. Katherine Hayles' discussion of the power of rhetorical frameworks (2004: 13).
14 "Poplars and willows are multipurpose species and form an important component of forestry and agricultural production systems worldwide, often owned by small-scale farmers. They provide a long list of wood and fibre products (sawn lumber, veneer, plywood, pulp and paper, packing crates, pallets, poles, furniture and small handicraft), non-wood products (animal fodder), environmental services (rehabilitation of degraded lands, forest landscape restoration, climate change mitigation) and are grown increasingly in bio-energy plantations for the production of biofuels. These attributes make poplars and willows ideally suited for supporting rural livelihoods, enhancing food security, alleviating poverty and contributing to sustainable land-use and rural development." Food and Agriculture Organization of the United Nations, International Poplar Commission, http://www.fao.org/forestry/ipc/en/ (accessed January 16, 2016).
15 In the Grabez case the court found that the testimony was likely arrived at through coercion and therefore perjurious, which served to confirm the Defendant's alibi and in the other the capacity for recall on the part of the eyewitness was deemed to be diminished as a consequence of their harrowing experience, thus also producing a ruling in favor of the defendant (ICTY 1998c: Paras 1879–2880).

Property and Possession

1 The research for this chapter was funded by two Discovery Grants from the Australian Research Council, "Urban Images and the Appearance of City Spaces" (2008–2010) and "Transforming City Spaces: Street Art, Urban Cultures and Transnational Networks" (2012–2014). I'm grateful to the ARC for their support. Thanks also to David Mence for his extensive contributions to this research over the years, most recently in the process of writing this chapter.
2 Unless otherwise indicated, all quotations from artists are from interviews with me, as part of my research on the emergence and reception of street art as a cultural practice.
3 There have been a number of notable pranks involving the display of items which do not belong to a museum: Banksy famously smuggled his own works into the Metropolitan Museum in New York, the Louvre in Paris, and the Natural History Museum in London (among others) and attached them to the walls with accompanying didactic texts.
4 On piracy and its historical nexus arising from the enclosure of common land in England, Wales, Ireland, and Scotland in the fifteenth and sixteenth centuries, see Linebaugh and Rediker (2000).
5 The nomad, in particular, has inspired a rich vein of postmodern thought from Nietzsche to Deleuze. See for example Deleuze (1977) and Cresswell (1997).
6 See further, on graffiti writers' intended audience, Young (2005) Chapter 3.

7 On the erosion of public space in cities, see Blomley (2004a, b), Harris (1995), Iveson (2007), Keenan (2010), Loukaitou-Sideris and Ehrenfeucht (2009), Watson (2006).
8 In R v *Charan Verdi* [2005] 1 Cr App R (S) 43, the defendant, who pleaded guilty to nine counts of criminal damage for spraying graffiti on London Underground trains, was sentenced to two years' detention and placed on an ASBO for ten years. In R v *Michael Holmes* [2006] EWCA Crim 2510, a man present merely to photograph a friend writing graffiti was placed on an ASBO for three years.
9 Second Reading of the Graffiti Prevention Bill, Assembly, October 10, 2007, 3437–3438.
10 See, for example, Blomley (2008), Hardt and Negri (2009), Harvey (2011), Holder and Flessas (2008), Linebaugh (2010), Linn (2007), Milun (2011), Mitchell (2008), Ostrom (2008). For some of the most recent work on the commons, see, Forsyth and Johnson (2014), McDermott (2014), Ostrom (2014), Wall (2014), Borch and Kornberger (2015), Cumbers (2014).
11 For a detailed reading of Lefebvre's conceptualizations of law, space and the right to the city, see Butler (2012).

Wrongs

1 On the right to truth, see "Report of the independent expert to update the Set of Principles to combat impunity," Diane Orentlicher, Addendum: "Updated set of principles for the protection and promotion of human rights through action to combat impunity," UN Doc. E/CN.4/2005/102/Add.1, February 8, 2005 (hereinafter "Updated Principles on Impunity"). For example, Principle 1 states that it is an obligation of the state "to ensure the inalienable right to know the truth about violations." Principle 4 states that "[i]rrespective of any legal proceedings, victims and their families have the imprescriptible right to know the truth about the circumstances in which violations took place and, in the event of death or disappearance, the victims' fate."
2 For example, Supreme Decree No. 355 of the Chile National Commission on Truth and Reconciliation: "Only upon a foundation of truth will it be possible to meet the basic demands of justice and create the necessary conditions for achieving true national reconciliation."
3 The impossibility of righting these latter wrongs is explored by Povinelli as she traces how "to be Indigenous requires passing through, and, in the passage, being scarred by the geography of the state." E.A. Povinelli, "Settler Modernity and the Quest for an Indigenous Tradition." *Public Culture*: 11, 19–48, 1999.
4 Primo Levi, *If This Is A Man and The Truce*. Lancashire, UK: Abacus, 1987. ("Monsters exist, but they are too few in number to be truly dangerous. More dangerous are the common men, the functionaries ready to believe and to act without asking questions.")

Legal Profession

1 Robert J. Spitzer said, "These laws encourage a 'shoot first and ask questions later' mentality, which may help explain why, in supposedly justifiable killings, the victim is more likely to be black when the shooter is white" (Spitzer 2015).
2 The Rodney King case was not the first time pictures were used as evidence. Edgar W. Butler, Hiroshi Fukurai and Richard Krooth mention the Scottsboro (1931) and Huey Newton (1968) cases as well as trials in Florida in the 1980s where police officers responsible for the deaths of African-Americans were found not guilty. Their acquittals led to riots in which eighteen people died (Butler et al 1994). See also Gooding-Williams 1993.

3 "At 41," writes Lou Cannon, "Stacey Koon took pride in being in control of himself and dangerous situations. As Koon saw it, the California Highway Patrol officer was injecting a gun into a situation that didn't require a lethal weapon. LAPD officers are taught not to approach a suspect with a drawn gun, and Melanie Singer's 'lousy tactic' offended Koon. 'Had she proceeded, either she was going to shoot Rodney King, or he was going to take her gun away and shoot her,' Koon said in 'Presumed Guilty,' a book he wrote about the incident" (Cannon 1998).

4 *Report of the Independent Commission on the Los Angeles Police Department.* 1991: 32–33.

5 One of the arguments put forward by the police against the accusation of racism is based on the crime rate of African-Americans and their average dangerousness. African-Americans account for 12 percent to 13 percent of the total US population but 45 percent of the total state and federal prison population. Figure quoted by Ogletree (1995: 13).

6 "LAPD's Use of Force Policy and Guidelines," 1979, quoted in *Report of the Independent Commission.* 1991: 26.

7 Ibid, vii. A recent account of police violence against African-Americans can be found in a book written by Ta-Nehisi Coates, in which she writes to her son: "The destroyers will rarely be held accountable. Mostly they will receive pensions. And destruction is merely the superlative form of a dominion whose prerogatives include friskings, detainings, beatings and humiliations. All of this is common to black people. All of this is old for black people. No one is held responsible." *Between the World and Me.* 2015, New York: Spiegel & Grau: 9.

8 This pertains to events that occurred on November 29 and 30, 1963, respectively. The argument *Life* invokes not to broadcast the Zapruder film is that the images would be too graphic. Only on December 6, 1963 did *Life* finally publish color frames.

9 Since the Second World War, the jurisprudence of the use of moving images as forensic evidence benefited from John Ford's experience in the secret services (Field Photographic Branch, OSS). The war movie cameramen's mission statement stipulated that recordings should be "a true, accurate, untouched, unchanged, undistorted picturization of the scene" (Delage 2014).

10 *Report of the Independent Commission.* 1991: xi.

11 (Ibid, p. xii).

12 "Therefore, it was not only the action of the three white officers who directly participated in the beating, but also the inaction of the bystanding officers that caused a public outcry," says Benjamin S. Wright, "Christopher Commission." Taylor Greene. 2009: 122. For a different take on the responsibility of the LAPD, see Lasley. 1998: 378–389.

13 *Fury* features a trial in which the main accused have their testimony contradicted by a film shot by news reporters and screened during the hearing. Particularly interesting is how Lang shows a possible overflow of the judge by the presence of a screen in a courtroom. The screen's white rectangle located on the back of the room is put in parallel with the wall, also white, located above the judge, as though the solemnity of its judicial space could be possibly desacralized (Delage 2014).

14 The LAPD officers that are tried are: Sgt. Stacey C. Koon, forty-one years old; Officers Laurence M. Powell, twenty-nine, Theodore J. Briseno, thirty-nine, and Timothy E. Wind, thirty-one. Three of them have been suspended from the force without pay, and Officer Wind, a rookie without tenure, has been dismissed.

15 When cross-examined by Michael Stone, Timothy Singer's standpoint turns out to be similar to that of his wife: "I knew it was against CHP policy to strike someone in the head

and it could, results be ... could be deadly. So I just knew it was wrong so that's exactly what went through my mind: 'How can he be doing this?'" (Linder 2001).

16 "The general rule ... is that ... motion pictures are admissible in evidence, within the sound discretion of the court, where such pictures are relevant to the issues, and are an accurate reproduction of persons and objects testified to in oral examination before the jury," 108 Ohio App. 241, 161 N.E.2d 413 (1959) (quoted in Paradis 1965).

17 The Holliday video is a non-broadcast tape, with a low resolution. No proper digitalization could be made of it at the time, which slightly reduces the quality of the image, always blurry when you freeze it. The sound is even worse than the image, particularly at the distance where Holliday stands. In the courtroom, the screen is just an ordinary TV, which does not allow the jury to have a good view of the images. Thus, it is mostly the comments made by the defendants—of course in coordination with the showing of video clips—that are offering a narrative.

18 Actually, this has become a recurrent explanation in most of the subsequent cases of deadly force against African-Americans by police. For Delores Jones-Brown, "In the criminal cases that resulted, it seems that the officers needed only to utter the word 'fear' to be determined not liable for criminal conduct. There is little serious inquiry as to whether the fear was rational or whether it was based on or influenced by racial stereotypes or other constitutionally impermissible assumptions" (Jones-Brown 2009).

19 Terry White believes that whoever participates in a crime has the same responsibility as he who perpetrates it: "Earlier we briefly talked about aiding and abetting and an aider or abettor is just as liable for a crime as someone who directively and actively commits the act."

20 Of the four defendants, officer Briseno is the only one who turned against his colleagues, considering that they had acted "out of control."

21 The American press is empathetic with this final plea to jurors. For at least one of the jurors, interviewed on condition of anonymity after the trial, "The video was weakened as a piece of evidence because Mr. King did not testify for the prosecution." On the contrary, for Los Angeles mayor Tom Bradley, himself a former police officer, "The jury's verdict will never blind us to what we saw on that videotape. The men who beat Rodney King do not deserve to wear the uniform of the LAPD" (Mydans 1992a).

22 This was the case in Nuremberg for the first film screened as evidence on November 29, 1945, preceded by an affidavit signed by Robert H. Jackson, US Chief of Counsel, directors John Ford and George Stevens, on behalf of the official teams that they directed, respectively the Special Coverage Unit and Field Photo Branch, and E.R. Kellogg, film editor.

23 For a connection between 1965 and 1992, see Jacobs (2000).

24 This porosity between the court and the civil society, which some judges may fear could alter the serenity of hearings, occasionally plays a role in the reshuffling of roles across levels of justice. For instance, the presentation of the filmed evidence of a massacre in The Hague forced the Serbian national justice to pursue, arrest, and prosecute criminals identifiable on the video.

25 The LAPD ranks among the best funded, receiving $1 million in 2015, but thirty-two states now get from federal aid. The "Body-Worn Camera Pilot Implementation Program," which receives $55 million in federal funding, is intended as a "commitment to building trust and transparency between law enforcement and the communities they serve," "Justice Department Awards over $23 Million in Funding for Body Worn Camera Pilot Program

to Support Law Enforcement Agencies in 32 States," Department of Justice, September 21, 2015.

26 This poses several sets of problems. If American organizations want to quickly show images filmed of a fatal altercation between a police officer and an African-American, this approach can facilitate the live, online dissemination of violent images filmed in other contexts (suicide, terrorism, etc.), from with the social networks have a duty to protect their users.

BIBLIOGRAPHY

1900. "Neue Freie Presse." *Translated Leo Unglaub and Logan Kennedy*, December 8, 1900.
1992. Mabo v Queensland (No. 2) [175 CLR 1]. High Court of Australia.
1993. Coe v Commonwealth [118 ALR 193]. High Court of Australia.
1994. Walker v New South Wales [182 CLR 45]. High Court of Australia.
1994. Campbell v Acuff-Rose Music, Inc.: US Supreme Court.
1996. Wik Peoples v Queensland [187 CLR 1]. High Court of Australia.
2002. De Rose v South Australia [FCA 1342]. In *O'Loughlin, J.*: Federal Court of Australia.
2003. De Rose v State of South Australia [FCAFC 286]. In *Wilcox, Sackville, and Merkel JJ*: Federal Court of Australia.
2004. *The Bhopal Disaster—BBC—The Yes Men*. www.youtube.com/watch?v=LiWlvBro9eI: BBC World.
2005. De Rose v State of South Australia (No. 2) [FCAFC 110]. In *Wilcox, Sackville and Merlek JJ*: Federal Court of Australia.
2005. De Rose v State of South Australia (No. 3) [FCAFC 137]. In *Wilcox, Sackville and Merkel JJ*: Federal Court of Australia.
2005. Gawirrin Gumana v Northern Territory of Australia (No. 2) [FCA 1425]. Federal Court of Australia.
2009. Chamber of Commerce v Servin: Complaint. United States District Court for the District of Colombia.
2013. Migration Amendment (Unauthorised Maritime Arrivals and Other Measures) Bill 2013. In *The House of Representatives, The Parliament of the Commonwealth of Australia*. Canberra, Australia: http://parlinfo.aph.gov.au/parlInfo/download/legislation/bills/r4920_aspassed/toc_pdf/12192b01.pdf;fileType=application%2Fpdf.
Aboriginal Land Commissioner (Gray, Peter). 1987. Warlmanpa (Muckaty Pastoral Lease) Land Claim: Report by the Aboriginal Land Commissioner to the Minister for Aboriginal Affairs and to Minister for the Northern Territory. Canberra: Australian Government Publishing Service.
Aboriginal Land Commissioner (Gray, Peter). 2007. Alcoota Land Claim: Report and Recommendation of the Former Aboriginal Land Commissioner to the Minister for Families, Community Services and Indigenous Affairs and to the Administrator of the Northern Territory. Canberra: Australian Government Publishing Service.
Aboriginal Land Commissioner (Olney, Howard). 1990. Wakaya/Alyawarre Land Claim Findings, Recommendation and Report of the Aboriginal Land Commissioner to the Minister of Aboriginal Affairs and to the Administrator of the Northern Territory Canberra: Australian Government Publishing Service.
Aboriginal Land Commissioner (Toohey, John). 1979. Borroloola Land Claim: Report by the Aboriginal Land Commissioner to the Minister for Aboriginal Affairs and to Minister for the Northern Territory. Canberra: Australian Government Publishing Service.

Aboriginal Land Commissioner (Toohey, John). 1979. *Land Claim by the Alyawarra and Kaititja: Report by the Aboriginal Land Commissioner to the Minister for Aboriginal Affairs*. Canberra: Australian Government Publishing Service.

Adorno, Theodor W. and Max Horkheimer. 1989. *Dialectic of Enlightenment*, 2nd edn. London: Verso.

Aeschylus. 1900. *Die Orestie*. Translated by Ulrich von Wilamowitz-Moellendorf and directed by Paul Schlenther. Vienna: Burgtheater.

Aeschylus. 1953 [458 BC]. *Oresteia*. Translated by Richard Lattimore. Chicago, IL: University of Chicago.

Aeschylus. 1977. *Oresteia*. Translated by Robert Fagles. Harmondsworth: Penguin.

Aeschylus. 1981. *The Oresteia*. Translated by Tom Harrison and directed by Peter Hall. London: National Theatre Production.

Aeschylus. 2000. *Oresteia*. Translated by Ted Hughes. London: Farrar, Straus & Giroux.

Aeschylus. 2003. *Oresteia*. Translated by Christopher Collard. Oxford: Oxford University Press.

Aeschylus. 2009. *Oresteia*. Translated by Christopher Collard. Cambridge, MA: Harvard University Press.

Agamben, Giorgio. 1998. *Homer Sacer: Sovereign Power and Bare Life*. Translated by Daniel Heller-Roazen. Stanford, CA: Stanford University Press.

Agamben, Giorgio. 2005. *State of Exception*. Translated by Kevin Attell. Chicago, IL: University of Chicago Press.

Agencies, TNN and 2012, February 28. "Stratfor was Dow's Bhopal spy: WikiLeaks." *The Times of India*. http://timesofindia.indiatimes.com/india/Stratfor-was-Dows-Bhopal-spy-WikiLeaks/articleshow/12062587.cms.

American Heritage® Dictionary of the English Language, Fifth Edition. "impersonation." www.thefreedictionary.com/impersonation.

Anaya, James S. 2004. *Indigenous Peoples in International Law*, 2nd edn. Oxford: Oxford University Press.

Anderson, Benedict. 2006. *Imagined Communities: Reflections on the Origin and Spread of Nationalism*. London and New York: Verso.

Arendt, Hannah. 1963. *Eichmann in Jerusalem: A Report on the Banality of Evil*. London: Faber & Faber.

Andocides. 1968. "On the Mysteries." In *Minor Attic Orators: In Two Volumes*. Cambridge, MA and London: Harvard University Press and William Heinemann Ltd, respectively.

Arendt, Hannah. 1971. *The Life of the Mind*. San Diego, New York, London: Harcourt Brace and Company.

Arendt, Hannah. 1973. *The Origins of Totalitarianism*. Orlando, FL: Harcourt Brace and Company.

Arendt, Hannah. 1977. "What is Freedom?" In *Between Past and Future: Eight Exercises in Political Thought*. London: Penguin.

Arendt, Hannah. 1979. "On Hannah Arendt." In *Hannah Arendt. The Recovery of the Public World*, edited by Melvyn A. Hill. New York: St. Martin's Press.

Arendt, Hannah. 1994. "Understanding Politics." In *Essays in Understanding 1930–1945*. New York: Schocken Books.

Aristodemou, Maria. 1999. "The Seduction of Mimesis: Theater as Woman and the Plat of Difference and Excess in Aeschylus' 'Oresteia'." *Cardozo Studies in Law and Literature* 11: 1–33.

Aristodemou, Maria. 2000. *Law and Literature: Journeys from Her to Eternity*. Oxford: Oxford University Press.

Aspinall, Edward. 2010. "The Irony of Success." *Journal of Democracy* 21(2): 20–34. doi: 10.1353/jod.0.0157.

Attali, Jaques. 1985. *Noise: The Political Economy of Music*. Translated by Brian Massumi. Manchester: Manchester University Press.

Attoh, Kaufi A. 2011. "What *Kind* of Right is the Right to the City?" *Progress in Human Geography* 35(5): 669–685. doi: https://doi.org/10.1177/0309132510394706.

Attwood, Bain and Andrew Markus. 2007. *The 1967 Referendum: Race, Power and the Australian Constitution*. Canberra: Aboriginal Studies Press, AIATSIS.

Austi, N.J.L. 1962. *How to Do Things with Words*, edited by J.O. Urmson and Marina Sbisà, 2nd edn. Cambridge, MA: Harvard University Press.

Bal, Mieke. 1990. "De-disciplining the Eye." *Critical Inquiry* 16(3): 506–531.

Bal, Mieke. 1991. *Reading "Rembrandt": Beyond the Word-Image Opposition*. Cambridge: Cambridge University Press.

Bal, Mieke. 1999. *Quoting Caravaggio: Contemporary Art, Preposterous History*. Chicago, IL and London: University of Chicago Press.

Baltimore Sun. 1993. "The Second 'Rodney King Trial'." *The Baltimore Sun*, February 24, 1993. http://articles.baltimoresun.com/1993-02-24/news/1993055202_1_law-enforcement-enforcement-officer-police-chief.

Barsh, Russel Lawrence. 1986. " Indigenous Peoples: An Emerging Object of International Law." *American Society of International Law* 80(2): 369–385. doi: 10.2307/2201975.

Benjamin, Walter. 1999. *The Arcades Project*. London: Belknap Press.

Benjamin, Walter. 2003 [1940]. "On the Concept of History." In *Selected Writings*, edited by Howard Eiland and Michael W. Jennings. Cambridge: Harvard University Press.

Benjamin, Walter. 2007 [1940], *Illuminations*, edited by Hannah Arendt. New York: Schocken Books.

Bennett, Jane. 2002. *Vibrant Matter*. Durham, NC: Duke University Press.

Bergson, Henri. 1911. *Creative Evolution*. Translated by Arthur Mitchell. London: Macmillan & Co.

Bergson, Henri. 2010 [1946]. *The Creative Mind: An Introduction to Metaphysics*. Translated by Mabelle L. Andison. New York: Dover.

Berkowitz, Roger. 2006. *The Gift of Science: Leibnitz and the Modern Legal Tradition*. Cambridge, MA: Harvard University Press.

Berlin, Isaiah. 1976. *Vico and Herder: Two Studies in the History of Ideas*. London: Chatto & Windus.

Berlin, Isaiah. 1991. *The Crooked Timbre of Humanity*. New York: Alfred A. Knopf.

Berman, Harold J. 1983. *Law and Revolution: The Formation of the Western Legal Tradition*. Cambridge, MA: Harvard University Press.

Bernstein, Richard. 1983. *Beyond Objectivism and Relativism: Science, Hermeneutics, and Praxis*. Philadelphia, PA: University of Pennsylvania Press.

Bijsterveld, Karin. 2008. *Mechanical Sound: Technology, Culture and Public Problems of Noise in the Twentieth Century*. Cambridge, MA: MIT Press.

Bley, Helmut. 1996. *Namibia under German Rule*. Berlin: LIT Verlag.

Blomley, Nicholas. 2004a. "Un-real Estate: Proprietary Space and Public Gardening." *Antipode* 36(4):614–641. doi:10.1111/j.1467-8330.2004.00440.x.

Blomley, Nicholas. 2004b. *Unsettling the City: Urban Land and the Politics of Property*. New York: Routledge.

Blomley, Nicholas. 2008. "Enclosure, Common Right and the Property of the Poor." *Social & Legal Studies* 17 (3):311–331. doi: https://doi.org/10.1177/0964663908093966.
Blomley, Nicholas. 2011. *Rights of Passage: Sidewalks and the Regulation of Public Flow*. New York: Routledge.
Boal, Augusto. 1979. *Theatre of the Oppressed*. Translated by A. and Maria-Odila Leal McBride Charles. London: Pluto Press.
Bohler-Muller, Narnia. 2007. "On Desire, Transcendence and Sacrifice." *Law & Critique* 18: 253–274.
Borch, Christian and Martin Kornberger. 2015. *Urban Commons: Rethinking the City*. London: Routledge.
Bourdieu, Pierre. 1977. *Outline of a Theory of Practice*. Translated by Richard Nice. Cambridge: Cambridge University Press.
Boyd, Andrew and Dave Oswald Mitchell (eds.). 2013. *Beautiful Trouble: A Toolbox for Revolution* (Pocket Edition). New York and London: OR Books.
Brecht, Bertolt. 1964. *Brecht on Theatre: The Development of an Aesthetic*. Translated by John Willett. Edited by John Willett. New York: Farrar, Straus and Giroux.
Brennan, Sean. 2011. "Constitutional Reform and its Relationship to Land Justice." *Land, Rights, Laws: Issues of Native Title* 5(2):1–16.
Bridge, F.R. 1972. *From Sadowa to Sarajevo: The Foreign Policy of Austria-Hungary, 1866–1914*. London: Routledge & Kegan Paul.
Brink, Joram Ten and Joshua Oppenheimer (eds.). 2012. *Killer Images: Documentary Film, Memory and the Performance of Violence*. London and New York: Wallflower Press.
Brookes, Graham and Peter Barfoot. 2016. *GM Crops: Global Socio-Economic and Environmental Impacts 1996–2014*. Dorchester, UK: PG Economics.
Brown, Wendy. 2004. "'The Most We Can Hope For': Human Rights and the Politics of Fatalism." *The South Atlantic Quarterly* 103(2):451–463.
Bruner, Jerome. 1986. *Actual Minds, Possible Worlds*. Cambridge, MA: Harvard University Press.
Bruner, Jerome. 1991. "The Narrative Construction of Reality." *Critical Inquiry* 18(1):1–21. doi: 10.1086/448619.
Bryson, Norman. 1983. *Vision and Painting: The Logic of the Gaze*. New Haven: Yale University Press.
Bull, Michael and Les Back (eds.). 2003. *The Auditory Culture Reader*. Oxford: Berg.
Burke, Paul. 2011. *Law's Anthropology: From Ethnography to Expert Testimony in Native Title*. Canberra: The Australian National University E Press.
Burke, Paul. 2014. The Submission of Dr. Paul Burke to the Australian Law Reform Commission Review of the Native Title Act 1993 (submission 33). www.alrc.gov.au/inquiries/native-title-act-1993/submissions: Australian Law Reform Commission website.
Burrow, J.W. 2000. *The Crisis of Reason: European Thought, 1848–1914*. New Haven and London: Yale University Press.
Bush, George H.W. 1992. "Address to the Nation on the Civil Disturbances in Los Angeles, California." The American Presidency Project. www.presidency.ucsb.edu/ws/?pid=20910.
BusinessDictionary. agreement. www.businessdictionary.com/definition/agreement.html: WebFinance, Inc.
Butler, Chris. 2012. *Henri Lefebvre: Spatial Politics, Everyday Life and the Right to the City*. London: Routledge.
Butler, Edgar W., Hiroshi Fukurai, and Richard Krooth. 1994. "The Rodney King Beating Verdicts." In *The Los Angeles Riots: Lessons for the Urban Future*, edited by Edgar W. Butler,

Hiroshi Baldassare, Peter A. Morrison, and James A. Regalado, 73. Boulder, CO: Westview Press.

Butler, Judith. 1997. *A Politics of the Performative*. New York: Routledge.

Butler, Judith. 2006. *Gender Trouble: Feminism and the Subversion of Identity*. New York: Routledge.

Cage, John. 1968. *Silence: Lectures and Writings*. London: Marion Boyars.

Cage, John. 2013 [1961]. *Silence: Lectures and Writings*. Middletown, CN: Wesleyan University Press.

Campbell, Kirsten. 2012. "The Laws of Memory: The ICTY, the Archive, and Transitional Justice." *Social & Legal Studies* 22 (2):247–269. doi: https://doi.org/10.1177/0964663912464898.

Cannon, Lou. 1998. "The King Incident: More Than Met the Eye on Videotape." *The Washington Post*, January 25, 1998.

Cardozo, Benjamin. 1921. *The Nature of the Judicial Process*. New Haven, CT: Yale University Press.

Cardozo, Benjamin. 1924. *The Growth of the Law*. New Haven, CT: Yale University Press.

Cardozo, Benjamin. 1928. *The Paradoxes of Legal Science*. Clark, NJ: The Lawbook Exchange.

Carver, Richard. 2000. "Broadcasting and Political Transition: Rwanda and Beyond." In *African Broadcast Cultures: Radio in Transition*, edited by Richard and Graham Furniss Fardon, 188–197. Cape Town: David Philips Publishers.

Castleman, Craig. 1984. *Getting Up: Subway Graffiti in New York*. Boston: MIT Press.

Castoriadis, Cornelius. 1997. *World in Fragments: Writings on Politics, Society, Psychoanalysis, and the Imagination*. Stanford, CA: Stanford University Press.

Charlesworth, Hilary, Christine Chinkin, and Shelley Wright. 1991. "Feminist Approaches to International Law." *American Journal of International Law* 85(4): 613–645. doi: 10.2307/2203269.

Chastanet, François. 2007. *Pixação: São Paulo Signature*. Toulouse: XGpress.

Chatterton, Paul. 2010. "Seeking the Urban Common: Furthering the Debate on Spatial Justice." *City* 14(6): 625–628. doi: 10.1080/13604813.2010.525304.

Chion, Michel. 1994. *Audio-Vision: Sound on Screen*. Translated by Claudio Gorbman. New York: Columbia University Press.

Chion, Michel. 2011. "Let's Have Done with the Notion of 'Noise'." Translated by James A. Steintrager. *Differences* 22 (2–3): 240–248. doi: 10.1215/10407391-1428906a.

Chrétien, Jean-Pierre. 1995. *Rwanda: Les Médias du Génocide*. Paris: Karthala.

Christopher Commission. 1991. Report of the Independent Commission on the Los Angeles Police Department. The Independent Commission on the Los Angeles Police Department.

Clunies Ross, Margaret. 1978. "The Structure of Arnhem Land Song-Poetry." *Oceania* 49(2): 128–156. doi: 10.1002/j.1834-4461.1978.tb01383.x.

Clunies Ross, Margaret. 1987. "Research into Aboriginal Songs: The State of the Art." In *Songs of Aboriginal Australia, Issue 32, Oceania monographs*, edited by Margaret Clunies Ross, Tasmin Donaldson and Stephen Aubrey Wild. Sydney: Sydney University Press.

Coates, Ta-Nehisi. 2015. *Between the World and Me*. New York: Spiegel & Grau.

Coleridge, Samuel Taylor. 1983. *The Collected Works of Samuel Taylor Coleridge: Biographia literaria, or, Biographical Sketches of My Literary Life and Opinions*, edited by James and W. Jackson Bate Engell. Vol. 7. Bolligen: Routledge & Kegan Paul.

Coles, Romand. 2016. *Visionary Pragmatism: Receptive Resonance, Circulation and the Dynamics of Transformation*. Durham, NC: Duke University Press.

Conacher, D.J. 1987. *Aeschylus' Oresteia: A Literary Commentary*. Toronto: University of Toronto Press.

Connolly, William. 2002. *Neuropolitics: Thinking, Culture, Speed*. Minneapolis, MN: University of Minnesota Press.

Consolidated Laws, New York. Criminal impersonation in the second degree. In *Penal Law §* 190.25. http://codes.findlaw.com/ny/penal-law/pen-sect-190-25.html#sthash.3YcoLANi. dpuf: Thomas Reuters Westlaw.

Cooke, Maeve. 1997. "Authenticity and Autonomy: Taylor, Habermas, and the Politics of Recognition." *Political Theory* 25: 258–288.

Cooke, Michael. 1995. "Aboriginal Evidence in the Cross-Cultural Courtroom." In *Language in Evidence: Issues Confronting Aboriginal and Multicultural Australia*, edited by Diana Eades. Sydney: University of NSW Press.

Coonfield, Gordon. 2006. "Thinking Machinically, or, the Techno-aesthetic of Jackie Chan: Toward a Deleuze-Guattarian Media Studies." *Critical Studies in Media Communication* 23 (2006): 285–301. doi: http://dx.doi.org/10.1080/07393180600933105.

Cooper, Davina. 2006. "'Sometimes a Community and Sometimes a Battlefield': From the Comedic Public Sphere to the Commons of Speakers' Corner." *Environment and Planning D: Society and Space* 24 (5):753–775. doi: https://doi.org/10.1068/d1004.

Cooper, Davina. 2007. "Opening up Ownership: Community Belonging, Belongings, and the Productive Life of Property." *Law & Social Inquiry* 32(3): 625–664. doi: 10.1111/j.1747-4469.2007.00072.x.

Cornucopia Institute, The. 2012. September 12. Stanford's "Spin" on Organics Allegedly Tainted by Biotechnology Funding. *Cornucopia News* (www.cornucopia.org/2012/09/stanfords-spin-on-organics-allegedly-tainted-by-biotechnology-funding/).

Cover, Robert M. 1983. "The Supreme Court, 1982 Term—Foreword: Nomos and Narrative." *Harvard Law Review* 97: 1–4.

Cover, Robert M. 1993. "Nomos and Narrative." In *Narrative, Violence, and the Law: The Essays of Robert Cover*, edited by Michael Ryan Austin Sarat, and Martha Minow, 95–173. Michigan: The University of Michigan Press.

Cresswell, Tim. 1997. "Imagining the Nomad: Mobility and the Postmodern Primitive." In *Space and Social Theory: Interpreting Modernity and Postmodernity*, edited by Georges Benko and Ulf Strohmayer, 360–379. Malden, MA: Blackwell.

Cumbers, Andrew. 2014. "Constructing a Global Commons in, against and beyond the State." *Space and Polity* 19(1): 62–75. doi: http://dx.doi.org/10.1080/13562576.2014.995465.

Dallaire, Roméo. 2003. *Shake Hands with the Devil: The Failure of Humanity in Rwanda*. New York: Random House.

Damisch, Hubert. 2002. *A Theory of /Cloud/: Towards a History of Painting*. Translated by Janet Lloyd. Stanford, CA: Stanford University Press.

Daughtry, J. Martin. 2014. "Thanatosonics: Ontologies of Sonic Violence." *Social Text* 32(2) (119): 25–51. doi: 10.1215/01642472-2419546.

Davis, Kathleen. 2008. *Periodization and Sovereignty: How Ideas of Feudalism and Secularization Govern the Politics of Time*. Philadelphia: University of Pennsylvania Press.

Davis, Megan. 2016. "Listening but Not Hearing: When Process Trumps Substance." *Griffith REVIEW* 51:73–87.

Davis, Megan and George Williams. 2015. *Everything you Need to Know about the Referendum to Recognise Indigenous Australians*. Sydney: NewSouth Publishing.

Dawson, Richard. 2014. *Justice as Attunement: Transforming Constitutions in Law, Literature, Economics and the Rest of Life*. New York: Routledge.

De Forges, Alison. 1999. *Leave None to Tell the Story: Genocide in Rwanda*. Vol. 3169, No. 189. New York: Human Rights Watch, and International Federation of Human Rights.

De Ville, Jaques. 2011. "Mythology and the Images of Justice." *Law & Literature* 23: 324–364.

Delage, Christian. 2014. *Caught on Camera: Film in the Courtroom from the Nuremberg Trials to the Trials of the Khmer Rouge*. Translated by Ralph Schoolcraft and Mary Byrd Kelly. Edited by Ralph Schoolcraft and Mary Byrd Kelly. Philadelphia: University of Pennsylvania Press.

Delaney, David. 2005. *Territory: A Short Introduction*. Malden MA: Blackwell.

Deleuze, Gilles. 1977. "Nomad Thought." In *The New Nietzsche: Contemporary Styles of Interpretation*, edited by David B. Allison, 142–149. Cambridge, MA: MIT Press.

Deleuze, Gilles. 2001. *Pure Immanence: Essays on a Life*. Translated by Anne Boyman. New York: Zone Books.

Derrida, Jacques. 1972. *Margins of Philosophy*. Translated by Alan Bass. Chicago, IL: University of Chicago Press.

Derrida, Jacques. 1976. *Of Grammatology*. Translated by Gayatri Chakravorty Spivak. Baltimore: Johns Hopkins University Press.

Derrida, Jacques. 1984. *Signéponge/Signsponge*. Translated by Richard Rand. New York: Colombia University Press.

Derrida, Jacques. 1992. "Force of Law: The Mystical Foundation of Authority." In *Deconstruction and the Possibility of Justice*, edited by Drucilla Cornell, Michel Rosenfeld, and David Gray Carlson. New York: Routledge.

Derrida, Jacques. 2002. "Forgiveness." In *On Cosmopolitanism and Forgiveness*. London and New York: Routledge.

Derrida, Jaques. 2009. *The Beast & the Sovereign*. Translated by Geoffrey Bennington. Vol. 1. Chicago, IL: and London: The University of Chicago Press.

Derrida, Jaques and Bernard Steigler. 2002. *Echographies of Television: Filmed Interviews*. Translated by Jennifer Bajorek. Malden MA: Polity Press.

Dew, Christine. 2007. *Uncommissioned Art: An A-Z of Australian Graffiti*. Melbourne: Melbourne University Press.

Dewey, John. 1926. "The Historic Background of Corporate Legal Personality." *Yale Law Journal* 25: 655–673. doi: 10.2307/788782.

Diamantides, Marinos. 2000. "The Subject May Have Disappeared but its Sufferings Remain." *Law & Critique* 11: 137–166. doi: 10.1023/A:1008937006566.

Diamantides, Marinos. 2003. "In the Company of Priests: Meaninglessness, Suffering and Compassion in the Thoughts of Nietzsche and Levinas." *Cardozo Law Review* 24: 1275–1307.

Diamantides, Marinos (ed.). 2007. *Levinas, Law, Politics*. London: Routledge.

Dickens, Luke. 2008. "'Finders Keepers': Performing the Street, the Gallery and the Spaces in-Between." *Liminalities: A Journal of Performance Studies* 4(1): 1–30.

Donaldson, Susan. 2000. *Alyawarr, Kaytetye, Warumungu, Wakay Native Title Claim: Tyaw and Antarrengeny Awely Performance*. Alice Springs: Central Land Council. (Exhibit A22).

Douglas, Susan J. 1987. *Inventing American Broadcasting 1899–1922*. Baltimore: Johns Hopkins University Press.

Douglas-Scott, Sionadh. 2013. *Law After Modernity*. Oxford: Hart.

Douzinas, Costas and Adam Gearey. 2005. *Critical Jurisprudence: The Political Philosophy of Justice*. Oxford: Hart.

Drumbl, Mark A. 2004–2005. "Collective Violence and Individual Punishment: The Criminality of Mass Atrocity." *Northwestern University Law Review* 99(2): 539.

Duncan, Ivison, Paul Patton and Will Sanders (eds.) 2000. *Political Theory and the Rights of Indigenous Peoples*. Cambridge: Cambridge University Press.

Dupuy, Jean-Pierre. 2013. *The Mark of the Sacred*. Translated by M.B. Debevoise. Stanford, CA: Stanford University Press.

Dworkin, Ronald. 1985. *Law's Empire*. Cambridge, MA: Belknap Press.

Dyzenhaus, David. 1997. *Legality and Legitimacy: Carl Schmitt, Hans Kelsen and Hermann Heller in Weimar*. Oxford: Clarendon Press.

Dyzenhaus, David (ed.). 1998. *Law as Politics: Carl Schmitt's Critique of Liberalism*. Durham, NC: Duke University Press.

Dyzenhaus, David. 2006. *The Constitution of Law: Legality in a Time of Emergency*. Cambridge: Cambridge University Press.

Eckersley, Robyn. 1992. *Environmentalism and Political Theory: Toward and Ecocentric Approach*. Albany: SUNY Press.

Electronic Frontier Foundation, The. (n.d.) Chamber of Commerce v. Servin. (www.eff.org/cases/chamber-commerce-v-servin). Accessed October 2, 2015.

Elliott, Craig. 1999. *Alyawarr, Kaytetye, Warumungu, Wakaya Native Title Application Anthropology Report*. Alice Springs: Central Land Council. (Exhibit A1).

Enciso, L. Angélica. 2013, December 24. Firme, la suspensión de permisos para cultivo de maíz transgénico. *La Jornada, Política* (www.jornada.unam.mx/2013/12/24/politica/020n1pol).

European Commission Legal Service, The. 2013. "Codification." European Commission Legal Service, Last Modified June 19, 2013, accessed November 10, 2016. http://ec.europa.eu/dgs/legal_service/codifica_en.htm.

Ewans, Michael. 1982. *Wagner and Aeschylus: The Ring and Oresteia*. London: Faber & Faber.

Fecske, Steve, Steven Antoniou, James Earl Jones, Les Beigel, and Daryl F. Gates (Dirs.). 1993. *Outcry L.A.: Riots, Trials, Recovery*. United States: Edge Films.

Feenberg, Andrew. 1991. *Critical Theory of Technology*. Oxford: Oxford University Press.

Félix, Guattari. 2009. *Chaosophy: Texts and Interviews 1972–1977*. Translated by David L. Sweet, Jarred Becker, and Taylor Adkins. Edited by Sylvère Lotringer. Paris: Semiotext(e).

Felman, Shoshana. 2001. "A Ghost in the House of Justice: Death and the Language of Law." *Yale Journal of Law & the Humanities* 13: 241–282.

Felman, Shoshana. 2002. *The Juridical Unconscious: Trials and Traumas in the Twentieth Century*. London: Harvard University Press.

Ferrell, Jeff. 1996. *Crimes of Style: Urban Graffiti and the Politics of Criminality*. Boston: Northeastern University Press.

Ferrell, Jeff and Robert D. Weide. 2010. "Spot Theory." *City* 14 (1–2): 48–62. doi: 10.1080/13604810903525157.

Finnegan, Ruth. 1970. *Oral Literature in Africa*. Oxford: Clarendon Press.

Fitzpatrick, Peter. 2001. "Bare Sovereignty: Homo Sacer and the Insistence of Law." *Theory & Event* 5(2). doi: 10.1353/tae.2001.0011.

Ford, Mark. 2012. *Uprising: Hip Hop & the LA Riots*. USA: Creature Films.

Forsyth, Tim and Craig Johnson. 2014. "Elinor Ostrom's Legacy: Governing the Commons and the Rational Choice Controversy." *Development and Change* 45 (FORUM 2014): 1093–1110. doi: 10.1111/dech.12110.

Foster, Sheila. 2011. "Collective Action and the Urban Commons." *Notre Dame Law Review* 87:57–135.

Foucault, Michel. 1978. *The History of Sexuality*. Volume 1: *An Introduction*. Translated by Robert Hurley. London: Penguin.

Frank, Jerome. 2009 [1932]. *Law and the Modern Mind*. New Brunswick, NJ: Transaction.

Fraser, Nancy. 1997. *Justice Interruptus: Critical Reflections on the "Post-Socialist" Condition*. London: Routledge.

Freud, Sigmund. 1953 [1900]. *The Interpretation of Dreams*. Translated by James Strachey. Vol. 4: *The Standard Edition of the Complete Psychological Works of Sigmund Freud*. London: Hogarth Press.

Freud, Sigmund. 1961 [1929]. *Civilization and its Discontents*. Translated by James Strachey. Vol. 21: *The Standard Edition of the Complete Psychological Works of Sigmund Freud*. London: Hogarth Press.

Freud, Sigmund. 1964 [1934–38]. *Moses and Monotheism*. Translated by James Strachey. Vol. 23: *The Standard Edition of the Complete Psychological Works of Sigmund Freud*. London: Hogarth Press.

Freud, Sigmund. 2001. *The Standard Edition of the Complete Psychological Works of Sigmund Freud*. Translated by James Strachey. Vol. 21. New York: Vintage Classics.

Frith, Simon. 1996. *Performing Rites: Evaluating Popular Music*. Oxford: Oxford University Press.

Frodl, Gerbert and Gustav Klimt. 1992. *Klimt*. London: Vintage.

Gadamer, Hans-Georg. 1975 [1960]. *Truth and Method*. New York: Crossroad.

Gallie, Walter Bryce. 1955. "Essentially Contested Concepts." *Proceedings of the Aristotelian Society* 56:167–198.

Galligan, Ann M. 1994. "Using Courtroom Video in the Classroom: The Rodney King Case." *Journal of Criminal Justice Education* 5(2): 265–270. doi: http://dx.doi.org/10.1080/10511259400083271.

Gatens, Moira. 1996. *Imaginary Bodies: Ethics, Power and Corporeality*. London: Routledge.

Gates, Kelly. 2013. "The Cultural Labor of Surveillance: Video Forensics, Computational Objectivity, and the Production of Visual Evidence." *Social Semiotics* 23(2):242–260. doi: http://dx.doi.org/10.1080/10350330.2013.777593.

Gay, Peter. 2010. *Modernism: The Lure of Heresy*. London: W.W. Norton.

Geertz, Clifford. 1973. *The Interpretation of Cultures*. New York: Basic Books.

Geertz, Clifford. 1983. *Local Knowledge: Further Essays in Interpretive Anthropology*. New York: Basic Books.

Geny, François. 1954 [1899]. *Méthode d'interprétation et sources en droit privé positif: essai critique*, 2nd edn. Baton Rouge, LA: Louisiana State Law Institute.

Gevers, Christopher. 2014. "International Criminal Law and Individualism: An African Perspective." In *Critical Approaches to International Criminal Law: An Introduction*, edited by Christine Schwöbel, 221–245. Abingdon: Routledge.

Gewirtz, Paul. 1988. "Aeschylus' Law." *Harvard Law Review* 101:1043–1055. doi: 10.2307/1341428.

Ghai, Anita. 2002. "Disabled Women: En Excluded Agenda of Indian Feminism." *Hypatia* 17(3): 49–66. doi: 10.1111/j.1527-2001.2002.tb00941.x.

Goddard, Cliff. 1992. *Pitjantjatjara/Yankunytjatjara to English Dictionary*, 2nd edn. Alice Springs: Institute for Aboriginal Development.

Goddard, Cliff. 1996. *Pitjantjatjara/Yankunytjatjara to English Dictionary*, 2nd edn. Alice Springs: IAD Press.

Goldhill, Simon. 2004. *Language, Sexuality, Narrative: The Oresteia*. Cambridge: Cambridge University Press.

Goldstein, Daniel. 2007. "Human Rights as Culprit, Human Rights as Victim: Rights and Security in the State of Exception." In *The Practice of Human Rights: Tracking Law between the Global and the Local*, edited by Mark Goodale and Sally Engle Merry. Cambridge: Cambridge University Press.

Goldstone, R.J. 1995. Indictment: The Prosecutor of the Tribunal against Mile Mrkšić, Miroslav Radić and Veselin Šljivančanin, Case No. IT-95-13a. The Hague: ICTY, United Nations.

Gooding-Williams, Robert (ed.). 1993. *Reading Rodney King, Reading Urban Uprising*. New York: Routledge.

Goodman, Steve. 2010. *Sonic Warfare: Sound, Affect and the Ecology and Fear*. Cambridge, MA: MIT Press.

Goodrich, Peter. 2014. *Legal Emblems and the Art of Law: Obiter depicta as the Vision of Governance*. Cambridge: Cambridge University Press.

Goose, Stephen D. and Frank Smyth. 1994. "Arming Genocide in Rwanda: The High Cost of Small Arms Transfers." *Foreign Affairs* 73(5): 86–96. doi: 10.2307/20046833.

Gordon, Gregory S. 2010. "Music and Genocide: Harmonizing Coherence, Freedom and Nonviolence in Incitement Law." *Santa Clara Law Review* 50(3): 607. doi: http://dx.doi.org/10.2139/ssrn.2006348.

Goya, Francisco. 1814. *Second and Third of May 1808*. Madrid: Museo del Prado.

Grassi, Ernesto. 1988. *Renaissance Humanism: Studies in Philosophy and Poetics*. Binghamton, NY: Medieval & Renaissance Texts & Studies.

Green, Jennifer. 2009a. "Between and Earth and the Air: Multimodality in Arandic Sand Stories." Doctor of Philosophy (unpublished), School of Languages and Linguistics, University of Melbourne.

Green, Jennifer. 2009b. *Central and Eastern Anmatyerr to English Dictionary*. Alice Springs: IAD Press.

Green, Jenny. 2010. *Central and Eastern Anmatyerr to English Dictionary*. Alice Springs: IAD Press.

Greenberg, Karen and Joshua Dratel (eds.). 2005. *The Torture Papers: The Road to Abu Ghraib*. Cambridge: Cambridge University Press.

Greene, Helen Taylor and Shaun L. Gabbidon, (eds.). 2009. *Encyclopedia of Race*. Thousand Oaks, CA: SAGE Publications.

Greenpeace, International. 2004. *Greenpeace Supports the Cartagena Protocol on Biosafety*. Amsterdam: Stitchting Greenpeace Council.

Gregory, Sam. 2006. "Transnational Storytelling: Human Rights, Witness, and Video Advocacy." *American Anthropologist* 108(1): 195–204.

Grimm, Dieter. 2015. *Sovereignty: The Origin and Future of a Political and Legal Concept*. New York: Colombia University Press.

Guerra, Gustavo. 2014, March. Restrictions on Genetically Modified Organisms: Mexico. In *Legal Reports*. www.loc.gov/law/help/restrictions-on-gmos/mexico.php: The Law Library of Congress.

Habermas, Jürgen. 1975. *Legitimation Crisis*. Translated by Thomas McCarthy. Boston: Beacon Press.

Habermas, Jürgen. 1984. *The Theory of Communicative Action*, Volume 1: *Reason and the Rationalization of Society*. Translated by Thomas McCarthy. Boston: Beacon Press.

Habermas, Jürgen. 2008. "Secularism's Crisis of Faith: Notes on Post-Secular Society." *New Perspectives Quarterly* 25: 17–29. doi: 10.1111/j.1540-5842.2008.01017.x.

Halsey, Mark and Alison Young. 2006. "Our Desires Are Ungovernable: Writing Graffiti in Urban Space." *Theoretical Criminology* 10(3): 275–306. doi: https://doi.org/10.1177/1362480606065908.

Harbord, Graham. 2008. "Singing the Law." *Law Society of South Australia Bulletin* 30(4): 22–24.

Hardt, Michael, and Antonio Negri. 2009. *Commonwealth*. Cambridge, MA: Harvard University Press.

Hardwick, Lorna and Christopher Stray (eds.). 2011. *A Companion to Classical Receptions*. London: Wiley and Sons.

Haro, Lia and Coles, Romand. 2015. "Toward a Radical Democratic Groove: Receptivity and the Arts of Political Musicality." American Political Science Association Annual Meeting, San Francisco, California, August 24, 2015.

Harper, Douglas. corporation. In *Online Etymology Dictionary*. www.etymonline.com/index.php?term=corporation.

Harris, J.W. 1995. "Private and Non-Private Property: What Is the Difference?" *Law Quarterly Review* 111: 421–444.

Hart, H.L.A. 1961. *The Concept of Law*. Oxford: Oxford University Press.

Harvey, David. 2011. "The Future of the Commons." *Radical History Review* 109: 101–107. doi: 10.1215/01636545-2010-017.

Hausler, Kristin. 2012. "Indigenous Perspectives in the Courtroom." *Journal of Human Rights* 16(1): 51–72.

Haverkamp, Anselm and Cornelia Vismann. 1997. "Habeas Corpus: The Law's Desire to Have the Body." In *Violence, Identity and Self-Determination*, edited by Hent and Weber de Vries, Samuel. Stanford, CA: Stanford University Press.

Hayles, Katherine (ed.) 2004. *Nanoculture: Implications of the New Technoscience*. Bristol and Portland, OR: Intellect Books.

Hayner, Pricilla B. 2002. *Unspeakable Truths: Facing the Challenge of Truth Commissions*. New York and London: Routledge.

Heidegger, Martin. 1977. *The Question Concerning Technology and Other Essays*. Translated by William Lovitt. Hamden: Garland.

Henderson, Willie. 2000. "Metaphors, Narrative and Truth': South Africa's TRC." *African Affairs* 99(396): 457–465.

Hiatt, Lester and Betty Hiatt. 1966. Notes on songs of Arnhem Land. In Companion booklet to disc. Canberra: Australian Institute of Aboriginal Studies.

Hill, Melvyn A. (ed.) 1979. *Hannah Arendt: The Recovery of the Public World*. New York: St. Martin's Press.

Hirsch, Marianne. 1997. *Family Frames: Photography, Narrative, and Postmemory*. Cambridge, MA and London: Harvard University Press.

Hobbes, Thomas. 1968 [1651]. *Leviathan*. Edited by C.B. Macpherson: Pelican Classics.

Hobhouse, Emily. 1901. *Report of a Visit to the Camps of Women and Children in the Cape and Orange River Colonies*. London: Friars.

Hofmann, Werner. 1972. *Gustav Klimt*. New York: Graphic Society.

Holder, Jane B. and Tatiana Flessas. 2008. "Emerging Commons." *Social & Legal Studies* 17(3): 299–310. doi: https://doi.org/10.1177/0964663908093965.

Hollingsworth, Mary. 1994. *Patronage in Renaissance Italy: From 1400 to the Early Sixteenth Century*. London: John Murray.

Hookey, John. 1984. "Settlement and Sovereignty." In *Aborigines and the Law: Essays in Memory of Elizabeth Eggleston*, edited by Peter and Bryan Keon-Cohen Hanks. Sydney: Allen and Unwin.

Howes, David, and Constance Classen. 2014. *Ways of Sensing: Understanding the Senses in Society*. Oxford: Oxford University Press.

Human Rights and Equal Opportunity Commission. 1997. *Bringing Them Home: Report of the National Inquiry into the Separation of Aboriginal and Torres Strait Islander Children from Their Families*. Sydney: HREOC.

Human Rights Watch. 2004. "ICTY Justice at Risk: War Crimes Trials in Croatia, Bosnia and Herzegovina, and Serbia and Montenegro." *Human Rights Watch* 16 (7)(D), available https://www.hrw.org/sites/default/files/reports/icty1004.pdf.

Humphreys, Stephen. 2006. "Legalizing Lawlessness: On Giorgio Agamben's State of Exception." *European Journal of International Law* 17:667–687. doi: https://doi.org/10.1093/ejil/chl020.

Hutchson, Joseph. 1929. "The Judgment Intuitive: The Function of the 'Hunch' in Judicial Decision." *Cornell Law Quarterly* 14: 247–288.

Huxley, Aldous. 1970. *The Perennial Philosophy*. New York: Modern Library.

Huyse, Lucien. 2003. "The Process of Reconciliation." In *Reconciliation after Violent Conflict: A Handbook*, edited by Terri Barnes and Lucien Huyse David Bloomfield. Stockholm: International Institute for Democracy and Electoral Assistance (IDEA).

Hydaralli, Saeed. 2012. "What is Noise? An Inquiry into its Formal Properties." In *Reverberations: The Philosophy, Aesthetics and Politics of Noise*, edited by Michael Goddard, Benjamin Halligan and Paul Hegarty, 219–232. New York: Continuum.

ICTR. 1994, November 8. Statement of Rwanda. UN Doc S/PV, 3453.

ICTR. 1994, November 8. Statute of the International Criminal Tribunal for Rwanda. UN Doc S/RES/955, annex ("ICTR Statute"): United Nations.

ICTR. 1996, September 24. First Annual Report of the International Criminal Tribunal for the Prosecution of Persons Responsible for Genocide and Other Serious Violations of International Humanitarian Law Committed in the Territory of Rwanda. In *UN Doc A/51/399-S/1996/778*. annex: United Nations.

ICTR. 1998, September 2. Prosecutor v Akayesu (Judgment). ICTR-96-4-T, T Ch I.

ICTR. 2001, July 4. Prosecutor v Bikindi (Indictment). ICTR-01-72-I ("Bikindi indictment").

ICTR. 2003, December 3. Prosecutor v Nahimana (Judgment and Sentence). ICTR-99-52-T, T Ch I ("Media Judgment").

ICTR. 2007, December 7. Prosecutor v Karera (Judgment and Sentence). ICTR-01-74-T, T Ch I.

ICTR. 2008, December 2. Prosecutor v Bikindi (Judgment). ICTR-01-72-T, T Ch III ("Bikindi Judgment").

ICTR. 2008, December 18. Prosecutor v Bagosora (Judgment and Sentence). ICTR-98-41-T, T Ch I.

ICTR. 2011, September 30. Prosecutor v Bizimungu (Judgment and Sentence). ICTR-99-50-T, T Ch II.

ICTR. (Various dates). Prosecutor v Bikindi (Transcript). ICTR-01-72-T, T Ch III ("Bikindi transcript").

ICTR. (Various dates). Prosecutor v Nahimana (Transcript). ICTR-99-52-T, T Ch I.

ICTY. 1998a. Court Transcript 980421. The Hague: United Nations.

ICTY. 1998b. Court Transcript 980617IT. The Hague: United Nations.

ICTY. 1998c. Court Transcript 980618ED. The Hague: United Nations.

ICTY. 2009. Court Transcript 090324ED. The Hague: United Nations.

The Independent Commission on the Los Angeles Police Department. 1991. "The Christopher Commission on Tuesday issued a 228-page report on the activities of the Los Angeles Police Department. Here are the excerpts." *The Los Angeles Times*, July 10, 1991. http://articles.latimes.com/1991-07-10/news/mn-1962_1_lapd-officers-excessive-force-officers-laurence-m-powell.

Irigaray, Luce. 1985. *This Sex which is Not One*. Translated by Catherine Porter. Ithaca, NY: Cornell University Press.

Ivanisevic, Bogdan. 2004. "Justice at Risk: War Crimes Trials in Croatia, Bosnia and Herzegovina, and Serbia and Montenegro." *Human Rights Watch* 16(7): 1–31.

Iveson, Kurt. 2007. *Publics and the City*. Malden, MA: Blackwell.

Iveson, Kurt. 2013. "Cities within the City: Do-It-Yourself Urbanism and the Right to the City." *International Journal of Urban and Regional Research* 37(3): 941–956. doi: 10.1111/1468-2427.12053.

Ivison, D., Patton, P. & Sanders, W. 2000. *Political Theory and the Rights of Indigenous Peoples*. Cambridge: Cambridge University Press.

Jacobs, Ronald N. 2000. *Race, Media and the Crisis of Civil Society: From Watts to Rodney King*. Cambridge: Cambridge University Press.

James, William. 1925. *The Philosophy of William James*. New York: Modern Library.

James, William. 1956. *The Will to Believe*. New York: Dover.

Jones-Brown, Dolores. 2009. "The Right to Life?: Policing, Race and Criminal Justice." *Human Rights* 36(2): 6–9.

Judd, Denis and Keith Surridge. 2013. *The Boer War: A History*. New York: Palgrave Macmillan.

Kafka, Franz. 1953 [1921]. *Collected Stories*. New York: Schocken Books.

Kahan, Dan M. 2009. "Whose Eyes are you Going to Believe? *Scott V. Harris* and the Perils of Cognitive Illiberalism." Yale Faculty Scholarship Series Paper 97.

Kahn, Paul W. 1999. *The Cultural Study of Law: Reconstructing Legal Scholarship*. Chicago, IL: University of Chicago Press.

Kann, Robert A. 1981. "Carl Schorske's *Fin-de-Siècle Vienna*." *Central European History* 14(2):169–180. doi: https://doi.org/10.1017/S0008938900019622.

Kateb, George. 1972. *Utopia and its Enemies*. New York: Schocken Books.

Keeanga-Yamahtta, Taylor. 2016. *From Black Lives Matter to Black Liberation*. London: Haymarket Books.

Keen, John. 2003. "South Australia Developments—De Rose and Others v The State of South Australia and Ors [2002] FCA 1342." *Australian Resources and Energy Law Journal* 22(1): 320–323.

Keenan, Sarah. 2010. "Subversive Property: Reshaping Malleable Spaces of Belonging." *Social & Legal Studies* 19(4): 423–439. doi: https://doi.org/10.1177/0964663910372175.

Keenan, Thomas and Eyal Weizman. 2012. *Mengele's Skull: The Advent of a Forensic Aesthetics*. Frankfurt: Sternberg Press/Portikus.

Kellow, Christine L. and H. Leslie Steeves. 1998. "The Role of Radio in the Rwandan Genocide." *Journal of Communication* 48(3): 107. doi: 10.1111/j.1460-2466.1998.tb02762.x.

Kelsen, Hans. 1934. "Pure Theory of Law—Its Method and Fundamental Concepts." *Law Quarterly Review* 50: 474.

Kelsen, Hans. 1967. *Pure Theory of Law*. Los Angeles and Berkeley: University of California Press.

Kennedy, Ellen. 2004. *Constitutional Failure: Carl Schmitt in Weimar*. Durham, NC: Duke University Press.

Keon-Cohen, Bryan. 1984. "Indigenous Land Rights in Australia and Canada." In *Aborigines and the Law: Essays in Memory of Elizabeth Eggleston*, edited by Peter and Bryan Keon-Cohen Hanks. Sydney: Allen & Unwin.

Kim, David D. (Dir.) 2012. *Clash of Colors: LA Riots of 1992*. USA: DDK Productions.

King, Rodney with Lawrence J. Spagnola. 2012. *The Riot Within: My Journey from Rebellion to Redemption*. New York: Harper One.

Klimt, Gustav. 1897–98. Kompositionsentwurf.
Klimt, Gustav. 1898. Water in Motion.
Klimt, Gustav. 1898–1907. Philosophie.
Klimt, Gustav. 1899. Nuda Veritas. Austrian National Library.
Klimt, Gustav. 1899–1907. Medizin.
Klimt, Gustav. 1903–07. Jurisprudenz.
Knott, Marie Luise. 2014. *Unlearning with Hannah Arendt*. Translated by David Dollenmayer. Granta Books.
Koch, Grace. 2013. "We Have the Song, So We Have the Land: Song and Ceremony as Proof of Ownership in the Aboriginal and Torres Strait Islander Land Claims." In *AIATSIS Research Discussion Paper No. 33*. Canberra: AIATSIS Research Publications.
Kraus, Karl. 1903. *Die Fackel*, November 21, 1903, Issue 147. Translated by Leo Unglaub and Logan Kennedy.
Kristeva, Julia. 1980. *Desire in Language: A Semiotic Approach to Literature and Art*. Translated by Alice Jardine, Thomas Gorda, and Leon Roudiez. New York: Columbia University Press.
Kuhns, Richard F. 1962. *The House, the City, and the Judge: The Growth of Moral Awareness in the Oresteia*. Boston, MA: Bobbs-Merill.
Langton, Marcia. 2010. "The Estate As Duration: 'Being in Place' and Aboriginal Property Relations in the Areas of Cape York Peninsular in North Australia." In *Comparative Perspective on Communal Lands and Individual Ownership: Sustainable Futures*, edited by Lee and Maureen Tehan Godden, 75–97. Oxford and New York: Routledge-Cavendish.
Larkin, Brian. 2008. *Signal and Noise: Media, Infrastructure, and Urban Culture in Nigeria*. London: Duke University Press.
Lasley, James R. and Michael K. Hooper. 1998. "On Racism and the LAPD: Was the Christopher Commission Wrong?" *Social Science Quarterly* 79(2): 378–389.
Lebeck, Anne. 1971. *The Oresteia: A Study in Language and Structure*. London: Centre for Hellenic Studies.
Legal Information Institute, The. 21 U.S. Code § 321—Definitions; generally. In *Title 21, Chapter 9, Subchapter II*. www.law.cornell.edu/uscode/text/21/321: Cornell Law School.
Legal Information Institute, The. Libel. In *Wex*, edited by Cornell Law School. www.law.cornell.edu/wex/libel.
Legal Information Institute, The. 1948. 18 U.S. Code § 912—Officer or employee of the United States. In *June 25, 1948, Ch. 645, 62 Stat. 742; Pub. L. 103–322, title XXXIII, § 330016 (1) (H), Sept. 13, 1994, 108 Stat. 2147*. www.law.cornell.edu/uscode/text/18/912: Congress of the United States of America.
Leland, John. 2014, May 13. Top Court Champions Freedom to Annoy. *The New York Times* (www.nytimes.com/2014/05/14/nyregion/top-court-champions-freedom-to-annoy.html?smid=pl-share&_r=1).
Lemon, Don. 1992. *Race and Rage: The Beating of Rodney King*. USA: CNN.
Levin, Thomas Y. 2002. "Rhetoric of the Temporal Index: Surveillant Narration and the Cinema of 'Real Time'." In *Ctrl [space]: Rhetorics of Surveillance from Bentham to Big Brother*, edited by Thomas Y. Levin, Ursula Frohne, and Peter Weibel. Karlsruhe: ZKM.
Levinas, Emmanuel. 1969. *Totality and Infinity: An Essay on Exteriority*. Translated by Alphonso Lingis. Vol. 24, *Duquesne Studies*. Philosophical series. Pittsburgh: Duquesne University Press.
Levinas, Emmanuel. 1981. *Otherwise than Being or Beyond Essence*. Translated by Alphonso Lingis. The Hague: Martin Nijhoff.

Levinas, Emmanuel. 1988. "Useless Suffering." In *The Provocation of Levinas: Rethinking the Other*, edited by Robert Bernasconi and David Wood. London: Routledge.

Levinas, Emmanuel. 1989. *The Levinas Reader*. Edited by Sean Hand. Oxford: Blackwell Publishers.

Levinas, Emmanuel. 2001. *Is it Righteous To Be?: Interviews with Emmanuel Levinas*. Stanford, CA: Stanford University Press.

Levy, Daniel and Natan Sznaider. 2010. *Human Rights and Memory*. University Park, PA: The Pennsylvania State University Press.

Levy, Primo. 1987. *If This Is A Man; and The Truce*. Translated by Stuart Joseph Woolf. Lancashire: Abacus Press.

Li, Darryl. 2004. "Echoes of Violence: Considerations of Radio and Genocide in Rwanda." *Journal of Genocide Research* 6(1): 9–27. doi: http://dx.doi.org/10.1080/1462352042000194683.

Liberman, Kenneth. 1985. *Understanding Interaction in Central Australia: An Ethnomethodological Study of Australian Aboriginal People*. Boston, MA: Routledge & Kegan Paul.

Likhovski, Assaf. 2009. "Venus in Czernowitz: Sacher-Masoch, Ehrlich and the *Fin-de-siècle* Crisis of Legal Reason." In *Living Law: Reconsidering Eugen Ehrlich*, edited by Marc Hertogh, 49–73. Oxford and Portland, OR: Hart Publishing.

Lind, Allan and Tom Tyler. 1988. *The Social Psychology of Procedural Justice*. New York and London: Plenum Press.

Linder, Douglas O. 2001. "A Trial Account: The Trials of Los Angeles Police Officers' in Connection with the Beating of Rodney King." http://law2.umkc.edu/faculty/projects/ftrials/lapd/lapdaccount.html.

Linebaugh, Peter. 2010. "Enclosures from the Bottom Up." *Radical History Review* 108:11–27. doi: 10.1215/01636545-2010-007.

Linebaugh, Peter and Rediker, Marcus. 2000. *The Many-Headed Hydra: Sailors, Slaves, Commoners, and the Hidden History of the Revolutionary Atlantic*. New York: Beacon Press.

Linn, Karl. 2007. *Building Commons and Community*. Oakland CA: New Village Press.

Loos, Adolf. 1982. *Spoken into the Void: Collected Essays 1897–1900*. Translated by Jane O. Newman and John H. Smith. Cambridge, MA: MIT Press.

Loos, Adolf. 1998. *Ornament and Crime: Selected Essays*. Translated by Adolf Opel. California: Adriane Press.

Lorde, Audre. 2012. *Sister Outsider: Essays and Speeches*. Berkeley: Crossing Press.

Loukitau-Sideris, Anastasia and Irena Ehrenfeucht. 2009. *Sidewalks: Conflict and Negotiation over Public Space*. Cambridge, MA: MIT Press.

Luckerson, Victor. 2013, January 22. "Can You Go to Jail for Impersonating Someone Online?" *Time Business*.

Lukács, Georg. 1971. *History and Class Consciousness: Studies in Marxist Dialectics*. Translated by Rodney Livingstone. Cambridge, MA: MIT Press.

Lyotard, Jean-François. 1984. *The Postmodern Condition: A Report on Knowledge*. Minneapolis, MN: University of Minnesota Press.

McCormick, Carlo, Marc Schiller, Sara Schiller, and Ethel Seno. 2010. *Trespass: A History of Uncommissioned Urban Art*. Cologne: Taschen.

McDermott, Mary. 2014. "Introduction." *Commons Sense: New Thoughts about an Old Idea, Community Development Journal* 49 (suppl_1): i1–i11. doi: https://doi.org/10.1093/cdj/bsu010.

Macdonald, Nancy. 2001. *The Graffiti Subculture*. London: Palgrave Macmillan.

MacDowall, Lachlan. 2006. "In Praise of 70K: Cultural Heritage and Graffiti Style." *Continuum: Journal of Media & Cultural Studies* 20(4): 471–484. doi: http://dx.doi.org/10.1080/10304310600987320.

McGaw, Janet. 2008. "Complex Relationships between *Détournement and Récupération* in Melbourne's Street (Graffiti and Stencil) Art Scene." *Architectural Theory Review* 13(2): 222–239. doi: http://dx.doi.org/10.1080/13264820802216858.

Macintosh, Fiona et al. (eds.). 2004. *Agamemnon in Performance 458 BC–AD 2004*. Oxford: Oxford University Press.

McLagen, Meg. 2003. "Principles, Publicity, and Politics: Human Rights Media." *American Anthropologist* 105(3):605–612. doi: 10.1525/aa.2003.105.3.605.

McLuhan, Marshall. 1964. *Understanding Media: The Extensions of Man*. New York: New American Library.

McNeil, Donald G. 2002, March 17. "Killer Songs." *The New York Times Magazine*, accessed January 29, 2016. www.nytimes.com/2002/03/17/magazine/killer-songs.html?src=pm.

McNulty, Mel. 2000. "French Arms, War and Genocide in Rwanda." *Crime, Law and Social Change* 33(1):105–129. doi: 10.1023/A:1008394219703.

Mahmood, Saba. 2011. *Politics of Piety: The Islamic Revival and the Feminist Subject*. Princeton, NJ: Princeton University Press.

Manderson, Desmond. 2003. "From Hunger to Love: Myths of the Source, Interpretation, and Constitution of Law in Children's Literature." *Law and Literature* 15(1): 87–141. doi: 10.1525/lal.2003.15.1.87.

Manderson, Desmond (ed.). 2008. *Essays on Levinas and Law: A Mosaic*. New York: Palgrave Macmillan.

Manderson, Desmond. 2009. *Essays on Levinas and Law*. London: Palgrave Macmillan.

Manderson, Desmond. 2012. *Kangaroo Courts and the Rule of Law: The Legacy of Modernism*. London: Routledge.

Manderson, Desmond. 2013a. "From Zero Tolerance to Harm Reduction: 'The Asylum Problem'." *Refugee Survey Quarterly* 32(4): 1–21. doi: https://doi.org/10.1093/rsq/hdt019.

Manderson, Desmond. 2013b. "Groundhog day: Why the Asylum Problem is Like the Drug Problem." *Griffith REVIEW* 41: 84–110.

Manderson, Desmond. 2016. "Athena's Way: The Jurisprudence of the Oresteia." *Law Culture and the Humanities* 12: 1–24.

Mannheim, Karl. 2013. *Ideology and Utopia: Collected Works of Karl Mannheim*. Vol. 1. London: Routledge.

Mantziaris, Christos and David Martin. 2000. *Native Title Corporations: A Legal and Anthropological Analysis*. Sydney: Federation Press.

Marlowe-Storkovich, Tina. 2003. "'Medicine' by Gustav Klimt." *Artibus et Historiae* 24(47): 231–252. doi: 10.2307/1483769.

Marrero, Maria Teresa. 1994. "Public Art, Performance Art, and the Politics of Site." In *Negotiating Performance: Gender, Sexuality, and Theatricality in Latin/o America*, edited by Diana and Juan Villegas Taylor, 102–120. Durham, NC: Duke University Press.

Marshall, Thomas H. 1950. *Citizenship and Social Class: and Other Essays*. Cambridge: Cambridge University Press.

Massumi, Brian. 2002. *Parables for the Virtual: Movement, Affect, Sensation*. Durham, NC: Duke University Press.

Massumi, Brian. 2015. *Politics of Affect*. Cambridge: Polity.

Matheson, Kelly. 2015. "Video Evidence Case Study: Filing Long after a Crime in Croatia." *Witness*. https://blog.witness.org/2015/02/video-evidence-case-study-crime-croatia/.

Mégret, Frédéric. 2014. "International Criminal Justice: A Critical Research Agenda." In *Critical Approaches to International Criminal Law: An Introduction*, edited by Christine Schwöbel, 17–55. Abingdon: Routledge.

Meier, Christian. 2010. *Das Gebot des Vergessens und die Unabweisbarkeit des Erinnerns*. Munich: Siedler Verlag.

Melvern, Linda. 2000. *A People Betrayed: The Role of the West in Rwanda's Genocide*. London: Zed Books.

Melvern, Linda. 2005. "Radio Murder." *The Times Literary Supplement*, September 9, 2005, 25.

Melville, Herman. 2007. *Moby Dick: or the Whale*. New York: Random House Vintage Classics.

Mendeloff, David. 2004. "Truth-Seeking, Truth-Telling, and Postconflict Peacebuilding: Curb the Enthusiasm?" *International Studies Review* 6(3):355–380. doi: 10.1111/j.1521-9488.2004.00421.x.

Merleau-Ponty, Maurice. 2014. *Phenomenology of Perception*. Translated by Donald A. Landes. London and New York: Routledge.

Merriam, Alan P. 1964. *The Anthropology of Music*. Evanston, IL: Northwestern University Press.

Metzl, Frederic, Jamie. 1997. "Rwandan Genocide and the International Law of Radio Jamming." *American Journal of International Law* 91(4): 628–651. doi: 10.2307/2998097.

Milun, Kathryn. 2011. *The Political Uncommons: The Cross Cultural Logic of the Global Commons*. Farnham: Ashgate.

Minkkinen, Panu. 1994. "The Radiance of Justice: On the Minor Jurisprudence of Franz Kafka." *Social & Legal Studies* 3(3): 349–363. doi: https://doi.org/10.1177/096466399400300303.

Minkkinen, Panu. 1999. *Thinking without Desire: A First Philosophy of Law*. Oxford: Hart Publishing.

Minkkinen, Panu. 2008. "The Expressionless: Law, Ethics, and the Imagery of Suffering." *Law & Critique* 19(1): 65–85. doi: 10.1007/s10978-007-9021-7.

Minow, Martha. 1998. *Between Vengeance and Forgiveness: Facing History after Genocide and Mass Violence*. Boston, MA: Beacon Press.

Mitchell, Johnathan. 2008. "What Public Presence? Access, Commons and Property Rights." *Social & Legal Studies* 17(3): 351–367. doi: https://doi.org/10.1177/0964663908093968.

Mitchell, W.J.T. 2004. *What Do Pictures Want? The Lives and Loves of Images*. Chicago, IL: University of Chicago Press.

Mohanty, Chandra Talpade, Ann Russo, and Lourdes Torres. 1991. *Third World Women and the Politics of Feminism*. Bloomington and Indianapolis: Indiana University Press.

Mondzain, Marie-José. 2005. *Image, Icon, Economy: The Byzantine Origins of the Contemporary Imaginary*. Stanford, CA: Stanford University Press.

Moore, Sally Falk. 1973. "Law and Social Change: The Semi-Autonomous Social Field as an Appropriate Subject of Study." *Law & Society* 7(4): 719–746. doi: 10.2307/3052967.

More, Thomas. 1965 [1515]. *Utopia*. Translated by Paul Turner. Harmondsworth: Penguin.

Morphy, Frances. 2007. "Performing law: The Yolngu of Blue Mud Bay Meet the Native Title Process." In *The Social Effects of Native Title: Recognition, Translation, Coexistence* (CAEPR Monograph No. 27), edited by Ben and Frances Morphy Smith. Canberra: Australian National University Press.

Morphy, Howard. 1983. "'Now you Understand': An Analysis of the Way Yolngu have Used Sacred Knowledge to Retain their Autonomy." In *Aborigines, Land and Land Right*, edited by Nicolas and Marcia Langton Peterson. Canberra: Australian Institute of Aboriginal Studies.

Motyl, Howard (Dir.). 1998. *Image of an Assassination: A New Look at the Napruder Film*. USA: MPI Teleproductions.

Mouffe, Chantal. 2000. *The Democratic Paradox*. London and New York: Verso.

Moyle, Richard. 1979. *Songs of the Pintubi: Musical Life in a Central Australian Society*. Canberra: Australian Institute of Aboriginal Studies.

Moyle, Richard. 1983. "Songs, Ceremonies and Sites: The Agharringa Case." In *Aborigines, Land and Land Rights*, edited by Nicolas and Marcia Langton Peterson. Canberra: Australian Institute of Aboriginal Studies.

Moyle, Richard. 1986. *Alyawarra Music: Songs and Society in a Central Australian Community*. Canberra: Australian Institute of Aboriginal Studies.

Mydans, Seth. 1992a. "Prosecutor in Beating Case Urges Jury to Rely on Tape." *New York Times*, April 21, 1992.

Mydans, Seth. 1992b. "THE POLICE VERDICT; Los Angeles Policemen Acquitted in Taped Beating." *New York Times*, April 30, 1992.

Myers, Steve. 2011. "How Citizen Journalism has Changed since George Holliday's Rodney King Video." *Poynter*, March 3, 2011. www.poynter.org/2011/how-citizen-journalism-has-changed-since-george-hollidays-rodney-king-video/121687/.

Nancy, Jean-Luc. 1991. *The Inoperative Community*. Translated by Peter Connor, Lisa Garbus, Michael Holland and Simona Sawhney. Minneapolis, MN: University of Minnesota Press.

Nebehay, Christian. 1994. *Gustav Klimt: From Drawing to Painting*. London: Thames and Hudson.

Neuhouser, Frederick, Jay M. Bernstein, Michael Quante, Ludwig Siep, Terry Pinkard, Daniel Brundey, Andreas Wildt et al. 2009. *The Philosophy of Recognition: Historical and Contemporary Perspectives*, edited by Hans-Christoph Schmidt Am Busch and Christopher F. Zurn. Toronto: Rowman & Littlefield Publishers.

New Yorker, The. 2012. Sophie Calle's "The Address Book." An Excerpt. *Page-Turner* (www.newyorker.com/books/page-turner/sophie-calles-the-address-book-an-excerpt).

Nietzsche, Friedrich. 1968. *The Will to Power*. Translated by Walter Kaufmann and R.J. Holingdale. New York: Vintage.

Norris, Andrew (ed.). 2005. *Politics, Metaphysics, and Death: Essays on Giorgio Agamben's Homo Sacer*. Durham, NC: Duke University Press.

Novotny, Fritz and Johannes Dobai. 1968. *Gustav Klimt; With a Catalogue Raisonne of His Paintings*. Berlin: Praeger.

Now!, Democracy. 2009, October 20. "The Yes Men Pull Off Prank Claiming US Chamber of Commerce Had Changed Its Stance on Climate Change." democracynow.org.www.democracynow.org/2009/10/20/yes_men_pull_off_prank_claiming.

Nussbaum, Martha. 2013. *Political Emotions: Why Love Matters for Justice*. Cambridge, MA: Harvard University Press.

Ogletree, Charles Jr., Mary Prosser, Abbe Smith, and William Jr. Talley (ed.) 1995. *Beyond the Rodney King Story: An Investigation of Police Conduct in Minority Communities*. Boston: Northeastern University Press.

Oreskes, Naomi. 2015, October 9. Exxon's Climate Concealment. The Opinion Pages, *The New York Times*. (www.nytimes.com/2015/10/10/opinion/exxons-climate-concealment.html?_r=0).

Oreskes, Naomi and Eric M. Conway. 2011. *Merchants of Doubt: How a Handful of Scientists Obscured the Truth on Issues from Tobacco Smoke to Global Warming*. London: Bloomsbury.

Osiel, Mark J. 1997. *Mass Atrocity, Collective Memory, and the Law*. New Brunswick, NJ: Transaction.

Ostrom, Elinor. 1990. *Governing the Commons: The Evolution of Institutions for Collective Action*. Cambridge: Cambridge University Press.

Ostrom, Elinor. 2000. "Collective Action and the Evolution of Social Norms." *The Journal of Economic Perspectives* 14(3):137–158. doi: www.jstor.org/stable/2646923.

Ostrom, Elinor. 2008. "The Challenge of Common-Pool Resources." *Environment: Science and Policy for Sustainable Development* 50(4): 8–21. doi: http://dx.doi.org/10.3200/ENVT.50.4.8-21.

Ostrom, Elinor. 2014. "Collective Action and the Evolution of Social Norms." *Journal of Natural Resources Policy Research* 6(4): 235–252. doi: http://dx.doi.org/10.1080/19390459.2014.935173.

Oxford English Dictionary, The. 2017 March. "code, n.1." Oxford University Press, accessed October 26, 2015. www.oed.com.ezp.lib.unimelb.edu.au/view/Entry/35578?result=1&rskey=cil0O7&.

P3, Exhibit No. 1994, May 17. "Transcript of RTLM Broadcast of May 17, 1994." In Prosecutor v Bikindi. ICTR-01-72-0207: 19-20, 22.

P11(E), Exhibit No. 1997, June 2. "Transcript of RTLM Broadcast of 15 April 1994." In Prosecutor v Bikindi. ICTR-01-72-0070.

P72, Exhibit No. "Excerpts from Jean-Pierre Chrétien, Rwanda: Les Médias du Génocide (Karthala 1999)." In Prosecutor v Bikindi. ICTR-01-72.

Pack, Michael (Dir.). 1999. *The Rodney King Incident: Racism and Justice in America*. USA: Manifold Productions Inc.

Palumbo, Dominic (Dir.). 1992. *The Rodney King Case: What the Jury Saw in California v. Powell*. USA: Court Television Network.

Pakenham, Thomas. 1997. *The Boer War*. New York: Random House.

Paradis, Pierre R. 1965. "The Celluloid Witness." *University of Colorado Law Review* 37: 235–268.

Parker, James. 2011. "The Soundscape of Justice." *Griffith Law Review* 20(4):962–993. doi: http://dx.doi.org/10.1080/10383441.2011.10854727.

Parker, James E.K. 2015a. *Acoustic Jurisprudence: Listening to the Trial of Simon Bikindi*. Oxford: Oxford University Press.

Parker, James E.K. 2015b. "Towards an Acoustic Jurisprudence: Law and the Long Range Acoustic Device." *Law, Culture and the Humanities*:1–7. doi: https://doi.org/10.1177/1743872115615502.

Pasolini, Pier Paolo. 1976. "Observations sur le Plan-Séquence." In *L'Expérience Hérétique: Langue et Littérature*, 88–92. Paris: Traces, Payot Éditions.

Pearson, Noel. 1994. "A Troubling Inheritance." *Race and Class* 35(4):1–9. doi: https://doi.org/10.1177/030639689403500402.

Penalver, Eduardo Moises and Sonia Katyal. 2010. *Property Outlaws*. New Haven, CT: Yale University Press.

Peters, John Durham. 1999. *Speaking into the Air: A History of the Idea of Communication*. Chicago, IL: University of Chicago Press.

Peterson, Trudy Huskamp. 2008. *Temporary Courts, Permanent Records*. Washington, DC: History and Public Policy Program.

Phelps, Teresa Godwin. 2004. *Shattered Voices: Language, Violence, and the Work of Truth Commissions*. Philadelphia: University of Pennsylvania Press.

Pinch, Trevor and Karlin Bijsterveld (eds.). 2012. *The Oxford Handbook of Sound Studies*. Oxford: Oxford University Press.

Pontoppidan, Erik, Bishop of Bergen. 1753. *A Natural History of Norway*. Copenhagen.

Povinelli, Elizabeth A. 1999. "Settler Modernity and the Quest for an Indigenous Tradition." *Public Culture* 11(1):19–48. doi: 10.1215/08992363-11-1-19.

Power, Samantha. 2001. "Bystanders to Genocide: Why the United States Let the Rwandan Genocide Happen." *The Atlantic*, September 2001, 288(2): 89.

Proudhon, P.J. 1923. "What Is Government?" In *General Idea of the Revolution in the Nineteenth Century*. New York: Freedom Press.

Quijones, Don. 2014, September 1. Mexican Judge Departs from Script, Turns Monsanto's Mexican Dream into Legal Nightmare. *Wolf Street* (http://wolfstreet.com/2014/09/01/mexican-judge-departs-from-script-turns-monsantos-mexican-dream-into-legal-nightmare/).

Rainbowitz, Paula. 1994. *They Must Be Represented: The Politics of Documentary*. New York: Verso.

Rancière, Jacques. 2004. *The Politics of Aesthetics: The Distribution of the Sensible*. Translated by Gabriel Rockhill. London: Continuum Publishing.

Rancière, Jaques. 2014. "Aesthetic Separation, Aesthetic Continuity." In *The Emancipated Spectator*, 62. Verso.

Rawls, John. 1985. "Justice as Fairness: Political not Metaphysical." *Philosophy and Public Affairs* 14(3): 223–251.

Regan, Tom. 2004. *The Case for Animal Rights*, 2 edn. Berkeley and Los Angeles, CA: University of California Press.

Rentschler, Eric. 1996. *Ministry of Illusion*. Cambridge, MA: Harvard University Press.

Ritter, David. 2009. *Contesting Native Title: From Controversy to Consensus in the Struggle over Indigenous Land Rights*. Sydney: Allen and Unwin.

Roberts, Colin H. and T.C. Skeat. 1983. *The Birth of the Codex*. Oxford: Oxford University Press.

Rodowick, David. 2001. *Reading the Figural, Or, Philosophy After the New Media*. Durham, NC: Duke University Press.

Rodrigo, Javier. 2012. "El Relato y la Memoria. Pasados Traumáticos, Debates Públicos y Viceversa." *Ayer* 87: 239–249.

Roht-Arriaza, Naomi. 1995. *Impunity and Human Rights in International Law and Practice*: New York. Oxford University Press.

Rorty, Richard. 1979. *Philosophy and the Mirror of Nature*. Princeton, NJ: Princeton University Press.

Rose, Carol M. 1994. *Property and Persuasion: Essays on the History, Theory, and Rhetoric of Ownership*. Boulder, CO: Westview Press.

Rose, Deborah Bird. 1994. "Whose Confidentiality? Whose Intellectual Property? In Edmunds, M. *Claims to Knowledge, Claims to Country: Native Title, Native Title Claims and the Role of the Anthropologist*." Annual Conference of the Australian Anthropological Society, University of Sydney, September 28–30, 1994.

Roth, Kenneth. 2004. "Defending Economic, Social and Cultural Rights: Practical Issues Faced by an International Human Rights Organization." *Human Rights Quarterly* 26(1): 63–73. doi: 10.1353/hrq.2004.0010.

Roth, Michael S. 1994. "Performing History: Modernist Contextualism in Carl Schorske's *Fin-de-Siècle* Vienna." *The American Historical Review* 99(3):729–745. doi: 10.2307/2167767.

Rowse, Tim. 1987. "Assimilation and After." In *Australians from (1939)*, edited by Ann Curthoys, A.W. Martin and Tim Rowse, 133–149. Sydney: Fairfax, Syme & Weldon.

Rubin, Joel, Andrew Blankstein and Scott Gold. 2011. "Twenty Years after the Beating of Rodney King, the LAPD is a Changed Operation." *Los Angeles Times*, March 3, 2011. http://articles.latimes.com/2011/mar/03/local/la-me-king-video-20110301.

Said, Edward W. 1979. *Orientalism*. New York: Vintage.

Sandel, Michael. 1998. *Democracy's Discontent: America in Search of a Public Philosophy*. Cambridge, MA: Belknap Press.

Schacter, Rafael. 2008. "An Ethnography of Iconoclash." *Journal of Material Culture* 13(1): 2008. doi: https://doi.org/10.1177/1359183507086217.

Schacter, Rafael. 2013. *The World Atlas of Street Art and Graffiti*. New Haven, CT: Yale University Press.

Schafer, R. Murray. 1977. *The Soundscape: Our Sonic Environment and the Tuning of the World*. New York: Knopf.

Schechner, Richard. 1985. *Between Theater & Anthropology*. Pittsburgh, PA: University of Pennsylvania Press.

Schechner, Richard. 1993. *The Future of Ritual: Writings on Culture and Performance*. London and New York: Routledge.

Scheeres, Julia. January 30, 2002. Video Forensics: Grainy to Guilty. Wired (www.wired.com/2002/01/video-forensics-grainy-to-guilty/).

Schlenther, Paul. 1900. *Antikes Drama und Moderne Buhne*. Vienna: Neue Freie Presse.

Schmitt, Carl. 1969 [1912]. *Gesetz und Urteil: Eine Untersuchung zum Problem der Rechtspraxis*. Berlin: C.H. Beck.

Schmitt, Carl. 2005 [1922]. *Political Theology: Four Chapters on the Concept of Sovereignty*. Translated by George Schwab. Chicago, IL: University of Chicago Press.

Schmitt, Carl. 2008 [1932]. *The Concept of the Political*. Translated by George Schwab. Chicago, IL: University of Chicago Press.

Schmitt, Carl. 2014. "Law in the Flesh: Tracing Legitimation's Origin to 'The Act of Killing'." *No Foundations: An Interdisciplinary Journal of Law and Justice* NYLS Legal Studies Research Paper No. 13/14 #81:23 Pages.

Schorske, Carl E. 1961. "Politics and the Psyche in fin de siècle Vienna: Schitzler and Hofmannsthal." *The American Historical Review* 66(4): 930–946. doi: 10.2307/1845864.

Schorske, Carl E. 1973. "Politics and Patricide in Freud's Interpretation of Dreams." *The American Historical Review* 78(2): 328–347. doi: 10.2307/1861171.

Schorske, Carl E. 1978. "Generational Tension and Cultural Change: Reflections on the Case of Vienna." *Daedalus* 107(4): 111–122.

Schorske, Carl E. 1980. *Fin-de-Siècle Vienna: Politics and Culture*. New York: Alfred Knopf.

Schorske, Carl E. 1982. "Mahler and Klimt: Social Experience and Artistic Evolution." *Daedalus* 111(3): 29–50.

Schuppli, Susan. 2014. *Evidence on Trial*. Den Haag: Stroom.

Schuppli, Susan. 2015. "Law and Disorder." In *Realism Materialism Art*, edited by Christoph J.J. Cox and Suhail Malik. Berlin: Sternberg.

Schuppli, Susan. Forthcoming. *Material Witness: Forensic Media and the Production of Evidence*. London: MIT Press.

Schwartz, Hillel. 2011. *Making Noise: From Babel to the Big Bang & Beyond*. New York: Zone Books.

Schwartz, Louis-Georges. 2009. *Mechanical Witness. A History of Motion Picture Evidence in U.S. Courts*. Oxford: Oxford University Press.

Seibold, Birgit Susanne. 2011. *Emily Hobhouse and the Reports on the Concentration Camps during the Boer War 1899–1902: Two Different Perspectives*. Stuttgart: Ibidem-Verlag.

Serres, Michel. 1995. *Genesis*. Translated by Geneviève and James Nielson James. Ann Arbor: University of Michigan Press.

Sherwin, Richard. 1988. "Dialects and Dominance: A Study of Rhetorical Fields in the Law of Confessions." *University of Pennsylvania Law Review* 136(3): 729–849. doi: 10.2307/3312119.

Sherwin, Richard. 2000. *When Law Goes Pop: The Vanishing Line between Law and Popular Culture*. Chicago, IL and London: The University of Chicago Press.

Sherwin, Richard. 2006–2007. "A Manifesto for Visual Legal Realism." *New York Law School Public Law and Legal Theory* 40:1–18.

Sherwin, Richard. 2011. *Visualizing Law in the Age of the Digital Baroque: Arabesques & Entanglements*. New York: Routledge.

Sherwin, Richard. 2012/13. "Visual Jurisprudence." *New York Law School Law Review* 57:11–39.

Sherwin, Richard. 2013. "Performer la Loi. Présences et simulacres, sur scène et au tribunal." *Revue Communications* 92(1): 147–158.

Sherwin, Richard. 2014."Law in the Flesh: Tracing Legitimation's Origin to 'The Act of Killing.'" *No Foundations: An Interdisciplinary Journal of Law and Justice* 11 (June 2014).

Silvergate, Harvey A. 2012 [2005]. *FIRE's Guide to Free Speech on Campus*, edited by William Creely and Greg Lukianoff; 2nd edn, *Fire's Guides to Student Rights on Campus*. Foundation for Individual Rights in Education.

Simpson, Gerry. 1993. "*Mabo*, International Law, *Terra Nullius*, and the Stories of Settlement: An Unresolved Jurisprudence." *Melbourne University Law Review* 19(1): 195–210.

Simpson, Gerry. 2014. "Linear Law: The History of International Criminal Law." In *Critical Approaches to International Criminal Law: An Introduction*, edited by Christine Schwöbel, 159–179. Abingdon: Routledge.

Smulyan, Susan. 1994. *Selling Radio: The Commercialization of American Broadcasting 1920–1934*. New York: Smithsonian Institution Press.

Snyder, Gregory J. 2009. *Graffiti Lives: Beyond the Tag in New York's Urban Underground*. New York: New York University Press.

Spitzer, Robert J. 2015. "Stand Your Ground Makes No Sense." *The New York Times*, May 4, 2015.

Spivak, Gayatri Chakravorty. 1988. "Can the Subaltern Speak?" In *Marxism and the Interpretation of Culture*, edited by Cary Nelson and Lawrence Grossberg, 271–313. Urbana and Chicago, IL: University of Illinois Press.

Stanner, W.E.H. 1979. "The Yirrkala Land Case (1970)." In *White Man Got No Dreaming: Essays 1938–1973*. Canberra: Australian National University Press.

Stanner, W.E.H. 1984. "Religion, Totemism and Symbolism." In *Religion in Aboriginal Australia: An Anthology*, edited by Maxwell John Charlesworth. Lucia: University of Queensland Press.

Steintrager, James A. 2011. "Speaking of Noise: From Murderous Loudness to the Crackle of Silk." *Differences* 22(2–3): 249–275. doi: 10.1215/10407391-1428915.

Sterne, Jonathan. 1999. "Television under Construction: American Television and the Problem of Distribution, 1926–62." *Media, Culture & Society* 21(4): 503–530. doi: https://doi.org/10.1177/016344399021004004.

Sterne, Jonathan. 2003. *The Audible Past: Cultural Origins of Sound Reproduction*. London: Duke University Press.

Sterne, Jonathan (ed.). 2012. *The Sound Studies Reader*. London: Routledge.

Steyerl, Hito. 2009, November. "In Defence of the Poor Image." *E-Flux* 10: 9.

Stone, Christopher D. 1972. "Should Trees Have Standing? Toward Legal Rights for Natural Objects." *Southern California Law Review* 45: 450–501.
Straus, Leo. 1965. *Natural Right and History*. Chicago: University of Chicago Press.
Straus, Scott. 2006. *The Order of Genocide: Race, Power and War in Rwanda*. Ithaca, NY: Cornell University Press.
Straus, Scott. 2007. "What Is the Relationship between Hate Radio and Violence? Rethinking Rwanda's 'Radio Machete'." *Politics & Society* 35(3): 609–637. doi: https://doi.org/10.1177/0032329207308181.
Strehlow, Theodor G.H. 1971. *Songs of Central Australia*. Sydney: Angus and Robertson.
Strobl, Alice (ed.). 1980. *Gustav Klimt: Die Zeichnungen 1878–1903*. Vol. 1. Vienna: Verlag Galerie Welz.
Sutton, Peter. 1994. "The Relative Strength of Oral and Written Evidence." Proof and Management of Native Title Workshop, University House, Canberra, January 31—February 1, 1994.
Takahashi, Tess. 2006. "Impure Film: Medium Specificity and Intermediality in the North American Avant-Garde (1968–2008)." Ph.D. Dissertation, Brown University.
Tavares, Paulo. 2014. "Nonhuman Rights." In *Forensis: The Architecture of Public Truth*, edited by Forensic Architecture. Berlin: Sternberg.
Taylor, Charles. 1992a. *Sources of the Self: The Making of the Modern Identity*. Cambridge: Cambridge University Press.
Taylor, Charles. 1992b. *Multiculturalism: Examining the Politics of Recognition*. Edited by Amy Gutmann. Chichester and Princeton, NJ: Princeton University Press.
Taylor, Charles. 1994. "The Politics of Recognition." In *New Contexts of Canadian Criticism*. Toronto: University of Toronto Press.
Taylor, Charles. 1997. "The Politics of Recognition." In *New Contexts of Canadian Criticism*, edited by Donna Palmateer Pennee Ajay Heble, and J.R. (Tim) Struthers, 98–131. Toronto: Broadview Press.
Taylor, Charles. 2004. *Modern Social Imaginaries*. Durham, NC: Duke University Press.
Taylor, Charles. 2007. *A Secular Age*. Cambridge, MA, and London: Harvard University Press.
Taylor, Diana. 2016. *Performance*. Durham, NC: Duke University Press.
Taylor, Telford. 1945. "Memorandum for Mr. Justice Jackson, and the Board of Review. Subject: Order of Proof, Order of Witness, Use of Motion Pictures and Related Subjects." Library of Congress, RHJ 111, 3rd November, 1945.
Teitel, Ruti G. 2000. *Transitional Justice*. Oxford: Oxford University Press.
Tennyson, Alfred Lord. 1830. "The Kraken."
Thompson, Allan (ed.) 2007. *The Media and the Rwandan Genocide*. London: Pluto.
Thompson, Emily. 2004. *The Soundscape of Modernity: Architectural Acoustics and the Culture of Listening in America, 1990–1933*. Cambridge, MA: MIT Press.
Thurston, Thomas. 2004. "Hearsay of the Sun: Photography, Identity, and the Law of Evidence." *American Quarterly* in collaboration with the American Studies Crossroads Project at Georgetown University and the Center for History & New Media at George Mason University https://chnm.gmu.edu/aq/photos/.
Tihanyi, Catherine. 2004. "An Anthropology of Translation." *American Anthropologist* 106(4): 739–742. doi: 10.1525/aa.2004.106.4.739.
Timms, Edward. 1986. *Karl Kraus, Apocalyptic Satirist: Culture and Catastrophe in Hapsburg Vienna*. New Haven and London: Yale University Press.
Tocqueville, Alexis de. 2006 [1835]. "Democracy in America." In. www.gutenberg.org/ebooks/815?msg=welcome_stranger.

Tomasulo, Frank P. 1996. "I'll See It When I Believe it: Rodney King and the Prison-House of Video." In *The Persistence of History, Cinema, Television and the Modern Event*, edited by Vivian Sobchack. London: Routledge.

Tully, James. 1995. *Strange Multiplicity: Constitutionalism in an Age of Diversity*. Cambridge: Cambridge University Press.

Turkle, Sherry. 1997. *Life on the Screen*. New York: Simon and Schuster.

Turner, Victor. 1969. *The Ritual Process: Structure and Anti-Structure*. Ithaca, NY: Cornell University Press.

Turner, Victor. 1982. *From Ritual to Theatre: The Human Seriousness of Play*. New York: Performing Arts Journal Publications.

Turner, Victor. 1988. *The Anthropology of Performance*. New York: PAJ Publications.

Unger, Roberto. 1986. *The Critical Legal Studies Movement: Another Time, A Greater Task*. Cambridge, MA: Harvard University Press.

United Nations, The. 2015. "20 Years Challenging Impunity." United Nations Mechanisms for International Criminal Tribunals, accessed January 29, 2016. http://unictr.unmict.org/.

Van Marle, Karin. 2010. "Jurisprudence, Friendship and the University as Heterogeneous Public Space." Pretoria: University of Pretoria.

Various Authors, Beautiful Trouble. "Beautiful Trouble: A Toolbox for Revolution." http://beautifultrouble.org.

Verwimp, Philip. 2006. "Machetes and Firearms: The Organization of Massacres in Rwanda." *Journal of Peace Research* 43(1): 5–22. doi: https://doi.org/10.1177/0022343306059576.

Vico, Giambattista. 1976 [1744]. *The New Science of Giambattista Vico*. Translated by Thomas Goddard Bergin and Max Harold Fisch. Ithaca, NY: Cornell University Press.

Vico, Giambattista. 1990. *On the Study Methods of Our Time*. Translated by Elio Gianturco. Ithaca, NY: Cornell University Press.

Villa-Vicencio, Charles, Wilhelm Verwoerd, Robert Rotberg, and D. Thompson. 2003. *Looking Back and Reaching Forward: Reflections on the Truth and Reconciliation Commission of South Africa*. Capetown: Capetown University Press.

Vismann, Cornelia. 2004. "Breaks in Language at the Nuremberg Trials." In *Rechenschaften*, edited by S. Braese. Göttingen: Wallstein Verlag.

Von, Wright, Georg Henrik. 1971. *Explanation and Understanding*. Ithaca, NY: Cornell University Press.

Wagner, William Joseph. 1999–2000. "Pursuit of the Hunt, Interrupted: Changing Literary Images of Law." *Catholic University Law Review* 49: 945.

Wall, Derek. 2014. "Green Politics and the Republican Commons." *Commons Sense: New Thinking about an Old Idea, Community Development Journal* 49 (suppl_1): i81–i91. doi: https://doi.org/10.1093/cdj/bsu003.

Walsh, Michael. 1995. "'Tainted Evidence': Literacy and Traditional Knowledge in an Aboriginal Land Claim." In *Language in Evidence: Issues Confronting Aboriginal and Multicultural Australia*, edited by Diana Eades, 97–124. Sydney: UNSW Press.

Watson, Sophie. 2006. *City Publics: The (Dis)Enchantments of Urban Encounters*. New York: Routledge.

Weiner, Tim. 2001, June 15. Mexico City Journal; Pummeling the Powerful, With Comedy as Cudgel. *The New York Times, World*.

West's Encyclopedia of American Law, 2nd edn. "agreement." http://legal-dictionary.thefreedictionary.com/agreement.

West's Encyclopedia of American Law, 2nd edn. "Impersonation." http://legal-dictionary.thefreedictionary.com/Impersonation.

Whitaker, Benjamin. 1985. A Report into Genocide by Special Rapporteur Benjamin Whitaker, for the Sub-Commission on Prevention of Discrimination and Protection of Minorities. UN Doc.E/CN. 4/Sub. 2/1985/6: UN Economic and Social Council.

White, James Boyd. 1985. *When Words Lose Their Meaning: Constitutions and Reconstructions of Language, Character and Community*. Chicago, IL: University of Chicago Press.

White, James Boyd. 1989. *Heracles' Bow: Essays on the Rhetoric and Poetics of Law*. Madison, WI: University of Wisconsin Press.

Whitehead, Alfred North. 1978. *Process and Reality: An Essay in Cosmology*. New York: The Free Press.

Whitford, Frank and Gustav Klimt. 1990. *Gustav Klimt: Edition en langue anglaise*. London: Thames & Hudson.

Wiessner, Siegfried. 2008. "Indigenous Sovereignty: A Reassessment in Light of the United Nations Declaration on the Rights of Indigenous People." *Vanderbilt Journal of Transnational Law* 41: 1141–1176.

Wiessner, Siegfried. 2011. "The Cultural Rights of Indigenous Peoples: Achievements and Continuing Challenges." *European Journal of International Law* 22(1): 121–140. doi: https://doi.org/10.1093/ejil/chr007.

Wieviorka, Annette. 2006. *The Era of the Witness*. Translated by Jared Stark. Ithaca, NY and London: Cornell University Press.

Wilcox, Sackville and Merkel JJ. 2005. De Rose v South Australia (No. 2). Federal Court of Australia—Full Court.

Williams, Nancy. 1987. *Two Laws: Managing Disputes in a Contemporary Aboriginal Community*. Canberra: Institute of Aboriginal Studies Press.

Wooley, T. 2006. "Notes on De Rose Hill Native Title Claim." In *Your Legal Rights*.

Yeebo, Zaya, Abdul Tejan-Cole and BBC News. 2012. "Is Africa on Trial?" *BBC News*, March 27. www.bbc.com/news/world-africa-17446655 and www.bbc.com/news/world-africa-17513065.

"The Yes Men." accessed April 14, 2015. http://theyesmen.org/.

Young, Alison. 2005. *Judging the Image: Art, Value, Law*. New York: Routledge.

Young, Alison. 2014. "Cities in the City: Street Art, Enchantment, and the Urban Commons." *Law & Literature* 26(2): 145–161. doi: http://dx.doi.org/10.1080/1535685X.2014.888208.

Young, Iris Marion. 1990. *Justice and the Politics of Difference*. Princeton, NJ: Princeton University Press.

Zak, William F. 1995. *The Polis and the Divine Order: The Oresteia, Sophocles, and the Defense of Democracy*. London: Bucknell University Press.

Zalaquett, José. 1991. "Balancing Ethical Imperatives and Political Constraints: The Dilemma of New Democracies Confronting Past Human Rights Violations." *Hastings Law Journal* 43: 1425–1438.

Zavada, Roland J. 1998. "Dissecting the Zapruder Bell & Howell 8mm Movie Camera." Movie Machine Society Conference, Toronto. (www.jfk-info.com/zavada1.htm).

Zelizer, Barbie. 1999. "From the Image of Record to the Image of Memory: Holocaust Photography, Then and Now." In *Picturing the Past: Media, History & Photography*, edited by Bonnie Brennen and Hanno Hardt, 98. Urbana and Chicago, IL: University of Illinois Press.

INDEX

Aboriginal land claims 47–8
   Aboriginal customary law 51, 54
   Alcoota Land Claim 55–6
   Alyawarr 47, 48, 54, 57, 58–61, 63, 189
   Blue Mud Bay hearing 57
   Canada 187
   constitutional exclusion 49, 50
   De Rose 48, 53, 54, 57, 62–7, 190, 191
   Dreaming 48, 52–3
   judicial process 53–5
   Mabo 50–1, 53
   New Zealand 178
   performance evidence 53–8, 65–7, 67
   politics of recognition 48–9
   terra nullius 49, 50
academic freedom 96
acoustics. *See* soundscape
activist performance 88–98
Aeschylus: *Oresteia* 28, 32–3, 32–4
aesthetics 15, 23, 32
affect 3, 12–13, 25, 81, 160
Agamben, Giorgio 27, 34, 35, 36, 39, 40, 42, 186
agape 24. *See also* love
Andersen, Niels Pagh 161, 162
Arendt, Hannah 2, 17, 115
Aristodemou, Maria 187
art 27–8, 30, 39, 44, 54, 88, 129, 133, 135–6, 146, 163. *See also* situational art
atonal composition 3, 6
attunement 16, 24
audio recording 82–4
"audiovisual contract" 70
Austin, J. L. 195
Australia
   land claims (*see* Aboriginal land claims)
   treatment of migrants 35–6

Bal, Mieke 39
"bare life" 27, 28, 34, 35, 39, 40, 41, 43, 153
Baudelaire, Charles 11
Benjamin, Walter 2, 15, 27
Bergson, Henri 6
Berman, Harold 5

Bigelow, Katherine 14, 145
Bikindi, Simon 70, 72–3
bio-politics 12
black liberation 4
"Black Lives Matter" 170
Boal, Augusto 88
Boer War 34
Bourdieu, Pierre 67
Brecht, Bertolt 95, 164
Bruner, Jerome 7
Bryson, Norman 31
Burke, Kenneth 17
Bush, George H. W. 181–2
Bush, George W. 7
Butler, Judith 195

Cage, John 6
Calderón, Felipe 89
Capote, Truman 145
Capra, Frank 145
Cardozo, Benjamin 6
censorship 96, 153
Chrétien, Jean-Pierre 77
Cicero 9
civil liberties 97
Coates, Ta-Nehisi 199
codes of meaning 13, 17
codification 69
cognitive dissonance 148
Coleridge, Samuel Taylor 87
colonial power 48, 67, 187
common law tradition 5
commons 142–3
common sense 13, 14
communication 1, 17
community 11, 12, 17, 23–5, 42, 55, 139–40, 157
competing preferences 7, 8
concentration camps 34, 40
Congo, Anwar 14, 24, 147–8, 153–9, 164–5
"constitutive rhetoric" 12
construction of meaning 1, 5, 7, 12–13
constructivism 9

contextualized fairness 6
corporations 88–9, 93, 95
Cover, Robert 9, 187
crimes against humanity 102–3, 152, 153.
  See also genocide; war crimes
critical legal studies (CLS) 7, 39
Cubism 3, 6
cultural hegemony 67, 68
cultural legal studies 7
cultural literacy 13, 23
cultural prejudice 75, 79, 80
customary rights 51, 54, 142

Dadaism 3
dance 47–8, 53, 59, 65–6, 79, 89
Dante Alighieri 7, 9
Deleuze, Gilles 12, 197
democracy 12, 17
Derrida, Jacques 4, 12, 136, 180
dialogue 8, 10, 32, 70, 81
dignity 10, 68, 149, 166
disabilities 4
discursive communities 17
documentaries 145, 161
Dokmanović, Slavko 99–103, 115–28, 196
Dreaming 48, 52–3
Dupuy, Jean-Pierre 2

Eichmann Trial 111, 115
empathy 44, 164–6
"engineering of consent" 1
Enlightenment 3, 7, 16, 28
environmental policies 105, 124
Eros 24, 25, 37, 44
"esoteric" order 13, 15
ethics 1, 9, 18, 24–5, 40–1, 149, 167
evidence
  expert witnesses 99, 102, 103, 107, 109,
    110, 179
  trees as 100–5, 121–7
  visual media 99, 100, 104–5, 107, 113,
    115, 114, 116–17
exclusion 4, 137, 142, 144
"exoteric" order 13, 14
expert witnesses 99, 102, 103, 107, 109, 110,
  179

fake websites 92, 93, 94, 95
Felman, Shoshana 115
feminism 4, 10
feminist jurisprudence 7
films 13, 14, 25
  The Act of Killing 14, 146–9, 152, 154–7,
    159–62, 164
  Dark Blue 183
  documentaries 145–6, 165
  Fury 174
  ICTR: "20 Years Challenging Impunity"
    70–1, 76, 78, 73, 86
  The Killing Fields 145
  The Look of Silence 24, 146, 149–50, 152,
    153, 156–9, 160–2, 164
  Malcolm X 183
  Natural Born Killers 183
  Prelude to War 145
  The Thin Blue Line 145
  Three Kings 183
  Triumph of the Will 145
  Zero Dark Thirty 14, 145
formalism 8, 28, 44
Foucault, Michel 13, 17, 39
fragmentation 5, 6, 14
freedom of speech 94, 96, 97
Freud, Sigmund 25, 32, 81
  Interpretation of Dreams 28, 37–9

Geertz, Clifford 9
genocide 14, 24, 151, 152. See also crimes
    against humanity; war crimes
  concentration camps 34–5, 40
  incitement 72, 76, 83, 84
  perpetrators 14, 24, 152–4, 157, 165–7
  Rwanda 71, 72, 75, 77, 82, 84
Goebbels, Joseph 145
Goya, Francisco de 39
graffiti 129. See also situational art
  audience 138
  autonomy 136
  lack of authorization 136–8
  "legal walls" 137, 144
  media 131
  motivation 138, 141
  "pieces" 131
  proprietorship and criminal impropriety
    139, 140–2
  public space 139, 142–3
  surfaces and locations 133, 136, 138, 143
  "tagging" 129–32, 138
Grassi, Ernesto 9
Greek tragedy 32
Guattari, Félix 81

habeas corpus 40, 42
Habermas, Jürgen 8

Habimana, Kantano 82–3
Halsey, Mark 139, 141
Hardt, Michael 25
Heidegger, Martin 81
Hemispheric Institute of Performance and
    Politics 89, 97
Herder, Johann Gottfried 3, 16
heterogeneity 4, 11
historical cycles 3
historical materialism 15
Hobbes, Thomas 30
homo sacer 28, 34, 35, 40, 42, 44
humanism 16, 24
human rights 7, 10–11
human rights violations
    perpetrators 14, 24, 152–4, 157, 165–6
    truth and reconciliation commissions 150,
        151, 198
Human Rights Watch 77

icons 13
'ICTR'. *See* International Criminal Tribunal
    for Rwanda
'ICTY'. *See* International Criminal Tribunal
    for the former Yugoslavia
illiberalism 8, 23
image 12–13, 27, 30, 36, 70, 116–18, 143,
    148–50, 154, 156, 163, 170, 173, 162,
    184
immanence 12, 163
impersonation
    activist performance 88–98
    corporations 88–9, 93, 95
    fake websites 92, 93, 94, 95
    false impersonation 88
    intention to deceive, to profit, or to harm
        88
    legal censure 87, 88, 93, 97
    "suspension of disbelief" 87
    theater 88
    Yes Men 91–3, 97
incommensurability 3, 5, 7, 16, 23, 25
indigenous rights 4. *See also* Aboriginal land
    claims
instrumentalism 7, 8, 81, 83
International Criminal Tribunal for Rwanda
    ('ICTR')
    archival holdings 107, 118
    audio-visual technology 112
    Completion Strategy 107
    Court Records 106, 107, 111, 115
    courtroom 106

Dokmanović 99–103, 115–28, 196
evidence vault 108, 111
expert witnesses 99, 102, 103, 107, 109
metadata 118
non-human witnesses 99–100, 105
Office of the Prosecutor (OTP) 108
Rules of Procedure and Evidence 121
trees used as evidence 100–3, 121–7
visual media 99, 100, 104–5, 107, 113,
    115, 114, 116–17
International Criminal Tribunal for the former
    Yugoslavia ('ICTY'). 106
    audio recording 82–4
    Bikindi 70, 72–86
    film: "20 Years Challenging Impunity"
        70–1, 76, 78, 85, 86
    Media case 72, 74, 75, 78, 79, 80
    noise 73–6
    racial and cultural prejudice 75, 79, 80
    radio 73, 75–82, 85
"invisible theater" 88
irrational forces 6, 159, 166

Jackson, Robert H. 115, 176, 200
jurisprudence
    feminist jurisprudence 7
    legal recognition 39, 41
    "legal science" 33–4
justice 4, 6, 9, 11, 16, 27, 33, 44, 65, 85, 111,
    150–1, 157, 163–7, 169–77, 182–3

Kafka, Franz 32
Kelsen, Hans 33–4, 43
King, Rodney 14, 111, 170–85
Klimt, Gustav: *Jurisprudence/Jurisprudenz*
    27–8
    adverse criticism of 28–31
    aesthetics as critique 31
    allegorical figures 30
    "bare life" 27, 28, 34, 35, 39, 40, 41, 43
    commissioning 28
    critique of legal formalism 28, 33, 44
    destruction of the painting 29, 44
    focalization and perspectives 41, 43
    Freudian resonances 28, 32, 37–9
    Oresteia and 28, 32–3, 41–3
    sovereign power 27, 28, 34–5, 39–43,
        45
    surviving descriptions and reproduction 30
    use of color 30, 31
Koch, Grace 188, 189, 190
Kraus, Karl 28, 30, 31, 38

Lacan, Jacques 159
Lang, Fritz 174
Laub, Doris 115
Lee, Spike 183
Lefebvre, Henri 142, 143
legal emblems 36
legal formalism 8, 28, 44
legal pluralism 51
legal positivism 33
Legal Realism 6
legal recognition 39, 41
legal subjects 28
Levi, Primo 166
Levinas, Emmanuel 24, 25, 40, 167, 186–7
lex talionis 32, 41, 42
liberal democracy 17
liberalism 8, 10
love 25, 149–50, 164–5
Lukács, Georg 80
Lukianoff, Greg 96, 195

Mabo 50–1, 53
McLuhan, Marshall 75, 79–80
Mallarmé, Stéphane 6
Martinez, Daniel 88
Massumi, Brian 12
materiality 3
material witness 111, 115, 116
meaning-making processes 1, 5, 7, 13
mediated evidence 99, 118. *See also* audio recording; non-human witnesses; visual media
media theory 75, 79–80, 81, 118
memorialization 129
metadata 118
Mitchell, William 15, 142
modernism 31
Monsanto Corporation 88–91, 93–7, 194, 196
More, Thomas 31
Morphy, Frances 51, 57, 189
Morphy, Howard 187
Morris, Errol 145
Moyle, Richard 53, 188, 190
multiculturalism 4
multiple literacies (or modalities of expression) 5, 12, 25, 103

"naive realism" 118
native title. *See* Aboriginal land claims
natural law theory 8
natural objects 103, 105

"natural rights" 5
Nazi regime 30, 34, 44, 79, 115, 145
Negri, Antonio 25
Nietzsche, Friedrich 12, 23
noise 73–6
nomads 137, 197
nomoi 9
non-human witnesses 4, 99–100, 105
    material witness 111, 115
    trees 100–5, 121–7
normativity 4, 5, 6
Nuremberg Trials 10, 106, 111, 115, 145, 176, 196, 200
Nussbaum, Martha 25

Obama, Barack 169
objective truths 7
Oppenheimer, Joshua 13–14, 24, 145–67
    The Act of Killing 14, 146–9, 151, 154–7, 159–62, 164
    interview with 151–67
    The Look of Silence 24, 146, 149–50, 152, 153, 156–9, 161–2, 164
oral traditions 80
Oresteia 28, 32–3, 41–3
Ostrom, Elinor 142

painting 27–33, 36–41, 55, 56, 133, 138, 140
Pandectism 33
Parlá, José 137
Pasolini, Pier Paolo 181
Pasquini, Alice 138
Peñalver, Eduardo Moises 137
Perelman, Chaim 9
performance 89, 94, 95, 158–9
performance evidence 53–8, 65–7, 187–8, 190
Plato 9, 25
pluralism
    legal pluralism 51
    plurality of worlds 5, 9, 22
    radical pluralism 3, 5, 6–11, 16, 23, 24
police violence 169–70
    Rodney King case 14, 111, 169–85
political unconscious 14
politics of recognition 48–9
politics of significance 5, 15, 18
positivism 8, 10
post-colonialism 4, 39
post-modernism 3
post-structuralism 3
power 1, 13–15, 22
Power, Samantha 77

pragmatism 7
process theory 6
propaganda 1, 14, 78, 85
property 129
    proprietorship and criminal impropriety 139, 140–2
    public space 139, 142–4
Proudhon, Pierre-Joseph 40
prudent judgment 15
public policy 6
public space 139, 142–4

racial prejudice 75, 79, 80, 191
racism 169, 173, 174, 183, 199, 200
radical pluralism 3, 5, 6–11, 16, 23, 24
radio 73, 76–82, 85
Rancière, Jacques 87, 135, 143, 144
rationality 3
Rawls, John 8
recognition
    legal 39, 41
    politics of 48–9
"reification" 80
relativism 8, 16, 23
resistance 89
rhetorical fields 9
Riefenstahl, Leni 145
rights-bearing subjects 4
Rodríguez, Jesusa 89, 97, 98, 194
Roman law 34
Romanticism 3, 11
Rose, Carol 53, 142
rule making 8
rule of law 42
Rwanda
    Africanness 75, 79, 80, 191
    Gacaca courts 74
    genocide 71, 72, 75, 77, 82, 84
    Interahamwe 71, 73, 75
    International Criminal Tribunal (*see* ICTR)
    Radio Télévision Libre des Mille Collines (RTLM) 72, 75–85

Sandel, Michael 8
Schafer, R. Murray 83
Schechner, Richard 24, 94
"schizophonia" 83
Schmitt, Carl 5, 8, 23, 27, 33, 43
Schopenhauer, Arthur 41, 162
Schorske, Carl 31, 33, 186
Schwartz, Hillel 74
Schwartz, Louis-George 174

scientific expertise 99
    expert witnesses 99, 102, 103, 107, 109, 110
screen images 14. *See also* films; visual images
secularism 6, 13
secular liberalism 8, 10
Servin, Jacques 91, 92, 93, 95, 97, 196
Shakespeare, William xii, 24
Sherwin, Richard 7, 14, 17, 54, 67, 99, 118, 145–67, 180, 188
Shoah 3
Simpson, Gerry 82
situational art 134–5. *See also* graffiti; street art
    commissioning 135–6
    motivation 138, 141
    proprietorship and criminal impropriety 139, 140–2
    public space 139, 142–4
    sensibility 138–9, 143
    trespass 137
    urban space 135–8
social commons 143
social drama 94
social realism 31
song(s) 47, 48, 53, 56, 58, 64–6, 72, 82, 84–5
sonic imagination 70
soundscape 69–70
    audio recording 82–4
    "audiovisual contract" 70
    Bikindi case 70, 72–3
    noise 73–6
    radio 73, 76–82, 85
    "schizophonia" 83
sovereign power
    cultural hegemony 67
    Klimt's *Jurisprudence* 27, 28, 34–6, 39–43, 45
speech 73–5, 85, 97, 184
    land and sovereignty 49–51
    popular sovereignty 50
"state of emergency" 5
state violence 146, 150. *See also* police violence
Stevens, Wallace 6, 7
Strauss, Leo 7, 8
street art 129. *See also* situational art
    audience 138
    autonomy 136
    lack of authorization 136–8
    "legal walls" 137, 144
    media 131
    motivation 138, 141

"pieces" 131, 133, 134
proprietorship and criminal impropriety 139, 140–2
public space 139, 142–4
surfaces and locations 133, 136, 138, 143
"tagging" 129–32, 138, 139
Suharto, General 146
surrealism 3
"suspension of disbelief" 87
synaesthetic jurisprudence 15, 22

Tabbush, Paul 100, 102, 103, 117, 121–7
Taylor, Charles 6
Taylor, Telford 176, 179
technology 80–1
television 118, 170, 173, 181–2, 184
terra nullius 49, 50
text 12, 30, 79, 84, 89, 131, 136
textualism 69
theater 88
theology 14–15
Thompson, Allan 77
Tihanyi, Catherine 11
Tocqueville, Alexis de 11
Tomasulo, Frank P. 183
torture 10
trees
    legal rights and personhood 105
    used as evidence 100–5, 124–7
trespass 137
Trotha, Lothar von 35
truth and reconciliation commissions 150, 151, 198
truth claims 4
Turner, Victor 94
TV shows 14

universalism 7, 10, 12, 16
urban space
    ownership and exclusion 137, 139, 141, 143
    public space 139, 142–4
    situational art 135–8
utopianism 11, 31

Vamos, Igor 91, 93
Verene, Donald 9
Vico, Giambattista 3, 7, 9, 16
visual media
    decoding 184
    ICTY trial evidence 99, 100–5, 107, 110, 113–5, 117–28
    polysemy 170
    Rodney King case 173, 176–80
    video editing 161–2
visual rhetoric 99

Wagner, Richard 32
war crimes 102, 103, 106. *See also* crimes against humanity; genocide
Weaver, Richard 9
Weber, Max 7
"webs of significance" 9
Welles, Orson 87, 96, 145
White, James Boyd 9, 12
Williams, William Carlos 6
Wright, Benjamin S. 199

Yes Men 91–3, 97, 194–5

Zak, William 41
Zapruder, Abraham 173, 181, 199
Zaleta, Marroquin 97